SWIFT: THE CRITICAL HERITAGE

THE CRITICAL HERITAGE SERIES

GENERAL EDITOR: B. C. SOUTHAM, M.A., B.LITT. (OXON.)
Formerly Department of English, Westfield College, University of London

Volumes in the series include

JANE AUSTEN	B. C. Southam
BROWNING	Boyd Litzinger, *St. Bonaventure University* and Donald Smalley, *University of Illinois*
BYRON	Andrew Rutherford, *University of Aberdeen*
COLERIDGE	J. R. de J. Jackson, *Victoria College, Toronto*
DICKENS	Philip Collins, *University of Leicester*
THOMAS HARDY	R. G. Cox, *University of Manchester*
HENRY JAMES	Roger Gard, *Queen Mary College, London*
JAMES JOYCE (2 vols.)	Robert H. Deming, *University of Miami*
D. H. LAWRENCE	R. P. Draper, *University of Leicester*
MILTON	John T. Shawcross, *University of Wisconsin*
SCOTT	John O. Hayden, *University of California, Davis*
SWINBURNE	Clyde K. Hyder,
TENNYSON	J. D. Jump, *University of Manchester*
THACKERAY	Geoffrey Tillotson and Donald Hawes, *Birkbeck College, London*
TROLLOPE	Donald Smalley, *University of Illinois*

SWIFT

THE CRITICAL HERITAGE

Edited by
KATHLEEN WILLIAMS

Professor of English
University of California, Riverside

NEW YORK
BARNES & NOBLE, INC.

First published in Great Britain 1970
Published in the United States of America 1970
by Barnes & Noble, Inc., New York, N.Y.

© *Kathleen Williams 1970*

SBN 389 01092 8

1. Swift, Jonathan - Criticism

CUR P
08
1.W

Printed in Great Britain

General Editor's Preface

The reception given to a writer by his contemporaries and near-contemporaries is evidence of considerable value to the student of literature. On one side we learn a great deal about the state of criticism at large and in particular about the development of critical attitudes towards a single writer; at the same time, through private comments in letters, journals or marginalia, we gain an insight upon the tastes and literary thought of individual readers of the period. Evidence of this kind helps us to understand the writer's historical situation, the nature of his immediate reading-public, and his response to these pressures.

The separate volumes in the *Critical Heritage Series* present a record of this early criticism. Clearly for many of the highly productive and lengthily reviewed nineteenth- and twentieth-century writers there exists an enormous body of material; and in these cases the volume editors have made a selection of the most important views, significant for their intrinsic critical worth or for their representative quality—perhaps even registering incomprehension!

For earlier writers, notably pre-eighteenth century, the materials are much scarcer and the historical period has been extended, sometimes far beyond the writer's lifetime, in order to show the inception and growth of critical views which were initially slow to appear.

In each volume the documents are headed by an Introduction, discussing the material assembled and relating the early stages of the author's reception to what we have come to identify as the critical tradition. The volumes will make available much material which would otherwise be difficult of access, and it is hoped that the modern reader will be thereby helped towards an informed understanding of the ways in which literature has been read and judged.

B.C.S.

Contents

CONTENTS

Introduction

I

A collection of predominantly eighteenth-century criticism of Swift cannot make a large book. Swift wrote before the art of the reviewer was much developed, and while only a few periodicals existed in England. Thus while Lord Orrery's *Remarks on the Life and Writing of Dr. Jonathan Swift* (1752) was fairly extensively reviewed, *Gulliver's Travels* and *A Tale of a Tub* were too early to receive much of that kind of automatic attention in the periodicals which is to be expected in later years, when novels and other books of general interest would naturally be described and discussed. Some formal reviews of the *Travels, A Tale of a Tub*, and the *Miscellanies* do exist, some in French periodicals; but for the most part they are disappointingly uncritical, often consisting almost entirely of descriptions of the action of the work considered or of lengthy quotations. Sometimes the reviewer may draw upon a predecessor, usually without acknowledgement (this is very frequent in all kinds of eighteenth-century comment on Swift, formal or informal, critical or biographical). For reasons of this kind, such reviews as that of *Le Conte du Tonneau* in *Le Journal des Sçavans*, Tôme XX, 1721, or that of *Voyages du Capitaine Lemuel Gulliver en divers Pays éloigné*, in *Le Journal Littéraire*, Des Années 1723-8, Tôme XII, second part, have not been included, though a brief quotation from the latter is given in this Introduction. Many passages of criticism are fragmentary, occurring in the course of material otherwise purely biographical, descriptive, or abusive, or sometimes in pieces not primarily concerned with Swift.

On the other hand, there is more contemporary comment on Swift's work than has been included in the present volume. The problem is that much contemporary comment is not criticism at all, but deliberate misinterpretation, modulating into personal attack on the writer. Swift's writings did not, in his own time, have the status of literary works standing aloof from contemporary controversy; they were not solely works of art, amusement, or edification, like novels. They were seen as primarily political and partisan, and that in the almost unbelievably intense and frenetic eighteenth-century world of dedicated Whigs and

Tories. Never, perhaps, has there been a reading public more politically minded, and of course Swift himself contributed to this hectic atmosphere by the whole-heartedness of his own commitment to political causes. Thus, for example, John Oldmixon's criticism of the *Proposal for correcting, improving, and ascertaining the English Tongue* (*Reflections on Dr. Swift's Letter to Harley*, 1712) and Arthur Maynwaring's[1] comment on the same tract (*The British Academy*, 1712) are both Whig and anti-Tory documents, but they only enlarge upon a political element which is certainly present in the *Proposal*. Again, we do not now think of *A Tale of a Tub* or *Gulliver's Travels* as primarily political works, but political, along with much else, they certainly were, and it is hardly surprising that this is the aspect that filled the minds of his contemporaries. That the political aspect should dwarf the rest is natural enough: what is less forgivable is the way in which so often the major works are used, frequently distorted almost beyond recognition, as a stick with which to beat a political enemy. Religion, too, was, in the earlier eighteenth century, a political issue, and Swift's political and religious opponents and personal enemies had already in his own day used his works as proof of his wickedness as a political turncoat and an atheist priest—a view of him which became a part of the inaccurate but popular Swift legend.

Over the centuries, then, Swift's writings have been used to denigrate him as a man, and it is his misfortune and ours that his character and his career, as first interpreted by his enemies in the virulent atmosphere of eighteenth-century political thinking, have been so much more interesting than his literary achievement to the majority of those who have written about him in the past three hundred years. Swift the man early became a legend, but the Drapier Dean, hero of oppressed Ireland, rapidly took second place to the savage and miserly misanthrope, the mysteriously sadistic friend or lover or husband of three unfortunate women. Lives of Swift were printed, reviewed, discussed, and refuted, and the more horrifying a picture they presented the better. Lord Orrery's particularly offensive and unctuous account of his 'friend' Swift (No. 26) was reviewed and tutted over even in France before any really serious criticism of the works existed. On the other hand, it is only fair to say that some of the earliest comment on *Gulliver's Travels* which can be called literary criticism emerges as a result of the endeavour of Swift's friends to deny the existence in him of that hatred of mankind and that extreme inhumanity of word and action that had been most lengthily and systematically dwelled upon by Orrery. Sheridan, for instance, son of one of Swift's closest friends in Ireland, is forced by Orrery's account of the misanthropic Swift to discuss (No. 46) at some length the fourth book of *Gulliver's Travels*, which had so grieved the noble lord; and in doing so he makes certain critical, as well as moral, distinctions. In this way the 'Voyage to the Houyhnhnms' became, as it has remained, the crucial point in Swift criticism. But it first became so, not by virtue of being the greatest and most disturbing part of all his writings, but because it was the obvious place to refer to in attacking or supporting the character of its writer. Those who wished to attack had a ready-made weapon which those who wished to defend were compelled to counter in whatever way they could. Only comparatively recently has Swift criticism become sufficiently detached from the passions of the Swift legend to escape from this situation.

The search for eighteenth-century Swift criticism is therefore a rather frustrating one, and in this volume some comments by early-nineteenth-century writers have been included, to suggest that slowly a certain detachment from the political and personal events of Swift's life was enabling critics to turn their attention to the works. There is Sir Walter Scott's often perceptive and often underrated account (No. 59), and there is Hazlitt, who remarks (and one draws a breath of relief):

I do not carry my political resentments so far back: I can at this time of day forgive Swift for having been a Tory. I feel little disturbance (whatever I might think of them) at his political sentiments, which died with him, considering how much else he has left behind him of a more solid and imperishable nature. (No. 61.)

Coleridge (No. 62) has some brilliant fragmentary comment, and Nathan Drake (No. 57), a little earlier, some comparatively detailed work on the writings, including the poetry. William Monck Mason (No. 63), too, writes moderately and sensibly of the major works. But not everyone, even then, was as dispassionate as Hazlitt; Francis Jeffrey (No. 60), for example, remarks 'with these impressions of his personal character, perhaps it is not easy for us to judge quite fairly of his works'. Nor does the early nineteenth century bring the end of the outcries of moral affront; one has only to think of Thackeray. But by Hazlitt's time the atmosphere is clearly changing, and though critics still do not come to grips with the difficulties of the *Tale* and the *Travels* they are able to write calmly of Swift's style and his inventive skill. Indeed, in 1783 Hugh Blair (No. 45) was already able to regard the works dispassionately from his vantage-point as a rhetorician, and to discuss their stylistic interest, while as early as 1758 Dilworth (No. 30) wrote in painstaking detail, and with apparent admiration for Swift as a patriot, upon a number of the works. The history of Swift criticism even in the eighteenth century is not wholly one of prejudice and irrelevance; nor, unfortunately, is the criticism of the nineteenth century by any means wholly detached.

II

A Tale of a Tub

The earliest pieces in this volume are of comment upon *A Tale of a Tub*. Dr. William King (No. 1), himself a wit, seems to think that the book has some wit and learning, but that this exists in a setting of dirt and profanity. King makes no effort to examine the satiric purpose and methods of the *Tale*, yet his elaborate device for insisting on the dirtiness of the book is an implicit critical comment, though not, indeed, of a very high order. His accusation, which alludes presumably to such matters as the talk, full of oaths, which Swift invents for his character Peter, or the description of the Aeolists, is often repeated over the years. So is Atterbury's comment (No. 2) on the book's profanity (Atterbury also witnesses to the rapid popularity of the *Tale*) and William Wotton's objection that in shooting at the Church of Rome Swift has hurt the Church of England: 'I would not so shoot at an Enemy, as to hurt my self at the same time.' Wotton's well-known *Observations upon the Tale of a Tub* (No. 3) is a very detailed explanation of the satiric allusions in the religious allegory; Wotton, who is attacked in *The Battle of the Books*, naturally takes the *Tale* seriously, but his detailed comment is plainly intended to support one conclusion: 'So great a delight has this Unhappy writer, to play with what some part or other of Mankind have always esteemed as Sacred!' It is noticeable, too, that Wotton concentrates on the religious allegory and so discusses only a part of the work; so does the author of *A Complete Key to the Tale of a Tub* (No. 6). This is normal for the period; clearly the literary digressions were by no means as exciting and as controversial to the public mind as the allegory of the Churches, so closely related to the fascinating subject of party politics. A 'key' to the religious allegory would sell; a discussion of the complexities of the digressions would not (as well as being much more difficult to do). The *Tale*, an old-fashioned work when it was published, emerged into a world not altogether suited to it. Whether genuinely or as a move in the all-absorbing political and personal controversies of the time, many professed to be distrustful of wit, which considers nothing sacred; and the unfortunate results of this attitude may be seen in the subcritical exclamations of John Dennis (No. 5) and Sir Richard Blackmore (No. 7).

All his life Swift, with his friends Pope, Gay, and Arbuthnot, was subjected to foolish political attacks like that in *The Twickenham Hotch-Potch, for the Use of the Rev. Dr. Swift, Alexander Pope, Esq.; and Company, Being a Sequel to the Beggars Opera &c.* (1728), by Caleb d'Anvers (possibly Nicholas Amhurst). In the Introduction to this worthless production Swift and his friends are referred to as 'four Objects (an impertinent *Scotch*-Quack, a Profligate *Irish*-Dean, the Lacquey of a Superannuated Dutchess, and a little virulent Papist)'. It is in vain to look for criticism here, or in the heavily Whig *Life and Posthumous Works of Arthur Maynwaring, Esq.* (1715), where Swift appears as the mercenary writer of the *Examiner*, or in *Essays Divine, Moral and Political, by the Author of the Tale of a Tub, sometime the Writer of the Examiner, and the Original Inventor of the Band-Box-Plot* (1714), in which Swift is shown confessing that his works have led people to represent him as an '*Atheist,* or a *Lewd Town-Rake,* or both'. One of the works in question is that 'Divine Treatise, the *Tale of a Tub*'. Swift's connection with the Tory ministry, and above all perhaps with the *Examiner*, insured a thoroughly biased reading of the *Tale* from a number of those who lived by their pens or their politics.

Considering the controversial atmosphere which prevailed in England, it is hardly surprising that some of the most sensible remarks on the *Tale*, with *The Battle of the Books*, and *The Mechanical Operation of the Spirit*, come from the Continent. Juste van Effen published his French translation of the volume in 1721, and with it a Preface (No. 8) in which he refers to the digressions and their parodic intention, and describes them with some appreciation. Writing as a 'philosophic' and enlightened man, van Effen thinks that what is being attacked in the *Tale* is not religion, but extravagances which have in reality nothing to do with religion. He accepts, in fact, Swift's own position that it is the abuses of religion which he is satirizing in the allegory of the Churches. Jean le Clerc (No. 9), reviewing van Effen's translation, is less pleased with the *Tale*, but in his remarks on *The Mechanical Operation of the Spirit* he raises, very justly, the question which has concerned later critics of the piece: Just what is the object of Swift's satire? Voltaire (No. 14), for whom Swift was a politer Rabelais, a Rabelais with good judgement (he repeats the definition, with variations, several times), is pleased with the *Tale* largely on religious, or anti-religious, grounds. He clearly takes with a grain of salt Swift's claim to be attacking not religion but its abuses. Voltaire does not mention the digressions, and he makes much of the *Tale*'s derivation from the story of the three rings and from a story of Fontenelle. Wotton, some time earlier, had found different originals for both the *Tale* and the *Battle*; such denials of the originality of his works seem, to judge from the Apology to the *Tale*, to have hurt Swift particularly. To have borrowed a hint from no one was what he especially prided himself on. The chief complaint made by French critics is that put forward by Cartaud de la Villate (No. 21), that it is not properly organized.

After these reasonable and dispassionate considerations from the Continent, the *Tale* continues to be used, in England, in attacks on the foulness of its writer. The anonymous *Letter from a Clergyman to his Friend* (No. 12) devotes most of its space to *Gulliver's Travels*, but the *Tale* serves for an emphatic conclusion:

In a former Performance, he levelled his Jests at Almighty God: banter'd and ridiculed Religion and all that's good and adorable above; By this, he has abused and insulted those who are justly valued by us, as the best, the greatest below.

Those so neatly paralleled in this passage with Almighty God are apparently Sir Robert Walpole and his associates; to such heights had party warfare risen. Pope's friend Warburton (No. 13), too, couples the *Tale* and the *Travels* as impious works:

The religious *Author of the Tale of a Tub* will tell you, Religion is but a Reservoir of Fools and Madmen; and *the virtuous Lemuel Gulliver* will answer for the *State*, that it is a Den of Savages and Cut-throats.

Lord Orrery (No. 26), who did so much damage to Swift's reputation both as clergyman and as private person, is reasonably fair to the works, though that hypocritical pretence of erring on the side of generosity to his dead friend, which so infuriated Swift's supporters, is visible here, too. For example, he looks on the *Tale* as 'no *intended* satyr against Christianity, but as a satyr against the wild errors of the Church of Rome, the slow and incompleat reformation of the Lutherans, and the absurd, and affected zeal of the presbyterians'. But Orrery is at least one of the few who pay attention to, and praise in however modified a manner, the wit of the digressions. Dilworth (No. 30), who discusses

6

so many of the minor works, oddly makes no more than a mention of the *Tale*; but James Beattie (No. 38), while disapproving of the mingling 'of the most solemn truths with ludicrous ideas', regards the *Tale* as unequalled 'as a piece of humorous writing'. It is interesting, too, that Beattie testifies that this work is 'in the opinion of many, his best', but as usual in the period the brilliant and difficult digressions are ignored; 'the subject', says Beattie, 'is religion', and no mention is made of the satire on the abuses of learning. For Dr. Johnson (No. 40) it is a 'wild work', though Johnson, one senses with some reluctance, had to admire its rapidity of mind and copiousness of images.

George-Monck Berkeley (No. 48) defends the *Tale*, and a writer on the 'Character of Jonathan Swift' in the *European Magazine* (No. 50) praises it, though with the usual reminder of its obscenity and, in this instance, its obscurity. Thomas Sheridan, in his 1784 *Life of Swift* (No. 46), concentrates in the usual way upon the satire on religious matters in the *Tale*, and he is concerned less with description of the work than with Swift's motives in writing it and in keeping it by him for some years so as to publish it at the most propitious time. With some reason, Sheridan remarks that Swift 'set but little value on his talents as a writer . . . farther than as they might contribute to advance some nobler ends'. The end in view in this particular case he sees as being that of showing the excellency of the established Church, as compared with Catholicism and Dissent, in a way that all could understand and enjoy; wearisome argument is replaced in the *Tale* by 'the graces of the comick muse'. Thus the rival religions, which had been regarded as powerful and terrifying, were made merely contemptible by the power of ridicule. Sheridan has no word of rebuke for Swift's levity on religious matters, as is usual with his contemporaries; instead, he regards the *Tale* as a genuine and permanent contribution to the weakening of popery and fanaticism in England.

At the end of the century, William Godwin (No. 50), concerned primarily with Swift's style, finds the *Tale* a witty book partly spoiled by its use of slang; in 1805 Nathan Drake (No. 57) praises its spirited quality and the learning of the digressions, and Sir Walter Scott (No. 59) has nothing new to say, agreeing with Lord Orrery that the *Tale* is not in intention an anti-religious work, though it is, in Johnson's words, 'of dangerous example'. By 1806 Francis Jeffrey (No. 60) is able to say that the *Tale* 'has, by many, been considered as the first in point of merit' of Swift's works—an opinion with which Jeffrey disagrees partly on the interesting grounds that the *Tale*'s 'mimicry of tediousness and pedantry' is so successful that it becomes itself tedious. Hazlitt (No. 61), on the other hand, thinks the *Tale* 'one of the most masterly composi- tions in the language, whether for thought, wit, or style'. Critics of Swift have, indeed, been more in agreement in the past than they are now, a situation which perhaps itself points to the vitality of such works as the *Tale* and the *Travels*.

III

Gulliver's Travels

Few early comments on minor prose works of Swift exist, and they are perhaps not numerous enough for special notice here, though Richard Steele's famous approval of the gentlemanly *Project for the Advancement of Religion* (No. 4) is an exception to the generally prevailing silence; it does contain critical observation, and not the mere abuse which can generally be expected at this date. The poems receive more notice; Dilworth (No. 30) and later John Aikin (No. 55) (in considerable detail) and Nathan Drake (No. 57) (more generally) are examples of those who write rather sensibly, apart from occasional squeamishness, on the poetry. *The Drapier's Letters*, too, are occasionally treated from the middle of the century onwards.

But for the most part it was the *Travels* that engaged the attention of those who wrote upon Swift. At the time of the publication of the *Travels*, Swift himself was in Ireland and conducting a correspondence with his friends in England, notably with Pope, Bolingbroke, Arbuth- not, and Gay (No. 10). Because of the ironic tone which prevails in the letters of the group, it is difficult to be sure quite how to take some of their comments, but it is plain that *Gulliver's Travels* was a great and immediate success, that what took most people's fancy was the topical and political references, and that opinion of the book was considerably affected by political allegiance. Some disaffected Whigs, like the Tories, approve of it, notably the Duchess Dowager of Marlborough, once a formidable enemy of Swift and his Tory friends, but now delighted by his new satire on the Government and the Court. Gay refers to the Duchess's pleasure in the *Travels*, and her own written comments are included (No. 20). Another celebrated and quarrelsome woman, Lady Mary Wortley Montagu (No. 11), provides a good example of Whig strategy in dealing with the successful *Travels*. Lady Mary was under the impression that the work was a joint production of Swift, Arbuthnot, and Pope, now her enemy; and she ignores its literary merit and satiric brilliance, seeking to dismiss the book with a coarse joke.

In other letters to and from Swift, and in verses by Pope, there is abundant evidence in the way of joking references to show that *Gulliver's Travels* did not seem to Swift's own circle the solemn and savage book it appeared to later writers. Moreover, even the personal jibes or jokes or the political skits which the *Travels* aroused show the extraordinary popularity of the book, and its rapid sale, a phenomenon which Dr. Johnson still found remarkable years later. The fact that 'Remarks' and 'Keys' to the *Travels* were thought worth putting before the public is itself a further indication of the book's popularity. Pope wrote Lilliputian poems, and Arbuthnot, in *An Account of the State of Learning in the Empire of Lilliput; Together with the History and Character of Bullum the Emperor's Library-Keeper*, extended the Lilliputian satire to include that favourite object of Scriblerian wit, Richard Bentley. *Gulliver Decypher'd, or Remarks on a Late Book, intitled Travels into Several Remote Nations of the World, by Capt. Lemuel Gulliver, Vindicating the Reverend Dean on whom it is maliciously Father'd* (n.d.) professes to prove that the malicious attribution of the book to Swift cannot be sustained because there are ancient Greek copies of it extant; because there is 'not one Word of true Christianity in it, but several ludicrous and obscene passages, which are shocking even to common decency'; and because it casts reflections upon 'our present happy Administration, to which 'tis well known how *devoutly* he is attach'd and affected'. A work of such heavy irony as this can contain little of interest, and when in the same vein the author apparently seeks to discredit the *Travels* for its very popularity, the attempt badly misfires:

If our Judgment of Books was to be determin'd by their Success, *Gulliver's Travels* is certainly the best Piece that ever was written, except *Pilgrim's Progress*, the *Seven Champions, Jack the Giant-Killer*, and a few more: For 'tis very remarkable, that there have been several Thousands sold in a week; and it is already translated into the *French* Language, in which, we are told, *Robinson Crusoe* has been very successful. But 'tis well known, that Milton went off, at first, very slowly; that Dean Prideaux could hardly get a Purchaser for his *Connection*, &c., and that a famous Printer was lately undone by the Bible.

The Reason of this is, that there are more Fools than People Of Judgment in the World. . . .

A similar tribute, this time from a writer who seems to enjoy the *Travels* rather than to respond with hostility (his jokes are aimed, rather, at Bishop Wilkins, Sir Richard Blackmore, Edmund Curll, and other assorted characters), is contained in *A Key, being Observations and Explanatory Notes, upon The Travels of Lemuel Gulliver. By Signior*

Corolini, a noble Venetian now residing in London. In a Letter to Dean Swift (1726). Here we are told of the *Travels* that:

The town are infinitely more eager after them, than they were after *Robinson Crusoe*, but this I attribute to their *Ignorance*, for what *Hudibras* says of the Jugler, may with strict Justice be applied to the Readers of our Friend Lemuel,
> *That still the less they understand*
> *The more they 'dmire his Slight of Hand.*

For you are to know, that, under the Allegory of a Voyager, Mr. *Gulliver* gives us an admirable system of modern Politicks.

The author of *A Key* is not certainly known (the work is sometimes attributed to Arbuthnot), but he shows, where he feels inclined to do so, a better than usual grasp of part of Swift's purpose. He agrees, for example, with Gulliver's opinion that nothing is great or little otherwise than by comparison, and his verse epigraph to Book IV has been remarked upon as suggesting that he sees something of what Swift is doing by the relating of Houyhnhnm, Yahoo, and man:

> Here, Rochester's Remark's made good, at least,
> Man, differs more from Man, than Man from Beast.

And he makes his own amusing comparison of the Struldbrugs to 'those *English* ecclesiastics, who have asserted the *Independency* of the *Church* upon the State'.

'Signor Corolini', like Swift's acknowledged friends, seems to find all four voyages amusing reading. But from the beginning, if one is to accept the implications of Pope's, Gay's, Arbuthnot's, and Swift's letters, some people at least were struck by the so-called depreciation of 'human nature' and 'the works of the Creator'—that is, they saw, though in a confused enough way, that more is involved than immediate political comment, that *Gulliver's Travels* is about the nature of man, and not only of man as a political animal. The depreciation of the nature of man was to become the central concern for most of those who referred to *Gulliver's Travels*. Jonathan Smedley's (No. 16) personal animosity to Swift prevents him from having 'the least Sense of any Moral' in the fable, but Pope's mentor, Warburton (No. 13), not notable for literary sensitivity, makes one of the earliest references to Swift's design to 'degrade [his] species'.[2] Similarly the writer of a *Letter from a Clergyman to his Friend* (No. 12), while mainly concerned with the malignancy and destructiveness of the political satire, takes particular exception to the fourth voyage, which he thinks tedious, repetitive, and lacking in the wit and invention which make the first three at least potentially diverting were it not for their grossness and lewdness. In the fourth voyage 'the Author flags, he loses his vivacity, and in my Opinion maintains little of his former Spirit but the Rancour'. This pre-eminent importance of the fourth voyage, whether liked or hated, is further attested to by the charming skit called *Critical Remarks upon Gulliver's Travels; Particularly his Voyage to the Houyhnhnms Country*. This is a parody not of Swift but of the critical methods of Dr. Richard Bentley, who appears on the title-page as the author (the true author may have been John Arbuthnot). Compared with most of the minor ironic works of the period, this is polished and clever; as comment on Swift's work its chief interest, apart from its assumption that the reading public will be familiar with and particularly interested in Houyhnhnmland, is its pretence to clear Gulliver from the severe imputation of debasing human nature. It shows, too, how people continued to take sides for or against Swift in accordance with their personal friendships and political allegiances. Again, on the other side, *An Essay upon the Taste and Writings of the Present Times* (No. 17), a piece inscribed to Sir Robert Walpole, shows the resentment of Whig writers against the ascendancy which the Swift-Pope group ('not only Mr. *Pope*, but the whole Company') had established in the literary world, making themselves dreaded by their power of ridicule. It was to be long before any dispassionate criticism of Swift's writings, unaffected by personal and political considerations, could come into being. Henry Fielding (No. 24), a devoted admirer of Swift, was one of the earliest men of letters to consider the satires as works of literary art belonging to a well-founded tradition. With Fielding, Swift becomes a major comic writer, 'the greatest master of humour that ever wrote', to be placed in relation to such established figures as Lucian, Rabelais, and Cervantes. As Fielding's Billy Booth remarks, Pope had already set Swift in this important tradition when he compared him, in the beginning of *The Dunciad*, to Cervantes and Rabelais, but with Fielding Pope's compliment to a friend becomes a considered literary judgement.

But, as in the case of *A Tale of a Tub*, some of the earliest literary criticism proper comes from France. Voltaire, who was known to Swift and corresponded with him, was an early proselytizer among his countrymen. What he has to say is rather repetitious for this reason, but what he repeats is, like Fielding's, a considered view. Voltaire's general accounts of Swift's way of writing are always enthusiastic, but in writing to M. Thieriot his particular opinion of *Gulliver's Travels* is a little less whole-hearted. Being Voltaire, he is pleased by the satire, but he also notices the book's imaginative power and the poise of its style; in a second letter to Thieriot, however, he seems to be finding that fantasy—even fantasy as skilful as Swift's—will pall in the long run. 'Nothing unnatural may please long', he says in a thoroughly neo-classical comment.

Partly because of Voltaire's public advocacy of Swift, another French man of letters, the Abbé Desfontaines, took it upon himself in 1727 to translate *Gulliver's Travels*. Both as a translator and as a critic of the *Travels*, Desfontaines suffers from the limitation common to many French writers of the neo-classical period: he is unable to free himself from French conceptions of correctness and polish, and so does less than justice to Swift's imaginative power. In his translation he feels himself free to omit and to adjust to French taste wherever he wishes, and he makes of the *Travels* a much gentler book than it really is. The polite irony of Swift's draft letter to him (No. 15 (d)) is no more than he deserved. But his Preface to his translations, while marred by the same limitation, does contain some genuine and apposite critical comment. Despite what he sees as its occasional coarseness, triviality, and insularity, Desfontaines is aware of the book's originality, its inventiveness and its moral concern. The fourth book he finds the most brilliant as well as the boldest. From Desfontaines we hear nothing of the degrading of human nature; he regards Houyhnhnms and Yahoos as artistic devices. For example, 'man, if he is to be well drawn, must be portrayed as an animal other than man'. The book as a whole is concerned, thinks Desfontaines, with important moral and philosophical ideas, though they are presented in a comic way. Desfontaines has some further comment on the *Travels* in his Preface to his own book, *Le Nouveau Gulliver* (No. 15 (e)). In 1743 another French critic of the *Travels*, Paradis de Moncrif (No. 23), interestingly forestalls Dr. Johnson in denying genuine imagination to the use of big men and little men, while to him the fourth voyage consists of a mere frigid trick of reversal by which horses are given the reason of men, and men the instinct of horses.

After Desfontaines's translation several reviews appeared in France. *Le Journal Littéraire* for 1723–8 (Volume XII, ii, article lx) has a lengthy and disappointingly descriptive account of the work. Virtually its only interpretative comment is on the fourth voyage, which it sees, as does de Moncrif and as do others in the eighteenth century, as being a mere pointless reversal of horses and men:

These Houyhnhnms are horses, but horses endowed with reason and the faculty of speech. In their country there live also the Yahoos, a kind of animals who resemble men, without having the same degree of intelligence nor the ability to speak. That is to say that (at least according to the description of our author) the horses are men, and the men horses.

Later in the century French opinion seems to incline more firmly towards seeing *Gulliver's Travels* as essentially a philosophic work; this is partly due, no doubt, to the nature of Desfontaines's translation. This attitude is very marked in No. 33, a review of a reissue of the Desfontaines version. Again, in 1760 the Abbé Ladvocat's *Dictionnaire Historique-Portatif* (Volume II) gives a descriptive list in which *Gulliver's Travels* is called Swift's *Roman philosophique & historique de Guliver . . . connu de tout le Monde.* Diderot, on the other hand, chooses to take *Gulliver's Travels*, together with the *Modest Proposal* and the Bickerstaff papers, as a useful illustration of the English quality called 'humour' (*Encyclopédie ou Dictionnaire Raisonné des Sciences, des Arts et des Métiers*, 1765, Volume VIII, 353).

With Lord Orrery's self-righteous *Remarks on the Life and Writings of Dr. Jonathan Swift* (No. 26) the lines of demarcation between those who are for Swift and those who are against him, and particularly those who are for and against the fourth book of *Gulliver's Travels*, are more sharply drawn. To Arbuthnot the *Travels* had been 'a merry work', to Desfontaines a moral one, but Orrery takes up, with heavy emphasis, the opinion already expressed earlier that the aim of the fourth voyage is to depreciate human nature. Orrery's book is a substantial one, and both his title and the fact that he had been a friend of Swift's later years gave prestige to his account. This book was reviewed both in England and in France as an authoritative version of the life of the notorious Dean. It was Orrery, with his scandalous stories of Swift's treatment of Stella and Vanessa, and his insistence on the avarice and peevishness which seem to have overtaken Swift in his last years, who established the legend of the ambitious and inhumane misanthrope. Orrery's stories were fascinating and he gave people what they wished to hear; his account of Swift's life and character chimed well with the growing tendency of the century away from wit to sentimentality.

The misunderstanding of Swift's work which is so prevalent from the middle of the century on is doubtless a genuine misunderstanding, not the deliberate misrepresentation which, while Swift lived, was one of the chief weapons of his political and private enemies. As Fielding found, comic and satiric writing was less and less understood, and Orrery's account of Swift's life seemed only to confirm what many people felt in reading *Gulliver's Travels*. As might be expected, Samuel Richardson (No. 22) is one of those who feel the Dean's behaviour to his 'wife' (Stella) and Vanessa is 'of a piece with all those of his writings, in which he endeavours to debase the human, and to raise above it the brutal nature'. (Richardson's characters in the novels are also made to express horror and disgust at Swift's work; Clarissa's 'pity' for the celebrated Dr. Swift and Harriett Byron's comment on his dirty imagination are well known.) Richardson's letter also shows that there was opposition to Orrery's unctuously spiteful attitude, and there is other evidence of this—for example, in Lady Bradshaigh's reply to Richardson's letter which refers to the 'outcry' against Orrery. There are also verse attacks on Orrery and his 'scribbling Itch'—for example, *A Satire on L——d O——y's Remarks on the Life and Writings of Dean S——t*, a three-stanza poem added to *An Epistle from the Hon. R[ichard] E[dgcumbe]*, 1752, which contains two lines that must often be echoed by any reader of Swift criticism in the eighteenth and nineteenth centuries:

> Had S——ft provok'd to this Behaviour,
> Sure after Death, Resentment cools.

A more accomplished piece is *A Candid Appeal from the late Dean Swift to the Right Hon. the Earl of O——y* (1752). In this the ghost of Swift appears to say scornfully, in his own octosyllabic metre, that Orrery is:

> Skill'd to adapt obscurer Praise
> To Numbers low, and feeble Lays,
> Distinguish'd Censure to expose
> In smooth epistolary Prose.

to

> Refine elaborate Abuse
> Correct the wrong, reclaim the wild,
> And help to form the *favrite Child*;[3]
> Explain good Manners, teach good Sense,
> At poor departed Swift's expense.

The verses end in triumphantly Swiftian vein:

> The Dean is dead—and you may write.

But these attacks on Orrery build merely upon his ingratitude and hypocrisy; it remained for Delany, Deane Swift, and Sheridan to refute the noble lord in books as substantial as his own. Unfortunately, not one of these refutations appears to have achieved its end. Orrery had made his point vigorously and with apparent authority; the replies of Swift's friends seemed merely defensive, and the Swift legend survived.

IV

THE RELATION OF SWIFT'S LIFE AND WORKS

Orrery's ambitious *Remarks* contains comment on many of Swift's works, both in prose and in poetry, but he devotes a great deal of space to *Gulliver's Travels*, which he discusses in relation to Swift's life and character. He concedes that the general intention of the book was 'to correct vice, by showing her deformity in opposition to the beauty of virtue, and to amend the false systems of philosophy, by pointing out the errors, and applying salutary means to avoid them'. To do Orrery justice, this conception of *Gulliver's Travels*, as, at least in intention, an example of the genre of philosophical or moral voyage, is of some importance; nor is this his only just comment on the book. He sees the main point of Swift's methods in Lilliput and Laputa, and even in the Struldbrugs, but he is less concerned with these insights in themselves than with relating Swift's writings to a splenetic misanthropy resulting from disappointed ambition. Often one feels, in reading the *Remarks*, that if Orrery had carried his occasional insights further, a genuinely critical work, of some importance at this early date, might have resulted. Even in discussing the fourth voyage, where he is at his most self-righteous, he is able to see one of the problems that have concerned later critics: that the picture of the Houyhnhnms is not very 'inviting or amusing'.

It wants both shade and light to adorn it. It is cold and insipid. We there view the pure instincts of brutes, unassisted by any knowledge of letters, acting within their narrow sphere, merely for their immediate preservation. They are incapable of doing wrong, therefore they act right. It is surely a very low character given to creatures, in whom the author would insinuate some degree of reason, that they act inoffensively, when they have neither the motive nor the power to act otherwise. Their virtuous qualities are only negative.

Critics since Orrery's day have dealt with this unattractive or negative quality in the Houyhnhnms in a variety of ways. Orrery does not deal with it at all, but uses it as an excuse for further moralizing. He deserves credit for perceptiveness in this and other places, but he has only himself to blame for the fact that he has rarely received it.

The first to refute Lord Orrery with some attempt at systematic inclusiveness was Patrick Delany (No. 27). Delany is, like Orrery, concerned primarily with Swift's life, and in critical matters he is a good example of Swift's misfortune in being so ill served by his friends. Delany dislikes the 'Voyage to the Houyhnhnms' even more than Orrery does. 'I am sick of this subject', he remarks at one point, an intensification of Orrery's 'I am heartily tired of this last part of *Gulliver's* travels'. Like some of his predecessors, Delany equates the Yahoos straight-forwardly with man and the Houyhnhnms apparently with horses, and he embarks on a muddle-headed and rather pointless discussion of the real superiority of the human body to that of the horse. 'This voyage', he says:

is considered as a satire of Swift's upon the human frame. I would fain hope, that it was intended only as a satire upon human corruptions: be that as it may, it is most certainly in effect a panegyrick upon the human frame, by shewing the inability even of the noblest structures of inferior animals: to answer the purposes of a reasonable life in this world.

The dismissive 'be that as it may' is a curious phrase; Delany sets aside, perhaps as insoluble, the major question of whether or not the fourth voyage is a moral rather than a physical satire. In practice, Delany devotes considerable space to the weakness of Swift's attempts 'to equal the Houyhnhnm structure to the human'. Perhaps the only critical comment of real interest Delany makes is concerned with the Houyhnhnms:

And he deprives them of all those tender passions, and affections, without which life would be a load: and which, when he lost, his own became so.

But like Orrery, Delany takes this line of thought no further. Really close and acute discussion of Swift's intention in portraying the Houyhnhnms as he did was not to come until Thomas Tyler's letter to the *Academy* on 18 August 1883.[4] Delany constantly turns criticism of *Gulliver's Travels* into moral indignation, as in the final phrase of the last quotation above, or in his singularly offensive assumption that Swift's last illness was 'the signal chastisement of his total infatuation' (Orrery had made the same assumption, applauded by Samuel Richardson). Curiously enough, Delany concludes in this way:

But however, the satire upon vice and the amendment of mankind by it, was his main view even in that abominable picture, which he drew of the Yahoos; may, I think, be fairly concluded from his own verses on the death of the Doctor SWIFT, which he puts in the mouth of an impartial man.

This conclusion is drawn not from the work itself but from an outside source; presumably Delany regarded the fourth voyage as a satiric failure.

Delany's reference to Swift's verses on his own death as having been put 'in the mouth of' a *persona* raises another curious point: of all those who wrote on either the *Travels* or the *Tale* in the eighteenth century, not one makes a firm distinction between Swift and the 'supposed authors' of these two works. What even Delany, a sufficiently obtuse critic, could see in the case of one of Swift's poems, neither he nor the other writers seem to take into account in dealing with the major works; it does not occur to Delany that the 'infatuation' may be not Swift's, but Gulliver's. This approach was not to be made explicit for many years; one may assume that at least some of Swift's immediate contemporaries and friends made the distinction in reading, but they do not make it in writing.

Delany was rapidly followed by Swift's contumacious cousin, Deane (No. 28), who vigorously takes issue with both his predecessors in his *Essay upon the Life and Writings and Character of Dr. Jonathan Swift.* Though at times excessively aggressive, Deane Swift does not make an effort to deal with *Gulliver's Travels* as a literary work by an important author. 'I shall only observe in the general', he begins firmly,

that the famous Gulliver is a direct, plain and bitter satire against the innumerable follies and corruptions in law, politicks, learning, morals and religion.

He accords the *Travels* the status which it had originally had among Swift's friends, that of a comic satire whose aim was partly to amuse: 'his intention', says Deane Swift,

was either to laugh vice and immorality if it were possible quite out of the world; or at least to avenge the cause of virtue on all the patrons and betters of iniquity.

Then he goes on to deal briskly with each book in turn, perhaps spending too much time in refuting some of the more crass judgements of Lord Orrery, ('this incomparable judge of excellencies and defects in the productions of the learned'), but sometimes succeeding in showing just how crass they were. And it is Deane Swift who realizes that the work of his clerical cousin may well have relevance to the Bible. In discussing the King of Brobdingnag's description of man as a grovelling insect, he refers to John the Baptist, in relation to the Yahoos, he produces a host of references to the Old and New Testaments; so that the author of the *Travels* becomes a 'preacher of righteousness', a 'watchman of the Christian faith', whose duty it was to show up the depravities of men as his predecessors, the prophets and the apostles, had done, in order to 'enforce the obligation of religion and virtue upon the souls of men'. Thus the depreciator of men made in God's image becomes in Deane Swift's eyes God's own prophet.

Thomas Sheridan (No. 46) was not, chronologically, the next writer on *Gulliver's Travels*, but it is he who next attempts, as Orrery, Delany, and Swift had done, a full-scale biographical treatment. Sheridan is concerned with *Gulliver's Travels* chiefly as the main cause of the attribution of misanthropy to Swift,

chiefly founded upon his supposed satire on human nature, in the picture he has drawn of the Yahoos. This opinion has been so universally adopted by almost all who have read *Gulliver's Travels*, that to controvert it would be supposed to act in opposition to the common sense and reason of mankind.

Sheridan, however, boldly undertakes to controvert it none the less. The simple and reasonable yet in its way epoch-making case that he undertakes to prove is that:

the whole apologue of the Houyhnhnms and Yahoos, far from being intended as a debasement of human nature, if rightly understood, is evidently designed to show in what the true dignity and perfection of man's nature consists, and to point out the way by which it may be attained.

Sheridan sees acutely enough that in the first three books Swift has shown mankind in its actual mixture of 'vices, follies, and absurdities', 'not without some mixture of good qualities, of virtue and wisdom, though in small proportion to the others, as they are to be found in life'. Thus Sheridan goes beyond the political and topical issues which had concerned so many of his predecessors, and sees that the first three books, as well as the fourth, are concerned with the nature of man. He then goes on to point out, with considerable accuracy and precision, how in Book IV Swift divides those qualities of the human mind which have been more discursively dealt with in the first three books, 'taking away the rational soul from the Yahoo, and transferring it to the Houyhnhnm', the bodies of man and horse being used to make the division of qualities clearer. 'The rational soul in the Houyhnhnm acts unerringly as by instinct; it intuitively perceives what is right, and necessarily acts up to the dictates of reason.' But if the Houyhnhnm is a portrait of un-adulterated virtue, the Yahoo is a portrait of unmixed vice; not man at all, but a non-existent creature, the product of the author's brain.

Sheridan perceives that Swift has gone out of his way to differentiate Yahoo from man: the Yahoo has no ray of reason and no speech, and it does not have the upright posture which had for centuries been considered the mark of man's God-centred intelligence. It differs from man, in fact, 'in all the characteristical marks which distinguish man from the rest of the animal world', resembling him only in its bodily shape and the vicious propensities of its nature. The logic of the author's end required that the 'vicious qualities of man's nature in their pure unmixed state' should be embodied in a brute, governed by instinct uncontrolled by reason; similarly, that logic required that the creature should be human in shape, to bring the lesson home to man. The end of the whole invention is to show man in its acutest form the choice between virtue and vice with which he is continuously faced. The fourth voyage is not a degrading of man, but a lesson to him; the Yahoo is no more a man than the Houyhnhnm is a horse (though, as we have seen, earlier commentators persisted in seeing them so). Sheridan makes his point, perhaps, at excessive length, but it was a point thoroughly worth making, and previous outcries against the fourth voyage (and indeed further outcries still to come) showed that it was necessary to belabour it. How can it be, says Sheridan, that readers apparently accepted with equanimity the bold satire on human nature 'in its actual state of exis- tence', in the giant king's observations to Gulliver, and yet exclaimed with horror at the allegory of the Yahoos?

Sheridan's point of view, obvious though it seems now, is an insight of genuine importance and originality in his own day. Until the fourth voyage could be seen as not a snarl of fury, but the work of a logical imagination proceeding according to necessary literary laws, no pro- gress could be made in critical evaluation. It would not be just, how- ever, to say that no previous critic had shown a similar balance and good sense. Hawkesworth (No. 31)—'the benevolent and judicious Dr. Hawkesworth' he is called by Sheridan, who quotes from him as well as from the intemperate and imperceptive Dr. Young—had in a brief, concise, and brilliant note on 'the picture of a Yahoo' to some degree anticipated Sheridan's more exact and extensive distinctions. Indeed, Hawkesworth's notes, though few and brief, are uniformly 'judicious', and it is matter for regret that he did not see fit, in his edition of Swift's *Works*, to give more of his own opinions instead of quoting so fully from the remarks of others, especially the egregious Orrery.

Soon after Hawkesworth's edition, and predating Sheridan's *Life* by twenty-six years, is the *Life of Swift* by W. H. Dilworth. Dilworth's criticism (No. 30) is largely derivative, but he deals with the works one by one with a patience infrequent in the eighteenth century, and writes at unusual length and with some perceptiveness on *The Drapier's Letters* and *The Modest Proposal*. He is equally sensible on the first three books of the *Travels*, including such episodes as that of the Struldbrugs, and regards the whole as a forceful satire on the vices of men. As for the fourth voyage, he is brief, pointed, and forthright on the 'affected squeamishness' of those who profess to be offended by it. Brutality *ought* to be shown in the most shocking and detestable light if 'the obligations of religion and virtue' are to be enforced upon the human mind. Dilworth's lengthy effort makes, on the whole, dull enough reading, and even he, comparatively enlightened though he seems to be, finds it necessary to take Swift to task for some nauseous and indecent ideas; indeed, he even (despite his sharpness with those who are offended by *Gulliver's Travels*) makes use of the familiar phrase: Swift at times 'degrades humanity'. But he pays Swift the compliment of a serious and conscientious handling, and sees *Gulliver's Travels* as, to quote his anonymous French contemporary (No. 33), 'a book of censure and morality'.

It is none the less something of a relief to turn to the lighter touch of Lord Lyttelton in his *Dialogues of the Dead* (No. 32), two lively squibs in which Swift converses with Addison and Mercury and Lucian discusses Swift with Rabelais (to whom he is preferred). Lyttelton, like Fielding, sees Swift as an author to be laughed with and delighted in, not to be solemnly anathematized in the manner of Young.

But along with criticism of comparative skill, like that of Sheridan and Hawkesworth, or of charm, like that of Lyttelton, there are heard the voices of Richardson and of Edward Young—voices which were to swell to a chorus in the nineteenth century. Young's famous passage on the fourth voyage (No. 31) is as sanctimonious as the *Remarks* of Orrery. Swift has 'blasphemed a nature little lower than that of angels', has made a monster of Milton's human face divine. This is the familiar accusation of 'depreciating human nature', made more rhapsodic and emotional in an age which increasingly stressed that in man which is little lower than the angels, forgetting that which is little higher than the beasts. This kind of impressionistic outcry has had to serve as criticism of Swift through much of the time since his death; few of those who wrote about him in the eighteenth century, few even in the nineteenth, seem to be writing from a close study of the text. In James

Harris (No. 42) we find a more precise critical style than Young's, but no more critical intelligence; for Harris, as for others before him, Swift is merely trying 'to render the nature of *men odious*, and the nature of *beasts admirable*'. In such company it is a relief to find the brief, sensible comments of Fielding or of Goldsmith (No. 34), who briefly presents an anti-romantic Swift, describing Nature 'just as it was', or Lord Monboddo's brisk recommendation of Swift's simple and circumstantial style as well suited to a true history as it is to a false (No. 37), or Ralph Griffith's honest admiration (No. 35), or Samuel Badcock's delight in Swift's creative wit (No. 41). George-Monck Berkeley (No. 48) is still concerned to refute, by a rather niggling logic, the old charges of misanthropy and impiety, and a reviewer of his book (Thomas Ogle) is still concerned to dismiss the refutation: 'What trifling is this!' Similarly, the anonymous writer in the *European Magazine* for November 1790 (No. 50) finds that the hateful lesson of the 'Voyage to the Houyhnhnms' outweighs its other merits, and chooses the second voyage as by far the best. In none of the voyages is Swift credited with much imaginative power, and here he, as any satirist would be, is brought up short against the dogmatic criterion of the end of the century: 'The mind that is not turned either to the sublime or the pathetic, cannot certainly rank in the first class of writers of imagination.'

On the whole, those who write specifically of the fourth voyage in the later part of the century continue to blame it. James Beattie (No. 38) appears to make a distinction between the fourth and the first three voyages, in which the satire, as he rightly says, 'is levelled at human pride and folly; at the abuses of human learning; at the absurdity of speculative projectors; at those criminal or blundering expedients in policy which we are apt to overlook, or even to applaud, because custom has made them familiar'. Beattie is aware that satire, and perhaps pre-eminently Swift's satire, works to strip the veil of familiarity from our actions. But where satire goes beyond particularities it becomes, for Beattie, a kind of blasphemy, since it impugns not only human nature but the God who created it. Like other eighteenth-century writers, Beattie raises some questions of potential interest—for example, he sees the Houyhnhms as being 'destitute of every religious idea', though there is ascribed to them 'the perfection of reason, and of happiness'. Considered in terms of literary, philosophic, and moral intention, such remarks could have led to interesting critical comment, but Beattie, like others, is too promptly horrified by rational Houyhnhnms and irrational Yahoos alike to think the matter through. Only a malevolent heart, he tells us, could triumph in the satire of the fourth voyage, and his indignation leads him to see it as an ill-conceived and indeed absurd fable, as well as a wicked one. But even when, as so often, the 'Voyage to the Houyhnhnms' is dismissed with horror, justice is done to the circumstantial and consistent detail with which the countries of Lilliput and Brobdingnag are described. Beattie writes well, though briefly, on this, and Samuel Johnson (No. 40) would seem to be in a minority (though he is not quite alone) in dismissing Swift's 'device of relative size' with his famous and devastating comment, 'When once you have thought of big men and little men, it is very easy to do all the rest'.

It is unfortunate that Johnson never had occasion to write at length on Swift's prose works, his only formal criticism of Swift being in the *Lives of the Poets*, so that we lack only full expression of his considered views on *Gulliver's Travels*. His one statement that the third voyage gave least pleasure and the fourth most disgust is in line with the general tendency of eighteenth-century comment, and suggests that even from Johnson we would not have received a really critical and literary reading of the fourth voyage. He writes well, however, on Swift's prose style, and in this, too, he is typical of several eighteenth-century critics. Once safely away from the question of the moral or immoral tendencies of the *Travels* or the *Tale*, they could devote themselves comfortably to pointing out the virtues of Swift's style, its ease, manliness, and clarity, or sometimes its defects in correctness. Hugh Blair, lecturing on rhetoric and publishing his lectures in 1783 (No. 45), not only deals generally with the qualities of Swift's style, but chooses a quite minor work, the *Proposal for Correcting the English Tongue*, for close stylistic examination. One should not leave the eighteenth century, however, without remarking upon a happy descriptive phrase coined for the *Travels* by the writer (he signs himself with the initials P.L.) of the Preface to a short novel called *The English Hermit* (1786). Here, remarking first upon the popularity of Defoe's novels 'among the lower rank of reader', P.L. goes on to say 'it is as certain that the morality in masquerade, which may be discovered in the Travels of Lemuel Gulliver, has been an equal entertainment to the superior class of mankind'.

V

NINETEENTH-CENTURY VIEWS
The nineteenth century in Swift criticism begins trivially enough.

Charles Henry Wilson's *Swiftiana* (No. 54) is a compendium of un-original anecdotes and critical dicta, both often trite and inaccurate (for example, 'scarcely one metaphor is to be found in [Swift's] works'). Alexander Chalmers (No. 53) is equally unoriginal, while Richard Payne Knight (No. 56) contributes one good comment on the plausibility of Swift's fiction in the *Travels*. John Aikin (No. 55) and Nathan Drake (No. 57) have, however, some of the conscientiousness of a Dilworth. Aikin deals with the poetry, and much of it is not to his liking, but he recognizes Swift as the master of 'familiar poetry' unrivalled in its easy grace and vigour, its consummate naturalness in the handling of rhymes, and its colloquial freedom. Though he ignores the powerful satiric poems which he finds indelicate, Aikin's selection among the rest, and his comments upon those he chooses to consider, show good critical taste and understanding. Nathan Drake, too, is selective about what he treats, and in him one finds again the opinion that Swift is 'prone to vilify and degrade human nature', a fault for which no abilities can atone.

After these slight beginnings, however, we come to the criticism of a man of more capacious mind, Sir Walter Scott. Scott devoted much of his prodigious energy to work on Swift; his annotated edition appeared in 1814, and his *Life of Swift*, which comprised the first volume of that edition, contains critical as well as biographical material. He has remarks also on individual works, including, of course, *Gulliver's Travels*. His criticism is not always consistent with itself, and he has many obvious limitations; but here for the first time since Sheridan's *Life* and Hawkesworth's notes we are dealing with a man of original mind who, whatever the shortcomings of his criticism by modern standards, is at least endeavouring to come to grips with real critical issues and who is capable of large insights. Scott has little of interest to say on *A Tale of a Tub*, but he is interesting on *The Drapier's Letters*, the poems, which he regards as unrivalled in their kind, though he finds the indelicate ones perverse, and on the *Journal to Stella* and the *Sermons*, which are very rarely taken notice of in the period under review; and all these comments are included in No. 59 of this volume. This may appear to give a disproportionate amount of space to Scott, but it is of interest to see some of Swift's less spectacular works treated seriously and methodically for virtually the first time. The work on which Scott chiefly concentrates, however, is *Gulliver's Travels*, which he treats, again with method and at considerable length, both in the *Life* and in the introduction to the *Travels* themselves. In both—but with particular force in the Introduction—he shows that abhorrence of the Yahoos which has rendered so many incapable of looking critically at the details of the fourth voyage, and of considering freely for what purposes that voyage and its animals were created. Although in the *Life* Scott concedes an intended moral purpose to the voyage, he regards it as ill conceived; and his explanation of the picture of the Yahoos is the now-familiar one of 'incipient mental disease'. A more literary objection to the fourth voyage is that its fiction is 'gross and improbable', especially (as Beattie had suggested) in the case of the Houyhnhnms, who 'are represented with attributes inconsistent with their natural structure'. But Scott is unable to bring to a book he finds so loathsome the considerable power of close attention he devotes to the other three. It is in this that his strength as a critic of the *Travels* lies; he reads the first three books closely, and points out several details which are still repeated today as examples of Swift's skill as a writer of fiction and particularly his mastery of verisimilitude through the observations and reactions of Gulliver to what he sees in Lilliput and Brobdingnag. Scott, like most people, regards the 'Voyage to Laputa' as inferior to the two preceding books, but he brings the same close attention to it, distinguishing between the kinds of scientific activity with which it deals and pointing out the satire on the 'projectors, or undertakers', like those who floated the notorious South Sea Scheme. Scott, for all his failure with the 'Voyage to the Houyhnhnms', is an informed and intelligent critic of Swift. He takes his task seriously, reads attentively, and for the most part (the fourth voyage and some of the poems are an exception) without prejudice, and comments with perception and good sense. Despite the developments made in the present century in Swift criticism, Scott, like Sheridan, still makes on the whole a respectable figure in his period.

Scott quotes in the *Life* from John Dunlop who, in his *History of Fiction*, a work well known in its time, compares Swift's use of 'circumstantial detail of facts' in *Gulliver's Travels* with Defoe's in *Robinson Crusoe*. Dunlop is further represented in this volume by a conventional discussion of Swift's indebtedness to Cyrano de Bergerac (No. 58). Two years later Francis Jeffrey (No. 60) introduces in his review of Scott's edition an objection to the fourth voyage of *Gulliver's Travels* which might be considered typical of him: the voyage fails not so much because it degrades human nature in an exaggerated way as because it is simply dull. Indeed, the whole of the *Travels* is a failure as satire, and it owes its appeal to its 'plausible description of physical wonders'. The aim of the writer in the whole of the *Travels* is, none the less, 'to degrade and vilify human nature'. Jeffrey is scarcely a competent critic of Swift, yet his arbitrary views do provide a late example of the absurdities produced even as late as 1816 by a splenetic dislike of Swift's personality and of the legendary stories which still passed as a reputable account of his life. Hazlitt, on the contrary, has no personal dislike of Swift, his life, or his politics, and he sees Swift as a satirist of power who in *Gulliver's Travels* tears 'the scales from off his moral vision' and, weighing human life, finds nothing solid or valuable in it but virtue and wisdom. Hazlitt, writing of *Gulliver's Travels* only incidentally in *Lectures on the English Poets*, does not apply himself closely to the *Travels* in supporting his opinion of its power, but at least he sees it as a serious moral work and has no patience with the 'quacks in morality' who 'preach up the dignity of human nature' and 'pamper pride and hypocrisy'. Perhaps one of the most penetrating and healthy general remarks made about Swift in the whole period to which this volume is devoted is by Hazlitt:

There is nothing more likely to drive a man mad than the being unable to get rid of the idea of the distinction between right and wrong, and an obstinate, constitutional preference of the true to the agreeable.

Coleridge (No. 62) unfortunately has left only scattered remarks on Swift, but they are enough to make one wish for more. He appreciates Swift's wit, and his brief comments on the Houyhnhnms are of real interest: in them Swift gives 'the misanthropic ideal of man—that is, a being virtuous from rule and duty, but untouched by the principle of love', and again: 'critics in general complain of the Yahoos; I complain of the Houyhnhnms'.

The few contributions from the early nineteenth century which have been included in this volume to complete the picture of early Swift criticism are closed by the careful work of William Monck Mason (No. 63). Mason is a historian rather than a critic, and much of his commentary is derivative, but he is capable of pointing out the rather muddled thinking of Scott on the fourth voyage, and in his notes (perhaps the best part of his work on Swift) he can produce original and perceptive comments. For example, he brings to bear upon *Gulliver's Travels* Swift's now-famous letter to Pope about his hatred for mankind and his love for 'John, Peter, Thomas, and so forth', and suggests:

To represent, in strong colours, the actually degraded state of human nature, and yet, to shew the great value of charitable forbearance towards the faults of particular individuals, seems to be the moral which Swift had in view, and that which the Travels of Captain Lemuel Gulliver were intended chiefly to inculcate.

Outside *Gulliver's Travels*, too, Mason has some good things to say
about the 'cold, phlegmatic style of a political projector', the 'business-
like manner' and the 'unconsciousness of the barbarity of his own project' which Swift feigns so brilliantly and with such fine satiric strategy
in *A Modest Proposal*.

And so a survey of eighteenth-century and early-nineteenth-century
criticism of Swift is not, after all, wholly barren. There is much political
and personal spite, much outrage, genuine or feigned, much that a
modern reader will scarcely call critical at all. But throughout the
period, and increasingly in the later part of it, there are rewarding
glimpses of genuine critical application and intelligence. The critical
distinctions which we make were not made then; yet from time to time
there can be found occasional and undeveloped insights which anticipate later theories.

During the nineteenth century, following the critical efforts of Scott,
Hazlitt, and Coleridge, there are disappointingly few pieces of properly
critical thinking on the subject of Swift as a writer or as a man. Dislike
for the 'dirt' and coarseness of his work becomes, if anything, more
marked and more widespread. Taine, Gosse, the biographer John
Forster, Augustine Birrell and others refer in terms of passionate revul-
sion to much of the work, while Thackeray, who advises readers to
ignore the fourth voyage of *Gulliver's Travels*, and Macaulay, who
proclaims that Swift's mind was 'richly stored with images from the
dunghill and the lazarhouse', have become almost proverbial examples
of both the squeamishness and the violence of nineteenth-century reac-
tion to Swift. The comic writer and the playful companion becomes a
morose figure of almost diabolical spleen.

In this thick atmosphere nothing approaching a close reading of the
texts appears to have been possible. Nearest to it is the letter of the
biblical scholar and Shakespearian editor Thomas Tyler, printed in the
Academy for 18 August 1833. The letter is described and part of it is
quoted by Milton Voigt in *Swift and the Twentieth Century*. In it Tyler
looks closely at the fourth voyage and concludes that:

As the life according to original and essential human nature, the life of the
Yahoos, is exhibited as revolting, so the life according to perfect reason—that
of the Houyhnhnms—is set forth as impracticable and even absurd.[5]

But if Tyler's is a lone critical voice in the second part of the nineteenth
century, the comparatively shrewd and sensible biographical work be-

gun by Scott and Monck Mason was continued by John Forster, Craik, and Leslie Stephen.

VI

TO THE PRESENT DAY

In our own century, careful biographical work, painstaking checking of records, pruning away of legendary melodrama has continued. Critically, too, great advances have been made, and there is no doubt that the greatest contribution of our period has been the recognition that the writings are not screams of pain or fury, but works of art; and, especially, that Swift is not necessarily identifiable with Gulliver, the author of *A Tale of a Tub*, the modest proposer, or any other of his invented authors; that these themselves, indeed, may be the objects of their creator's satire. Opinions still differ on many specific points—for example, whether, and if so in what way, the *Tale* may be regarded as a unity, what precisely *Gulliver's Travels* means. But Swift criticism is now firmly established on a close examination of the text, and due importance is given to Swift's art as being, precisely, that of the satirist and the skilled rhetorician. His rhetorical methods are examined, his satirical techniques related to those of other writers. Whatever further developments are in store, and one hopes that there will be many, the day is long past when abuse or a cry of distress could masquerade as serious criticism of our greatest prose satirist.

This Introduction has concentrated chiefly, for obvious reasons, on criticism of *A Tale of a Tub* and *Gulliver's Travels*; but among the extracts which deal with these major works will be found occasional references to the other prose works and the poems. Some of these have been mentioned in this Introduction, but for the most part they are so brief, and occur so rarely, that they have not been separately considered, nor have they been separately included in the text. There are one or two exceptions to this general rule: for instance, apart from those already mentioned, the French *Journal Anglais* in 1777 devotes considerable space to a translation of *A Modest Proposal* and some brief but sensible remarks upon its method. This is such a rarity in the case of the minor works that the critical comments are given in No. 39. Another exception is Hugh Blair's lengthy and detailed consideration of the style of *The Proposal for Correcting the English Tongue*. But for the most part the occasional remarks on the minor works which do exist have been left as incidental comments in the general criticism of writers like Johnson, Dilworth, Sheridan, or Scott.

NOTES ON EDITIONS

Swift's works, almost all published anonymously, seem to have been widely read in his own lifetime and throughout the eighteenth century. His most popular pieces ran through several editions. Among the poems, *Cadenus & Vanessa* appeared seven times in 1726, and *The Conduct of the Allies*, which sold exceptionally well, appeared in five editions in 1711 and one in 1712–13. According to the introduction to Herbert Davis's sixth volume of the *Works* a second edition was called for after only two days, and this edition was sold out in five hours. In a few months, six editions were sold out, making eleven thousand copies. Editions also appeared in Edinburgh and Dublin in 1712, and in the same year it was translated into French and Spanish. *The Drapier's Letters* appeared in Dublin twice in 1724 and once in 1725 and 1730, and in London also in 1730.

The major works must also have been much read. *A Tale of a Tub* ran to three editions in 1704 and one in 1705, and it appeared again in 1710, 1711, 1724, 1727, 1733, 1739, 1743, 1747 and 1755, apart from pirated editions, several editions in Ireland and Scotland, and the French, German, and Dutch translations; *Gulliver's Travels*, published in 1726 in two editions, also appeared in 1727 (twice), 1738, 1742, 1743, 1747, 1748, 1751 (twice), 1755, 1756, 1757, 1759, 1760, 1765, and thereafter yearly until 1768.

As the century advanced, complete editions of Swift's *Works* were frequently printed, about fifteen editions being produced between 1735 (Faulkner's edition) and 1787 (the second appearance of Sheridan's edition) in London, Edinburgh and Dublin.

NOTES

1. Maynwaring, a passionate and active Whig, seems to have hated Swift (whom, according to Oldmixon, he used to call 'one of the *wickedest wretches* alive') as a writer for the *Examiner*. In the 38th number of the *Medley* he attacks Swift (who he believed had already attacked him in the *Examiner*) for the 'Cursing and Swearing' in *A Tale of a Tub*, which he calls 'a Satyr upon Religion', made to please *'Deists, Socinians, and Free-Thinkers'*.

2. If Captain Gulliver may be admitted as a commentator on the criticism his book has received, it is of interest that in his 'Letter to his Cousin Sympson' (which Swift wrote for the 1735 edition) he remarks: 'you are loading our Carrier every week with Libels, and Keys, and Reflections, and Memoirs, and Second Parts; wherein I see myself accused of reflecting upon our great

States-Folk; of degrading human Nature, (for so they have still the Confidence to stile it) and of abusing the Female Sex'. (*Works*, ed. H. Davis, Vol. XI, 7.)

3. Orrery's life of Swift was published in the form of instructive letters to his son, Hamilton Boyle.

4. See Milton Voigt, *Swift and the Twentieth Century* (Detroit: Wayne University Press, 1964), 10.

5. op. cit., 11.

NOTE ON THE TEXT

The materials printed in this volume follow the original texts in all important respects. Lengthy extracts from the works of Swift have been omitted whenever they are quoted merely to illustrate the work in question. Typographical errors in the originals have been silently corrected, but contemporary spellings have been allowed to stand.

1. Dr. William King on *A Tale of a Tub*

1704

'Some Remarks on *A Tale of a Tub*', *The Original Works in Verse and Prose of Dr. William King* (3 vols), 1776, i, 213–18.

Dr. William King (1663–1712) was an advocate at Doctors' Commons and a writer of some wit and skill. Like Swift, he was an enemy of Richard Bentley, one of the butts in *The Battle of the Books*, and he and Swift were later on good terms. In this squib, however, he writes as a collector of night-soil who finds the *Tale* too dirty even for him.

It may lie in the power of the meanest person to do a service or a dis-service to the greatest, according as his inclination or his due respect may lead him; which is the true occasion of my writing you this Letter, to shew you that a person in the lowest circumstances in the world may still have a concern to do good; as I hope it is yours to do so to every body else. Although I believe you know not me; yet I have known you from a child, and am certain you cannot forget Mr. Seyley the chimney-sweeper; any more than you can your neighbour the small-coalman at Clerkenwell, at whose musick-meeting I have often performed a part in your hearing, and have seen you several times at the auction of his Books, which were a curiosity that I could have wished you had been able to have purchased.

I own that I am a person, as far as my capacity and other circum-stances will give me leave, desirous of my own improvement and know-ledge, and therefore look into all Books that may contribute towards them. It is natural for every person to look after things in their own way. . . .

Now, Sir, I must own, that it has been my fortune to find very few that tend any way to my own employment; I have not been able to meet with *Tartaretus*, a Book mentioned by Dr. Eachard; nor with several Authors quoted by Mr. Harrington; that great commonwealth's-man, in his incomparable treatise of *The Metamorphosis of A-Jax*.

But at last it happened that, as I was returning from my *nightly* vocation, which, beginning between eleven and twelve in the evening, generally employs me till the dawn of the succeeding morning; and being melancholy that I had not found so much gold that night as I might be supposed to have done either by my wife or my neighbours; I saw a fellow pasting up the title-pages of Books at the corners of the streets; and there, among others, I saw one called *A Tale of a Tub*, which imagining to be a satire upon my profession, I ordered one of my myrmidons to attack the fellow, and not to box him, but give him two or three gentle strokes over the nostrils; till at last the fellow, being of a ready wit, as having to do with all sorts of Authors, promised to go to Mr. Nutt's for one of the copies; and that, if he did not convince me that it was a more scandalous libel upon the Author of that foolish Tale, than it could be upon anyone else, he would engage that I should set him astride upon one of my barrels, whenever I should meet him publishing any thing printed for the same Stationer.

Sir, pardon me, if I fancy you may, by what I have said, guess at my profession: but I desire you not to fear, for I declare to you that I affect cleanliness to a nicety. I mix my ink with rose or orange-flower-water, my scrutoire is of cedar-wood, my wax is scented, and my paper lies amongst sweet bags. In short, I will use you with a thousand times more respect than the Bookseller of *A Tale of a Tub* does a noble Peer, under the pretence of a Dedication; or than the Author does his Readers.

It was not five o'clock when I had performed a severe penance; for I had read over a piece of nonsense, inscribed 'To his Royal Highness Prince Posterity'; where there is so considerable an aim at nothing, and such an accomplishment of that design, that I have not in my library met any thing that equals it. I never gave over till I had read his *Tale*, his *Battle*, and his *Fragment*: I shall speak of the series and style of these three treaties hereafter. But the first remarkable story that I found was that, about the twenty-second page, concerning a fat fellow crowding to see a Mountebank. I expected to have found something witty at the end: but it was all of a piece; so stuffed with curses, oaths, and imprecations, that the most profligate criminal in New-prison would be ashamed to repeat it.

I must take notice of one other particular piece of nonsense, and no more; where he says, 'That the ladder is an adequate symbol of faction and of poetry. Of faction, because . . . *Hiatus in MS.* . . . Of poetry, because its orators do *perorare* with a song.' The true reasons why I do not descend to more particulars is, because I think the three treatises (which, by their harmony in dirt, may be concluded to belong to one Author) may be reduced to a very small compass, if the common-places following were but left out. But the Author's first aim is, to be profane; but that part I shall leave to my betters, since matters of such a nature are not to be jested with, but to be punished.

The second is, to shew how great a proficient he is, at hectoring and bullying, at ranting and roaring, and especially at cursing and swearing. He makes his persons of all characters full of their oaths and impreca-tions; nay, his very spider has his share, and, as far as in the Author lies, he would transmit his impiety to things that are irrational.

His third is, to exceed all bounds of modesty. Men who are obliged by necessity to make use of uncommon expressions, yet have an art of making all appear decent; but this Author, on the other side, endeavours to heighten the worst colours, and to that end he searches his ancient Authors for their lewdest images, which he manages so as to make even impudence itself to blush at them.

His next is, a great affectation for everything that is nasty. When he spies any object that another person would avoid looking on, that he embraces. He takes the air upon dung-hills, in ditches, and common-shoars, and at my Lord Mayor's dog-kennel. In short, almost every part has a tincture of such filthiness, as renders it unfit for the worst of uses.

By the first of these, he shews his *religion*; by the second, his *conver-sation*; by the third, his *manners*; and by the fourth, his *education*.

Now were the Crow, who at present struts so much in the gutter, stripped of these four sorts of feathers, he would be left quite naked: he would have scarce one story, one jest, one allusion, one simile, or one quotation. And I do assure Mr. Nutt, that, if he should employ me in my own calling; I would bargain not to foul my utensils with carrying away the Works of this Author. Such were my sentiments upon reading these pieces; when, knowing that no sponge or fair water will clean a Book, when foul ink and fouler notions have sullied the paper, I looked upon the fire as the properest place for its purgation, in which it took no long time to expire.

Now, Sir, you may wonder how you may be concerned in this long story; and why I apply myself to you, in declaring my sentiments of this Author. But I shall shew you my reason for it, before I conclude this my too tedious epistle.

Now, Sir, in the dearth of wit that is at present in the town, all people are apt to catch at any thing that may afford them any diversion;

and what they cannot find, they make: and so this Author was bought up by all sorts of people, and every one was willing to make sense of that which had none in it originally. It was sold, not only at court, but in the city and suburbs; but, after some time, it came to have its due value put upon it: the Brewer, the Soap-boiler, the Train-oil-man, were all affronted at it; and it afforded a long dispute at our Coffee-house over the Gate, who might be the Author.

A certain Gentleman, that is the nearest to you of any person, was mentioned, upon supposition that the Book had Wit and Learning in it. But, when I displayed it in its proper colours, I must do the company that justice, that there was not one but acquitted you. That matter being dispatched, every one was at liberty of guessing. One said, he believed it was a Journey-man-taylor in Billeter-lane, that was an idle sort of a fellow, and loved writing more than stitching, that was the Author; his reason was, 'because here he is so desirous to mention "his Goose and his Garret"': but it was answered, 'that he was a member of the Society'; and so he was excused. 'But why then,' says another, 'since he makes such a *parable* upon coats, may he not be Mr. Amy the Coat-seller, who is a Poet and a Wit?' To which it was replied, 'That that gentleman's loss had been bewailed in an Elegy some years ago.'—'Why may not it be Mr. Gumly the Rag-woman's husband in Turnball-street?' says another. 'He is kept by her; and, having little to do, and having an Officer in Monmouth's Army, since the defeat at Sedgemore, has always been a violent Tory.' But it was urged 'that his style was harsh, rough, and unpolished; and that he did not understand one word of Latin.'—'Why then,' cries another, 'Oliver's porter[1] had an Amanuensis at Bedlam, that used to transcribe what he dictated: and may not these be some scattered notes of his Master's?' To which all replied, 'that, though Oliver's porter was crazed, yet his misfortune never let him forget that he was a Christian.' One said, 'It was a Surgeon's man, that had married

---

[1] This man, whose christian name was Daniel, learned much of the cant that prevailed in his master's time. He was a great plodder in books of divinity, especially in those of the mystical kind, which are supposed to have turned his brain. He was many years in Bedlam, where his library was, after some time, allowed him; as there was not the least probability of his cure. The most conspicuous of his books was a bible given him by Nell Gwynn. He frequently preached, and sometimes prophesied; and was said to have foretold several remarkable events, particularly the fire of London. See Lesley's *Snake in the Grass*, p. 330; where we learn, that people went often to hear him preach, 'and would sit many hours under his window with great devotion'. Mr. Lesley had the curiosity to ask a grave matron, who was among his auditors, 'what she could profit by hearing that madman?' She, with a composed countenance, as pitying his ignorance, replied, 'That Festus thought Paul was mad!' Granger, IV. 210. [King's note.]

a Midwife's nurse': but, though by the style it might seem probable that two such persons had a hand in it; yet, since he could not name the persons, his fancy was rejected. 'I conjecture,' says another, 'that it may be a Lawyer, that——' When, on a sudden, he was interrupted by Mr. Markland, the Scrivener, 'No, rather, by the oaths, it should be an Irish evidence.' At last there stood up a sprant young man, that is Secretary to our Scavenger, and cries, 'What if after all it should be a Parson!¹ for who may make more free with their trade? What if I know him, describe him, name him, and how he and his friends talk of it, admire it, are proud of it.'—'Hold, cry all the company; that function must not be mentioned without respect. We have enough of the dirty subject; we had better drink our coffee, and talk our politicks.'

I doubt not, Sir, but you wish the discourse had broke off sooner. Pardon it; for it means well to you, however exprest: for I am to my utmost, &c.

¹ The Clergyman here alluded to is not the real Author, who was not at the time suspected, but Mr. Thomas Swift, rector of Puttenham in Surrey, whom the Dean, XVI, 2, calls his 'parson cousin', and who appears to have taken some pains to be considered as the author of the *Tale of a Tub*. See XVII, 528. [King's note.]

2. Francis Atterbury on *A Tale of a Tub*

1704

The Epistolary Correspondence, Visitation Charges, Speeches, and
Miscellanies of the Right Reverend Francis Atterbury, D.D., Lord
Bishop of Rochester (3 vols), 1784, iii.

Atterbury (1662–1732) was made Dean of Carlisle in 1704 and
Bishop of Rochester in 1713. All three of the letters quoted here
are addressed to his close friend, Sir Jonathan Trelawny, Bishop
of Exeter and later of Winchester. His fragmentary remarks on
the then anonymous *Tale* seem especially significant, for here a
prominent member of the religious and political 'establishment'
is less concerned about the work's 'prophaneness' and more sensitive to its wit and learning than many critics outside the clergy.
In later years Atterbury and Swift became good friends and
frequent correspondents.

---

15 June 1704

I beg your Lordship (if the book is come down to Exon) to read the
Tale of a Tub. For, bating the profaneness of it in some places, it is a book
to be valued, being an original in it's kind, full of wit, humour, good
sense, and learning. It comes from Christ Church; and a good part of it
is written in defence of Mr. Boyle against Wotton and Bentley. The
town is wonderfully pleased with it [203].

29 June 1704

The authors of *A Tale of a Tub* are now supposed generally at Oxford
to be one Smith, and one Philips; the first a Student, the second a
Commoner, of Christ-Church [214].

1 July 1704

The author of *A Tale of a Tub* will not as yet be known; and if it be the
man I guess, he hath reason to conceal himself, because of the prophane
strokes in that piece, which would do his reputation and interest in the
world more harm than the wit can do him good. . . . Nothing can
please more than that book doth here at London [218].

3. William Wotton on *A Tale of a Tub*

1705

A Defense of the Reflections upon Ancient and Modern Learning, In Answer to the Objections of Sir W. Temple, and Others. With Observations upon The Tale of a Tub, printed in A Tale of a Tub, ed. A. C. Guthkelch and D. Nicol Smith, 1920, 314–23.

William Wotton (1666–1727) is, naturally, ill disposed to *A Tale of a Tub,* since he and Dr. Bentley had both been ridiculed in *The Battle of the Books,* published with the *Tale.* Both had been involved in the dispute with Sir William Temple and others over the relative merits of ancient and modern learning, which had occasioned the *Battle,* and the *Tale,* too, may be regarded as an anti-modern work.

This way of printing Bits of Books that in their Nature are intended for Continued Discourses, and are not loose Apophthegems, Occasional Thoughts, or incoherent Sentences, is what I have seen few Instances of; none more remarkable than this, and one more which may be supposed to imitate this, *A Tale of a Tub,* of which a Brother of Dr. *Swift's* is publicly reported to have been the Editor at least, if not the Author. In which Dr. *Bentley* and my self are coursely treated, yet I believe I may safely answer for us both, that we should not have taken any manner of notice of it, if upon this Occasion I had not been obliged to say something in answer to what has been seriously said against us.

For, believe me, Sir, what concerns us, is much the innocentest part of the Book, tending chiefly to make Men laugh for half an Hour, after which it leaves no farther Effects behind it. When Men are jested upon for what is in it self praiseworthy, the World will do them Justice: And on the other hand, if they deserve it, they ought to sit down quietly under it. Our Cause therefore we shall leave to the Public very willingly, there being no occasion to be concerned at any Man's Railery about it. But the rest of the Book which does not relate to us, is of so irreligious a nature, is so crude a Banter upon all that is esteemed as

Sacred among all Sects and Religions among Men, that, having so fair an Opportunity, I thought it might be useful to many People who pretend they see no harm in it, to lay open the Mischief of the Ludicrous Allegory, and to shew what that drives at which has been so greedily brought up and read. In one Word, God and Religion, Truth and Moral Honesty, Learning and Industry are made a May-Game, and the most serious Things in the World are described as so many several Scenes in *A Tale of a Tub*.

That this is the true Design of that Book, will appear by these Particulars. The *Tale* in substance is this; 'A Man had three Sons, all at a Birth, by one Wife; to whom when he died, because he had purchased no Estate, nor was born to any, he only provided to each of them a New Coat, which were to last them fresh and sound as long as they lived, and would lengthen and widen of themselves, so as to be always fit.' By the Sequel of the *Tale* it appears, that by these three Sons, *Peter, Martin,* and *Jack; Popery,* the *Church of England,* and our *Protestant Dissenters* are designed. What can now be more infamous than such a *Tale.* The Father is *Jesus Christ,* who at his Death left his WILL or TESTAMENT to his Disciples, with a Promise of Happiness to them and the Churches which they and their Successors should found for ever. So the Tale-teller's Father to his three Sons, 'You will find in my WILL full Instructions in every Particular concerning the wearing and managing of your Coats; wherein you must be very exact, to avoid the Penalties I have appointed for every Transgression or Neglect, upon which your *Future Fortunes* will *entirely* depend.' By his Coats which he gave his Sons, the Garments of the *Israelites* are exposed, which by the Miraculous Power of God waxed not old, nor were worn out for Forty Years together in the Wilderness. The number of these Sons born thus at one Birth, looks asquint at the TRINITY, and one of the Books in our Author's Catalogue in the Off-page over-against the Title, is a Panegyric upon the Number THREE, which Word is the only one that is put in Capitals in that whole Page.

In the pursuit of his Allegory, we are entertain'd with the Lewdness of the Three Sparks. Their Mistresses are the *Dutchess d' Argent,* Madamoizelle *de Grands Titres,* and the Countess *d' Orgueil* i.e. *Covetousness, Ambition* and *Pride,* which were the Three great Vices that the Ancient Fathers inveighed against as the first Corrupters of Christianity. Their Coats having such an extraordinary Virtue of never wearing out, give him large Scope for his Mirth, which he employs in burlesquing *Religion, Moral Honesty* and *Conscience,* which are the strongest Ties by which Men can be tied to one another. *Is not Religion a Cloak, Honesty a Pair of Shoes worn out in the Dirt, Self-love a Surtout, Vanity a Shirt, and Conscience a Pair of Breeches?* Which last Allusion gives him an opportunity that he never misses of talking obscenely.

His Whim of Clothes is one of his chiefest Favourites. 'Man', says he, 'is an Animal compounded of two *Dresses*, the *Natural* and the *Celestial-Suit*, which were the Body and the Soul.' And 'That the Soul was by daily Creation and Circumfusion they proved by Scripture, because *In them we live, and move, and have our Being.*' *In them* (i.e. *in the Clothes of the Body:*) Words applicable only to the Great God of Heaven and Earth, of whom they were first spoken by *St. Paul*. Thus he introduces his Tale; then that he might shelter himself the better from any Censure here in *England*, he falls most unmercifully upon *Peter* and *Jack*, i.e. upon *Popery* and *Fanaticism*, and gives *Martin*, who represents the *Church of England*, extream good Quarter. I confess, Sir, I abhor making Sport with any way of worshipping God, and he that diverts himself too much at the Expense of the *Roman Catholics* and the *Protestant Dissenters*, may lose his own Religion e're he is aware of it, at least the Power of it in his Heart. But to go on.

The first Part of the *Tale* is the *History of Peter*. Thereby *Popery* is exposed. Every body knows the *Papists* have made great Additions to Christianity. That indeed is the great Exception which the Church of *England* makes against them. Accordingly *Peter* begins his Pranks with *adding a Shoulderknot to his Coat*, 'whereas his Father's Will was very precise, and it was the main Precept in it with the greatest Penalties annexed, not to add to, or diminish from their Coats one Thread, without a positive Command in the WILL'. His Description of the Cloth of which the Coat was made, has a farther Meaning than the Words may seem to import. 'The Coats their Father had left them were of very good Cloth, and besides so neatly sown, you would swear they were all of a Piece, but at the same time very plain, with little or no Ornament.' This is the Distinguishing Character of the Christian Religion. *Christiana Religio absoluta & simplex,* was *Ammianus Marcellinus's* Description of it, who was himself a Heathen. When the *Papists* cannot find any thing which they want in Scripture, they go to *Oral Tradition:* Thus *Peter* is introduced dissatisfied with the tedious Way of looking for all the Letters of any Word which he had occasion for in the *Will*, when neither the constituent Syllables, nor much less the whole Word were there *in Terminis*, and he expresses himself thus: 'Brothers, if you remember, we heard a Fellow say when we were Boys, that he heard my Father's Man say, that he heard my Father say, that he would advise his Sons to get *Gold-Lace* on their Coats, as soon as ever they could procure Money to buy it.' Which way of coming at any thing that was not expressly in his Father's WILL, stood him afterwards in great stead.

The next Subject of our *Tale-Teller's* Wit is the *Glosses* and *Interpretations of Scripture*, very many absurd ones of which kind are allow'd in the most Authentic Books of the Church of *Rome*: The sparks wanted Silver Fringe to put upon their Coats. Why, says *Peter*, (seemingly perhaps to laugh at Dr. *Bentley* and his Criticisms); 'I have found in a certain Author, which shall be nameless, that the same Word which in the Will is called *Fringe*, does also signifie a *Broomstick*, and doubtless ought to have the same Interpretation in this Paragraph.' This affording great Diversion to one of the Brothers; 'You speak', says *Peter*, 'very irreverently of a *Mystery*, which doubtless was very useful and significant, but ought not to be overcuriously pry'd into, or nicely reason'd upon.' The Author, one would think, copies from Mr. *Toland*, who always raises a Laugh at the Word *Mystery*, the Word and Thing whereof he is known to believe to be no more than *A Tale of a Tub*.

Images in the Church of *Rome* give our *Tale-teller* but too fair a Handle. 'The Brothers remembered but too well how their Father abhorred the Fashion of Embroidering their Clothes with *Indian* Figures of Men, Women and Children; that he made several Paragraphs on purpose, importing his utter Detestation of it, and bestowing his Everlasting Curse to his Sons, whenever they should wear it.' The Allegory here is direct. The *Papists* formerly forbad the People the use of Scripture in a Vulgar Tongue; *Peter* therefore *locks up his Father's Will in a strong Box brought out of* Greece *or* Italy: Those countries are named, because the *New Testament* is written in *Greek*; and the *Vulgar Latin*, which is the Authentic Edition of the Bible in the Church of *Rome*, is in the Language of Old *Italy*. The Popes in their *Decretals* and *Bulls* have given their Sanction to very many gainful Doctrines which are now receiv'd in the Church of *Rome*, that are not mentioned in Scripture, and are unknown to the Primitive Church. *Peter* accordingly pronounces *ex Cathedra*, that *Points tagged with Silver were absolutely Jure Paterno*, and so they wore them in great numbers. The Bishops of *Rome* enjoy'd their Privileges in *Rome* at first by the Favour of Emperors, whom at last they shut out of their own Capital City, and then forged a Donation from *Constantine the Great*, the better to justifie what they did. In imitation of this, *Peter*, 'having run something behindhand with the World, obtained leave of a certain Lord to receive him into his House, and to teach his Children. A while after the Lord died, and he by long Practise upon his Father's Will, found the way of contriving a Deed of Conveyance of that House to himself and his Heirs: Upon which he took possession, turned the Young Squires out, and receiv'd his Brothers in their stead.' *Pennance* and *Absolution* are plaid upon under the Notion of a Sovereign Remedy for the Worms, especially in the Spleen, which by observing of *Peter's* Prescriptions, would void insensibly by Perspiration ascending through the Brain. By his *Whispering Office* for the Relief of Eves-droppers, Physicians, Bawds and Privy Councellors, he ridicules *Auricular Confession*, and the Priest who takes it is described by the Ass's Head. Holy-Water he calls an 'Universal Pickle', *to preserve Houses, Gardens, Towns, Men, Women, Children and Cattle, wherein he could preserve them as sound as Insects in Amber*; and because Holy-Water differs only in Consecration from Common Water, therefore our Tale-teller tells us that his Pickle by the Powder of *Pimperlimpimp* receives new Virtues, though it differs not in Sight nor Smell from the Common Pickle which preserves Beef and Butter, nor Herrings. The *Papal Bulls* are ridiculed by Name, so there we are at no loss for our *Tale-teller's* Meaning. *Absolution in Articulo Mortis*, and the *Taxa Camerae Apostolicae* are jested upon in Emperor *Peter's* Letter. The *Pope's Universal Monarchy*, and his *Triple Crown*, and *Key's* and *Fisher's Ring* have their turns of being laughed at; nor does his Arrogant way of requiring Men to kiss his Slipper escape Reflexion. The *Celibacy of the Romish Clergy* is struck at in *Peter's* turning his own and Brothers Wives out of Doors. But nothing makes him so merry as *Transubstantiation*: *Peter* turns his Bread into Mutton, and, according to the Popish Doctrine of Concomitance, his Wine too, which in his way he calls *pauming his damned Crusts upon the Brothers for Mutton*. The ridiculous multiplying of the *Virgin Mary's* Milk among the Papists, he banters under the Allegory of a *Cow* which gave as much Milk at a Meal as would fill Three thousand Churches: and the *Wood of the Cross* on which our Saviour suffered, is prophanely likened to an 'Old Signpost that belonged to his Father, with Nails and Timber enough upon it to build Sixteen large Men of War'. And when one talked to *Peter* of *Chinese* Waggons which were made so light as to sail over Mountains, he swears and curses four times in Eleven Lines, that the *Chapell* of *Loretto* had travelled Two Thousand *German* Leagues, though built with Lime and Stone, over Sea and Land.

But I expect, Sir, that you should tell me, that the *Tale-teller* falls here only upon the Ridiculous Inventions of Popery; that the Church of *Rome* intended by these things to gull silly Superstitious People; and to rook them of their Money; that the World had been but too long in Slavery; that our Ancestors gloriously redeemed us from that Yoak; that the Church of *Rome* therefore ought to be exposed, and that he deserves well of Mankind that does expose it.

All this, Sir, I own to be true: but then I would not so shoot at an Enemy, as to hurt my self at the same time. The Foundation of the Doctrines of the Church of *England* is right, and came from God: Upon this the Popes, and Councils called and confirmed by them, have built, as St. *Paul* speaks, *Hay and Stubble*, perishable and slight Materials, which when they are once consum'd, that the Foundation may appear, then we shall see what is faulty, and what is not. But our *Tale-teller* strikes at the very Root. *'Tis all* with him *a 'Farce, and all a Ladle'*, as a very facetious Poet says upon another occasion. The *Father*, and the *WILL*, and *his Son Martin*, are part of the *Tale*, as well as *Peter* and *Jack*, and are all usher'd in with the Common Old Wives Introduction, *Once upon a Time*. And the *main Body of the Will* we are told consisted in *certain admirable Rules about the wearing of* their Coats. So that let *Peter* be mad one way, and *Jack* another, and let *Martin* be sober, and spend his *Time* with Patience and Phlegm in picking the Embroidery off his Coat never so carefully, *'firmly resolving to alter whatever was already amiss, and reduce all their future Measures to the strictest Obedience prescribed therein'*. Yet still this is all part of *A Tale of a Tub*, it does but enhance the *Teller's* Guilt, and shews at the bottom his contemptible Opinion of every Thing which is called Christianity.

For pray, Sir, take notice that it is not saying he personates none but Papists or Fanatics, that will excuse him; for in other Places, where he speaks in his own Person, and imitates none but himself, he discovers an equal mixture of Lewdness and Irreligion. Would any Christian compare a *Mountebank's-Stage*, a *Pulpit*, and a *Ladder* together? A *Mountebank* is a profess'd Cheat, who turns it off when he is press'd, with the Common Jest, *Men must live*; and with this Man the Preacher of the Word of God is compared, and the Pulpit in which he preaches is called *an Edifice* (or Castle) *in the Air:* This is not said by *Peter*, or *Jack*, but by the Author himself, who after he has gravely told us, that he has had Poxes ill cured by trusting to Bawds and Surgeons, reflects with *'unspeakable Comfort*, upon his having past a long Life with a *Conscience void of Offence towards God and towards Man'*.

In his own Person, the Author speaks in one of his Digressions of

Books being not bound to Everlasting Chains of Darkness in a Library; but that when the Fulness of Time should come, they should happily undergo the Tryal of Purgatory, in order to ascend the Sky'. In another Digression our Author describes one of his Madmen in *Bedlam*, who was distemper'd by the Loose Behaviour of his Wife, to be like *Moses: Ecce Cornuta erat ejus Facies*; which is the rendring of the *Vulgar Latin* of that which in the *English* Bible is called *the shining of his Face* when he came down from the Mount. Our Author himself asserts, that the 'Fumes issuing from a Jakes, will furnish as comely and useful a Vapor, as Incense from an Altar'. And 'tis our Author in his own Capacity, who among many other Ludicrous Similes upon those that get their Learning out of *Indices*, which are commonly at the End of a Book, says, 'Thus Human Life is best understood by the *Wise-man*'s Rule of *regarding the End*'. 'Tis in the *Fragment*, which has nothing to do with the *Tale*, that Sir *Humphrey Edwin* is made to apply the Words of the *Psalmist*, *Thy Word is a Lanthorn to my Feet, and a Light to my Paths*, to a Whimsical Dark Lanthorn of our Authors own contrivance; wherein he poorly alludes to *Hudibras's Dark-Lanthorn of the Spirit, which none see by but those that bear it*. His whole VIIIth Section concerning the *Aeolists*, in which he banters Inspiration, is such a Mixture of Impiety and Immodesty, that I should have as little regard to you, Sir, as this Author has had to the Public, if I should barely repeat after him what is there. And it is somewhat surprizing that the Citation out of *Irenaeus*, in the Title-Page, which seems to be all *Gibberish*, should be a Form of Initiation used anciently by the *Marcosian* Heretics. So great a delight has this Unhappy Writer, to play with what some part or other of Mankind have always esteemed as Sacred!

And therefore when he falls upon *Jack*, he deals as freely with him, and wounds Christianity through his Sides as much as he had done before through *Peter*'s. The *Protestant Dissenters use Scripture-Phrases* in their Serious Discourses and Composures more than the Church of *England-men*. Accordingly *Jack* is introduced, making 'his Common Talk and Conversation to run wholly in the Phrase of his WILL, and circumscribing the utmost of his Eloquence within that compass, not daring to let slip a Syllable without Authority from thence'. And because he could not of a sudden recollect *an Authentic Phrase*, for the Necessities of Nature, he would use no other: Can any thing be prophaner than this? Things compared always shew the Esteem or Scorn of the Comparer. To ridicule Praedestination, *Jack* walks blindfold through the Streets; the Body of our Dissenters having till of late been

Calvinists in the Questions concerning the *Five Points*. 'It was ordained, said he, some few days *before* the Creation (*i.e.* immediately by God himself) that my Nose and this very Post should have a Rencounter: and therefore Providence thought fit to send us both into the World in the same Age, and to make us Country-men and Fellow Citizens.' This is a direct Prophanation of the Majesty of God. '*Jack* would run Dog-mad at the Noise of Music, especially a Pair of Bagpipes.' This is to expose our Dissenters Aversion to Instrumental Music in Churches. The Agreement of our Dissenters and the Papists, in that which Bishop *Stillingfleet* called the *Fanaticism of the Church of Rome*, is ludicrously described for several Pages together, by *Jack*'s likeness to *Peter*, and their being often mistaken for each other, and their frequent meeting when they least intended it. In this, singly taken, there might possibly be little harm, if one did not see from what Principle the whole proceeded.

This 'tis which makes the difference between the sharp and virulent Books written in this Age against any Sect of Christians, and those which were written about the beginning of the Reformation between the several contending Parties then in *Europe*. For tho' the Rage and Spight with which Men treated one another was as keen and as picquant then as it is now, yet the Inclination of Mankind was not then irreligious, and so their Writings had little other effect but to encrease Men's Hatred against any one particular Sect, whilst Christianity, as such, was not hereby at all undermined. But now the Common Enemy appears barefaced, and strikes in with some one or other Sect of Christians, to wound the whole by that means. And this is the Case of this Book, which is one of the Prophanest Banters upon the Religion of *Jesus Christ*, as such, that ever yet appeared. In the *Tale*, in the *Digressions*, in the *Fragment*, the same Spirit runs through, but rather most in the *Fragment*, in which all extraordinary Inspirations are the Subjects of his Scorn and Mockery, whilst the Protestant Dissenters are, to outward appearance, the most directly levelled at. The Bookseller indeed in his Advertisement prefixed to the *Fragment*, pretends to be *wholly ignorant of the Author, and he says, he cannot conjecture whether it be the same with that of the two foregoing Pieces, the Original having been sent him at a different Time, and in a different Hand.* It may be so; but the Stile, and Turn, and Spirit of this *Fragment*, and of the *Tale* being the same, no body, I believe, has doubted of their being written by the same Author: If the Authors are different, so much the worse, because it shews there are more Men in the World acted by the same Spirit. But be the Author one or more, the Mask is more plainly taken off in the *Fragment*. The Writer uses the

Allegory of an *Ass's bearing his Rider up to Heaven*: And presently after he owns his Ass to be allegorical, and says, 'That if we please, instead of the Term *Ass*, we may make use of *Gifted* or *Enlightened Preacher*, and the Word *Rider* we may exchange for that of *Fanatic Auditory*, or any other Denomination of the like Import'. And now *having settled this Weighty Point*, (as he contemptuously calls it) he enquires *by what Methods this Teacher arrives at his Gifts, or Spirit, or Light*. Enthusiasm with him is an Universal Deception which has run through all Sciences in all Kingdoms, and every thing has some *Fanatic Branch annexed to it*; among which he reckons the *Summum Bonum, or an Enquiry after Happiness*. The *Descent of the H. Ghost* after our Blessed Saviour's Ascension in the Shape of Cloven Tongues, at the First *Pentecost*, in the Second of the *Acts*, is one of the Subjects of his Mirth: And because in our Dissenting Congregations, the Auditory used formerly with great Indecency to keep on their Hats in Sermon Time, therefore, says he, 'They will needs have it as a Point clearly gained, that the Cloven Tongues never sat upon the Apostles Heads, while their Hats were on', using that Ridiculous Argument to prove that the Dissenting Ministers are not divinely inspired. And he does not mince the Matter when he says, 'That he is resolved immediately to weed this Error out of Mankind, by making it clear, that this Mystery of venting Spiritual Gifts is nothing but a Trade acquired by as much Instruction, and master'd by equal practice and Application as others are.' Can any thing be more blasphemous than his *Game at Leap-Frog between the Flesh and Spirit?* This affects the Doctrine of St. *Paul*, and not the Private Interpretations of this or that Particular Sect; and this too is described in the Language of the Stews, which with now and then a Scripture-Expression, compose this Writer's Stile. Thus when the *Snuffling* of Men who have lost their Noses by Lewd Courses is said to have given rise to that Tone which our Dissenters did too much affect formerly, He subjoins, 'That when our Earthly Tabernacles are disordered and desolate, shaken out of Repair, the *Spirit* delights to dwell within them, as Houses are said to be haunted, when they are forsaken and gone to decay.' And in his Account of Fanaticism, he tells us, *That the Thorn in the Flesh serves*, for a Spur to the Spirit. Is not this to ridicule St. *Paul's* own Description of his own Temptation; in which the Apostle manifestly alludes to a Passage in the Prophet *Ezekiel*?

What would Men say in any Country in the World but this, to see their Religion so vilely treated from the Press? I remember to have seen a *French* Translation of the Learned Dr. *Prideaux* (the present Worthy

Dean of *Norwich's*) *Life of Mahomet,* printed in *France,* I think at *Paris,* in the Advertisement before which, the Translator tells the Public, That he did not translate the *Letter to the Deists,* thereto annexed in *English,* because, says he, our Government suffers no such people, and there is no need of Antidotes where there is no Poison. Be this true or false in *France,* it matters not to our present Purpose; but it shews that no Man dares publickly play with Religion in that Country. How much do the *Mahometans* reverence the *Alcoran*? Dares any Man among them openly despite their Prophet, or ridicule the Words of his Law? How strictly do the *Banians,* and the other Sects of the *Gentile East-Indians* worship their Pagods, and respect their Temples? This Sir, you well know, is not Superstition nor Bigottry. It is of the Essence of Religion, that the utmost Regard should be paid to the *Name and Words of God,* both which upon the slightest, and the most ridiculous Occasions, are play'd upon by Common Oaths, and Idle Allusions to Scripture Expressions in this whole Book. I do not carry my Charge too far. . . .

Before I leave this Author, be he who he will, I shall observe, Sir, that his *Wit* is *not his own,* in many places. The *Actors* in his *Farce, Peter, Martin,* and *Jack,* are by Name borrowed from a Letter written by the late Witty D. of *Buckingham,* concerning Mr. *Clifford's Human Reason*: And *Peter's* Banter upon *Transubstantiation,* is taken from the same D. of *Buckingham's Conference with an Irish Priest,* only here *Bread* is *changed into Mutton* and *Wine,* that the Banter might be the more crude; there a *Cork* is *turned into a Horse.* But the *Wondrings* on the one side, and the *Asseverations* on the other, are otherwise exactly alike. And I have been assured that the *Battel in St.* James's *Library* is *Mutandis* taken out of a *French* Book, entituled, *Combat des Livres,* if I misremember not.

4. Richard Steele on *A Project for the Advancement of Religion*

1709

The Tatler, 5, 21 April, 1709. *The British Essayists*, 1803, i, 120–1.

WILL'S COFFEE-HOUSE, 20 APRIL.

This week being sacred to holy things, and no public diversions allowed, there has been taken notice of even here a little Treatise called, *A Project for the Advancement of Religion*: dedicated to the Countess of Berkeley. The title was so uncommon, and promised so peculiar a way of thinking, that every man here has read it; and as many as have done so have approved it. It is written with the spirit of one who has seen the world enough to undervalue it with good-breeding. The author must certainly be a man of wisdom as well as piety, and have spent much time in the exercise of both. The real causes of the decay of the interest of religion are set forth in a clear and lively manner, without unseasonable passions; and the whole air of the book, as to the language, the sentiments, and the reasonings, shows it was written by one whose virtue sits easy about him, and to whom vice is thoroughly contemptible. It was said by one of this company, alluding to that knowledge of the world the author seems to have, 'The man writes much like a gentleman, and goes to Heaven with a very good mien'.

5. John Dennis on the *Examiner*

1712

From a letter 'To the *Examiner*. Upon his wise Paper of the Tenth of January, 1712', Edward Niles Hooker, ed., *The Critical Works of John Dennis* (2 vols), 1943, ii, 397–8.

John Dennis (1657–1734) was an interesting literary critic with a very bad temper, who crossed swords with Pope as well as with Swift. The *Examiner* had attributed to him the authorship of a pamphlet called *The Englishman's Thanks to the Duke of Marlborough*, and Dennis denies that he wrote it. The extract given is a good example of the abuse which took the place of criticism in so much early eighteenth-century comment on Swift. Dennis believes Swift to be the author of the *Examiner* and attacks him as a political and religious turncoat. Much of what he says clearly refers to *A Tale of a Tub*.

By thy Impudence, thy Ignorance, thy sophistical arguing, thy pedantick declamatory Style, and thy brutal *Billingsgate* Language thou canst be none but some illiterate Pedant, who has liv'd twenty Years in an University; by thy being a turbulent hot-brain'd Incendiary, a hot-brain'd Incendiary with a cool Heart, one may easily guess at the University which gave thee thy Education. By thy wonderful Charity, thou canst be nothing but a scandalous Priest, hateful to God and detestable to Men, and agreeable to none but Devils, who makest it thy Business to foment Divisions between Communities and private Persons, in spight of that Charity which is the fundamental Doctrine of that Religion which thou pretendst to teach. How amazing a Reflection is it, that, in spight of that Divine Doctrine, the Christian World should be the only part of the Globe embroil'd in endless Divisions. From whence can this proceed, but from Priests like thee, who are the Pests of Society and the Bane of Religion. But 'tis not enough to say thou art a Priest, 'tis time to point out what Priest thou art. Thou art a Priest then who mad'st thy first Appearance in the World like a dry

Joker in Controversy, a spiritual Buffoon, an Ecclesiastical *Jack Pudding*, by publishing a Piece of waggish Divinity, which was writ with a Design to banter all Christianity; yes, thou nobly began'st as *Judas Iscariot* ended; began'st by crucifying thy God afresh, and selling him to *John Nutt* for ten Pound and a Crown, and so under-selling half in half thy execrable Predecessor. Hadst thou but had half his common Sense, thou hadst had his Remorse and consequently his Destiny; instead of which thou fell'st from selling and betraying thy God to selling and betraying thy old Friends. So that hadst thou liv'd in the time of *Judas*, thou wouldst infinitely have surpass'd him in Villany, thou wouldst have betray'd both Christ and all his Apostles, nay, wouldst have undermin'd, and undersold, and betray'd even *Judas* the Betrayer himself.

When thou wert come piping hot from betraying both Friends and God, thou wert often heard to cry most impudently, but most truly, out, that the Church was in Danger. Any one may swear, when it has such Priests, that 'tis not in Danger, but upon the very brink of Ruine; and that if it were not supported by God himself, it would immediately tumble.

Yet 'tis hard to be angry with such a Miscreant, when I reflect, that he who has us'd me so, has us'd his God worse. For thou hast denied his very Being; which is to degrade him below the meanest of his own Creatures, not only below Fools and Ideots, but even below Vermin, Insects, Mites, and all the Creatures of the material invisible World, even below the *Examiner*. For nothing must always be less than Something, let Something be never so little.

6. The aim of *A Tale of a Tub*

1714

A Complete Key to the Tale of a Tub, 3rd edition, 1714, pp. 4–6.

This has been variously attributed to Edmund Curll, the notorious bookseller, and to Thomas Swift, Jonathan's cousin, who is here given the chief credit for writing *A Tale of a Tub*. The Preface of the Bookseller to the Reader professes to show 'The cause and design of the whole work, which was perform'd by a couple of young clergymen in the year 1697; who, having been Domestic Chaplains to Sir William Temple, thought themselves oblig'd to take up his quarrel, in relation to the controversy then in dispute between him and Mr. *Wotton*, concerning ancient and modern Learning'. The present extract is taken from the Preface, less as an example of critical acumen than as an illustration of how early comment on the *Tale* concentrates almost entirely on the religious allegory. The *Key* itself is sketchy, and very similar to the explanations in Wotton's *Observations*.

The one of 'em began a *Defence* of Sir *William*, under the title of *A Tale of a Tub*; wherein, he intended to couch the General History of Christianity, shewing the Rise of all the remarkable Errors of the *Roman Church* in the same Order they enter'd, and how the Reformation endeavour'd to root 'em out again, with the different Temper of *Luther* from *Calvin* (and those more violent Spirits) in the way of his Reforming. His Aim was to ridicule the stubborn Errors of the *Roman Church*, and the Humours of the *Fanatick Party*; and to shew that their Superstition has somewhat very radical in it, which is common to both of 'em, notwithstanding the Abhorrence they seem to have for one another.

The Author intended to have it very regular, and withal so particular that he thought not to pass by the Rise of any one single Error, or its Reformation. He design'd at last, to shew the Purity of the Christian Church in the Primitive Times; and consequently how weakly Mr.

Wotton pass'd his Judgment, and how partially, in preferring the *Modern* Divinity before the *Ancient*, with the confutation of whose Book he intended to conclude. But when he had not yet gone half way, his Companion borrowing the *Manuscript* to peruse, carried it with him to *Ireland*, and having kept it seven years, at last publish'd it imperfect; for indeed he was not able to carry it on after the intended Method: because *Divinity*, tho' it chanc'd to be his Profession had been the least of his Study. However, he added to it *The Battle of the Books*, wherein he effectually persues the main Design, of lashing Mr. *Wotton*; and having added a jocose Epistle Dedicatory to my Lord *Sommers*, and another to Prince *Posterity*, with a pleasant Preface, and interlarded with four *Digressions*: 1. Concerning *Criticks*: 2. In the *Modern* Kind: 3. In Praise of *Digressions*: 4. Concerning the Original, Use and Improvement of *Madness* (with which he was not unacquainted) in a *Commonwealth*; concluding the Book with a *Fragment* of the first Author's, being a *Mechanical Account of the Operation of the Spirit*, and which he intended should have come in about the Middle of the *Tale* as a Preliminary to *Jack's* Character.

Having thus shewn the Reasons of the little order observ'd in the Book, and the Imperfections of the *Tale*, 'tis so submitted to the Reader's Censure.

7. Sir Richard Blackmore on
A Tale of a Tub
1716

'An Essay upon Wit', in *Essays Upon Several Subjects*, 1716, 217–18.

Blackmore (d. 1729), a physician and prolific dunce-poet who was
to be heartily ridiculed by Pope, can see in *A Tale of a Tub* only a
satire upon religion. Blackmore was one of those (there were many
in the early eighteenth century) who regarded wit with suspicion
as destructive and often scurrilous.

Another pernicious Abuse of Wit is that which appears in the Writings
of some ingenious Men, who are so hardy as to expose from the Press
the most venerable Subjects, and treat Vertue and Sobriety of Manners
with Raillery and Ridicule. Several, in their Books, have many
sarcastical and spiteful Strokes at Religion in general, while others make
themselves pleasant with the Principles of the Christian. Of the last kind
this Age has seen a most audacious Example in the Book intitul'd, *A
Tale of a Tub*. Had this Writing been publish'd in a Pagan or Popish
Nation, who are justly impatient of all Indignity offer'd to the Establish'd Religion of their Country, no doubt but the Author would have
receiv'd the Punishment he deserv'd. But the Fate of this impious
Buffoon is very different; for in a Protestant Kingdom, zealous of their
Civil and Religious Immunities, he has not only escap'd Affronts and
the Effects of publick Resentment, but has been caress'd and patroniz'd
by Persons of great Figure and of all Denominations. Violent Party Men,
who differ'd in all Things besides, agreed, in their Turn, to shew
particular Respect and Friendship to this insolent Derider of the Worship of his Country, till at last the reputed Writer is not only gone off
with Impunity, but triumphs in his Dignity and Preferment. I do not
know, that any Inquiry or Search was ever made after this Writing, or
that any Reward was ever offer'd for the discovery of the Author, or

that the infamous Book was ever condemn'd to be burnt in Publick: Whether this proceeds from the excessive Esteem and Love that Men in Power, during the late Reign, had for Wit, or their defect of Zeal and Concern for the Christian Religion, will be determin'd best by those, who are best acquainted with their Character.

8. A translator's opinions of
A Tale of a Tub

1721

The translator's Preface to *Le Conte du Tonneau, Contenant tout ce que les Arts, et les Sciences ont de plus mystérieux. Avec plusieurs autres Pièces très-curieuses. Par le fameux Dr. Swift*, 1721.

This translation, greatly superior to the earlier *Les Trois Justaucorps*, is by Juste van Effen (1684–1735). Though, like most French commentators, he is over-apologetic for Swift's lack of correctness, strange to a French taste, his Preface does contain genuine critical observation.

If ever a book needed a preface, I dare say it is this one. It is true that it is already loaded with all sorts of preliminary discourses, but they are by no means designed to reveal to us the true views of the author; rather, they are parts of the work, and the satiric ironies which they contain have the same purpose as has the book as a whole.

The English rightly regard the book as a masterpiece of subtle pleasantry, and, despite the flatness which a translation must inevitably give to witty productions of this kind, I think the reader will agree that it is difficult to find in any language a work so full of fire and imagination. At the same time it is true that there could be nothing more eccentric; the narration is continually interrupted by digressions, which take up more room than the main subject, but this oddity is not the result of an unruly mind which runs away with itself and whose reason cannot master its enthusiasm. The disorderliness is assumed in order to ridicule the most modern English authors, who take pleasure in digressions of this kind simply to give volume to their works.

Moreover, these digressions are of so special a turn, and full of such ingenious and uncommon fun, that it is impossible for a reader with enough penetration and judgment to understand the delicate strength of these ironies to be impatient to return to the main subject.

Most of these incidental discourses serve to ridicule the Moderns, and above all those among them who monopolize the good name of critics. The author of this work is a great partisan of the Ancients. Perhaps he is an extreme partisan; it would be wrong to come to a decision on this because the case is still *sub judice*; it is not yet, and perhaps never will be, completed. However that may be, the supporters of the Ancients have never had a more able defender. Until now the advocates of this faction have been mere dabblers, who could only utter coarse insults and oppose to their antagonists an ostentatious rampart of useless quotations founded upon pedantic pride. They were people so familiar with the learned tongues that they could scarcely turn a period in their own, and unfortunately for them they had to deal with men of wit, spirit, and style, who could make their way into the reader's mind through elegant badinage and delicate raillery.

Our author is the first of his party who has been able to bring over to his side those who like to laugh, and able to fight the Moderns with their own weapons.

Those against whom he chiefly directs his attack are the critics by profession, a race of small minds, whose scanty intelligence, animated by a good dose of malignity, occupies itself in bringing together the weak points of the most famous authors without doing the least justice to the art which gives life to the whole body of their works, or to the admirable passages which embellish them everywhere. The author rightly lays a heavy hand on those cowardly vermin who aspire to wit; and I am persuaded that the most enlightened of the Moderns will be as grateful to him as the most zealous partisans of venerable antiquity.

The principal piece to be found in the first volume is called *A Tale of a Tub*, for reasons which will be found in the author's Preface; its aim is to ridicule the superstition and fanaticism which so much degrade a religion which, in its primitive institution, was adorned in nothing more than a reasonable simplicity. This whole work is an allegory perfectly well sustained from beginning to end, and calculated to bring back from a disguised paganism those who glory in calling themselves Christians. The work can make them renounce certain metaphysical subtleties which dazzle the most those who understand them the least, and certain empty fancies which are dignified by the name of inspiration, though they are in reality only the effect of certain vapours common to those of a moody and melancholy constitution.

[There follows an outline of the plot of the religious allegory]

. . . One can readily see in this allegory that the Simple coats stand for the Christian religion in its primitive purity; the father's will for the New Testament; the ornaments for the ceremonies and dogmas of Catholicism; Lord Peter for the Pope, or the Roman Church; Martin, for the Lutheran religion, Jack for the reformed religion, and so on.

The author appears here to favour Martin at the expense of Jack, whose ill-considered zeal is everywhere mocked. The reason is that he wishes to plead the cause of the Anglican Church, which has followed the Lutherans in keeping many Catholic ceremonies, the reform of which was thought too dangerous; while the Calvinists by aiming at too rigorous a reform have taken themselves to the limits of reformation. Moreover he draws up under the banners of Jack all the different kinds of fanatics, whom he regards as having arisen from the reformed religion as it was established in England under the name of Presbyterianism.

I am convinced that what I have just said about this *Tale* will greatly surprise most people who have heard it spoken of. Pious people in England regard the work as the extreme effort of a libertine imagination, whose sole intention is to lay the foundations of irreligion on the ruin of all Christian sects. Given the way in which the generality of men owning a religion are constituted, this is the judgment they must necessarily come to. Ordinarily each human being embraces the opinions of his sect *en bloc*, and he believes it impossible to be of such or such a religion if one hesitates on the least article of faith. We inherit our religion from our parents; they deliver its solid and reasonable dogmas confused with fanaticism and superstition. We are credulous and thoughtless heirs, who do not distinguish what is truly beautiful and useful in this treasure from the false coin, which for the most part is brighter and more striking than the pure gold. In this unfortunate prejudice, a man who examines and dares to find anything to find fault with in the smallest unfamiliar detail of each Christian sect, passes in our opinion for a free-thinker, who absolutely rejects all the sects and who is unworthy to be called a Christian.

But it is impossible for an enlightened man, who takes evidence as the sole guide to his opinions, to find anywhere a body of doctrine and religious ceremonies in which the strongest attention could not feel the least fault or weakness.

All the leaders of sects have been men; it is natural for vanity, spite, and the spirit of contradiction to throw them into a certain aberration, and a man who is in a calm and philosophic state of mind can perceive this without pain.

I can promise all those capable of knowing this truth, that they will find nothing here which has the least air of freethinking or of irreligion. The author never touches one of the dogmas which all the Christian sects regard as fundamental. He makes fun of the Roman Church, which he regards as a body of doctrine invented to subject reason to human authority and stupid credulity; while in connection with the different branches of the Protestant religion he ridicules the spirit of enthusiasm and fanaticism which makes piety incompatible with common sense. I imagine that every judicious person will be obliged to the author for this. Indeed one could not render a greater service to the only religion which is reasonable and worthy of the majesty of God and the excellence of human nature, than to free it of superstition and vain fancy, which not only debase it but destroy it from top to bottom by tearing up its unique and solid foundation, reason and good sense. Piety is, so to speak, the healthy state of the soul; superstitious and fanatical men have made of it a burning fever, and whoever tries to cure it effectively deserves the highest praises.

Some people will no doubt make the objection that it is unseemly to laugh at religious matters, and that instead of making fun of them the author would have done well to lay bare extravagances by grave and serious reasoning. The reply follows of itself from that which I have already established, that matters of religion are not in question here; what is in question are certain extravagances and mental aberrations which have nothing in common with religion, and which are almost as contrary to it as irreligion itself. To say nothing of the method of reasoning seriously with men who do not accept good sense as the natural judge of their sentiments and who regard it as a crime to have recourse to it. If there is anything that can rouse their reason from the lethargy into which they deliberately throw it, it is the sharp wit of raillery.

I admit that the author might have been a little more prudent in his banter, and not mingled with his ironies certain ribald turns of phrase which shock a delicate imagination; I have softened these as much as possible, and I dare to hope that the modesty of the French public will not be up in arms against my expressions.

I agree further that in my opinion the author would have done wisely to except from his joking all the passages from the Holy Scripture. It is true that he never jests with the natural sense of them, which in the end is the only sense to be respected; he ridicules only the disgraceful application that weak minds make of it; but all readers are not capable of making this distinction, which is sometimes a subtle one, and it is charitable and prudent to spare them scandals of this kind.

It is of little consequence who is the author of this work; I will say, however, that it has been attributed to the celebrated Sir William Temple, but that the general opinion is that it was written by Doctor Swift, an Anglican clergyman and one of the finest wits in Great Britain. Whether there really are large sections of this book which are lost, or whether the author has pretended to leave a large number of gaps to make the work more like an ancient manuscript, I do not know, and the public too can remain ignorant of the matter without loss.

. . . The English are extravagant and free to excess in their wit as in their conduct and manners; their irrepressible imagination expends itself wholly in comparisons and metaphors, and I am surprised that the more able of them have such great veneration for the Ancients, whose natural and noble simplicity they imitate so ill. I admit that ordinarily their figurative expressions, despite the oddity of imagination that they display, are admirably exact, but in most cases the sense is very forced, and their justness has to be searched for. However these passages strike and charm English readers, whose turn of mind is similar to that of the authors, they can only be displeasing to foreigners of a more exact and less impetuous turn, and a competent translator feels himself obliged to use a degree less warmth. The British wits perceive this, and regard the result of prudence as a lack of genius and imagination; they complain of something which should perhaps be praised.

9. A Swiss view of *A Tale of a Tub* and *The Battle of the Books*

1721

Bibliothèque Ancienne et Moderne, 1721, xv, 441–5.

This review of the French translation of the *Tale*, *Le Conte du Tonneau*, and of other pieces published with it, is by Jean le Clerc (1657–1737), a Swiss professor of philosophy at the Remonstrant Seminary in Amsterdam. Le Clerc was a biblical commentator of somewhat unconventional views.

The title of this work embarrassed the translator as it has many others. But its explanation, we believe, appears in the preface. Those who go whale fishing used to throw out an empty tub to amuse the enormous fish and distract it from attacking their ship. The author pretends that the allegorical fish to be understood here is the *Leviathan* of Hobbes, a book written to establish tyranny and irreligion, and the ship civil society, for the preservation of which this book is thrown at the head of the Hobbeists, to give them something to do which distracts them from attacking civil society—to which the author of the preface ought to have been able to add religion. The fact is that *A Tale of a Tub*, which is the English title, signifies in ordinary usage only an old wives' tale, and that the author of the preface is misleading the reader; an odd game which goes on throughout the book, where we often do not know whether the author is making fun or not, nor of whom, nor what his intention is. If we read the pretended dedication of the bookseller to Lord Somers, that of the author to Prince Posterity, the preface and the introduction which follows it, we will know well enough whom the author has undertaken to make fun of, though he wished to hide it under an impenetrable cloud. He wants to mock many things, where the ridiculous is mixed with the serious; but as he is one of the English, who do not very well know how to distinguish good from bad, in some places he turns everything into scurrilous jokes, while in others he

59

mocks only what deserves to be mocked. In the allegorical story of those brothers Peter, Martin, and Jack, which takes up with the digressions the whole of the first volume, one sees by the names what he refers to. One must admit that he often brings out the truth of each, though in a style as caustic as it is burlesque; but some people have believed that the author sought to destroy rather than to enlighten. It can be said in his favour, none the less, that when the people concerned have become what they should be, and not before, the author should be condemned to make them reparation and to praise their sentiments and manners as much as he has ridiculed them.

In the second volume, which deals more particularly with Great Britain, the first discourse is on *The Mechanical Operation of the Spirit*, and ridicules the fanatics, in whom a strong and troubled imagination, melancholy, and vehement passions excite extraordinary impulses which enable them to pass as inspired in the eyes of the people—as we have seen happen for some years. Habit, joined to such natural dispositions, allows a man to accustom himself to them so well that he ends by deceiving not only others but himself, and imagines himself inspired when he is merely agitated by feelings which are in large part mechanical. If the author is attacking only this kind of mechanical operation of the spirit he is undoubtedly right; but if he is going further and putting forward principles which destroy true prophecy, he is manifestly wrong. His ironic and figurative style can often seem too vigorous, and contains allusions that do not always appear regular and just. But how difficult it is, everywhere, to judge what his views are; it is better to believe that they are not so bad as they have, to some people, appeared to be.

The second piece is of quite a different character. It is an allegorical story of a battle that is pretended to have taken place between personified ancient and modern books in the Royal Library of St. James's, in England, where the Ancients won a complete victory over the Moderns, defended by Mr. Bentley and Mr. Wotton. The boldness of the fiction could scarcely be carried further, and there are no ancient fables equal to it.

10. The reception of *Gulliver's Travels*

1726

The Correspondence of Jonathan Swift, ed. Harold Williams, 1963,
iii, 180–9.
(a) Extract from a letter of John Arbuthnot to Swift, 5 November
1726.
(b) Extract from a letter of Pope to Swift, 16 November 1726.
(c) Extract from a letter of John Gay to Swift, 17 November 1726.
(d) Extract from a letter of Swift to Pope, 27 November 1726.

Gulliver's Travels was a great success from the time of its publication; clearly it was the topical references that first caught the
fancy of a period so fascinated by political controversy. Swift's
friends, though they keep up the pretence that the author is unknown, were in the secret of the work. In view of the habitually
joking and ironic tone of their letters to each other, it is difficult
to know how seriously to take the gentleman who looked for
Lilliput on the map or the bishop who 'hardly believed a word
of it'.

(a) JOHN ARBUTHNOT TO SWIFT

London, 5 November 1726

. . . I will make over all my profits to you, for the property of *Gulliver's Travels*, which I believe, will have as great a Run as John Bunian.
Gulliver is a happy man that at his age can write such a merry work. . . .

The princess immediately seized on your plade for her own use, &
has orderd the young Princess to be clad in the same, when I had the
honor to see her She was Reading *Gulliver*, & was just come to the
passage of the Hobbling prince, which she laughed at. I tell yow freely
the part of the projectors is the least Brilliant. . . .

Gulliver is in every body's Hands. Lord Scarborow who is no inventor of Storys told me that he fell in company with a Master of a ship,
who told him that he was very well acquainted with Gulliver, but that

the printer had Mistaken, that he lived in Wapping, & not in Rother-hith. I lent the Book to an old Gentleman, who went immediately to his Map to search for Lilly put. . . .

(b) ALEXANDER POPE TO SWIFT

16 November 1726

. . . I congratulate you first upon what you call your Couzen's wonderful Book, which is *publica trita manu* at present, and I prophecy will be in future the admiration of all men. That countenance with which it is received by some statesmen, is delightful; I wish I could tell you how every single man looks upon it, to observe which has been my whole diversion this fortnight. I've never been a night in London since you left me, till now for this very end, and indeed it has fully answered my expectations.

I find no considerable man very angry at the book: some indeed think it rather too bold, and too general a Satire: but none that I hear of accuse it of particular reflections (I mean no persons of consequence, or good judgment; the mob of Criticks, you know, always are desirous to apply Satire to those that they envy for being above them) so that you needed not to have been so secret upon this head. . . .

(c) JOHN GAY TO SWIFT

17 November 1726

About ten days ago a Book was publish'd here of the Travels of one Gulliver, which hath been the conversation of the whole town ever since. The whole impression sold in a week; and nothing is more diverting than to hear the different opinions people give of it, though all agree in liking it extreamly. 'Tis generally said that you are the Author, but I am told, the Bookseller declares he knows not from what hand it came. From the highest to the lowest it is universally read, from the Cabinet-council to the Nursery. The Politicians to a man agree, that it is free from particular reflections, but that the Satire on general societies of men is too severe. Not but we now and then meet with people of greater perspicuity, who are in search for particular applications in every leaf; and it is highly probable we shall have keys published to give light into Gulliver's design. Your Lord [Bolingbroke] is the person who least approves it, blaming it as a design of evil consequence to depreciate human nature, at which it cannot be wondered that he takes most offence, being himself the most accomplish'd of his species, and so losing more than any other of that praise which is due both to the dignity and virtue of a man. Your friend, my Lord Harcourt, commends it very much, though he thinks in some places the matter too far carried. The Duchess Dowager of Marlborough is in raptures at it; she says she can dream of nothing else since she read it; she declares, that she hath now found out, that her whole life hath been lost in caressing the worst part of mankind, and treating the best as her foes; and that if she knew Gulliver, tho' he had been the worst enemy she ever had, she would give up all her present acquaintance for his friendship. You may see by this, that you are not much injur'd by being suppos'd the Author of this piece. If you are, you have disoblig'd us, and two or three of your best friends, in not giving us the least hint of it while you were with us; and in particular Dr. Arbuthnot, who says it is ten thousand pitys he had not known it, he could have added such abundance of things upon every subject. Among Lady-critics, some have found out that Mr. Gulliver had a particular malice to maids of honour. Those of them who frequent the Church, say, his design is impious, and that it is an insult on Providence, by depreciating the works of the Creator. Notwithstanding I am told the Princess hath read it with great pleasure. As to other Critics, they think the flying island is the least entertaining; and so great an opinion the town have of the impossibility of Gulliver's writing at all below himself, that 'tis agreed that Part was not writ by the same Hand, tho' this hath its defenders too. It hath pass'd Lords and Commons, *nemine contradicente*; and the whole town, men, women, and children are quite full of it.

Perhaps I may all this time be talking to you of a Book you have never seen, and which hath not yet reach'd Ireland; if it hath not, I believe what we have said will be sufficient to recommend it to your reading, and that you order me to send it to you. . . .

(d) SWIFT TO ALEXANDER POPE

Dublin, 27 November 1726

I am just come from answering a Letter of Mrs. Howard's writ in such mystical terms, that I should never have found out the meaning, if a Book had not been sent me called *Gulliver's Travellers*, of which you say so much in yours. I read the Book over, and in the second volume observe several passages which appear to be patched and altered, and the style of a different sort (unless I am much mistaken) Dr. Arbuthnot likes the Projectors least, others you tell me, the Flying island; some think it wrong to be so hard upon whole Bodies or Corporations, yet the general opinion is, that reflections on particular persons are most to be blamed: so that in these cases, I think the best method is to let censure and opinion take their course. A Bishop here said, that Book was full of improbable lies, and for his part, he hardly believed a word of it; and so much for Gulliver.

11. Lady Mary Wortley Montagu on *Gulliver's Travels*

1726

Complete Letters of Lady Mary Wortley Montagu, ed. Robert Halsband, 1966, ii, 71–2.

Lady Mary Wortley Montagu (1689–1762) was a Whig and, at this time, an enemy of Pope. Like Edward Young, she guesses at a joint authorship of Swift, Arbuthnot, and Pope for *Gulliver's Travels.* This extract from her letter to her sister, Lady Mar, of November 1726, is a good example of the personal and political animosity which guided so much of the town in its response to Swift's work. The sharpness of Swift's political and moral comment is dismissed with a scurrilous joke on Book IV of the *Travels.*

Here is a book come out, that all our people of taste run mad about. Tis no less than the united Work of a dignify'd clergyman, an Eminent Physician, and the first poet of the Age, and very wonderful it is, God knows. Great Eloquence have they employ'd to prove themselves Beasts, and show such a veneration for Horses, that since the Essex Quaker no body has appear'd so passionately devoted to that species;[1] and to say truth, they talk of a stable with so much warmth and Affection I can't help suspecting some very powerfull Motive at the bottom of it.

---

[1] Lady Mary here refers to 'News from Colchester. Or, A Proper New Ballad of Certain Carnal Passages betwixt a Quaker and a Colt, at Horsly near Colchester, in Essex' [1659], by John Denham (*Poems and Translations,* 5th ed., 1709, 105–10). [Editor's note.]

12. An anonymous opinion of *Gulliver's Travels*

1726

A Letter from a Clergyman to his Friend, with an Account of the Travels of Capt. Lemuel Gulliver: and a Character of the Author. To which is added, the True Reasons why a certain Doctor was made a Dean, 1726, 6–19.

The anonymous author of this letter, which regards *Gulliver's Travels* entirely in the light of an attack on the Government, pretends that his friend has asked him to give 'a just character of the reputed Author of these *Travels*'. The clergyman claims to have been 'conversant with him [Swift] in publick and private Life; in his early Days, as well as since; when he first appear'd in the world; at home and abroad; in the Camp and Cabinet; a little when he was in Favour, more since in Disgrace. . . . But here for the sake of our Cloth I must beg Leave to draw a Viel [sic] and to keep it on, as much, and as long, as the nature of my design will admit: Was I indeed to follow the Captain's Example, what vile, what cruel things might I not suggest of him? What hard Things could I not Prove?'

Thus having said as much as I think needful by way of Introduction, I would turn my Thoughts more immediately to the work before me; I have, as you directed me, Sir, read it over with the greatest Distinction, and Exactness I was able: I've enter'd as much, as was possible for me, into the Spirit and Design of the Author: By the strictest Examination I've endeavoured to sift every material Passage; and I persuade my self the Drift of the Author has appear'd plain to me thro' the whole. From which I conclude, that had Care been taken to have adapted them to modest virtuous Minds, by leaving out some gross Words, and lewd Descriptions, and had the Inventor's Intention been innocent, the first three Parts of these *Travels* would undoubtedly have proved diverting, agreeable, and acceptable to all; there is a great deal of wit and more Invention in them; though, as is pretty usual in so large a work of this Sort, there are some unnatural Incidents, and here and there an Inconsistency with it self.

In the fourth Part, which is more than half of the second Volume, the Author flags, he loses his Vivacity, and in my Opinion maintains little of his former Spirit, but the Rancour. This indeed appears most plentifully in this Part; and the Captain seems so wholly influenced by it, that he makes a sort of Recapitulation of Invectives he had vented before; and having receiv'd a fresh supply of Gall, appears resolv'd to discharge it, though he has no way than by varying the Phrase, to express in other words, the unjust sentiments he had disclosed before: In this long tedious Part the Reader loses all that might have been engaging to him in the three former; the Capacity and Character given there of Brutes are so unnatural; and especially the great Preheminence asserted of them, to the most virtuous and noble of humane Nature, is so monstrously absurd and unjust, that 'tis with the utmost Pain a generous Mind must endure the Recital; a Man grows sick at the shocking things inserted there; his Gorge rises; he is not able to conceal his Resentment; and closes the Book with Detestation and Disappointment.

But to return to the three former Parts, as I have said all I can with Justice say, on their Behalf; allow me now to shew a little of the great malignity, and evil tendency of their Nature: Here I might be abundantly prolix, had I not absolutely determined to be otherwise, the Field is large, the Matter very copious: Here, Sir, you may see a reverend Divine, a dignify'd Member of the Church unbosoming himself, unloading his Breast, discovering the true Temper of his Soul, drawing his own Picture to the Life; here's no Disguise, none could have done it so well as himself: Here's the most inveterate Rancour of his Mind, and a hoard of Malice, twelve Years collecting, discharged at once; Here's ENVY, the worst of all Passions, in Perfection; ENVY, the most beloved Darling of Hell; the greatest Abhorrence of Heaven; ENVY, the Crime Mankind should be the most ashamed of, having the least to say in Excuse for it; the Canker of the Soul, most uneasy to the Possessor; a Passion not to be gratify'd, nor possible of Pleasure; the peculiar one would imagine of infernal Beings, and much of their Punishment. ENVY, is ever levell'd at Merit, and superior Excellence; and the most deserving are, for being such, the properest object of ENVY.

View now, Sir, the Doctor, as I shall henceforward call him; and upon examination, I fear 'twill be found, that his Conduct too fully answers the Description of this detestable Passion: I shall be very plain and expressive; an honest Man will no more conceal the truth, than deny it, when the Former may prove prejudicial to the Innocent: Whether the Government may ever think proper publickly to Chastise the Doctor for his Insolence, I know nothing of; perhaps such Snarling may be thought too low to engage such a Resentment: However this I am fully persuaded of, that as no Good Government ought to be so insulted and male-treated; so there is no honest Man among us but should contribute the utmost in his Power to bring the Author, and those concerned with him to exemplary Punishment, in order to deter others from the like pernicious Practices for the future.

What can be viler in the Intention? What may be worse in the Consequence, than an Attempt to interrupt the Harmony and good Understanding between His Majesty and his Subjects, and to create a Dislike in the People to these in the Administration; especially to endeavour at this in such a Juncture as the present? What could in all Probability be the Issue of bringing such Matters to bear, but the throwing ourselves and all *Europe* into a Flame? Ruining our Credit, destroying our Trade, beggaring of private Families, setting us a cutting one another's Throats; by which we should become an easy Prey to the common Enemy, who would at once subvert our Constitution, the happiest, the best in the World; destroy our Church Establishment; and subject us to all the Cruelty and sufferings the unbounded Lust of Tyrants, and the insatiable Avarice of Priests could load us with. . . .

The Doctor divests himself of the Gentleman and Christian entirely, and in their stead assumes, or if my Instructions are right, I should rather have said, discloses the reverse to them both; a Character too gross to be describ'd here and is better conceiv'd than express'd; he makes a Collection of all the meanest, basest, Terms the Rabble use in their Contests with one another in the Streets, and these he discharges without any other Distinction than only, that they who are Persons of the greatest Worth and Desert are loaded with the greatest Number of 'em. . . .

He spares neither Age nor Sex, neither the Living or the Dead; neither the Rich, the Great, or the Good; the best of Characters is no Fence, the Innocent are the least secure; even his Majesty's Person is not sacred, the Royal Blood affords no Protection here; he equally endeavours to bring into Contempt with the People, his Majesty, the Royal Family, and the Ministry.

The next great Attack, as all People understand it, is no less than upon a *British* Parliament; this August Assembly, the Wisest, the Noblest, the most Awful in the World, he treats with Words of the utmost Scurrility, with *Billingsgate* terms of the lowest Sort; this Body of the best Gentlemen in the Kingdom he calls Pedlars, Pickpockets, Highwaymen, Bullies; Words never spoke of a British Parliament before, and 'twould be a National Reproach they should now pass unpunished: This is beyond all Bounds; who that are *English* Men can with Temper think of such an Insult upon the Body of their Representatives; the Centre of the National Power; the great Preserver of our Laws, Religion, and Liberties, and of all that as Men and Christians we ought to hold dear and valuable.

I wish I could keep in better Terms with my old Companion, my Inclination's good t'wards it, but notwithstanding that, and all my Resolutions, I find it impracticable; his Conduct is so enormously bad, 'tis insufferable; humane Nature must be worse than he has represented it, and I never saw it look so ghastly before, to bear with him.

All that have read these *Travels* must be convinc'd I do the Doctor no Injustice by my Assertions: His Method of forming his characters seems to be new, it looks as if he first drew up a Set of ill Names and reproachful Epithets, and then apply'd them as he thought proper, without regarding at all, whether the Persons they were so apply'd to, deserv'd such Treatment or not; . . . he knew very well t'would sufficiently answer his End if by boldly and roundly asserting whatever he thought proper, and sticking at no Method of Defamation he should make the whole appear plausible and gain Adherents; and therefore with the utmost Assurance he affirms this Woman to be a Whore, that a Bawd, this Man a Pimp, that a Pathick tho' neither of them ever gave any Reason to be thought such, or were ever thought such, before. . . .

I look upon what I have hitherto said as necessary to my Undertaking; indulge me now, Sir, in a digression that seems naturally enough to present itself, and may be better made here than afterwards; the transition is easy, from the private, allow me to pass to the publick Life, of the Person [Walpole] I have been speaking: Here I might make a general Challenge and say; Who can Charge him with wanting of Wisdom, Judgment, Knowledge, Integrity, Uprightness, Justice, or Clemency, and a long &c.? But this would be but faint to the Latitude I may with Justice take the other way: This great Man, is the wise Director of the publick Affairs; he is the Delight of his Royal Master, and the Darling of the People; he is an Honour to his Nation, adds a

Lustre to the Crown, and is deservedly valued by us and all Europe, as a general publick Blessing, born for the Good, the Happiness of Mankind; and arrived to a Capacity of serving his Country best, when his Country stands in most need of his Service. . . .

I can't conclude without observing to you, Sir, that this Work is so far a finishing Stroke with the Doctor, that he seems by it to have compleated his Character: In a former Performance, he levelled his Jests at Almighty God: banter'd and ridiculed Religion and all that's good and adorable above; By this, he has abused and insulted those, who are justly valued by us, as the best, the greatest below.

13. William Warburton on Swift and human nature

1727

A Critical and Philosophic Enquiry into the Causes of Prodigies and Miracles, as related by Historians. With An Essay towards restoring a Method and Purity in History, 1727, 26–33.

William Warburton (1698–1779), later Bishop of Gloucester, was a theological controversialist of somewhat arrogant habit. He was to become the guide of Pope's last years, and his literary executor. The hectoring and heavily ironic tone of his comments on the line of thought he sees Swift as representing makes them perhaps less than literary criticism, but they are of representative interest.

But there is a Sect of Anti Moralists, who have *our Hobbes*, and the *French Duke de la Rochfoucault*, for their leaders, that give it but Encouragement, would soon rid our Hands of this Inconvenience [Love of our Country], and most effectively prevent all Return from that Quarter: For whereas it was the Business of ancient Philosophy, to give us a due Veneration for the Dignity of *human Nature*; they described it as it really was, beneficent, brave, and *a Lover of its Species*: a Principle, become sacred since our divine Master made it the Foundation of his Religion: These Men, for what Ends we shall see presently, endeavouring to create a Contempt and Horror for it, have *painted* it base, *cowardly, envious,* and *a Lover of its self* . . . Thy Pride, perhaps, won't suffer thee to *degrade thy Species*; nor thy Partiality to thy Country, to *abuse thy* Governors. Your Masters, *the Ancients*, said it, and you, alas! believed it, that Mankind was more free from Malignity than Meakness; and less able, than dispos'd to mend: But hearken to better Instructors, and learn to efface these silly Prejudices.

The religious author of A Tale of a Tub will tell you, *Religion* is but a Reservoir of Fools and Madmen; and *the virtuous Lemuel Gulliver* will answer for the *State*, that it is a Den of Savages and Cut-throats. What

71

think you, Reader: is not the System round and great? And now the Fig-leaf is so cleanly plucked off, what remains but bravely to strike away the rotten Staff, that yet keeps our old doting Parents on their last Legs?

Seriously let it be as they say, that Ridicule and Satire are the Supplement of publick Laws; should not then, the Ends of both be the same: the Benefit of Mankind? But where is the sense of a general Satire, if the whole Species be degenerated? And where is the Justice of it, if it be not? The Punishment of Lunaticks is as wise as the one; and a general Execution as honest as the other. In short, a general Satire, the work only of ill Men or little Genius's, was proscrib'd of Old, both by the *Critic* and the *Magistrate*, as an offence equally against Justice and common Sense.

The immortal Socrates employed his wit to better Purpose. His Vein was rich, but frugal. He thought the Laugh came too dear, when bought at the Expence of Probity: And therefore laid it all out in the Improvement and Reform of Manners.

14. Voltaire on Swift

1727, 1734, 1756, 1767, 1777

Oeuvres Completes (52 vols.), 1880:
- (*a*) Letter to M. Thieriot (February 1727), xxxiii, 165.
- (*b*) Letter to M. Thieriot [written in English] (March 1727), xxxiii, 167.
- (*c*) Letter XXII (1734), *Mélanges*, xxii, 174–5.
- (*d*) 'Des Beaux-Arts en Europe du Temps de Louis XIV', *Siecle de Louis XIV* (1756), xiv, 560.
- (*e*) Letter V, 'Sur Swift', *Lettres . . . sur Rabelais et sur d'autres auteurs accusés d'avoir mal parlé de la réligion chrétienne* (1726), xxvi, 489–91.
- (*f*) '*La Vie et les Opinions de Tristram Shandy*, traduites de l'anglais de Sterne, pour M. Frenais' (1777), *Articles Extraits du Journal de Politique et de Literature*, Part I, xxx, 381.

Voltaire (1694–1778) was a great admirer of Swift, with whom he exchanged letters. This admiration was no doubt based on what he thought to be a free spirit of irreverence in Swift, and he writes most of the religious allegory of *A Tale in a Tub*, but it is curious that he sees so little in *Gulliver's Travels*. Like Pope, Voltaire compares Swift to Rabelais.

(a)

If you wish to carry out the plans of which you tell me, by translating an English book, *Gulliver* is perhaps the only one that suits you. He is the English Rabelais, as I have already told you; but his work is not mixed with rubbish, like Rabelais', and this book would be entertaining in itself, because of the singular strokes of imagination it is full of, the lightness of its style, etc., even if it were not in addition a satire on human kind.

(b)

. . . You will find in the same parcel the second volume of *M. Gulliver*, which (by the by, I don't advise you to translate) strikes at the first;

the other is overstrained. The reader's imagination is pleased and charmingly entertained by the new prospect of the lands which Gulliver discovers to him; but that continued series of new fangles, follies of fairytales, of wild inventions pall at last upon our taste. Nothing unnatural may please long; it is for this reason that commonly the second parts of romances are so insipid. . . .

(c)

This [the topicality of his works] is why we in France will never have a very good understanding of the books of the ingenious Dr. Swift, called the English Rabelais. He too has the honour of being a clergyman though he makes fun of everything, but Rabelais was not superior to his age, while Swift is very much superior to Rabelais. Our Rector of Meudon, in his extravagant and unintelligible book, was lavish with extreme gaiety and an even greater irrelevance; he was prodigal of learning, dirt, and tediousness. A good story of a couple of pages is bought at the expense of volumes of foolishness; there are only a few persons, and those of a strange taste, who pride themselves on understanding and esteeming the whole work. The rest of the nation laughs at Rabelais' jokes, and despises the book. He is regarded as the chief of buffoons; one can only regret that a man with so much wit made such miserable use of it. He is a drunken philosopher, who wrote only when he was drunk.

Mr. Swift is Rabelais in his right senses, and living in good company. It is true he has not Rabelais' gaiety, but he has all the subtlety, the judgment, the taste, the power to select, which are lacking in our Rector of Meudon. His verses are of an unusual and almost inimitable turn; pleasantry is his speciality in verse and in prose, but to understand him properly one should make a short trip to his country.

In that country—what will seem strange to the rest of Europe—it was not considered odd that the Reverend Dr. Swift, Dean of a Cathedral, should make fun in his *Tale of a Tub* of Catholicism, Lutheranism, and Calvinism; he tells us in his own vindication that he has not touched Christianity itself. He pretends to have respected the father while giving a hundred strokes of the birch to the three children. People of a difficult turn of mind believed that the stick was so long it reached to the father as well.

The famous *Tale of a Tub* is an imitation of the old story of the three invisible rings, which a father left to his three children. The three rings were the Jewish faith, the Christian, and the Mahometan. It is also an imitation of the story of Méro and Énegu, by Fontenelle. Méro was an anagram of Rome and Énegu of Geneva. They are two sisters who claim the succession to their father's kingdom. Méro reigns first. Fontenelle presents her as a sorceress who does conjuring tricks with bread and performs incantations with the help of dead bodies. This is exactly Swift's Lord Peter, who gives a piece of bread to his two brothers and says to them 'Friends, here is some excellent Burgundy; this partridge is of an admirable flavour.' The same Lord Peter, in Swift, performs all that Méro does in Fontenelle.

(d)

There are several pieces in Dean Swift of which we find no example in antiquity: he is Rabelais perfected.

(e)

It is true, sir, that I have said nothing to you about Swift. He deserves an article to himself; he is the only witty English writer of this kind [writers accused of speaking ill of Christianity]. It is a strange thing that the two men most to be *reproached* for having turned the Christian religion into ridicule should have been two clergymen with cure of souls. Rabelais was rector of Meudon, and Swift was Dean of the Cathedral in Dublin. Both hurled more taunts against Christianity than Molière did against medecine, and both lived and died peacefully, while other men have been persecuted, pursued, put to death, for a few ambiguous words.

> *Quelquefois l'un se brise où l'autre s'est sauvé,*
> *Et par où l'un périt un autre est conservé.*
>
> (*Cinna*, acte II, Scene i.)[1]

Dean Swift's *A Tale of a Tub* is an imitation of *The Three Rings*. The story of the three rings is very ancient, and dates from the time of the Crusades. It concerns an old man who, dying, left a ring to each of his three children. They fight about which is the finest ring, but after long struggles they recognise that all three rings are exactly alike. The good old man is theism, the three children are the Jewish, Christian, and Mahometan religions. . . .

The story of *The Three Rings* is to be found in several ancient collections. Dr. Swift has substituted for the rings three coats. The frontispiece to this piece of blasphemous raillery is worthy of the work; it is a

---

[1] By Corneille. 'Sometimes one man is destroyed where another is saved, and one perishes by the same means that preserve another.' [Editor's note.]

print representing three methods of public speaking. The first is the theatre of harlequins and clowns, the second is a preacher speaking from a pulpit made of a half-cask, and the third is the ladder from the top of which a man about to be hanged makes his last speech to the people.

A preacher between a clown and a condemned criminal does not make an impressive figure. The main part of the book is an allegorical history of the three principal sects which divide southern Europe, the Roman, the Lutheran, and the Calvinist. He says nothing of the Greek Church, which is in possession of six times more land than any one of the others, and he ignores Mahometanism, much more widespread than the Greek Church.

The three brothers, to whom their good old father has left three coats all of one piece and of one colour, are Peter, Martin, and Jack, that is to say the Pope, Luther, and Calvin. The author has attributed to his three heroes more extravagances than Cervantes did to his Don Quixote, or Ariosto to his Roland, but Lord Peter is the worst treated of the three brothers. The book is very badly translated into French; it was impossible to find equivalents for the comic passages which give it its flavour. The comedy often turns upon the quarrels between the Anglican and the Presbyterian Churches, and customs and events of which we know nothing in France. Often, too, it depends upon word-play peculiar to the English language. For example, the word signifying a papal bull also means in English *un bœuf* (bull). This is a source of puns and jokes entirely lost for a French reader.

Swift was much less learned than Rabelais, but his wit is sharper and subtler; he is the Rabelais of good company.

(f)

Works of this kind [comic works like *Tristram Shandy*] were not un-known among the English. The famous Dean Swift composed several of this sort. He has been called the English Rabelais, but it must be acknowledged that he is considerably superior to Rabelais. As gay and as amusing as our priest of Meudon, he wrote in his own language with much more purity and delicacy than the author of *Gargantua* did in his, and we have verses of his worthy of Horace in their elegance and simplicity.

15. Abbé Desfontaines and *Gulliver's Travels*

1727, 1730, 1787

(a) Abbé Desfontaines, 'Preface du Traducteur', *Voyages de Gulliver*, 1727, i, pp. v–xxviii.

(b) *Mercure de France* (May 1727), 955–67.

(c) *Journal des Sçavans* (July 1727), 409–16.

(d) *The Correspondence of Jonathan Swift*, ed. Harold Williams (6 vols.), 1963.
   1. Desfontaines to Swift, 23 June 1727, iii, 217.
   2. Swift to Desfontaines, July 1727, iii, 226.

(e) Abbé Desfontaines, 'Preface de l'editeur', *Le Nouveau Gulliver, ou Voyages de Jean Gulliver, fils du Capitaine Gulliver* (1730). *Voyages Imaginaires, Songes, Visions, et Romans Cabalistiques*, ed. Charles George Garnier, 1787, xv, 24–6.

(f) Charles George Garnier, 'Avertissement de l'editeur', *Voyages de Gulliver. Voyages Imaginaires* . . . , xiv, vii–viii.

The Abbé Pierre-Francois Guyot Desfontaines (1685–1745) was educated by the Jesuits and became a professor of rhetoric at Bourges, but in 1715 he entered upon a new career as a man of letters, producing a series of critical reviews. His outspoken critical judgements made him a number of enemies, among them Voltaire. Desfontaines's translation of *Gulliver's Travels* is, to say the least, a free one, confidently adapted to what he thought the more correct and delicate taste of France, but his Preface, though hardly tactful, does contain some of the genuinely critical comment which is so rare during Swift's lifetime.

In this section are also included two French reviews of Desfontaines's translation; both appeared in 1727. These anonymous pieces include summaries of the work and, in the extracts given, also treat such matters as style and moral values.

An exchange of letters between Desfontaines and Swift also occurred in 1727. Desfontaines had heard, to his alarm, that Swift intended to visit France, and in the hope of placating Swift beforehand for the derogatory comments on his work, he sent Swift a letter and a second edition of the translation, in which he had omitted a large part of the paragraph in the Preface commenting on the puerility and bad taste of much of the *Travels*. He was too late, however; Swift had already seen an earlier edition, and replied in a letter of polished but crushing irony.

The Abbé Desfontaines himself wrote, after the publication of *Gulliver's Travels*, an imitation of it called *Le Nouveau Gulliver, ou Voyages de Jean Gulliver, fils du Capitaine Gulliver* (1730), a book of philosophic voyages. In his Preface, as 'editor' of Jean Gulliver's travels, he writes of *Gulliver's Travels* itself. *Le Nouveau Gulliver* was amazingly popular; it appeared in English and Italian translations as early as 1731, and it was reissued several times in France. Charles George Garnier included it as Volume XV in his thirty-nine volume series of *Voyages Imaginaires*, and it is from this edition that the extract here is taken. *Gulliver's Travels*, as translated by Desfontaines, comprise Volume XIV of the series, and Garnier's comments on it are included in the 'Avertissement' which concludes this section.

(*a*)

The author of this work is the famous Mr. Swift, Englishman and Dean of St. Patrick's in Dublin, all of whose writings either in the form of belles lettres or upon political matters are well known and highly esteemed in England. . . .

At the end of last year, Mr. Swift published in London the *Travels of Captain Lemuel Gulliver*, which I am to deal with now. An English nobleman living in Paris, having received the *Travels* almost immediately after publication, did me the honour of speaking to me about them as an agreeable and witty work. The opinion of this nobleman, who has himself a great deal of wit, taste, and literary knowledge, predisposed me in favour of the book. Some other Englishmen of my acquaintance, whose intelligence I esteem equally, had the same opinion of it; and as they knew that I had been learning their language for some time they urged me to make this ingenious work known in France, through a translation that could come up to the original.

At the same time, a friend of M. de Voltaire showed me a recent letter, written from London, in which that famous writer spoke very highly of Mr. Swift's new book, and asserted that he had never read anything more amusing and witty, and that if it was well translated into French it would be a brilliant success.

All that made me, at the beginning of February this year, not only desire to read it, but even to plan to translate it, if I felt myself capable of it and if I found it to my taste. I read it and found no difficulty in it. But I admit that the first thirty pages gave me no pleasure. The arrival of Gulliver in the Lilliputian empire, the description of that country and of its inhabitants, of six inches high, and the circumstantial detail of their feelings and conduct towards a stranger who to them was a giant, all that seemed to me rather frigid and mediocre, and made me afraid that the whole work would be of the same kind.

But when I had read a little further, my ideas changed, and I recognized that people were right to praise the book to me. I found in it entertaining and judicious things, a well sustained fiction, fine ironies, amusing allegories, a sensible and liberal morality, and, throughout, playful and witty satire. In a word, I found a book quite new and original in its kind. I hesitated no longer; I set to work to translate it purely for my own advantage, that is to say to perfect my knowledge of the English language, which is beginning to be fashionable in Paris and has lately been learned by several people of merit and distinction.

I read several passages of my translation to well-informed friends who are good judges of pleasantry. I observed the first impression that the work produced on them and according to my custom I paid more attention to that impression than to the favourable reflections that followed. At last, determined by their opinions and advice, I resolved to finish my translation and risk giving it to the public.

Nevertheless I cannot conceal here the fact that I found in this work of Mr. Swift some weak and even very bad parts; impenetrable allegories, insipid allusions, puerile details, low thoughts, boring repititions, coarse jokes, pointless pleasantries: in a word things which translated literally into French would have appeared indecent, paltry, impertinent, would have disgusted the good taste which reigns in France, would have covered me with confusion, and would certainly have drawn just reproaches on my head if I had been so weak and imprudent as to expose them to the eyes of the public.

I know that some people will reply that all these passages which shock us are allegorical, and are witty to those who understand them. For me, who have not the clue (any more than have those gentlemen who defend them) and who neither can nor will find the explanation of all these fine mysteries, I confess that I believed it proper to take the course of suppressing them entirely. If I have by any chance left any of this kind of thing in my translation, I beg the public to consider that it is natural for a translator to let himself be won over, and to feel sometimes too much indulgence for his author. For the rest, I thought myself capable of making good these deficiencies and replacing the losses by the help of my imagination, and by certain turns that I gave to things which displeased me. I have said enough about this to make clear the nature of my translation.

I understand that a translation is at this very time being printed in Holland. If it is literal, and if it is being made by some ordinary translator of that country, I pronounce judgement, without having seen it, that it is very bad, and I am certain that when it appears I shall not be contradicted or corrected.

I said that this work of Mr. Swift is new and original in its kind. I am not ignorant, however, of the fact that we already have some pieces of this sort. Without speaking of Plato's *Republic*, Lucian's *True History* and its supplement, there is the *Utopia* of Chancellor More, the *New Atlantis* of Chancellor Bacon, the *History of the Sevarambes*, the voyages of Sadeur and of Jacques Macé, and finally the *Voyage to the Moon* of Cyrano de Bergerac. But all these works are in a different style, and those who wish to compare them to this will find that they have nothing in common with it except the idea of an imaginary voyage and an imaginary country.

Certain people of serious, solid, and weighty mind, who are enemies of all fiction or who condescend, at most, to tolerate ordinary fictions, will perhaps be put off by the audacity and novelty of the inventions they will see here. Pigmies of six inches, giants of a hundred and fifty feet, a flying island inhabited by geometricians and astronomers, an academy of systems and fancies, an island of magicians, immortal men, finally horses endowed with reason in a country where animals in human shape are not reasonable creatures—all this will disgust solid minds who want above all truth and reality, or at least verisimilitude and possibility.

But I ask them if there is much verisimilitude and possibility in the stories of fairies, enchanters, and hippogryphs. How many highly esteemed works exist which are based only on the invention of these creatures of the fancy? Ariosto and Tasso are full of these fictions which offend against verisimilitude. What shall I say of the more usual poetic fictions? Do we not find there centaurs, sirens, tritons, dryads, naiads, muses, a Pegasus, gorgons, fauns, satyrs, living rivers, genies, and indeed pigmies and giants, as we find here? That is the poetic system. If we condemn it, we must now reduce all fictions to the boring intrigues of romance; we must look with the utmost scorn at Ovid's *Metamorphoses*, and those which are scattered through the poems of Homer and Virgil, since all this is based solely on inventions which are wholly lacking in verisimilitude.

But Rabelais' *Pantagruel* must also seem an insipid and execrable book, in those very parts of it which the experts admire. Is not Gargantua a giant bigger even than those of Brobdingnag? We see him mounted on a mare which is capable of carrying the two great bells of Nôtre Dame in Paris, and of pulling down with its tail half of the forest of Orleans. This picture can give little pleasure to our critics!

Is the journey to the flying island any more absurd in its assumption than Cyrano de Bergerac's *Voyage to the Moon*? Yet this burlesque invention has been relished by everyone. As for the voyage to the country of rational horses, or Houyhnhnms, I admit that it is the boldest of the book's inventions, but it is also the one in which Swift's art and wit are most brilliant. For myself, when I began to read this voyage, I found it hard to conceive how the author would be able to sustain and develop this strange fiction, and give it an air of, at least, the verisimilitude proper to fabulous stories. Rational horses, and their dealings with a traveller, seemed to me an invention impossible to sustain. But in the end I knew that I had willingly admitted the hypothesis; in fact man, if he is to be well drawn, must be portrayed as an animal other than man. Moreover, in the supplement to Lucian's history there is a republic of animals, and the fables of Aesop, La Fontaine, and some of M. de la Motte's, make beasts talk and reason.

I think then that for all these reasons one should not censure *Gulliver's Travels* precisely because its fictions are not believable. They are, it is true, fantastic fictions, but they provide exercise for the imagination and give a good opportunity to the author, and on this count alone they must be enjoyed if they are handled with judgment, if they are entertaining, and above all if they lead to a judicious moral. For it is this that, it seems to me, is found here. However as an author and a translator are one, I do not expect to be believed on my word alone.

The first two voyages are based on the idea of a very sure principle of natural philosophy, the knowledge that there is no absolute size, and that all measurement is relative. The author has worked on this idea, and has drawn from it all that he could, to entertain and instruct his readers, and to make them feel the vanity of human grandeur. In these two voyages he seems in a way to regard men through a telescope. First he turns the object-glass to his eye, and consequently sees them as very small: this is the voyage to Lilliput. Then he turns the telescope around, and then he sees very big men: this is the voyage to Brobdingnag. This furnishes him with pleasing images, allusions, reflections.

As for the other voyages, the author intended here, still more than in the first two, to censure various customs of his country. The flying island of Laputa seems to be the English court, and can have no reference to any court elsewhere. One feels too that in the third voyage the author is directing himself at certain maxims held by the Dutch sailors who trade with Japan; maxims which are only too much practised in reality, and which it is to be presumed the Republic does not authorize.

In all voyages, and above all in that to Houyhnhnm-land, the author attacks man in general, and makes us aware of the absurdity and the wretchedness of the human mind. He opens our eyes to enormous vices that we are accustomed to regard as, at most, slight faults, and makes us feel the value of a purified reason, more perfect than our own.

All these great and serious ideas, however, are here treated in a comic and burlesque way. They are not fairy tales, which commonly contain no moral conclusions and which in that case are good only to amuse children: indeed we ought to prevent even children from reading them for fear of familiarising their minds with frivolous things. In general all fiction is insipid when it leads to nothing useful. But this will not be said, I think, about the fictions now under discussion. Intelligent men will find them witty, and the common run of readers will be entertained by them.

I am not surprised, therefore, to learn that in three weeks ten thousand copies of the original English version of *Gulliver's Travels* were sold in London and circulated in England and elsewhere. Since everything in this book has a direct and immediate reference to practices in the three kingdoms, and to the customs of their inhabitants, and has no relevance to our usages and customs except so far as man in general is concerned, I am far from thinking that my translation could have such a prodigious success in this country. I can say nevertheless, without flattering myself too much, that it has a certain merit which the original lacks; I have given my reasons above. . . .

But what I deny beforehand are the wicked and unjust applications that some people would perhaps like to make in certain parts of the book. The world today is full of allusion-makers, subtle-minded and fanciful men, who, full of bad intentions, themselves, attribute as much to others, and give themselves up with pleasure to the most hateful and forced interpretations. If everything is to be condemned that can give occasions for far-fetched and fantastic allusions, one must condemn not only the great part of works of imagination but nearly all histories, in which one necessarily finds portraits rather like modern people, and deeds similar to those which are going on before our eyes.

It is clear that this book was written not for France, but for England, and that what it contains of direct and particular satire does not touch us. Next, I protest that if I had found in my author any sharp strokes which seemed to me to carry a marked and natural allusion, and whose bearing I had felt to be injurious to anyone in this country, I would have suppressed them without hesitation, just as I have struck out everything that seemed to me gross and indecent.

What pleased me in the original was that I have perceived nothing in it that could be prejudicial to true religion. What the author says of Big-Endians, High-Heels, and Low-Heels in the Empire of Lilliput clearly refers to the unfortunate differences which divide England into Conformists and Nonconformists, into Tories and Whigs. This is an absurd spectacle in the eyes of a profane philosopher; but it excites compassion in a Christian philosopher attached to true religion and to unity which is only to be found in the Roman Church. I do not press this reflection, which is too serious for the preface to a book such as this.

I think, moreover, that no one will be upset by certain details to do with seafaring, or by some small indifferent circumstances which the author relates and which I have left in my translation. He seems in this to have affected to imitate real travellers, and to have intended to mock their scrupulous exactitude, and the minute details with which they load their accounts.

The way in which Gulliver ends the relation of two of these voyages is a natural portrayal of the effects of habit. On leaving the Kingdom of Brobdingnag all men seem to him pigmies; and when he has left Houyhnhnm-land, where he heard so much that was bad about human nature, he could no longer tolerate it when he returned among men. But he makes us feel at last that all impressions wear away in time.

Although I have done all I could to adjust this work of Mr. Swift to the taste of France, I do not claim to have made of it quite a French work. A foreigner is always a foreigner; whatever wit and polish he may have, he always retains something of his own accent and manners. . . .

(b)

These four Voyages are full of judicious morality, subtle ironies, and excellent pleasantries. The images are agreeable and laughable; and although the book's assumptions are bold and extraordinary they are so well handled that they deceive the mind and seem like the truth. . . . The description of the Struldbrugs or Immortals in the Kingdom of Lugg-nagg is, again, a lively piece which gives an admirable picture of the miseries of old age, and makes one aware of the folly of wishing for a long life. . . .

The fourth Voyage is considered the finest. It is concerned with the land of the Houyhnhnms, that is to say the land of rational horses. In this country there are Yahoos who have human faces but no reason. Here the author develops, with a hundred agreeable turns, a moral as fine as it is elevated. He makes us feel all the faults of humanity, in such a way that the reader is inspired with a supreme scorn for man. There is nothing in this last Voyage that is not beautiful and striking.

This book is not only an amusing work; it is a very useful one. Descriptions, fictions, conversations, reflections, all proceed from a bold and delicate pen and from a profound mind. The work is written with purity, elegance, and above all with infinite clarity and vivacity.

(c)

If we seek in reading about a journey only to absorb all these facts, we will doubtless be very dissatisfied with Gulliver. We will not fail to reproach his book with being a tissue of absurd and uninstructive fictions, and we will feel ourselves ill rewarded for the time we have spent in reading his vain imaginations. But those who are less curious to know the facts about a savage nation they will never see than to acquire a deep knowledge of men with whom they will always have to live; those who have more taste for the study of the human heart in general than for searching into extravagant customs practised by a barbarous nation; those in fact who prefer to useless descriptions the most judicious reflections on morality, politics, virtue, and all that relates to civil society; those readers will infallibly find that Gulliver is superior to ordinary travellers.

The historical, or if you prefer it the fabulous, part of this work is not, therefore, what merits the reader's chief attention. It must be thought of as an ingenious invention, able to make pleasurable the solid and important maxims which it contains, and which appear to be the author's sole concern. It is true that the most serious arguments are found here interlaced with the most daring and improbable fictions, but this mixture should disgust no one. Certainly truth is not sure to please everyone by its air of truth alone. When it is adorned only by its own beauty it often risks seeming austere. It almost always needs some foreign graces to make the approach to it more agreeable, and it never steals more pleasurably into the mind than in presenting itself with a certain amiable playfulness.

If it can be said that this advantage is generally necessary to all truths, how useful it must be to those which tend to oppose human weaknesses and passions? What precautions have to be taken, what circumspection used, to fight them without shocking those who delight in and idolise them!

Our author, who aims precisely at the folly of men and the depravity of their customs, had accordingly to cover his purpose with some sort of stratagem, to attack such powerful enemies, and we are persuaded that it would have been difficult for him to find one more suitable. His philosophical reflections, his moral precepts, his political maxims, his sublime ideas of honour, honesty, and all the duties of civil life, his praise of virtue, his horror of vice in general and the biting satire, sprinkled throughout the work, against many particular faults, all these things are led up to by entertaining preambles, and sustained by amusing inventions, entirely suited to the task of giving relish to the rules of conduct that he proposes and of predisposing those who think themselves ill-treated. . . .

[Examples of satiric strokes in the first three books are included here, from the factions of the Low and High Heels to the Struldbrugs as a demonstration that a long life is not necessarily a happy one]

. . . The last voyage is unquestionably the one which contains most criticism, morality, and virtuous sentiments. The Houyhnhnm reflections on lying, the astonishment he feels at the enumeration of our vices, his remarks on our disputes and wars and on their causes, his thoughts about the inequality in our fortunes, all these are so many wise lessons, in which the greatest philosophers could find profit. . . .

It still remains to say a word about the characters in this work. The inhabitants of Lilliput and those of Brobdingnag are so different in stature that it would be more fitting if their customs were a little less similar. It is true that in a close examination one can find some contrast, but in our opinion it could be better sustained and more conspicuous. Lilliput, for example, is inhabited by a small industrious people, enterprising and warlike, whose king maintains a standing army. In Brobdingnag the people enjoy themselves watching a little man who is put on show in the cities; they think only of this pastime, and the king laughs at those princes who keep soldiers guarding their frontiers, and maintain armies in time of peace: these contrasts are perceptible. But after noticing what a great deal of liveliness there is in men six inches high, we would not have been irritated to find less among those of 150 feet. These latter should not excel, like the former, in mathematics: since the pigmies seem to be given over to the liveliest passions, such as ambition, jealousy, injustice and cruelty, the giants should have been exempt from them, and when we have been made aware of the pride of the emperor of Lilliput in the ostentatious titles he takes to himself at the head of his edicts, the titles of majesty and highness should have been proscribed in Brobdingnag otherwise than by a book which by criticising them presupposes that at least they are in use.

It seems, too, that the character of the Houyhnhnms contradicts itself in various places. Reason, they say (condemning the variety of our opinions) is unchanging; truth is one: from which they conclude that disputes are useless, and they do not even understand what uncertainty is. Yet they have a parliament, which makes its deliberations and debates questions on which different opinions are put forward; and even on the subject of Gulliver some wish to cripple him while others judge that he should be banished from the country. They cannot suffer the existence of inequality in fortune; why then do such different conditions exist among them? They have hired servants, and it does not appear that the laqueys are the equals of their masters. A horse obliged to be a servant because he is small has no less cause to complain than a man compelled by others to work because he was not born rich.

The same people know nothing of lying, and have no term to express it in their language. With this idea in our minds, we are rather shocked to see the Dapple-Grey accept a confidence from Gulliver and promise to keep it a secret. We are afraid that some curious Houyhnhnm may come to question Gulliver's confidant about this mystery, and consequently reduce him to lying in order to keep his word or to breaking faith in order to tell the truth.

We could continue to cite similar irregularities, but we are afraid we have already been too long; and moreover these slight faults are so far effaced by the merit of the book that it would be unjust to give a scrupulous account of them.

(d) 1

Sir, I have the honour of sending you the second edition of your work, which I have translated into French. I would have sent you the first, if

I had not been obliged, for reasons that I cannot tell you, to insert in the preface a passage with which you would have had cause to be displeased; this I did very much against my will. Since the book is selling without opposition, these reasons no longer exist, and I immediately suppressed this passage in the second edition, as you will see. I have also corrected the passage on Mr. Carteret, concerning which my memory was so faulty. In many places, sir, you will find my translation not a very close one, but everything which pleases in England does not meet with the same approval here, whether because our customs are different, or because allusions and allegories which are obvious in one country are not so in another; or finally because of the differences in taste between the two countries. I wished to give the French a book for their own use, and this made me write a free and loose translation. I have even taken the liberty to make my own additions, according as your imagination enlivened my own. It is to you alone, sir, that I owe the honour that I have received from this translation, which has sold here at an astonishing speed, three editions have already been brought out. I have such great esteem for you, and I am so much obliged to you, that if the suppression that I have made did not meet with your entire satisfaction I will willingly do still more to erase even the memory of the passage in the preface. Moreover I beg you, sir, to pay attention to the justice which I have done you in that same preface.

(d) 2

. . . Translators for the most part give excessive praises to the works that they translate, and perhaps imagine that their reputation depends in some way on that of the authors they have chosen. But you have felt your powers, which put you above such precautions as these, to be capable of correcting a bad book, a much more difficult task than that of composing a good one. You have not been afraid to give to the public a work which, you assure your readers, is full of foolishness, puerilities, etc. We agree here that taste is not always the same in different nations, but we are inclined to believe that good taste is everywhere the same among people of wit, judgment, and learning. If then, the works of Mr. Gulliver are calculated only for the British Isles, that traveller must pass for a very wretched writer. The same vices and the same follies reign everywhere, at least in all the civilised countries of Europe, and the author who writes only for a town, a province, a kingdom, or even a century, so far from deserving to be translated, does not even deserve to be read.

The supporters of this Gulliver, who are still very numerous among us, maintain that his book will last as long as our language, because his merit consists not in certain ways or manners of thinking and speaking, but in a series of observations on the imperfections, the follies, and the vices of man.

You judge rightly that the people of whom I have just spoken do not much approve your criticism, and you will be surprised, no doubt, to know that they regard this ship's surgeon as a grave author, who never abandons his seriousness, who uses no disguise, who does not pride himself on being a wit, and who is content to communicate to the public, in a simple and unaffected narration, the adventures which happened to him and the things that he saw or heard during his travels.

(e)

What has been admired in the genius of Mr. Swift is that, in the first *Gulliver*, he had the skill to make things which are obviously impossible in some way convincing, by deceiving the imagination and seducing his reader's judgment by an arrangement of circumstantial and consecutive inventions. . . .

It is enough to hope that this little work may have some of the success which the translation of Mr. Swift's book had in France. I am not ignorant that the public was very divided on the subject of that book, that some ranked it with the best works that had appeared for a long time, and that others regarded it as a collection of childish and insipid fictions. These latter followed the inventions merely, without considering their wit and their allegorical meaning, which is none the less so easy to understand almost everywhere in the work. They complained that their interest had not been captured by intrigues and complicated situations; they wanted a novel written according to the rules, and they found only a series of allegorical voyages, without any amorous adventure.

(f)

Of all the works of which this class [imaginary voyages] is composed, we believe there is not one which better deserves the approbation of our readers than the travels of Captain Lemuel Gulliver. Hardly had this production appeared in England than it was greeted with all the eagerness that is shown for masterpieces: several editions were quickly exhausted, but they scarcely satisfied the hunger of the public. The Abbé Desfontaines conceived the idea of translating the work into our tongue, but for some time he hesitated, fearing that the subtlety of the critical censure would escape us and lose its value in a foreign idiom; he was also discouraged by the extreme improbability of the fiction. A story which offends so carelessly against all the rules of physical possibility appeared to him to be the product of an over-bold imagination, which had managed to please in England but would shock the refinement of French taste. Happily the translator was mistaken; his translation was as completely successful as the original work had been, showing him that we were as well able as the English to fathom the mixture of criticism, morality, and philosophy which Dr. Swift had enveloped in the most extravagant of stories. The fiction in itself did not seem to us unworthy to entertain people of taste; there were to be found in it wit, gaiety and new ideas which could only have been produced by a lively and agreeably varied imagination.

16. Jonathan Smedley on *Gulliver's Travels*

1728

Gulliveriana: or, a Fourth Volume of Miscellanies. Being a Sequel of the Three Volumes, published by Pope and Swift, 1728.

Jonathan Smedley (1689–1729), Dean of Clogher, was a violent Whig and a violent enemy of Swift. His *Gulliveriana*, a pretended further volume of Pope's and Swift's *Miscellanies*, is a collection of invented and collected scurrility of which this example is the nearest to critical comment.

I Never wonder'd at any thing more than at a second Edition of *Gulliver's Travels*, and at seeing them in the Hands of Men and Women who had arriv'd at Years of Discretion, and had not, 'till then, discover'd any Tokens of *Stupidity* or *Idiotism*.

There must be some *Witchery* in it, said I to myself, for People who do not seem to be downright Fools, to waste so many Hours on a Book made up of Folly and Extravagance.

Humour has drawn aside many of both Sexes, to amuse themselves with *Quevedo's, Lazarello's, Tales of a Tub,* &c. But for Persons who do not appear to be perfectly stupid, to be led away by *Tom Thumbs in a Thimble*, and a *Fairy Giant* in a *Cowslip Cup*, which the Reverend Dean has invented for their Entertainment, without Humour or Allegory, is the most monstrous thing that ever happen'd in the bookish World.

It is no jesting Matter to see Boys and Girls lose their Play-time to divert themselves with the pious Divine's *Lilliputians, Brobdingnaggians, Houynhnms,* &c. and fill their Heads with an old Man's Dreams. The great Merit of these notable Works of his, is his stringing a Parcel of Consonants together, to make hard Names for the Countries and Countrymen he comes to in his Voyages. A Thought he doubtless took from the School-Boys spelling the Word *Drunk, double dd double rr,* &c. If one considers the Matter ever so little, will it not appear, I do not say Idle only, but Wicked, for a Man whose Vocation it is to preach the Holy Gospel, to spend so much precious Time purely to tempt Youth to mispend it? for certainly he could not be so vain as to flatter himself with Hopes that his Books would be read by any one that was far in the *Teens*. What little Moral he intends in his Fable, is as mystical as the *Sphinx's* Riddles of old, and when it is found out, does not teach Religion and Virtue, but the very Reverse of them.

As he has not in any one of his Writings shewn the least Conscience to his Readers with regard to their Morals or Understandings, so it will never be expected from him; but if he would not have them better than they are, it is not in his Function to make them worse; and if he can't make them merry without making them Fools, he should leave them to *Buffoons* and *Harlequins*, whose Province it is, and by no Means that of a *Dean*.

This pious Author seems to have taken his Hint, if not from the celebrated History of *Tom Thumb*, from the Author who a few Years ago obliged the World with the Travels of *Robinson Cruso*. What the former said was in Nature, and, by the Novelty of the Adventures, reasonably excited the Reader's Curiosity; whereas the Doctor has nothing in his Tale so credible as *Fortunatus's Cap, the Lancashire Witches Broomstick*, or Archdeacon *Echard's* Story of *Oliver Cromwel* and the *Devil*. The World in the Moon seems much more to be a Part of our World, as it has been described to us, than any of *Gulliver's* Worlds. The Author of *Cruso* intersperses here and there some Sentiments of Piety in his Work; in the *Doctor's* there is not one but what is brought in rather to be laugh'd at than inculcated. *Cruso*, does nothing but what might be done by a rational Creature in the like Circumstances: *Gulliver* goes mad after Fairies, Giants, Horses; and gets nothing Abroad but a mortal Hatred to his wedded Wife, whom he leaves, in Breach of his matrimonial Vow, and runs away with a Mare. Something of that Kind happen'd once in *Ireland*, and a much greater Dignitary than the Dean, was hang'd for it; but the Remorse and Penitence of that Offender forbid any farther Remembrance of it.

If it is pretended that the *Moral* in the *Fable* excuses the *Impertinence*, I would ask the Dean's greatest Admirers, whether they believe that the Boys and Girls, or the more elderly sort of People in the *Bookish* World, who judge like Boys and Girls, were ever taken with any Thing in the *Doctor's* Travels, but the Impertinence, or ever had the least Sense of any *Moral* in his Fable?

The other Excuse for it is, the pretty Language; his *Lilliputians* and his *Horses* talk all like fine Gentlemen; for *Gulliver* no sooner sets Foot on any Ground, than he is sent for to Court, and is not made to Dance

Attendance like the Dean of St. *Patrick's* at the Castle of *Dublin*. In *Lilliput* he carries about the Queen in his Breeches Pocket, and in *Brobdingnagg*, he is himself carried about on the Nipple of one of the Maids of Honour. He must needs learn to speak finely from such courtly Conversation. But after all, were his Language as Gentleman-like as his Friend *Alexander's* in his Letters; had he got the *Fierte's* and the *Riants* and all that, it would not make amends for stuffing People's Heads with Straws, and taking their Minds off from Things useful as well as pleasant. Poor *Curll's* Head was stuck in a Pillory for a Book which could not do a hundredth Part of the Mischief, as not having had a hundredth Part of the Readers.

17. Swift as political dictator

1728

An Essay upon the Taste and Writings of the Present Times, but with
a more particular view to Political and Dramatic Writings. Occasion'd
by a late Volume of Miscellanies by A. Pope, Esq: and Dr. Swift.
Inscribed to the Right Honourable Sir Robert Walpole. By a
Gentleman of C——st C——h, Oxon., 1728, 5–8.

This anonymous supporter of the Government sees Pope, Swift,
and their friends as self-made literary and political powers.

Indeed, not only Mr. *Pope*, but the whole Company seems of late Years
to have shamefully lagg'd in the Race of Fame, and have endeavoured,
by I know not what kind of Jockey-Play, to deter all others from any
further Pursuit. Hence arise those innumerable swarms of Jest, Lampoons, &c., which they have dispers'd over the face of the whole
Nation, and have been the perpetual Scourge of those, who have had the
Insolence to attempt any thing serious or useful without their Leave.—
By such Pieces of Ridicule they have almost erected themselves into
Judges; so that the young Adventurer in Fame is oblig'd to take out his
Passport from them, or he runs the Risque of being *whipp'd* by every
petty Scribler. But of all those Tyrants that have, in any Age or Nation,
made themselves dreadful by any of the various Parts of Ridicule, there
was perhaps never one that equall'd in Power our most facetious
Countryman Dr. *Swift*. For by this one single Talent he has reign'd
absolute in the witty world for upwards of 30 Years.—He has open'd a
Vein of Humour, which in the most humorous Nation of the World
was never heard of before. And of all the mirthful Men I ever read of I
think that inimitable Character of *Biron* in Shakespear is more applicable
to none than the Doctor:

> His Eye begets Occasion for Wit;
> For every Object that the one doth catch
> The other turns to a mirth-moving Jest,

93

Which his fair Tongue, (Conceits' Expositor),
Delivers in such apt and gracious words
That aged Years play truant to his Tales,
And younger Hearings are quite ravished.
L's Lr. Lost.

But it has been the Doctor's Misfortune (as it is of most absolute Sovereigns) to make an ill Use of his Power over us.—'Tis the Temper of the British Nation to be always most pleased with those political Writers, who labour to convince them that they are an unhappy People, and to put them out of Harmony with the present Scheme of Government. This Caprice springs from a Kind of Wantonness in Prosperity, and is always most discovered under a happy Adm——n. Yet how violent soever this Temper may be, we never suffer any but our own Countrymen to speak of us to our Disadvantage; like some surly Fathers, who engross to themselves the sole Privilege of abusing their own Children. This secret in our Temper the Doctor perfectly understands and has accordingly made an excellent Use of it. For by a continual succession of ludicrous Pamphlets, containing sometimes sly Insinuations of Mismanagement, and at other times bold Jokes upon the Ministry, he has been the most popular Author, or (to use his friend Mr. *Mist's* Encomium upon him) has *made* the *greatest Noise* of any writer in this Age. By his peculiar skill in libelling, he was able to make the expertest General upon Earth, as ridiculous as any pacifick Hero of them all; and by a Story about a Cock and a *Bull*, turned a War, which makes the most shining Figure in the *British* Annals, into as errant a Farce as ever was acted at *Bartholomew's*. Thus he is a kind of *Midas* reversed, and, by I know not what Magick, whatsoever he touches immediately turns to brass: Thus a religious[1] Prelate weeping over the Iniquities of a degenerate Age, comes out from the Doctor's Hands a pitiful whining Grub-Street Scribler: Thus he formerly proved the Duke of Marlborough to be no general; and thus he now proves a W——le no Statesman.

I know not whether or no my Apprehensions are vain, but I fear that the Doctor has of late begun to degenerate, and to lose that happy Scurrility, of which he was formerly Master.

---

[1] Bishop of St. Asaph. See Misc. Pref. to *John Bull*. [Original note.]

18. Anonymous criticisms of Houyhnhnmland

1735

Critical Remarks upon Gulliver's Travels; Particularly his Voyage to the HOUYHNHMS Country. Part I. By Doctor *Bentley*, 3rd edition, 1755.

Critical Remarks has been attributed to Swift's friend, Dr. Arbuthnot, but the author is not certainly known. It is an ironic piece of some skill, aimed partly at the pedantry of Dr. Bentley's annotations of ancient and modern authors, but also underlining the moral purpose of the fourth book of *Gulliver's Travels*. The quotation from Chaucer is, of course, an invention, giving a good opportunity for ridicule of learned annotation; much of the work, here omitted, consists of authentic references to ancient authors who praised horses, ironically equated with Houyhnhnms to demonstrate the truth of Gulliver's account of those creatures.

The following short Treatise, is particularly designed for those, who are Masters of the *Classical* Learning, and perfectly acquainted with the Beauties of the antient Authors.

DEDICATION

To a Person, thus qualified I was desirous to inscribe it; and after the strictest Enquiry common Fame hath directed me to You.

I do not pretend to have the Honour of Your Friendship; nor, can I hope to merit it by this Performance. And, contrary to the received Maxims of all Dedicators, I will freely confess; that, if any other Person might be found, whose Virtues were more universally owned and esteemed, or of whose Learning and Polite Taste the World conceived a better Opinion, Your *Lordship* had probably escaped this impertinent Application, From,

My Lord,

Your LORDSHIP'S *most Obedient, and most Humble Servant,*

R. B.

The Travels of Captain *Gulliver*, have been, so much, the Amusement of both Sexes, for some Years past, that I need not acquaint the Reader, either with the Character of the Author, or his Book. However, I cannot forbear giving my Opinion of that Performance, and I shall endeavour to do it with all possible Candour and Conciseness.

Criticism altho' so much decryed by the unlearned, and so injudiciously managed by some Writers, is an Art of infinite Advantage to the World; because, it directs the Judgments of those who might otherwise be misled, as well to disrelish Compositions which merit our Esteem, as to approve of those which are only worthy of our Contempt.

The *Antients* have received new Beauties from their Commentators; as Diamonds, rough from the *Mine*, derive new Lustre from the Polishing. *Horace*, among the *Romans*, and *Milton*, among the Poets of our own Nation, are held in just Admiration and Esteem; but, I believe it will be confessed, that each of those eminent Authors, owe many of the Beauties discernable in the present Editions of their Works, to the Labour and Learning of their modern Publishers.

Those Errors, which arose either from the Ignorance of *Copyists*, of the Conceit of *Interpolators,* or the Avarice and Negligence of *Printers*, would be handed down to Posterity as a Reproach to the Genius of those Great Men, if they had not been accurately detected and restored, by the unwearied Application of judicious *Criticks.*

This may suffice as an Apology for my present Undertaking. I am far from denying Captain *Gulliver* his just Merit, or envying him that uncommon Applause, which, I must own, he hath deservedly obtained. . . .

Yet, I think the World ought to be acquainted with some Particulars relating to that Performance, which, as yet, have escaped the general Observation: and may be a Means to instruct us, how to form a more equitable Judgment of the Merits, and Defects of that Work.

I had thoughts, of publishing my Remarks on the Beauties and Blemishes of it, soon after its Appearance; but, the Town was then so universally prejudiced in its Favour, that I perceived, it would be impossible to prevail with the Publick, to alter its Opinion.

An agreeable new Book, is received and treated like an agreeable young Bride: Men are unable to discern, and unwilling to be told of, those Faults in either, which are obvious enough after a more intimate Acquaintance. So that, I may at present hope for more Attention to what I propose, than I could possibly have expected in its first Success.

In a late Edition of *Gulliver*, printed in *Dublin*, I observe an *additional Letter*, from the *Captain* to his Friend Mr. *Sympson*, which was never before published. In which he complains of the various Censures passed upon his Travels, and particularly of that Part which treats of his *Voyage* to the Country of the *Houyhnhms*. That Nation which he describes as the Seat of Virtue, and its Inhabitants as Models to all the World for Justice, Truth, Cleanliness, Temperance, and Wisdom, are (he lays) *reputed no better than mere Fictions of his own Brain; and the* Houyhnhms *and* Yahoos *deemed to have no more Existence than the Inhabitants of* Utopia.

I readily own, that if we were to judge of the Manners of remote Countries, by the Conduct either of our neighbouring Nations, or our own; it might seem somewhat incredible, that Virtue could have any Kind of Esteem or Interest in any Part of the World. And therefore, a Nation wholly influenced by Truth and Honour, might as justly seem a Prodigy to us, as the Speech and Policy of the Nations of *Houyhnhm-land*; and so far, it might appear an Imaginary Kingdom rather than a Real one.

But, as I think a good Author's Veracity, ought not to be questioned unjustly, which might hinder all profitable Effects from his Writings: And as I am entirely unconcerned, whether the *Captain's* Reputation might be more advanced, by its passing for a Fiction, than a Fact; I shall undertake to convince the Learned, by sufficient Testimonies, that such a Nation as he calls the *Houyhnhms*, was perfectly known by the *Antients*; that, the Fame of their publick and private Virtues was spread thro' ATHENS, ITALY, and BRITAIN; and that the wisest Poets and Historians, of those Nations, have left us ample Authorities to support this Opinion.

The first Author I shall cite, is *Chaucer*: A Poet of our own Nation, who was well read in the antient Geography, and is allowed by all Criticks, to have been a Man of universal Learning, as well as inimitable Wit and Humour.

The Passage; is literally thus, as I transcribed it from a very fair, antient, Copy in the *Bodleian Library*, having carefully compared it, with different Editions, now in the Libraries of Lord *Sunderland*, Lord *Oxford*, and St. *James's*.

Certes, (qd. John) I nat denye
That, (a) touchende of the (b) Stedes Countrye,
I Rede, as thylke old (c) Cronyke Seythe,
Plonge afore our (d) Crysten Feythe,
Ther ben, as ye shull understonde,
An Ple, (e) ycleped (f) Courtyr's Londe,
Wher (g) nis ne (h) dampnynge (i) Covetyse;
He, (k) Letchere Notte, in (l) Sainctes Gise;
He, seely Squier, Lyche (m) browdered Ape,
Who maken (n) Goddes Boke, a (o) Jape;
He, (p) Lemman vyle, mishandlynge Youthe,
He, Women, (q) (Brutell mare in Sothe);
He, Flatterer, ne unlettred (r) Clerke,
Who (s) Rychen hym, withouten werke;
For Uyce, in thought, ne als in Dede,
Was never none in Londe of Stede.

Chaucer.

[pp. 1-9.]

(a) Concerning. (b) Horses. (c) Chronicle. (d) Christian. (e) Called. (f) Horses. (g) Is not. (h) Damnable. (i) Covetousness. (k) Lewd Person. (l) Religious. (m) Embroidered. (n) The Bible. (o) A Jest. (p) Harlot. (q) Brittle. (r) Parson. (s) Doth Enrich. [Original notes.]

Captain Gulliver mentions the exalted *Chastity* of both Sexes, with high Encomiums, *The Violation of Marriage,* saith he, *or any Unchastity, was never heard of.* This singular Perfection, sufficiently distinguishes them from human Creatures; and plainly evinces, that the Descriptions given of this Nation in the antient Authors, cannot possibly be applied with the least Shew of Justice, to any other People whatsoever.

I might produce many Passages from the Writings of the wisest *Greeks* and *Latins,* to confirm the *Traveller's* Testimony, and to prove, that it was the received Opinion of the World, many Ages before he happened to live among that *chaste* and *virtuous* People. . . .

Thus, have I by the best *Classical* Authority demonstrated my Assertion, that the Nation of *Houyhnhms* was well known to the Antients of *Greece, Italy,* and *England;* that their Virtues were universally known and esteemed; and that the most potent Princes of the Earth, have been proud of their Friendship. So that the great *modern Traveller* need be under no Manner of Uneasiness, at the Censures of the World, since the learned Part of Mankind, must, from these Authorities be effectually convinced, that he might actually have been an Eye-witness of all he hath attested.

I know many, who believed his Account of the *Houyhnhms* to be

98

merely fabulous, and who extolled his Invention, as, supposing such a Nation to exist only in his own Brain. And, how far he might be pleased to have his Imagination commended, at the Expence of his Veracity, I will not determine: But, I think, in Justice to himself, as well as the World, he ought to have *prevented* this *Criticism*, and frankly acknowledged the *Truth* of his Narration, altho' it might have somewhat lessened his Reputation as an *Author*.

I do not doubt, but this will clear *Gulliver* from another severe Imputation, which he lay under, for debasing human Nature, by making *Men* inferior to *Horses*. Because, in this Treatise, it is so plain, that *Antiquity* differed extreamly from so partial an Opinion; and, it is so manifest, that the whole History is a *Fact*, and not a *Fiction*, that, if we think Mankind disgraced by the Comparison, it is to their own Vices, and not to the *Traveller's* Relation, we ought to impute it.

I expect that all future *Commentators*, will copy the Example I have given them in this *Critical Essay*; and hereafter, be at least as studious to shew their own *Learning*, as to illustrate that of their *Author*.

I am pretty well assured, that the *Judicious* will readily join with me in Opinion; and I must own, that I think it the *highest Honour* to the *Critick*, and the surest *Test* of his *Genius*, to demonstrate the *Truth*, and *Existence* of those things, which the whole World beside determine to be *False* and *Fictitious*.

19. George Faulkner on Swift's poetry

1735

The Works of Jonathan Swift, D.D., D.S.P.D. (4 vols.), 1735, ii, i–ii.

George Faulkner (1699?–1775) had a long and colourful career as a printer and bookseller in Dublin. He was the first to publish a 'collected' edition of Swift's works; Faulkner's edition is far from complete, *A Tale of a Tub* and *The Battle of the Books* being the most conspicuous omissions. In accordance with Swift's wishes, no critical or prefatory comment is included. The extract here is from Faulkner's Advertisement to Vol. II, which consists entirely of Swift's poetry.

The following poems chiefly consist either of Humour or Satyr, and very often of both together. What Merit they may have, we confess ourselves to be no Judges of in the least; but out of due Regard to a Writer, from whose Works we hope to receive some Benefit, we cannot conceal what we have heard from several Persons of great Judgment; that the Author never was known either in Verse or Prose to borrow any Thought, Simile, Epithet, or particular Manner of Style; but whatever he writ, whether good, bad, or indifferent, is an Original in itself.

Although we are very sensible that, in some of the following Poems, the Ladies may resent certain satyrical Touches against the mistaken Conduct in some of the fair Sex: And that, some warm Persons on the prevailing Side may censure this Author, whoever he be, for not thinking in publick Matters exactly like themselves: Yet we have been assured by several judicious and learned Gentlemen, that what the Author hath here writ, on either of those two Subjects, had no other Aim than to reform the Errors of both Sexes.

20. The Duchess of Marlborough on Swift

1736

Memoirs of Sarah, Duchess of Marlborough, together with her Characters of her Contemporaries and her Opinions, ed., with Introduction, William King, 1930, 313–15.

Sarah, Duchess of Marlborough (1660–1744), was in her younger days opposed to Swift's Tory friends, through whom she lost power in Queen Anne's reign. But in later life she found herself estranged from the Whig Government, and disposed to see some truth in Swift's account of things at Court. The extracts are from the Duchess's characters of her contemporaries and are dated 1736.

Dean Swift gives the most exact account of kings, ministers, bishops and the courts of justice that is possible to be writ. He has certainly a vast deal of wit; and since he could contribute so much to the pulling down the most honest and best-intentioned ministry that ever I knew, with the help only of Abigail and one or two more, and has certainly stopped the finishing stroke to ruin the Irish in the project of the halfpence, in spite of all the ministry could do, I could not help wishing that we had had his assistance in the opposition; for I could easily forgive him all the slaps he has given me and the Duke of Marlborough, and have thanked him heartily whenever he would please to do good. I never saw him in my life; and though his writings have entertained me very much, yet I see he writes sometimes for interest; for in his books he gives my Lord Oxford as great a character as if he was speaking of Socrates or Marcus Antoninus. But when I am dead the reverse of that character will come out with vouchers to it under his own hand.

The style of the Lord's address puts me in mind of Dean Swift's account, who I am prodigiously fond of, which he gives of the manner in which he was introduced to the King of Luggnagg.

I most heartily wish that in this park I had some of the breed of those charming creatures Swift speaks of and calls the Houyhnhnms, which I understand to be horses, so extremely polite, and which had all manner of good conversation, good principles, and that never told a lie, and charmed him so that he could not endure his own country when he returned. He says there is a sort of creature there called Yahoos, and of the same species with us, only a good deal uglier; but they are kept tied up; and by that glorious creature the horses are not permitted to do any mischief. I really have not been pleased so much a long time as with what he writes.

21. François Cartaud de la Villate on *A Tale of a Tub*

1736

Essai Historique et Philosophique sur le Goust, 1736, 187.

François Cartaud de la Villate (1700?–37), Canon of Aubusson until he resigned his benefit to go to Paris, was a witty and para-doxical writer who had already published, in 1733, *Pensées Critiques sur les Mathematiques*, a science to which he denied certainty. His inability to perceive the design of *A Tale of a Tub* is common to many of his contemporaries.

A Tale of a Tub has some ingenious qualities, but in general the book is badly written. One thought is drowned in an ocean of superfluous matters. Moreover, there is no art in the style, nothing subtle in the detail, no orderly arrangement in the design.

The English sometimes know how to think, but they do not always know what development they ought to give to their thoughts. In this they are like tumblers who cannot submit to a regular rhythm.

22. Samuel Richardson on Swift

1740, 1748, 1752, 1754

(a) *Pamela* (1740), 4 vols., 1930.
(b) *Clarissa* (1748), 8 vols., 1930.
(c) *Sir Charles Grandison* (1754), 6 vols., 1929.
(d) *The Correspondence of Samuel Richardson*, 6 vols., 1804.

The personal biases of Richardson (1689–1761) are very thinly
veiled in his novels, where a distaste for Swift's personality and
works is an almost unquestioned assumption; it is common to
characters as diverse as Robert Lovelace and Harriett Byron, who
both speak of 'his abominable Yahoo story'. Richardson's 'real'
correspondence differs little from that of his fictional characters
in this respect.

(a) [LETTER FROM MRS. B—— TO MR. B—— ON THE EDUCATION OF
WOMEN AND ON THE ADVANTAGES PAMELA WILL DERIVE FROM
MR. B.'S 'REFLECTED GLORY'.]

I could multiply Instances of this Nature [Ladies sometimes being better
educated and more intelligent than gentlemen], were it needful, to the
Confutation of that low, and I had almost said *unmanly* Contempt, with
which a certain celebrated Genius treats our Sex in general, in most of
his Pieces that I have seen; particularly in his *Letter of Advice to a new-
marry'd Lady:* A Letter written in such a manner, as must disgust,
instead of instructing; and looks more like the Advice of an Enemy to
the *Sex,* and a bitter one too, than a Friend to the *particular Lady.* But I
ought to beg Pardon for this my Presumption, for Two Reasons; first,
Because of the truly admirable Talents of this Writer; and next, Because
we know not what Ladies the ingenious Gentleman may have fallen
among in his younger Days.

[Vol. IV, 367.]

(b) MR. LOVELACE TO JOHN BELFORD, 28 AUGUST
[On Lovelace's having heard rumours that Clarissa may be reunited with
her family. This immediately follows the onset of Clarissa's illness.]

What I mean by all this, is, to let thee see, what a stupid figure I shall make to all my own family, if my Clarissa has been capable, as Gulliver in his abominable Yahoo Story phrases it, of saying the *thing that is not.* By my Soul, Jack, if it were only that I should be *outwitted* by such a novice at plotting, and that it would make me look silly to my kins-women here, who know I value myself upon my contrivances, it would vex me to the heart; and I would instantly clap a Feather-bed into a coach-and-six, and fetch her away, sick or well, and marry her at my leisure.

[Vol. VII, 265.]

MR. BELFORD TO ROBERT LOVELACE, 10 SEPTEMBER
[Part of a description of the death-bed scene of Mrs. Sinclair, who is surrounded by 'no less than eight of her cussed daughters . . . haggard well-worn strumpets'. The contrast with Clarissa's dignified demise, which precedes it, is obvious.]

I am the more particular in describing to thee the appearance these creatures made in my eyes when I came into the room, because I believe thou never sawest any of them, much less a group of them, thus un-prepared for being seen. I, for my part, never did before; nor had I now, but upon this occasion, been thus *favoured.* If thou *hadst,* I believe thou wouldst hate a profligate woman, as one of Swift's Yahoos, or Virgil's obscene Harpyes, squirting their ordure upon the Trojan trenchers; since the persons of such in their retirements are as filthy as their minds—Hate them as much as I do; and as much as I admire, and next to adore a truly-virtuous and elegant woman. For to me it is evident, that as a neat and clean woman must be an angel of a creature, so a sluttish one is the impurest animal in nature.

[Vol. VIII, 56.]

MISS HOWE TO JOHN BELFORD, 12 OCTOBER
[Part of a long letter extolling Clarissa's character.]

But she was a severe Censurer of pieces of a *light* or *indecent* turn, which had a tendency to corrupt the morals of youth, to convey polluted images, or to wound religion, whether in itself, or thro' the sides of its professors, and this whoever were the authors, and how admirable soever the execution. She often pitied the celebrated Dr. Swift for so employing his admirable pen, that a pure eye was afraid of looking into his works, and a pure ear of hearing any thing quoted from them. 'Such authors,' she used to say, 'were not *honest* to their own talents, nor grateful to the God who gave them.' Nor would she, on these occasions, admit their beauties as a palliation; on the contrary, she held it as an aggravation of their crime, that they who were so capable of *mending the heart*, should in any places shew a *corrupt one* in themselves; which must weaken the influences of their good works; and pull down with one hand what they built up with the other.

[Vol. VIII, 237–8.]

(*c*) MISS HARRIETT BYRON TO MISS LUCY SELBY
[Here Harriett relates to Lucy the account Charlotte (Sir Charles's sister) has given her of Sir Thomas Grandison's crude behaviour towards her during the Lord L.'s courtship of her.]

Thus spoke the *rakish*, the *keeping* father, Lucy, endeavouring to justify his private vices by general reflexions on the Sex. And thus are wickedness and libertinism called a knowlege of the world, a knowlege of human nature. Swift, for often painting a dunghil and for his abominable Yahoo story, was complimented with this knowlege. But I hope, that the character of human nature, the character of creatures made in the image of the Deity, is not to be taken from the overflowings of such dirty imaginations.

[Vol. II, 89.]

(*d*) RICHARDSON TO LADY BRADSHAIGH, 23 FEBRUARY 1752
I join with your Ladyship most cordially in all you say of the author [Orrery], of the Dean, and of the Dean's savage behaviour to his unhappy wife, and Vanessa; as it is of a piece with all those of his writings, in which he endeavours to debase the human, and to raise above it the brutal nature. I cannot think so hardly as some do of Lord Orrery's observation: that the fearful deprivation which reduced him to a state beneath that of the merest animal seemed to be a punishment that had terrible justice in it.

[Vol. VI, 152–3.]

RICHARDSON TO MRS. DELANY, 29 JUNE 1754
I am confident that the *Observations* [Evidently Patrick Delany's *Observations on Lord Orrery's Remarks* (1754), which was anonymous at the time] must be extremely approved, when known and read. But

yet, from Ireland, I expect the greatest demand: for Swift is not so much a favourite with *us* as with the *Irish*. The men of wit and taste will always admire him, and in every country—but they are few.

[Vol. IV, 87.]

23. Paradis de Moncrif on *Gulliver's Travels*

1743

'Reflexions sur Quelques Ouvrages Faussement Appellez: Ouvrages d'Imagination', *Oeuvres Mêlées, tant en Prose qu'en Vers*, 1743, 4–8.

De Moncrif (1687–1770) was secretary to the Court of Clermont, reader to the Queen, and a member of the French Academy. The title of de Moncrif's essay, delivered before the Academy in 1741, indicates its intention, which is to deny the claim of novels of the marvellous and supernatural, fairy stories, and imaginary voyages (including *Robinson Crusoe* and *Gulliver's Travels*) to be properly works of imagination. He lists four sources, or methods, by reference to which such works can be readily produced without recourse to the imagination. *Gulliver's Travels* is attacked, as a work of imagination, by referring it to two of these simple sources.

The first source of what is falsely called a work of imagination is a simple reversal of principles or customs common to all, or at least practically all, nations. Certain characteristics are dissociated from beings to whom they are known to belong, and are then given to other beings to whom Nature has refused such advantages: two methods which presuppose no inventiveness of mind, and which have sufficed for the composition of almost all the imaginary voyages that are read with pleasure. It is these methods which produce descriptions of countries where women rule men and become magistrates and generals. . . . It is a similar reversal of ideas that carries the whole economy of that Republic where, under the name of Houynhnhnis [*sic*] horses have human reason, and men the instinct of horses. The theory which serves to produce such frigid stories betrays itself. It seems to me that the kind of imagination fitted to trump up such contrasts is like the wit of those whose only idea of shining is to take the opposite view to whatever is put forward. They believe themselves to be arguing, when they are only contradicting. . . .

The third source is simply the art of enlarging or reducing the figures of certain beings. Obviously I am speaking of the *big men* and *little men* of *Gulliver*. I will confess that a work whose whole invention consists in showing me men bigger than giants and smaller than pigmies seems to me to begin and end on the first page; all the rest is restatement. I concede that a witty man, like the author of *Gulliver*, instead of considering objects as they naturally present themselves, has enough curiosity to observe them through a telescope, now through the enlarging end, and now through the diminishing one; but with all this searching, if he makes me see in these same objects only what I could see with the help of my own eyes, I do not see how one can regard as a stroke of genius his idea of hurrying unnecessarily to the telescope, still less the notion of using both ends.

24. Henry Fielding on Swift

1745, 1751, 1752

(a) Obituary of Swift, *The True Patriot* (No. 1), 5 November 1745.

(b) Captain Booth in prison discourses on Swift, *Amelia*, Book VIII, Ch. V (1930), II, 74–5 (first published, 1751).

(c) *The Covent-Garden Journal* (No. 10), 4 February 1752.

(d) *The Covent-Garden Journal* (No. 52), 30 June 1752.

Fielding (1707–54) was an admirer of Swift and was influenced by him, as his earlier satiric work shows.

(a)

A few Days since died in Ireland, Dr. Jonathan Swift, Dean of St. Patrick's in Dublin. A Genius who deserves to be ranked among the first whom the World ever saw. He possessed the Talents of a Lucian, a Rabelais, and a Cervantes, and in his Works exceeded them all. He employed his Wit to the noblest Purposes, in ridiculing as well Superstition in Religion as Infidelity, and several Errors and Immoralities which sprung up from time to time in his Age; and lastly, in the Defence of his Country, against several pernicious Schemes of wicked Politicians. Nor was he only a Genius and a Patriot: he was in private Life a good and charitable Man, and frequently lent Sums of Money without Interest to the Poor and Industrious; by which means many Families were preserved from Destruction. The Loss of so excellent a Person would have been more to be lamented, had not a Disease that affected his Understanding, long since deprived him of the Enjoyment of Life, and his Country of the Benefit of his great Talents; But we hope this short and hasty Character will not be the last Piece of Gratitude paid by his Contemporaries to such eminent Merit.

(b)

As Booth was therefore what might well be called, in this age at least, a man of learning, he began to discourse our author on subjects of literature. 'I think, sir,' says he, 'that Dr. Swift hath been generally allowed, by the critics in this kingdom, to be the greatest master of humour that ever wrote. Indeed, I allow him to have possessed most admirable talents of this kind; and, if Rabelais was his master, I think he proves the truth of the common Greek proverb—that the scholar is often superior to the master. As to Cervantes, I do not think we can make any just comparison; for, though Mr. Pope compliments him with sometimes taking Cervantes' serious air——' 'I remember the passage,' cries the author;

> O thou, whatever title please thine ear,
> Dean, Drapier, Bickerstaff, or Gulliver;
> Whether you take Cervantes' serious air,
> Or laugh and shake in Rabelais' easy chair.

'You are right, sir,' said Booth; 'but though I should agree that the doctor hath sometimes condescended to imitate Rabelais, I do not remember to have seen in his works the least attempt in the manner of Cervantes. But there is one in his own way, and whom I am convinced he studied above all others—you guess, I believe, I am going to name Lucian. This author, I say, I am convinced, he followed; but I think he followed him at a distance: as, to say the truth, every other writer of this kind hath done in my opinion; for none, I think, hath yet equalled him.'

(c)

After what I have here advanced, I cannot fairly, I think, be represented as an Enemy to Laughter, or to all those Kinds of Writing that are apt to promote it. On the contrary, few Men, I believe, do more admire the Works of those great Masters who have sent their Satire (if I may use the Expression) laughing into the World. Such are that great Triumvirate, Lucian, Cervantes, and Swift. These Authors I shall ever hold in the highest Degree of Esteem; not indeed for that Wit and Humour alone; which they all so eminently possess, but because they all endeavoured, with the utmost Force of their Wit and Humour, to expose and extirpate those Follies and Vices which chiefly prevailed in their several Countries.

(d)

And as I am thus unwilling to think that Lucian was the Imitator of any other, I shall not be much more ready to grant, that others have been the Imitators of him. The Person whom I esteem to be most worthy of this Honour is the immortal Swift. To say Truth, I can find no better

Way of giving the English Reader an Idea of the Greek Author, than by telling him, that to translate Lucian well into English, is to give us another Swift in our own Language. I will add, however invidious it may appear, that when I allow to this excellent English Writer the Praise of imitating the Greek, I allow him that Praise only which the best imitator can possibly claim, of being Second to his Original. Our Author will perhaps for ever continue to deserve the Title of inimitable, (*i.e.* unequalled) which the learned Mr. Moyle hath given him.

25. David Hume on Swift

1751, 1752, 1768

(a) *Political Discourses* 1752.
    1. Discourse V, 'Of the Balance of Trade', 81–2.
    2. Discourse X, 'Of the Populousness of Antient Nations',
       201n.–2n.
(b) *Letters of David Hume* (2 vols.), ed J. Y. T. Greig, 1932.
    1. To Gilbert Elliot of Minto, February 1751, I, 153.
    2. To William Robertson, November or December 1768, II,
       194.

When Hume (1711–76) 'corrected' his *Political Discourses* prior to
their 1777 publication in his *Philosophical Works*, he tactfully
stated: 'Nothing can be more entertaining on this head than Dr.
Swift; an author so quick in discerning the mistakes and absurdities of others' (III, 341). Since the 1777 edition has been the basis
of most modern editions of Hume's works, the original wording
of this extract from Discourse V is not widely known, but Hume's
revision provides a kind of index to the rise in Swift's reputation.
One feels from reading both the *Discourses* and the *Letters* that for
Hume Swift was a figure to be reckoned with if not admired.
Gilbert Elliot, Earl of Minto and Governor-General of India, to
whom Hume discloses his desire to satirize priests, had been a
schoolmate of Hume. William Robertson, whose style Hume
criticizes in conjunction with Swift's, wrote histories of America
and of his native Scotland.

(a)

Nothing can be more entertaining on this head than Dr. *Swift*, an
author, who has more humour than knowledge, more taste than
judgment, and more spleen, prejudice, and passion than any of these
qualities. He says, in his *short view of the state of* Ireland, that the whole
cash of that kingdom amounted but to 500,000 *l.* that out of this they
remitted every year a neat million to *England*, and had scarce any other

source to compensate themselves from, and little other foreign trade but the importation of *French* wines, for which they pay'd ready money. The consequence of this situation, which must be own'd disadvantageous, was, that in a course of three years, the current money of *Ireland*, from 500,000 *l.* was reduc'd to less than two. And at present, I suppose, in a course of near 30 years, it is absolutely nothing. Yet I know not how, that opinion of the advance of riches in *Ireland*, which gave the doctor so much indignation, still seems to continue, and gain ground amongst every body.

[Discourse V, 'Of the Balance of Trade'. 81–2.]

'Tis dangerous to rely upon writers, who deal in ridicule and satire. What will posterity, for instance, infer from this passage of Dr. *Swift?* 'I told him, that in the kingdom of *Tribnia* (*Britain*) by the Natives call'd *Langdon* (*London*) where I had sojourned some time in my travels, the bulk of the people consist, in a manner, wholly of discoverers, witnesses, informers, accusers, prosecutors, evidences, swearers, together with their several subservient and subaltern instruments, all under the colours, the conduct, and pay of ministers of state and their deputies. The plots in that kingdom are usually the workmanship of those persons, &c.', *Gulliver's travels.* Such a representation might suit the government of *Athens*; but not that of *England*, which is a prodigy, even in modern times, for humanity, justice and liberty. Yet the doctor's satire, tho' carry'd to extremes, as is usual with him, even beyond other satirical writers, did not altogether want an object. The bishop of *Rochester*, who was his friend and of the same party, had been banish'd a little before by a bill of attainder, with great justice, but without such a proof as was legal, or according to the strict forms of common law.

[Discourse X, 'Of the Populousness of Antient Nations', 201n.–2n.]

(*b*) TO GILBERT ELLIOT OF MINTO, FEBRUARY 1751

I have frequently had it in my Intentions to write a Supplement to *Gulliver*, containing the Ridicule of Priests. Twas certainly a Pity that Swift was a Parson. Had he been a Lawyer or Physician, we had nevertheless been entertain'd at the Expense of these Professions. But Priests are so jealous, that they cannot bear to be touch'd on that Head; and for a plain Reason: Because they are conscious they are really ridiculous. That Part of the Doctor's Subject is so fertile, that a much inferior Genius, I am confident, might succeed in it.

(I, 153)

You know that you and I have always been on the footing of finding in each other's productions *something to blame and something to commend*; and, therefore, you may perhaps expect also some seasoning of the former kind; but really neither my leisure nor inclination allowed me to make such remarks, and I sincerely believe you have afforded me very small materials for them. However, such particulars as occur to my memory I shall mention. *Maltreat* is a Scotticism which occurs once. What the devil had you to do with that old-fashioned dangling word *wherewith*? I should as soon take back *whereupon, whereunto,* and *wherewithal.* I think the only tolerable decent gentleman of the family is *wherein,* and I should not choose to be often seen in his company. But I know your affection for *wherewith* proceeds from your partiality to Dean Swift, whom I can often laugh with, whose style I can even approve, but surely can never admire. It has no harmony, no eloquence, no ornament, and not much correctness, whatever the English may imagine. Were not their literature still in a somewhat barbarous state, that author's place would not be so high among their classics. But what a fancy is this you have taken of saying always *an hand, an heart, an head?* Have you *an ear?* Do you not know that this *n* is added before vowels to prevent the cacophony, and ought never to take place before *h* when that letter is sounded? It is never pronounced in these words, why should it be wrote? Thus, I should say, *a history,* and *an historian*; and so would you too, if you had any sense. But you tell me that Swift does otherwise. To be sure, there is no reply to that; and we must swallow your *hath* too upon the same authority. I will see you d——d sooner.—But I will endeavour to keep my temper.

(II, 194.)

26. Lord Orrery on Swift

1752

Remarks on the Life and Writing of Dr. Jonathan Swift, Dean of St. Patrick's, Dublin. In a Series of Letters from John Earl of Orrery to his Son, the Honourable Hamilton Boyle, 1752.

John Boyle, fifth Earl of Orrery (1701–62), was the son of Charles Boyle, editor of the spurious *Letters of Phalaris* which precipitated the hostilities between Temple and the 'moderns', Bentley and Wotton. Charles Boyle appears in *The Battle of the Books*. Lord Orrery had been a sycophantic friend of Swift's later years, but the inaccuracy and personal spite of his *Remarks* aroused much opposition. Delany and Deane Swift both wrote in partial refutation of him. The *Remarks*, being framed as personal letters, are digressive in form and contain much general commentary on classical philosophers and poets, and some personal observations to Orrery's son; they have therefore been extensively cut. Orrery's plan, in discussing the works of Swift, is to take the works in the order they occur in Faulkner's edition; this order has been retained in the extracts.

If we consider his prose works, we shall find a certain masterly conciseness in their style, that has never been equalled by any other writer. The truth of this assertion will more evidently appear, by comparing him with some of the authors of his own time. Of these Dr. TILLOTSON, and Mr. ADDISON, are to be numbered among the most eminent. ADDISON has all the powers that can captivate and improve: his diction is easy, his periods are well turned, his expressions are flowing, and his humour is delicate. TILLOTSON is nervous, grave, majestic, and perspicuous. We must join both these characters together to form a true idea of Dr. SWIFT: yet as he outdoes ADDISON in humour, he excels TILLOTSON in perspicuity. The Archbishop indeed confined himself to subjects relative to his profession: but ADDISON and SWIFT are more diffusive writers. They continually vary in their manner, and treat different topics in a different style. When the writings of ADDISON terminate in party, he loses himself extremely and from a delicate, and just comedian, deviates into one of the lowest kind.[1] Not so Dr. SWIFT: he appears like a masterly gladiator. He wields the sword of party with ease, justness and dexterity: and while he entertains the ignorant and the vulgar, he draws an equal attention from the learned and the great. When he is serious, his gravity becomes him. When he laughs, his readers must laugh with him. But, what shall be said for his love of trifles, and his want of delicacy and decorum? Errors, that if he did not contract, at least he encreased in *Ireland*. They are without a parallel. I hope they will ever remain so. The first of them, arose merely from his love of flattery, with which he was daily fed in that kingdom: the second, proceeded from the misanthropy of his disposition, which induced him peevishly to debase mankind, and even to ridicule human nature itself. Politics were his favourite topic, as they gave him an opportunity of gratifying his ambition, and thirst of power: yet even in this road, he has seldom continued long in one particular path. He has written miscellaneously, and has chosen rather to appear a wandering comet, than a fixed star. Had he applied the faculties of his mind to one great, and useful work, he must have shined more gloriously, and might have enlightened a whole planetary system in the political world.

The poetical performances of Dr. SWIFT ought to be considered as occasional poems written either to please, or vex some particular persons. We must not suppose them designed for posterity: if he had cultivated his genius in that way, he must certainly have excelled, especially in satyr. We see fine sketches, in several of his pieces: but he seems more desirous to inform, and strengthen his mind, than to indulge the luxuriancy of his imagination. He chooses to discover, and correct errors in the works of others, rather than to illustrate, and add beauties to his own. Like a skilful artist, he is fond of probing wounds to their depth, and of enlarging them to open view. He prefers caustics, which erode proud flesh, to softer balsamics, which give more immediate ease. He aims to be severely useful, rather than politely engaging: and as he was either not formed, or would not take pains to excel in poetry, he became, in some measure, superior to it; and assumed more the air and manners of a critic, than of a poet. Had he lived in the same age with HORACE, he would have approached nearer to him, than any other poet: and if we may make an allowance for the different

---

[1] See the papers intitled *The Freeholder*. [Orrery's note.]

course of study, and different form of government, to which each of these great men were subject, we may observe, in several instances, a strong resemblance between them. Both poets are equally distinguished for wit and humour. Each displays a peculiar felicity in diction: but, of the two, HORACE is the more elegant and delicate: while he condemns, he pleases. SWIFT takes pleasure in giving pain: The dissimilitude of their tempers might be owing to the different turns in their fortune. SWIFT early formed large views of ambition, and was disappointed. HORACE, from an exiled low state, rose into affluence, and enjoyed the favour and friendship of AUGUSTUS. Each poet was the delight of the principal persons of his age. *Cum magnis vixisse* was not more applicable to HORACE, than to SWIFT. They both were temperate: both were frugal; and both were of the same Epicurean taste. HORACE had his LYDIA, SWIFT had his VANESSA. HORACE had his MECÆNAS, and his AGRIPPA. SWIFT had his OXFORD, and his BOLINGBROKE. HORACE had his VIRGIL. SWIFT had his POPE.

(62-7.)

You seem not only desirous, but impatient, that I should pass critically through all the works of my friend SWIFT. Your request is unreasonable if you imagine, that I must say something upon every individual performance. There are some pieces that I despise, others that I loath, but many more that delight and improve me: and these last shall be discussed particularly. The former are not worthy of your notice. They are of no further use than to shew us, in general, the errors of human nature; and to convince us, that neither the height of wit, nor genius, can bring a man to such a degree of perfection, as vanity would often prompt him to believe.

In a disquisition of the sort which you require, I shall avoid as much as possible any annotations upon that kind of satyr, in which the Dean indulged himself against particular persons: most of whom it is probable provoked his rage by their own misconduct, and consequently owed to their own rashness the wounds which they received from his pen: but I have no delight in those kind of writings, except for the sake of the wit, which, either in general, or in particular satyr, is equally to be admired. The edge of wit will always remain keen, and its blade will be bright and shining, when the stone, upon which it has been whetted, is worn out, or thrown aside and forgotten. Personal satyr against evil magistrates, corrupt ministers, and those giants of power, who gorge themselves with the entrails of their country, is different from that personal satyr, which too often proceeds merely from self-love, or ill-nature: the one, is written in defence of the public, the other, in defence of ourselves. The one, is armed by the sword of justice, and encouraged not only by the voice of the people, but by the principles of morality: the other, is dictated by passion, supported by pride, and applauded by flattery. At the same time that I say this, I think every man of wit has a right to laugh at fools, who give offence, or at coxcombs, who are public nusances. SWIFT indeed has left no weapon of sarcasm untried, no branch of satyr uncultivated: but while he has maintained a perpetual war against the mighty men in power, he has remained invulnerable, if not victorious.

(77–9)

. . . the whole treatise [*A Discourse of the Contests and Dissensions between the Nobles and Commons in Athens and Rome*] is full of historical knowledge, and excellent reflexions. It is not mixed with any improper sallies of wit, or any light airs of humour: and in point of style and learning, is equal, if not superior, to any of his political works.

Subsequent to *the discourse concerning Athens and Rome*, is a paper written in the year 1703, in derision of the style and manner of MR. ROBERT BOYLE. To what a height must the spirits of sarcasm arise in an author, who could prevail upon himself to ridicule so good a man as MR. BOYLE? But, the sword of wit, like the scythe of time, cuts down friend and foe, and attacks every object that accidentally lies in its way. However, sharp and irresistible as the edge of it may be, MR. BOYLE will always remain invulnerable.

The sentiments of a church-of-England-man, with respect to religion and government, was written in the year 1708. It is adapted to that particular period. The style of the whole pamphlet is nervous, and, except in some few places, impartial. . . .

This tract is very well worth your reading and attention: and it confirms an observation which will perpetually occur, that SWIFT excels in whatever style or manner he assumes. When he is in earnest, his strength of reason carries with it conviction. When in jest, every competitor in the race of wit is left behind him.

The argument against abolishing Christianity is carried on with the highest wit and humour. Graver divines threaten their readers with future punishments: SWIFT artfully exhibits a picture of present shame. He judged rightly in imagining that a small treatise, written with a spirit of mirth and freedom, must be more efficacious, than long sermons, or laborious lessons of morality. He endeavours to laugh us into religion; well knowing, that we are often laughed out of it. As you have not read the pamphlet, excuse a quotation, to which may be prefixed the old proverb *ex pede Herculem,* '*I would fain know* (says the Dean) *how it can be pretended, that the churches are misapplied. Where are more appointments and rendezvouses of gallantry? Where more care to appear in the foremost box with greater advantage of dress? Where more meetings for business? Where more bargains driven of all forts? And where so many conveniencies or incitements to sleep?*'

The papers which immediately follow are entirely humorous, and relate to PARTRIDGE the almanac maker: and although they are not only temporary, but local, yet by an art peculiar to SWIFT himself, they are rendered immortal, so as to be read with pleasure, as long as the English language subsists.

To these, succeeds *A project for the advancement of religion, and the reformation of manners,* written in the year 1709, and dedicated to the Countess of BERKLEY. The author appears in earnest throughout the whole treatise, and the dedication, or introduction, is in a strain of serious panegyric, which the Lady, to whom it is addressed, undoubtedly deserved. But as the pamphlet is of the satirical kind, I am apt to imagine, that my friend the Dean put a violence upon himself, in chusing to appear candidly serious, rather than to smile under his usual mask of gravity. Read it, and tell me your opinion: for methinks, upon these occasions, I perceive him writing in shackles.

The tritical essay on the faculties of the mind, will make you smile.

The letter to the Earl of OXFORD *for correcting, improving, and ascertaining the* English *tongue* might have been a very useful performance, if it had been longer, and less eclypsed by compliments to the noble person to whom it is addressed. It seems to have been intended as a preface to some more enlarged design: at the head of which such an introduction must have appeared with great propriety. A work of this kind is much wanted, as our language, instead of being improved, is every day growing worse, and more debased. We bewilder ourselves in various orthography; we speak, and we write at random; and if a man's common conversation were to be committed to paper, he would be startled *for to* find himself guilty in *a few* sentences, of so many solicisms and such false English. . . .

There are two other letters in this volume extremely worthy of your notice. The one is, *To a young gentleman lately entered into holy orders.* The other is, *To a young lady on her marriage.* The former, ought to be read by all the young clergymen in the three kingdoms, and the latter, by all the new married women. But, here again is the peculiar felicity of SWIFT's writings; the letters are addressed only to a young clergyman and a young lady, but they are adapted to every age and understanding. They contain observations that delight and improve every mind; and they will be read, with pleasure and advantage, by the oldest, and most exemplary divines, and by the most distinguished, and most accomplished ladies.

[94–103].

I began one of my former letters, my dear HAMILTON, by a declaration that it was impossible for me to pass a very minute comment upon the various pieces that he has written; and I must renew the same declaration in regard to his poems. They are not only mingled improperly, in points of dates, and subjects, but many, very many of them, are temporary, trifling, and I had almost said puerile. Several of them are personal, and consequently scarce amusing; or at least, they leave a very small impression upon our minds. Such indeed as are likely to draw your attention, are exquisite, and so peculiarly his own, that whoever has dared to imitate him in these, or in any of his works, has constantly failed in the attempt. Upon a general view of his poetry, we shall find him, as in his other performances, an uncommon, surprizing, heteroclite genius: luxurious in his fancy, lively in his ideas, humorous in his descriptions, and bitter, exceeding bitter in his satyr. The restlessness of his imagination, and the disappointment of his ambition, have both contributed to hinder him from undertaking any poetical work of length or importance. His wit was sufficient to every labour: no flight could have wearied the strength of his pinions: perhaps if the extensive views of his nature had been fully satisfied, his airy motions had been more regular, and less sudden. But, he now appears, like an eagle that is sometimes chained, and at that particular time, for want of nobler, and more proper food, diverts his confinement, and appeases his hunger, by destroying the gnats, butterflies, and other wretched insects, that unluckily happen to buzz, or flutter within his reach.

While I have been reading over this volume of his poetry, I have considered him as an *Ægyptian* hieroglyphic, which, though it had an unnatural, and frequently an indecent appearance, yet it always contained some secret marks of wisdom, and sometimes of deep morality. The subjects of his poems are often nauseous, and the performances beautifully disagreeable.

The Lady's Dressing Room has been universally condemned, as deficient in point of delicacy, even to the highest degree. The best apology that can be made in its favour, is to suppose, that the author exhibited his CELIA in the most hideous colours he could find, lest she might be mistaken as a goddess, when she was only a mortal. External beauty is very alluring to youth and inexperience; and SWIFT, by pulling off the borrowed plumes of his harpy, discovers at once a frightful bird of prey, and by making her offensive, renders her less dangerous and inviting. Such, I hope, was his design; but let his views and motives have been ever so beneficial, his general want of delicacy and decorum, must not hope even to find the shadow of an excuse; for it is impossible not to own, that he too frequently forgets that politeness and tenderness of manners, which are undoubtedly due to human kind. From his early, and repeated disappointments, he became a misanthrope. If his mind had been more equal and content, I am willing to believe, that he would have viewed the works of nature with a more benign aspect.

[121–4.]

The third volume of SWIFT's works contains *The travels of* LEMUEL GULLIVER *into several remote nations of the world.* They are divided into four parts; the first, a voyage to *Lilliput*; the second, a voyage to *Brobdingnag*; the third, to *Laputa* and other islands; the fourth, and most extraordinary, to the country of the *Houyhnhnms.* These voyages are intended as a moral political romance, in which SWIFT seems to have exerted the strongest efforts of a fine irregular genius. But while his imagination and his wit delight, the venomous strokes of his satyr, although in some places just, are carried into so universal a severity, that not only all human actions, but human nature itself, is placed in the worst light. Perfection in every attribute is not indeed allotted to particular men: but, among the whole species, we discover such an assemblage of all the great, and amiable virtues, as may convince us, that the original order of nature contains in it the greatest beauty. It is directed in a right line, but it deviates into curves and irregular motions, by various attractions, and disturbing causes. Different qualifications shine out in different men. BACON and NEWTON (not to mention BOYLE) shew the divine extent of the human mind: of which power SWIFT could not be insensible; but as I have often told you, his disappointments rendered him splenetic, and angry with the whole world.

Education, habit, and constitution, give a surprizing variety of characters; and, while they produce some particular qualities, are apt to check others. Fortitude of mind seldom attends a sedentary life: nor is the man, whose ambitious views are crossed, scarce ever afterwards indued with benevolence of heart. The same mind, that is capable of exerting the greatest virtue, by some defect in the first steps of education, often degenerates into the greatest vice. These effects take their source from the causes almost mechanical. The soul, in our present situation, is blended and enclosed with corporeal substance, and the matter of which our body is composed, produces strange impulses upon the mind: but the instances that might illustrate, and explain the different effects arising from this formation, are too digressively extensive for my present plan.

To correct vice, by shewing her deformity in opposition to the beauty of virtue, and to amend the false systems of philosophy, by pointing out the errors, and applying salutary means to avoid them, is a noble design This was the general intent, I would fain flatter myself, of my hieroglyphic friend.

GULLIVER'S travels are chiefly to be looked upon as an irregular essay of SWIFT's peculiar wit and humour. Let us take a view of the two first parts together. The inhabitants of *Lilliput* are represented, as if reflected from a convex mirror, by which every object is reduced to a despicable minuteness. The inhabitants of *Brobdingnag*, by a contrary mirror, are enlarged to a shocking deformity. In *Lilliput* we behold a set of puny insects, or animalcules in human shape, ridiculously engaged in affairs of importance. In *Brobdingnag* the monsters of enormous size are employed in trifles.

LEMUEL GULLIVER has observed great exactness in the just proportion, and appearances of the several objects thus lessened and magnified: but he dwells too much upon these optical deceptions. The mind is tired with a repetition of them, especially as he points out no beauty, nor use in such amazing discoveries, which might have been so continued as to have afforded improvement, at the same time that they gave astonishment. Upon the whole, he too often shews an indelicacy that is not agreeable, and exerts his vein of humour most improperly in some places, where (I am afraid) he glances at religion.

In his description of *Lilliput*, he seems to have had *England* more immediately in view. In his description of *Blefuscu* he seems to intend the people and kingdom of *France:* yet the allegory between these nations is frequently interrupted, and scarce any where compleat. Several just strokes of satyr are scattered here and there upon errors in the conduct of our government: and, in the sixth chapter of his voyage to *Brobdingnag*, he gives an account of the political state of *Europe:* his observations are delivered with his usual spirit of humour and severity. He appears most particularly affected with the proceedings of the courts of judicature, and complains of being almost ruined by a Chancery suit, which was *determined in his favour with costs.* It must be confessed, that instances of this kind are too frequent in our courts of justice, and they leave us no room to boast of the execution of our present laws, however excellent the laws, in their own original foundation, may have been. *Judgement, when turned into wormwood, is bitter,* but delays, as Lord BACON observes, turn it into vinegar: it becomes sharp, and corroding: and certainly it is more eligible to die immediately by the wound of an enemy, than to decay lingering by poison, administered from a seeming friend.

The seventh chapter of the voyage of *Brobdingnag* contains such sarcasms on the structure of the human body, as too plainly shew us, that the author was unwilling to lose any opportunity of debasing and ridiculing his own species.

[132–7.]

Let us return back therefore to the *Lilliputians*, and the *Brobdingnaggians*; where you will find many ridiculous adventures, even such as must have excited mirth from HERACLITUS. Where indelicacies do not intervene, the narrative is very entertaining and humorous. Several just strokes of satyr are scattered up and down upon political errors in government. In some parts, GULLIVER seems to have had particular incidents, if not particular persons, in his view. His observations on education are useful: and so are his improvements on the institutions of LYCURGUS. Upon reading over the two first parts of these travels, I think that I can discover a very great resemblance between certain passages in GULLIVER'S voyage to *Lilliput*, and the voyage of CYRANO DE BERGERAC to the sun and moon.

CYRANO DE BERGERAC is a French author of a singular character, who had a very peculiar turn of wit and humour, in many respects resembling that of SWIFT. He wanted the advantages of learning, and a regular education: his imagination was less guarded, and correct, but more agreeably extravagant. He has introduced into his philosophical romance, the system of DESCARTES (which was then much admired) intermixt with several fine strokes of just satyr on the wild, and immechanical enquiries of the philosophers, and astronomers of that age:

and in many parts he has evidently directed the plan, which the Dean of St. PATRICK's has pursued.

I am sorry, and yet, in candour, I ought to observe, that GULLIVER, in his voyage to *Lilliput*, dares even to exert his vein of humour so liberally, as to place the Resurrection (one of the most encouraging principles of the Christian religion) in a ridiculous, and contemptible light. Why should that appointment be denied to man, or appear so very extraordinary in the human kind, which the Author of nature has illustrated in the vegetable species, where the seed dies and corrupts, before it can rise again to new beauty and glory? But I am writing out of my province; and that I may be tempted no farther, here let me end the criticism upon the two first parts of GULLIVER's travels, the conclusion of which, I mean GULLIVER's escape from BROBDINGNAG, is humorous, satyrical, and decent. . . .

The third part of GULLIVER's travels are in general written against chymists, mathematicians, mechanics, and projectors of all kinds.

SWIFT was little acquainted with mathematical knowledge, and was prejudiced against it, by observing the strange effects it produced in those, who applied themselves entirely to that science. No part of human literature has given greater strength to the mind, or has produced greater benefits to mankind, than the several branches of learning that may pass under the general denomination of mathematics. But the abuses of this study, the idle, thin, immechanical refinements of it, are just subjects of satyr. The real use of knowledge is to invigorate, not to enervate the faculties of reason. Learning degenerates into a species of madness, when it is not superior to what it possesseth. The scientific powers are most evident, when, they are capable of exerting themselves in the social duties of life. . . .

He cannot be supposed to condemn useful experiments, or the right application of them: but he ridicules the vain attempts, and irregular productions of those rash men, who, like IXION, embracing a cloud instead of a goddess, plagued the world with centaurs, whilst JUPITER, from the embraces of a JUNO, and an ALCMENA, blessed the earth with an HEBE, and an HERCULES.

However wild the description of the *flying island*, and the manners, and various projects of the philosophers of *Lagado* may appear, yet it is a real picture embellished with much latent wit and humour. It is a satyr upon those astronomers and mathematicians, who have so entirely dedicated their time to the planets, that they have been careless of their family and country, and have been chiefly anxious, about the œconomy and welfare of the upper worlds. But if we consider SWIFT's romance in a serious light, we shall find him of opinion, that those determinations in philosophy, which at present seem to the most knowing men to be perfectly well founded and understood, are in reality unsettled, or uncertain, and may perhaps some ages hence be as much descried, as the axioms of ARISTOTLE are at this day. Sir ISAAC NEWTON and his notions may hereafter be out of fashion. There is a kind of mode in philosophy, as well as in other things: and such modes often change more from the humour and caprice of men, than either from the unreasonable, or the ill-founded conclusions of the philosophy itself. The reasonings of some philosophers have undoubtedly better foundations than those of others: but I am of opinion (and SWIFT seems to be in the same way of thinking) that the most applauded philosophy hitherto extant has not fully, clearly, and certainly explained many difficulties in the phænomena of nature. . . .

The sixth chapter is full of severity and satyr. Sometimes it is exerted against the legislative power: sometimes against particular politicians: sometimes against women: and sometimes it degenerates into filth. True humour ought to be kept up with decency, and dignity, or it loses every tincture of entertainment. Descriptions that shock our delicacy cannot have the least good effect upon our minds. They offend us, and we fly precipitately from the sight. We cannot stay long enough to examine, whether wit, sense, or morality, may be couched under such odious appearances. I am sorry to say, that these sort of descriptions, which are too often interspersed throughout all SWIFT's works, are seldom written with any other view, or from any other motive, than a wild unbridled indulgence of his own humour and disposition.

He seems to have finished his voyage to LAPUTA in a careless, hurrying manner, which makes me almost think, that sometimes he was tired with his work, and attempted to run through it as fast as he could; otherwise why was the curtain dropped so soon, or why were we deprived of so noble a scene as might have been discovered in the island of *Glubdubdrib, where the governor, by his skill in necromancy, had the power of calling whom he pleased from the dead.* . . .

I believe it would be impossible to find out the design of Dr. SWIFT, in summoning up a parcel of apparitions, that from their behaviour, or from any thing they say, are almost of as little consequence, as the ghosts in GAY's farce of the *What d'ye call it*. Perhaps, SWIFT's general design might be, to arraign the conduct of eminent persons after their death, and to convey their names, and images to posterity, deprived of those false colours, in which they formerly appeared. If these were his intentions, he has missed his aim; or at least, has been so far carried away by his disposition to raillery, that the moral, which ought to arise from such a fable, is buried in obscurity. . . .

The description of the STRULDBRUGGS, in the tenth chapter, is an instructive piece of morality: for, if we consider it in a serious light, it tends to reconcile us to our final dissolution. Death, when set in contrast to the immortality of the STRULDBRUGGS, is no longer the King of Terrors: he loses his sting: he appears to us as a friend: and we chearfully obey his summons, because it brings certain relief to the greatest miseries. It is in this description, that SWIFT shines in a particular manner. He probably felt in himself the effects of approaching age, and tacitly dreaded that period of life, in which he might become a representative of those *miserable immortals*. His apprehensions were unfortunately fulfilled. He lived to be the most melancholy sight that was ever beheld: yet, even in that condition, he continued to instruct, by appearing a providential instance to mortify the vanity, which is too apt to arise in the human breast.

[144–83.]

It is with great reluctance, I shall make some remarks on GULLIVER's voyage to the *Houyhnhnms*. In this last part of his imaginary travels, SWIFT has indulged a misanthropy that is intolerable. The representation which he has given us of human nature, must terrify, and even debase the mind of the reader who views it. His sallies of wit and humour lose all their force, nothing remaining but a melancholy, and disagreeable impression: and, as I have said to you, on other parts of his works, we are disgusted, not entertained; we are shocked, not instructed by the fable. I should therefore chuse to take no notice of his YAHOOS, did I not think it necessary to assert the vindication of human nature, and thereby, in some measure, to pay my duty to the great author of our species, who has created us in a very fearful, and a very wonderful manner.

We are composed of a mind, and of a body, intimately united, and mutually affecting each other. Their operations indeed are entirely different. Whether the immortal spirit, that enlivens this fine machine, is originally of a superior nature in various bodies (which, I own, seems most consistent and agreeable to the scale and order of beings) or, whether the difference depends on a symmetry, or peculiar structure of the organs combined with it, is beyond my reach to determine. It is evidently certain, that the body is curiously formed with proper organs to delight, and such as are adapted to all the necessary uses of life. The spirit animates the whole; it guides the natural appetites, and confines them within just limits. But, the natural force of this spirit is often immersed in matter; and the mind becomes subservient to passions, which it ought to govern and direct. . . .

In painting YAHOOS he becomes one himself. Nor is the picture, which he draws of the *Houyhnhnms*, inviting or amusing. It wants both light and shade to adorn it. It is cold and insipid. We there view the pure instincts of brutes, unassisted by any knowledge of letters, acting within their own narrow sphere, merely for their immediate preservation. They are incapable of doing wrong, therefore they act right. It is surely a very low character given to creatures, in whom the author would insinuate some degree of reason, that they act inoffensively, when they have neither the motive nor the power to act otherwise. Their virtuous qualities are only negative. SWIFT himself, amidst all his irony, must have confessed, that to moderate our passions, to extend our munificence to others, to enlarge our understanding, and to raise our idea of the Almighty by contemplating his works, is not only the business, but often the practice, and the study of the human mind. It is too certain, that no one individual has ever possessed every qualification and excellence: however such an assemblage of different virtues, may still be collected from different persons, as are sufficient to place the dignity of human nature in an amiable, and exalted station. We must lament indeed the many instances of those who degenerate, or go astray from the end and intention of their being. The true source of this depravity is often owing to the want of education, to the false indulgence of parents, or to some other bad causes, which are constantly prevalent in every nation. Many of these errors are finely ridiculed in the foregoing parts of this romance: but the voyage to the *Houyhnhnms* is a real insult upon mankind.

I am heartily tired of this last part of GULLIVER'S travels, and am glad, that, having exhausted all my observations on this disagreeable subject, I may finish my letter; . . .

[184–90.]

We have now gone through FAULKNER'S edition of SWIFT'S works, but there are still remaining three of his pieces, *A Tale of a Tub, The Battle of the Books in St. James's Library,* and *The Fragment,* which although not absolutely owned by the Dean, *aut Erasmi sunt aut Diaboli.*

The first of these, *A Tale of a Tub*, has made much noise in the world. It was one of SWIFT's earliest performances, and has never been excelled in wit and spirit by his own, or any other pen. The censures that have passed upon it, are various. The most material of which were such as reflected upon Dr. SWIFT, in the character of a clergyman, and a Christian. It has been one of the misfortunes attending Christianity, that many of her sons, from a mistaken filial piety, have indulged themselves in too restrained, and too melancholy a way of thinking. Can we wonder then, if a book composed with all the force of wit and humour in derision of sacerdotal tyranny, in ridicule of grave hypocrisy, and in contempt of flegmatic stiffness, should be wilfully misconstrued by some persons, and ignorantly mistaken by others, as a sarcasm and reflexion upon the whole Christian Church? SWIFT's ungovernable spirit of irony, has sometimes carried him into very unwarrantable flights of wit. I have remarked such passages with a most unwilling eye. But, let my affections of friendship have been ever so great, my paternal affection is still greater: and I will pursue candour, even with an aching heart, when the pursuit of it may tend to your advantage or instruction. In the style of truth therefore, I must still look upon *A Tale of a Tub*, as no *intended* insult against Christianity, but as a satyr against the wild errors of the church of *Rome*, the slow and incompleat reformation of the Lutherans, and the absurd, and affected zeal of the presbyterians. In the character of PETER, we see the pope, seated on his pontifical throne, and adorned with his triple crown. In the picture of MARTIN, we view LUTHER and the first reformers: and in the representation of JACK, we behold JOHN CALVIN and his disciples. The author's arrows are chiefly directed against PETER, and JACK. To MARTIN, he shews all the indulgence that the laws of allegory will permit.

The actions of PETER are the actions of a man intoxicated with pride, power, rage, tyranny, and self-conceit. These passions are placed in the most ridiculous light: and the effects of them produce to us the tenets and doctrines of papal *Rome*, such as purgatory, penance, images, indulgences, auricular confession, transubstantiation, and those dreadful monsters, the pontifical bulls. . . .

In the character of JACK a set of people were alarmed, who are easily offended, and who can scarce bear the chearfulness of a smile. In their dictionary, wit is only another name for wickedness: and the purer, or more excellent the wit, the greater, and more impious the *abomination*. However wide therefore the difference of PETER and JACK might have been in fashioning their coats, the two brothers most sincerely agreed in their hatred of an adversary so powerful as this anonymous author. They spared no unmannerly reflexions upon his character. They had recourse to every kind of abuse that could reach him. And sometimes, it was the work of SWIFT and his companions: sometimes not a syllable of it was his work, it was the work of one of his uncle's sons, a clergyman: and sometimes it was the work of a person, who was to be nameless. Each of these malicious conjectures reigned in its turn, and you will find, my HAMILTON, that bold assertions, however false, almost constantly meet with success; a kind of triumph that would appear one of the severest institutes of fate, if time, and truth, did not soon obliterate all marks of the victory.

The critisms of the Martinists, (whom we may suppose the members of the church of *England*) were, it is to be hoped, more candid: for MARTIN, as I have just now hinted, is treated with a much less degree of sarcasm than the other two brothers. . . .

The best, and what is more extraordinary, the most serious apology, that can be made for the author was written by himself, and is dated *June* 3, 1709, from which time, it has been constantly printed in a prefatory manner to the work itself. In this apology, Dr. SWIFT candidly acknowledges, that '*There are several youthful sallies, which, from the grave and the wife, may deserve a rebuke.*' And farther adds, that '*He will forfeit his life, if any one opinion can fairly be deduced from the book, which is contrary to religion or morality*'.

The dedication to *Prince Posterity* will please you: nor will you be less entertained by the several *digressions* which are written in ridicule of bad critics, dull commentators, and the whole fraternity of Grub-street philosophers. *The Introduction* abounds with wit, and humour: but the author never loses the least opportunity of venting his keenest satyr against Mr. DRYDEN, and consequently loads with insults the greatest, although the least prosperous, of our English poets. Yet who can avoid smiling, when he finds the *Hind and Panther* mentioned as *a compleat abstract of sixteen thousand schoolmen*, and when TOMMY POTS is supposed written by *the same hand*, as *a supplement to the former work*? I am willing to imagine, that DRYDEN, in some manner or other, had offended my friend Dr. SWIFT, who, otherwise, I hope, would have been more indulgent to the errors of a man, oppressed by poverty, driven on by party, and bewildered by religion.

But although our satirical author, now and then, may have indulged himself in some personal animosities, or may have taken freedoms not so perfectly consistent with that solemn decency, which is required from a clergyman, yet throughout the whole piece, there is a vein of ridicule and good humour, that laughs pedantry and affectation into the lowest degree of contempt, and exposes the character of PETER and JACK in such a manner, as never will be forgiven, and never can be answered.

The *Battle of the Books* took its rise from the controversy between Sir WILLIAM TEMPLE and Mr. WOOTON(*sic*): a controversy which made much noise, and employed many pens towards the latter end of the last century. This humorous treatise is drawn up in an heroic style, in which SWIFT, with great wit and spirit, gives the victory to the former. The general plan is excellent, but particular parts are defective. The frequent chasms puzzle and interrupt the narrative: they neither convey any latent ideas, nor point out any distant or occult sarcasms. Some characters are barely touched upon, which might have been extended, others are enlarged, which might have been contracted. The name of HORACE is scarce inserted, and VIRGIL is introduced only for an opportunity of comparing his translator DRYDEN, to *the Lady in a Lobster: to a Mouse under a Canopy of State: and to a shrivelled beau within the Penthouse of a full bottomed Perriwig.* These similes carry the true stamp of ridicule: but, rancour must be very prevalent in the heart of an author, who could overlook the merits of DRYDEN; many of whose dedications and prefaces are as fine compositions, and as just pieces of criticism as any in our language. The translation of VIRGIL was a work of haste and indigence: DRYDEN was equal to the undertaking, but unfortunate during the conduct of it. . . .

The two chief heroes among the modern generals, are WOTTON and BENTLEY. Their figures are displayed in the most disadvantageous attitudes. The former is described, 'full of spleen, dulness, and ill manners'. The latter is represented, 'tall, without shape or comeliness: large, without strength or proportion'. But, I will not anticipate your pleasure in reading a performance that you will probably wish longer, and more compleat.

The *Battle*, which is maintained by the antients with great superiority of strength, though not of numbers, ends with the demolition of BENTLEY and his friend WOTTON by the lance of your grandfather. . . .

The *Fragment*, or *a Discourse concerning the mechanical operation of the Spirit*, is a satyr against enthusiasm, and those affected inspirations, which constantly begin in folly, and very often end in vice. In this treatise, the author has revelled in too licentious a vein of sarcasm: many of his ideas are nauseous, some are indecent, and others have an irreligious tendency: nor is the piece itself equal in wit and humour either to *A Tale of a Tub*, or *The Battle of the Books*. I should constantly chuse rather to praise, than to arraign any part of my friend SWIFT's writings: but in those tracts, where he tries to make us uneasy with ourselves, and unhappy in our present existence, *there*, I must yield him up entirely to censure.

[300–25.]

Few men have been more known and admired, or more envied and censured, than Dr. SWIFT. From the gifts of nature, he had great powers, and from the imperfection of humanity, he had many failings. I always considered him as an *Abstract and brief chronicle of the times*: no man being better acquainted with human nature, both in the highest, and in the lowest scenes of life. His friends, and correspondents, were the greatest and most eminent men of the age. The sages of antiquity were often the companions of his closet: and although he industriously avoided an ostentation of learning, and generally chose to draw his materials from his own store, yet his knowledge in the antient authors evidently appears from the strength of his sentiments, and the classic correctness of his style.

[337–8.]

27. Patrick Delany on Swift

1754

Observations upon Lord Orrery's Remarks on the Life and Writings of Dr. Jonathan Swift, 1754.

Dr. Patrick Delany (1685?–1768) was a friend of Swift's later years. Much of his work is biographical, and intended to correct the malicious *Remarks* of Orrery, to whom the letters are addressed.

MY LORD,

The freedom which I took of censuring SWIFT's errors in my last, and some former Letters, will, I hope, give you full satisfaction (if it be possible you should want any) that wherever I am so unhappy as to differ from your Lordship in my accounts or opinion of him, I do it, from the sole impulse of truth, and justice. And when I presume to make additional observations, it is, where you appear to me to have touched too lightly and dwelt too little. And this, I apprehend, is the case in relation to the voyage to the *Houyhnhnms*, a piece more deform, erroneous, and (of consequence) less instructive, and agreeable, than any of his productions.

As I have marked the passages that seemed to me most faulty, and gave me most offence, I beg leave to point them out, as they come in my way: without any further preface, or apology.

The picture he draws of the *Yahoos*, is too offensive to be copied, even in the slightest sketch. And therefore I shall only observe, that whilst he is debasing the human form to the lowest degree of a defiled imagination, he yet allows some powers in it, of a very distinguished nature. Strength, activity, and *prodigious* agility.

You, my Lord, have sufficiently expatiated upon the powers of the human mind, which so remarkably distinguish and exalt our species above the whole animal world; and I am highly delighted with your quotation from SHAKESPEARE upon that head. Give me leave to throw out a few hints upon the structure of the human frame: which demonstrate that also very superior to the make of all other animals. Insomuch that he evidently excels every other species, not vastly exceeding himself in bulk, and the advantages arising from it in every power in which they excel all others. He can out-run a horse, (the *Hottentots* are known to do so) out-leap an antelope, out-swim a shark: leap into the sea, combat with, and conquer that fiercest and most destructive of sea-monsters, in his own element.

He can carry a load under his arms, and on his shoulders, which would break the back of a horse.

He can dart himself into the air; turn in it, heels over head, inverting the centre of gravity, with an amazing power; and then bring his feet firm to the ground, with the utmost security. Which no other animal in the universe can do, nor any thing like it; except the action of one kind of fowl, whose wings, then extended in the air, leave nothing surprising, or extraordinary in the action.

I own, I have often gone to see most of the famed rope-dancers, and posture-masters, upon this sole principle of admiring those amazing powers, with which God hath endowed the human frame; and such as the most active, and agile of all other animals, can, with the utmost force of human industry, be brought only to imitate very imperfectly.

Among other advantages devolved upon the human species, above the brutes, is, that of the erect figure of his body; which S W I F T well knew; and the reader of any science will little need to have explained to him. And yet S W I F T satirises even this advantage. But he had sense enough to put the objection made to it, into the mouth of a *Houyhnhnm*, who could know no better.

If it be asked to what purpose this display of powers in the human make?

I answer, to demonstrate the divine wisdom, in preparing such a body for the habitation of a reasonable soul, in which only it could exert all its faculties, to all the purposes of a reasonable creature con-demned to support his life by labour, and arts of various kinds: as also to shew, the superiority of man, in every respect.

Next to man, a horse is generally allowed the noblest animal of the inferior world. And yet what a clumsy condition does the human soul appear to be in, when supposed to be lodged in that form, utterly in-capable of the meanest of those innumerable and important actions, and offices, which distinguish the lowest class of mankind.

This voyage is considered as a satire of S W I F T's upon the human frame. I would fain hope, that it was intended only as a satire upon human corruptions: be that as it may, it is most certainly in effect a panegyrick upon the human frame, by shewing the utter inability even of the noblest structure of inferior animals: to answer the purposes of a reasonable life in this world. To answer even the lowest and meanest of those purposes. The utmost capacity, with which even SWIFT, with all his wit and invention, was able to endow his *Houyhnhnms*, was that of carrying a little oats between his hoof and his fetlock: and what a fine figure must he make, even in that action, hobbling aukwardly, upon three legs!

He talks indeed of their untying the *Yahoos*, and giving GULLIVER a bowl of milk: but was far from being able to endow them with the power of doing either.

He places them in houses, which they could not build; and feeds them with corn, which they could neither sow nor reap, nor save. He gives them cows, which they could not milk, and deposits that milk in vessels, which they could not make, &c.

But it were time thrown away, to expose the weakness of his attempts, to equal the *Houyhnhnm* structure to the human: nor could they be serious to any other purpose than that of abandoned satire.

Let us examine next, into the qualities and powers, with which he endows their mind.

He distinguishes their manners by two qualities: decency, and cleanliness: by which he plainly confesses, that both are the natural effects of reason. And yet he, at the same time, demonstrates himself to be mentally lost to both! What then becomes of his rational faculty? He gives cleanliness to creatures, who have no capacity of cleansing themselves, and deprives the only being of it, that hath that capacity.

The offensive smell with which he poisons them, and every thing about them, is ordinarily the natural effect of great negligence, in the article of cleanliness; and the providential chastisement of it: and yet he charges it upon the nature of the *Yahoos*; forgetting how he had before endowed his favourite VANESSA; when VENUS had sprinkled her with nectar, from her sprig of *Amaranthine* flowers.

> *From whence the tender skin assumes,*
> *A sweetness above all perfumes:*
> *From whence, a cleanliness remains,*
> *Incapable of outward stains.*

He charges them with monstrous claws, which can be of no use, but to offend, and injure their fellows: forgetting, that at the same time, he made their hands as useless, to any of their proper purposes (even that of climbing, with which he endows them) as if they were mandarines of *China*: a nation the sillyest, of all the silly pretenders to wisdom, that ever disgraced pride! estimating the superiority of their mental powers, by impairing those of the body: disabling the better sort of one sex in their feet, and those of the other, in their hands.

He endows his *Houyhnhnms* with friendship and benevolence; the necessary consequences of reason: and yet, he almost professed himself devoid of both. Amazing debasement!

And he deprives them of all those tender passions, and affections, without which life would be a load: and which, when he lost, his own became so.

And what are the effects of those superior powers of unbiased reason, with which he endows them? They met once a year, to run, and leap; and plunge themselves in cold water; and once in four years to make laws which nobody was bound to obey.

For the rest, his whole reasoning tends to no other purpose, than to establish that principle, long since exploded in the schools: that would infer, the disuse of all things most valuable and desirable in the world, from their abuse. Kings, ministers, laws, physick, wine, riches, love, &c. But what he means by the acuteness of his master *Houyhnhnm*, which daily convinced him of a thousand faults in himself, whereof he had not the least perception before; and which, with us, would never be numbered, even among human infirmities, I confess, I can neither comprehend, nor conceive.

Upon the whole, I am clearly of opinion, that he would more effectually have endeavoured to amend mankind, by putting the virtues, and the suited practice of one, even imaginary good man, in a fair and amiable light, than by painting the depravities of the whole species in the most odious colours, and attitudes! Who would not wish rather to be the author of one *Arcadia*, than fifty *Laputa*'s *Lilliputs*, and *Houyhnhnms*?

I am fully satisfied, that exaggerated satire, never yet did any good, nor ever will. The only satire that can do any good is that which shews mankind to themselves, in their true light; and exposes those follies, vices and corruptions of every kind, in all their absurdities, deformities, and horrors, which flattery, self-love, and passions of any kind, had hitherto hid from their eyes. That magnifying-glass, which enlarges all the deform features into monstrous dimentions, defeats its own purpose: for no man will ever know his own likeness in it: and, consequently, tho' he may be shocked, he will not be amended by it.

I cannot help thinking, that if SWIFT had recovered one hour of rational reflection, after the signal chastisement of his total infatuation, he would have numbered his latter works, among the follies of his life; and lamented himself in a strain something like those lines, which I have somewhere met with.

> O life how art thou made a scene,
> Of follies first and last;
> Rejoicing in the present train,
> Repining at the past.

I am sick of this subject; . . . But however, the satire upon vice and the amendment of mankind by it, was his main view even in that abominable picture, which he drew of the *Yahoos*; may, I think, be fairly concluded from his own verses on the death of the Doctor SWIFT, which he puts in the mouth of an impartial man.

[161–77.]

MY LORD,

The indignation which always seized me upon looking into those poems of SWIFT's, which have given most offence, and apparently not without good reason: hindered me till very lately, from ever reading them over. But upon reflection, I thought it incumbent upon me, as I had in some measure taken up the character (I will not say of a critic, but of a candid observer) upon the several reflections that have been past upon him in the world: to examine, and consider more carefully, those parts of his writings, which have been most censured; and which I had before past over in disgust. And, upon the whole, the judgment that rests upon my mind, after the most candid disquisition into them, is this.

That they are the prescriptions of an able physician, who had, in truth, the health of his patients at heart, but laboured to attain that end, not only by strong emeticks, but also, by all the most nauseous, and offensive drugs, and potions, that could be administred. But yet not without a mixture of the finest ingredients that could possibly be imagined, and contrived, to take off the offence, which the rest so justly gave.

Give me leave to instance in two passages of his poem called STREPHON and CLOE.

The first is as follows:

> *Fair decency, celestial maid,*
> *Descend from heav'n, to beauty's aid,*
> *Tho' beauty may beget desire,*
> *'Tis thou must fan the lover's fire:*
> *For beauty, like supreme dominion,*
> *Is best supported by opinion:*
> *If decency bring no supplies,*
> *Opinion falls, and beauty dies.*

The next is in the eight concluding lines of the same poem.

> *On sense and wit your passions sound,*
> *By decency cemented round,*
> *Let prudence with good-nature strive,*
> *To keep esteem and love alive.*
> *Then come old age when e'er it will,*
> *Your friendship shall continue still:*
> *And thus a mutual gentle fire,*
> *Shall never, but with life, expire.*

Although many other parts of this poem will be read with pain, these, I think, and some others, must always be remembered with pleasure and profit: and must be considered under the character of such medicines, as not only tend to remove the distemper in his patients, and strengthen their constitutions against them, for the future, but also, as preventives, plague-water, and other antipestilential prescriptions (by Physicians called alexipharmacks) to guard others from the infection.

[197–9.]

Your Lordship hath made so many and such judicious observations upon the excellency of SWIFT's style, that little, I think, can be added to them. That little, however, will I hope not be deemed altogether unworthy your attention.

His own definition of a good style was this. *Proper words in proper places.*

To profit by this definition, two things must be carefully examined, and attended to.

The first is carefully to consider the power, and propriety of words. And the next, the strength and harmony arising from their arrangement, and connexion with one another.

Both these after long study and practice were become such a habit in SWIFT, it cost him little pains, or attention, to display them in his composition; and yet, after all, that which gave his style its true and best distinction was the clearness and perspicuity arising from that conciseness in his style, which gives obscurity to almost every other; and which you therefore most properly call a masterly conciseness. I can compare it to nothing so properly, as to that character of a right line, which as it is the plainest, simplest, and easiest to be comprehended by the eye, is, at the same time, the shortest that can be drawn between any two points.

[271–2.]

28. Deane Swift on *Gulliver's Travels* and on Swift as a poet

1755

Essay upon the Life, Writings and Character of Dr. Jonathan Swift, 2nd edition, 1755.

Deane Swift (1707–83) was a cousin of Jonathan Swift and a descendant of Admiral Richard Deane. This essay, first published in 1755 and reprinted the same year, shows his excessive concern with the honour of his family. Here he attempts to refute the opinions of the Observator (Delany) and of Lord Orrery, whom he attacks as the 'sagacious critick'.

Having in the two or three former chapters sufficiently remarked on the political behaviour of Dr. SWIFT, I shall now proceed to make some critical observations upon his travels. But since the Doctor's writings are always so clear and significant, that few or no remarks are required to make then intelligible to all capacities; I shall only observe in the general that his famous GULLIVER is a direct, plain and bitter satire against the innumerable follies and corruptions in law, politicks, learning, morals and religion. And without dispute these manifold corruptions have in a course of ages, by the refinements and glosses of iniquitous men, arrived at last to such strength and effrontery as to render it impossible for all the wit and genius that ever warmed the imagination of a satirist to lash them with any degree of severity proportioned to that excess of perturbation and mischief which they severally occasion in the great circle of society. All therefore which can be done by a wise man (seeing that by nature he is appointed to act for the space of thirty, fifty, or seventy years some ridiculous, silly part in this fantastick theatre of misery, vice and corruption) is either to lament with HERACLITUS the iniqualities of the world; or which is the more chearful, and therefore I do presume the more eligible course to laugh with DEMOCRITUS, at all the knaves and fools upon earth. And

accordingly we find that Dr. SWIFT has in these *Travels* exerted a force
of ridicule and satire, pointed so directly against the depravities of
humankind, and supported with such an abundance of wit and pleasantry as indeed more than persuade us to believe that his intention was
either to laugh vice and immorality if it were possible quite out of the
world; or at least to avenge the cause of virtue on all the patrons and
abetters of iniquity.

GULLIVER's voyages to *Lilliput*, as well as the voyage to *Brobdingnag*,
the machinery and some particular sallies of nature, wit and humour
only excepted, is intirely political. His meaning throughout the whole,
especially where he glances at the history of his own times, the wars of
Europe and the factions of WHIG and TORY, is to be found so very near
the surface, that it would almost be an affront to the common reason of
those who are at all versed in the affairs of the world to offer at any
further explication.

HOWEVER, we find it asserted by that very sagacious critick so
often mentioned, that DR. SWIFT in his account of *Lilliput* 'dares even
to exert his vein of humour so liberally as to place the resurrection (one
of the most encouraging principles of the christian religion) in a
ridiculous and contemptible light'. What grounds there are for such
an accusation we shall see presently. That passage in GULLIVER, which
seems to be referred to runs in the following manner: 'They bury their
dead with their heads directly downwards; because they hold an opinion
that in eleven thousand moons they are all to rise again; in which
period the earth (which they conceive to be flat) will turn upside down,
and by this means they shall at their resurrection be found ready
standing on their feet. The learned among them confess the absurdity of
this doctrine; but the practice still continues in compliance to the vulgar.'
A paragraph which, if it were examined with judgment and candor,
would incline us to believe, that an opinion of a life to come is connected
so immediately with all our reasoning faculties, that supposing we had
never been blessed with any revelation from GOD we should believe
the resurrection to life eternal. But the *Lilliputians* believe that after
eleven thousand moons the earth will be turned upside down; and upon
that account they are buried with their heads directly downwards, in
order to be found standing upon their feet at the day of resurrection: an
opinion which I confess with the learned among themselves to be
whimsical and ridiculous enough. But follies and absurdities are always
mixed with idolatry and superstition. Perhaps it will be objected, that
in perusing GULLIVER we are *always* to understand *Lilliput* to be some

nation of *Christendom*, and consequently their religious opinions to be the Christian faith. But, this I will venture to say, that whoever reads the voyage to *Lilliput* in that light, will find himself to be grossly mistaken. For the *Lilliputians* (although we are not expressly told so by DR. SWIFT) were so far from being *Christians* of any denomination, that in fact they were rank idolaters; otherwise it is impossible, that a people secluded from all the rest of the world, except the island of *Blefuscu*, should imagine GULLIVER's watch to be the god that he worshipped. And therefore I cannot but infer, that instead of placing the resurrection in a ridiculous, contemptible light, GULLIVER hath fairly manifested the opinion of a state hereafter, (although connected with some vanities and absurdities, which are the effects of superstition) to be the ground-work of all religion founded upon the clear and strong dictates both of nature and reason.

We are also told by this incomparable judge of exellencies and defects in the productions of the learned, 'That the seventh chapter of the voyage to *Brobdingnag* contains such sarcasms on the structure of the human body, as too plainly shew us, that the author was unwilling to lose any opportunity of debasing and ridiculing his own species.' But whereabouts in the seventh chapter of the voyage to *Brobdingnag* the author of GULLIVER hath endeavoured to ridicule his own species I protest I cannot conceive. Perhaps the critick imagines the structure of the human body is ridiculed, because a man of six foot high cannot read a folio of twenty foot high with the help of a ladder. But such a representation of GULLIVER in the character of GRILDRIG is so far from being a defect in the author's judgment, or indeed a satyr upon the human species, that on the contrary, it is an incident manifestly designed to keep up the probability; neither without some contrivance of that kind was it possible that he could have been acquainted with their learning; and consequently must have been totally silent with regard to that point. I am inclined therefore to believe the critick's indignation was raised against DR. SWIFT, because in this chapter he introduces the king of *Brobdingnag* as treating GULLIVER with some sort of contempt. But whether DR. SWIFT can deserve our censure upon this account, shall be the subject of our next inquiry.

IN the former part of this chapter we are told by GULLIVER, that as a small tribute of acknowledgment, in return for so many marks of royal favour and protection, which he had received from the prince of *Brobdingnag*, he discovered to him the force of powder and the use of artillery; and besides, made him an offer to instruct his servants in the composition of gun-powder, and direct his workmen how to make cannons and demiculverins of a size proportionable to all other things in his majesty's kingdom. Whereupon the king of *Brobdingnag*, a prince whom he declares to be possessed of every quality which procures veneration, love, and esteem; of strong parts, great wisdom, and profound learning; endued with admirable talents for government, and almost adored by his subjects; was struck with horror at the description he had given of those terrible engines, and the proposal he had made. 'He was amazed (saith GULLIVER) how so impotent and grovelling an insect as I (these were his expressions) could entertain such inhuman ideas, and in so familiar a manner as to appear wholly unmoved at all the scenes of blood and desolation, which I had painted as the common effects of those destructive machines; whereof he said, some evil genius, enemy to mankind, must have been the first contriver. As for himself, he protested that although few things delighted him so much as new discoveries in art or in nature; yet he would rather lose half his kingdom than be privy to such a secret; which he commanded me, as I valued my life, never to mention any more.'

IN the above quotation we find the king of *Brobdingnag* perfectly enraged to think, so diminutive a creature as GULLIVER, in respect to the inhabitants of that empire could entertain such inhuman ideas, and appear wholly unmoved at all the scenes of blood and desolation, which he had painted as the common effects of those destructive machines; calls him in disdain a *grovelling insect*; an expression highly proper on that occasion from a patriot king, so great, so venerable, and so beneficent to his people. But if this be degrading the human species, I am at a loss to conceive in what manner we can defend that uncourtly address of JOHN the BAPTIST to his own countrymen, 'Ye generation of vipers, &c.' than which, nothing can be more sarcastick, it being the received opinion of those times, that vipers were of a nature so cruel and sanguinary, as to force their passage into the world by gnawing their way through the bowels that bred and nourished them, leaving their dam a lifeless carcass upon the earth. But, if the human species be neither ridiculed by a man of six foot high mounting a ladder for the conveniency of reading a gigantick folio; nor by the prince of *Brobdingnag*'s calling the diminutive GULLIVER on a particular occasion, *a little grovelling insect*; I declare the remarks of the critick are totally beyond my comprehension. However indeed, there is a paragraph in the seventh chapter of the voyage to *Brobdingnag*, which it is impossible to read, without calling to mind that wicked *Meditation on a Broomstick*, which is every day rising more and more in the estimation of the world.

THE design of GULLIVER in his voyage to *Laputa* is to ridicule the vain pretensions of chymists, mathematicians, projectors, and the rest of that speculative tribe, who spend their time in aerial studies, by no means calculated to improve the faculties of the mind, or to enlarge the number of ideas; mathematicians (I mean those only, and I desire my words may not be racked, who are entirely devoted to their circles, their telescopes and their laboratory) being a race of men, so very abstracted from all sublunary affairs, that scarce one in twenty of them can give you a rational answer. However indeed, a certain degree of mathematical knowledge is, without dispute, extreamly necessary in the pursuit of the *Æsculapian* science, architecture, and other species of mechanicks. But, when the soul rambles after a thousand chimæras, and the brain is wholly absorbed in the consideration of the several powers of attraction, repulsion, and the circulation of the heavenly bodies; or, when a projector with sooty hands and face is employed in his laboratory in producing a considerable degree of cold, in order to refrigerate the air, and qualify the raging of the dog-star; which exactly answers to the project of extracting sun-beams out of cucumbers; such follies and extravagances are certainly the objects of derision. And accordingly DR. SWIFT has laughed egregiously in the voyage to *Laputa*, and exerted a vein of humour, not against the whole tribe of chymists, projectors, and mathematicians in general; but against those, and those only, who despise the useful branches of science, and waste their lives in the pursuit of aerial vanities and extravagancies.

GULLIVER's account of his entertainment at *Glubdubdrib*, or the island of sorcerers, is strangely and whimsically diverting. ALEXANDER the GREAT, at the head of his army just after the battle of *Arbela, assured* GULLIVER *upon his honor, that he was not poysoned, but died of a fever by excessive drinking. And afterwards* HANNIBAL *passing the Alps, declared to him, that he had not a drop of vinegar in his camp.* How ridiculous, how contemptible, are these plagues of the world; these destroyers of the human race; when stripped of their royalty and command, as well as their ability to perpetrate any further mischief!...

GULLIVER's account of the STRULDBRUGGS in the tenth chapter of the voyage to LAPUTA; which is the finest lecture that ever was conceived by any mortal man to reconcile poor tottering creatures unto a chearful resignation of this wretched life, and perfectly agreeable to that sentiment of the inspired prophet, *The days of our life are threescore years and ten; and though men be so strong, that they live to fourscore years;*

yet is their life then but labour and sorrow; hath furnished the critick with
an opportunity of reproaching DR. SWIFT with those calamities, which
it was by no means in his power to avert. . . .

I have been told that some others, beside the grand remarker upon
the works of DR. SWIFT, have thought proper to censure GULLIVER'S
voyage to the HOUYHNHNMS. But whether indeed their animadver-
sions proceeded from the infirmity of their judgment, or from some
YAHOO depravity in their own nature, I shall not vouchsafe to enquire;
as the daily occurrences of this wretched world prove, illustrate, and
confirm all the sarcasms of the Doctor. Shall we praise that excellent
moralist, the humorous HOGARTH, for exposing midnight revels,
debaucheries, and a thousand other vices and follies of humankind, in a
series of hieroglyphicks, suited to the improvement and the correction
of the wild, the gay, the frolick, and the extravagant? And shall we
condemn a preacher of righteousness, for exposing under the character
of a nasty unteachable YAHOO the deformity, the blackness, the filthiness and corruption of those hellish, abominable vices, which inflame
the wrath of GOD against the children of disobedience; and subject
them without repentance, that is, without a thorough change of life and
practice, to everlasting perdition? Ought a preacher of righteousness;
ought a watchman of the Christian faith, (who is accountable for his
talents, and obliged to warn the innocent, as well as terrify the wicked
and the prophane) to hold his peace, like a dumb dog that cannot bark,
when avarice, fraud, cheating, violence, rapine, extortion, cruelty,
oppression, tyranny, rancour, envy, malice, detraction, hatred, revenge,
murder, whoredom, adultery, lasciviousness, bribery, corruption,
pimping, lying, perjury, subordination, treachery, ingratitude, gaming,
flattery, drunkenness, gluttony, luxury, vanity, effeminacy, cowardice,
pride, impudence, hypocrisy, infidelity, blasphemy, idolatry, sodomy,
and innumerable other vices are as epidemical as the pox, and many of
them the notorious characteristicks of the bulk of humankind? I would
ask these mighty softeners, these kind pretenders to benevolence; these
hollow charity-mongers; what is their real opinion of that OLD
SERPENT, which, like a roaring lion, traverseth the globe, seeking whom
he may devour? Was he not created by the ALMIGHTY pure, faultless,
intelligent? but is there now throughout the whole system of created
existences, any BEAST, any YAHOO, any TYRANT so vile, so base, so
corrupted? And whence originally proceeded the change? was it not
from the abuse of that freedom, without which no created INTELLI-
GENCE can be reputed faithful, wise, brave, or virtuous, in the eyes of

his CREATOR? And surely, if this once great, once glorious spirit hath been reduced for many thousands of ages, for aught we know to the contrary, below all the several gradations of created beings, whether intelligent, animal, or insensible; and exposed to the fury of that avenging, although merciful GOD, who is the fountain of all wisdom, goodness, and virtue; are we not to conclude by an exact parity of reason, that every moral agent is equally accountable to GOD for that degree of intelligence and perfection, which determine the nature of his existence? And upon this very principle, which cannot be denied without running into the last of absurdities; and which in fact is the reasoning of ST. PETER throughout his whole second chapter of his second epistle; that creature man, that glorious creature man, is deservedly more contemptible than a brute beast, when he flies in the face of his CREATOR by enlisting under the banner of the enemy; and perverts that reason, which was designed to have been the glory of his nature, even the directing spirit of his life and demeanour, to the vilest, the most execrable, the most hellish purposes. And this manifestly appears to be the groundwork of the whole satire contained in the voyage to the HOUYHNHNMS.

BUT, to silence these tasteless animadverters upon the works of an uncommon, heteroclite genius, I shall observe, that DR. SWIFT was not the first preacher, whose writings import this kind of philosophy. And, to confirm what I have asserted, I shall produce some unquestionable authorities, which in effect will justify all the sarcasms of the Doctor.

[206–21].

[There follow quotations from the Old and New Testaments]

BUT, to conclude these remarks upon the voyage to the HOUYHN-HNMS; if the brutality and filthiness of the YAHOOS be represented by the satyrick genius of DR. SWIFT in colours the most shocking and detectable; as they certainly are, and as in fact they ought to have been; the picture is the more striking, as well as the more terrible; and upon that account, more likely to enforce the obligation of religion and virtue upon the souls of men.

The merits of DR. SWIFT in the character of a poet are considerably great. His descriptions, wherein there constantly appear the distinguishing marks of his own peculiar talents, are extreamly just and lively; many of his groups are not to be excelled by any painter's imagination; his rhymes and his numbers are chaste and delicate; and in many places, when rather by accident than choice he rises from the earth, and soars into the regions of poetry, he is equal to the finest masters among the *Greeks* and *Romans*; his ideas are lofty, and his versification musically sonorous. And yet after all, he is not to be considered in the light of a professed poet; the multitude of his writings on various subjects both in verse and prose being an evident demonstration, that he was superior to any particular course of learning. He was born to be the encourager of virtue, and the terror of the wicked. He never sate musing in his elbow chair upon new subjects, for the exercise of his genius, and the advancement of his fame; but writ occasionally to please and to reform the world, as either politicks or humour gave the spur to his faculties. There are but few of his poems that seem to have been the labour of more than one day, how greatly soever they might have been corrected and polished afterwards to his own liking, before he transcribed them fair.

[225–7.]

PERHAPS it may be expected, that in a work of this kind we should run into a minute detail of his poetry, and single out many of the finest strokes of his uncommon, heteroclite genius. But, since every man of taste and learning has abilities in himself to be his own critick, and to admire the real beauties of an author, as well as to accompany his flights into the most distant regions of poetry, without guide or monitor; we shall be very sparing in references and quotations of that sort. It may not, however, be amiss to observe in general, before we proceed to any critical remarks, that SWIFT's poetical writings, which in their present situation are only a beautiful heap of confusion, rather distracting the eye, and flashing upon the imagination, than conducting our fancies into poetick scenes; and commanding our approbation, while they improve our faculties; might easily be reduced into a number of classes under their proper heads, and those which are too miscellaneous for any particular series might follow the rest to posterity in a course by themselves; in which order, for the sake of the DOCTOR's reputation, I would earnestly recommend them to be published by all future editors. Neither would the arrangement of his works in prose and verse (for indeed they are both very strangely confused through his own carelessness) be any difficult task to a man of common abilities with any degree of attention.

ONE of the most distinguishing characteristicks of DR. SWIFT was a bright and clear genius, so extreamly piercing, that every the most striking circumstance, arising from any subject whatever, quickly occurred to his imagination; and these he frequently so accumulated one upon another, that perhaps beyond all other poets, of all ages and countries, he deserves in this particular to be the most universally admired. And this choice of circumstances, if any stress can be laid on the opinion of LONGINUS, that great director of our taste and judgment, renders a composition truly noble and sublime. The most remarkable pieces of this sort, are, *The Furniture of a Woman's Mind*; BETTY *the Grizette*; *The Journal of a Modern Lady*; *His Poem on reading Dr.* YOUNG's *Satyres*; MORDANTO; *The Description of a City Shower*; *The Description of Quilca*; *The Description of the Morning*; and, *The Place of the Damned.* This power of the mind gave him also that desperate hand, as POPE terms it, in taking off all sorts of characters. To omit for the present those of a political nature; vid. *The Progress of Poetry*; *The Second Part of* TRAULUS; *The Progress of Love*; *The Character of* CORINNA; and, *The Beautiful young Nymph just going to Bed*; where you will find that his imagination could even dream in the character of an old battered strumpet. And from the same inexhaustible fund of wit, he acquired the historick arts both of designing and colouring, either in groups, or in single portraits. How exact, how lively, and spirited, is that group of figures in *The Journal of a Modern Lady*? . . .

THROUGHOUT all his poetical writings, although many of them be dedicated immediately to the fair sex, there cannot be found, to the best of my recollection, one single distich, addressed in the character of a lover to any one person. If he writ any poems of that sort in his younger days, they must have been destroyed, if they be not concealed. Those verses upon women, which are deemed the most satyrical, were written principally with a view to correct their foibles, to improve their taste, and to make them as agreeable companions at threescore, as at the age of five and twenty: and, by what I can hear, the most exceptionable of his poems in that way have produced some very extraordinary effects in the polite world; which was in truth the ultimate design of his writing *The Lady's Dressing-Room*, and other pieces, which are acknowledged to be somewhat liable to censure on account of their indelicacy.

AMONG the admirers of DR. SWIFT many have compared him to HORACE, making proper allowances for the respective ages in which they are severally flourished. The resemblance however between them is not so exceedingly strong, as that a similitude and manner of writing could have excited the least degree of emulation between them, further than to be equally renowned for their peculiar excellencies. Each of them had, independent of what is generally called a fine taste, a thorough knowledge of the world, superadded to an abundance of learning. Both the one and the other of these great men held the numerous tribe of poets, as well as that motley generation of men called criticks, in the utmost contempt; and at the same time have manifested themselves to be incomparable judges of all that is truly excellent, whether in books or men. Neither of them had the least regard for the STOICKS: and whatever may be said of their being of the EPICUREAN taste, which, if rightly understood, as far from being inconsistent with the highest virtue; neither of them was attached to any particular system of philosophy. HOMER was the darling author both of HORACE and SWIFT. HORACE declares in his epistle to LOLLIUS, that HOMER had abundantly more good sense and wisdom than all the philosophers; and SWIFT's opinion was, that HOMER had more genius than all the rest of the world put together. Yet neither the one nor the other of them have attempted to imitate his manner; but like heroes of a bold and true spirit, have industriously followed the bent of nature, and struck out originals of their own.

[231–7.]

29. John Hawkesworth on Swift

1755

The Works of Jonathan Swift, 6 vols., 1755.
(*a*) *An Account of the Life of Dr. Swift*, Vol. I, part 1.
(*b*) Notes on *Gulliver's Travels*, Vol. I, part 2.
(*c*) Notes on Swift's poetry, Vol. IV, part 1.
(*d*) Notes on *A Collection of Genteel and Ingenious Conversation*, Vol. VI, part 1.
(*e*) Notes on 'A Sermon on the Trinity', Vol. VI, part 1.

Hawkesworth (1715?–73) brought out the first edition of Swift's works which can make any claim to completeness. It consists of six two-part volumes, most of which are organized in 'variorum' fashion, with notes taken from Orrery, Deane Swift, Warburton, and others, along with Hawkesworth's own footnotes and occasional prefatory remarks. The 1755 edition was also published in twelve separate volumes, and it was supplemented by eight additional volumes (mostly correspondence, tracts, and posthumous pieces) before 1784, when Sheridan's edition of Swift's works appeared. To make the footnotes to *Gulliver's Travels* more coherent, reference is made both to Hawkesworth's edition and to Herbert Davis's edition of 1959.

(*a*)

Such was Dr Jonathan Swift, whose writings either stimulate mankind to sustain their dignity as rational and moral beings, by shewing how low they stand in mere animal nature; or fright them from indecency, by holding up its picture before them in its native deformity: And whose life, with all the advantages of genius and learning, was a scale of infelicity gradually ascending, till pain and anguish destroyed the faculties by which they were felt. While he was viewed at a distance with envy, he became a burthen to himself; he was forsaken by his friends, and his memory has been loaded with unmerited reproach: His life therefore does not afford less instruction than his writings, since to the wise it may teach humility, and to the simple content.

[Vol. I, part 1, 40.]

(b)
Gulliver's Travels, Book I

It has been remarked, that courage in whatever cause, though it sometimes excites indignation, is never the object of contempt; and this appears to be true, only because courage is supposed to imply superiority: for this *officer in the guards* becomes extremely ridiculous and contemptible by an act of the most daring curiosity, which sets him in comparison with Gulliver; to whom he was so much inferior, that a blast of the *man-mountain's* nostrils would have endangered his life; and if heroism itself is not proof against ridicule, those surely are *Lilliputians* in philosophy, who consider ridicule as the test of truth.

[Vol. I, part 2, 10 (Davis edn., 27).]

The masculine strength of features, which Gulliver could not see, till he laid his face upon the ground; and the awful superiority of stature in a being, whom he held in his hand; the helmet, the plume, and the sword, are a fine reproof of human pride; the objects of which are trifling distinctions, whether of person or rank; the ridiculous parade and ostentation of a pigmy, which derive not only their origin, but their use, from the folly, weakness, and imperfection of ourselves and others.

[Vol. I, part 2, 14 (Davis edn., 30).]

He who does not find himself disposed to honour this magnanimity [the Emperor's, in freeing Gulliver] should reflect, that a right to judge of moral and intellectual excellence is with great absurdity and injustice arrogated by him who admires, in a being six feet high, any qualities that he despises in one whose stature does not exceed six inches.

[Vol. I, part 2, 21 (Davis edn., 44-5).]

There is something so odious in whatever is wrong, that even those whom it does not subject to punishment, endeavour to colour it with an appearance of right; but the attempt is always unsuccessful, and only betrays a consciousness of deformity by shewing a desire to hide it. Thus the *Lilliputian* court pretended a right to dispense with the strict letter of the law to put Gulliver to death, though by the strict letter of the law only he could be convicted of a crime; the intention of the statute not being to suffer the palace rather to be burnt than pissed upon.

[Vol. I, part 2, 57 (Davis edn., 68–9).]

Gulliver's Travels, Book II

Our inattention to the felicity of sensitive beings merely because they are small is here forcibly reproved: many have wantonly crushed an insect, who would shudder at cutting the throat of a dog; but it should always be remembered, that the least of these

> In mortal sufferance feels a pang as great
> As when a giant dies.

[Vol. I, part 2, 72 (Davis edn., 87).]

By this reasoning the author probably intended to ridicule the pride of those philosophers, who have thought fit to arraign the wisdom and providence in the creation and government of the world; whose cavils are specious, like those of the *Brobdingnagian* sages, only in proportion to the ignorance of those to whom they are proposed.

[Vol. I, part 2, 89 (Davis edn., 103–4).]

Among other dreadful and disgusting images which custom has rendered familiar are those which arise from eating animal food: he who has ever turned with abhorrence from the skeleton of a beast which has been picked whole by birds or vermin, must confess that habit only could have enabled him to endure the sight of the mangled bones and flesh of a dead carcass which every day cover his table: and he who reflects on the number of lives that have been sacrificed to sustain his own, should enquire by what the account has been balanced, and whether his life is become proportionately of more value by the exercise of virtue and piety, by the superior happiness which he has communicated to reasonable beings, and by the glory which his intellect has ascribed to God.

[Vol. I, part 2, 92 (Davis edn., 109–10).]

The author's zeal to justify providence has before been remarked; and these quarrels with nature, or in other words with God, could not have been more forcibly reproved than by shewing, that the complaints upon which they are founded would be equally specious among beings of such astonishing superiority of stature and strength.

[Vol. I, part 2, 126 (Davis edn., 138).]

There are several little incidents which shew the author to have had a deep knowledge of human nature; and I think this is one [when Gulliver's box is taken into the Captain's cabin]. Although the principal advantages enumerated by *Gulliver* in the beginning of this chapter, of mingling again among his countrymen, depended on their being of the same size with himself, yet this is forgotten in his ardour to be delivered: and he is afterwards betrayed into the same absurdity by his zeal to preserve his furniture.

[Vol. I, part 2, 132 (Davis edn., 144).]

From the whole of these two voyages to Lilliput and Brobdingnag, arises one general remark, which, however obvious, has been overlooked by those who consider them as little more than the sport of a wanton imagination. When human actions are ascribed to pigmies and giants, there are few that do not excite either contempt, disgust, or horror. To ascribe them therefore to such beings, was perhaps the most probable method of engaging the mind to examine them with attention, and judge of them with impartiality, by suspending the fascination of habit, and exhibiting familiar objects in a new light. The use of the fable then is not less apparent, than important and extensive; and that this use was intended by the author, can be doubted only by those who are disposed to affirm, that order and regularity are the effects of chance.

[Vol. I, part 2, 139 (Davis edn., 149).]

In this passage there is a peculiar beauty, though it is not discovered at an hasty view. The appearance of *Alexander* with a victorious army immediately after the battle of *Arbela* produces only a declaration that he died by drunkenness; thus inadequate and ridiculous in the eye of reason is the ultimate purpose for which *Alexander* with his army marched into a remote country, subverted a mighty empire, and deluged a nation with blood; he gained no more than an epithet to his name, which after a few repetitions was no longer regarded even by himself: thus the purpose of his resurrection appears to be at least equally important with that of his life, upon which it is a satire not more bitter than just.

[Vol. I, part 2, 182 (Davis edn., 195).]

To this it may possibly be objected, that the perpetuity of youth, health, and vigour would be less a prodigy than the perpetuity of life in a body subject to gradual decay, and might therefore be hoped without greater extravagance of folly; but the sentiment here expressed, is that of a being to whom immortality though not perpetual youth was familiar, and in whom the wish to perpetual youth only would have been extravagant, because that only appeared from facts to be impossible.

[Vol. I, part 2, 199 (Davis edn., 211).]

If it be said, that although the folly of desiring life to be prolonged under the disadvantages of old age is here finely exposed; yet the desire of terrestrial immortality upon terms, on which alone in the nature of things it is possible, an exemption from disease accident and decay, is tacitly allowed. It may be answered, that as we grow old by imperceptible degrees, so for the most part we grow old without repining, and every man is ready to profess himself willing to die, when he shall be overtaken by the decripitude of age in some future period; yet when every other eye sees that this period is arrived, he is still tenacious of life, and murmurs at the condition upon which he received his existence: to reconcile old age therefore to the thoughts of a dissolution appears to be all that was necessary in a moral writer for practical purposes.

[ibid.]

Perhaps it may not be wholly useless to remark, that the sight of a *struldbrug* would not otherwise arm those against the fear of death, who have no hope beyond it, than a man is armed against the fear of breaking his limbs, who jumps out of a window when his house is on fire.

[Vol. I, part 2, 202 (Davis edn., 214).]

Gulliver's Travels, Book IV

Whoever is disgusted with this picture of a *Yahoo*, would do well to reflect, that it becomes his own in exact proportion as he deviates from virtue, for virtue is the perfection of reason. The appetites of those abandoned to vice, are not less brutal and sordid, than that of a *Yahoo* for asses flesh; nor is their life a state of less abject servility.

[Vol. I, part 2, 217 (Davis edn., 223–4).]

It would perhaps be impossible, by the most laboured argument or forcible eloquence to shew the absurd injustice and horrid cruelty of war as effectually, as by this simple exhibition of them in a new light: with war, including every species of iniquity and every art of destruction, we become familiar by degrees under specious terms, which are seldom examined, because they are learned at an age, in which the mind implicitly receives and retains whatever is imprest: thus it happens, that when one man murders another to gratify his lust, we shudder; but when one man murders a million to gratify his vanity, we approve and we admire, we envy and we applaud. If, when this and the preceding pages are read, we discover with astonishment, that when the same events have occurred in history we felt no emotion, and acquiesced in wars which we could not but know to have been commenced for such causes, and carried on by such means; let not him be censured for too much debasing his species, who has contributed to their felicity and preservation by stripping off the veil of custom and prejudice, and holding up in their native deformity the vices by which they become wretched, and the arts by which they are destroyed.

[Vol. I, part 2, 234–5 (Davis edn., 245).]

To mortify pride, which indeed was not made for man, and produces not only the most ridiculous follies, but the most extensive calamity, appears to have been one general view of the author in every part of these *Travels*. Personal strength and beauty, the wisdom and the virtue of mankind, become objects, not of pride, but of humility, in the diminutive stature, and contemptible weakness of the Lilliputians; in the horrid deformity of the Brobdingnagians; in the learned folly of the Laputians; and in the parallel drawn between our manners and those of the Houyhnhnms.

[Vol. I, part 2, 286 (Davis edn., 296).]

(c)
'The Lady's Dressing-Room'

No charge has been more frequently brought against the Dean, or indeed more generally admitted, than that of coarse indelicacy, of which this poem is always produced as an instance. Here then it is but justice to remark, that whenever he offends against delicacy, he teaches it; he stimulates the mind to sensibility, to correct the faults of habitual negligence; as physicians, to cure a lethargy, have recourse to a blister. And though it may reasonably be supposed; that few English ladies have such a dressing-room as Caelia's, yet many may have given sufficient cause for reminding them, that very soon after desire has been gratified, the utmost delicacy becomes necessary, to prevent disgust.

[Vol. IV, part 1, 113).]

'Strephon and Chloe'

This poem has, among others, been censured for indelicacy; but with no better reason than a medecine would be rejected for its ill taste. By attending to the marriage of Strephon and Chloe, the reader is necessarily led to consider the effect of that gross familiarity in which it is to be feared many married persons think they have a right to indulge themselves: he who is disgusted at the picture, feels the force of the precept, not to disgust another by his practice: and let it never be forgotten, that nothing quenches desire like indelicacy; and that when desire has been thus quenched, kindness will inevitably grow cold.

[Vol. IV, part 1, 149.]

If virtue, as some writers pretend, be that which produces happiness, it must be granted, that to practise decency is a moral obligation; and if virtue consists in obedience to a law, as the nuptial laws enjoin both parties to avoid offence, decency will still be duty, and the breach of it will incur some degree of guilt.

[Vol. IV, part 1, 157.]

'A Beautiful young Nymph going to Bed'

This poem, for which some have thought no apology could be offered, deserves on the contrary great commendation, as it much more forcibly restrains the thoughtless and the young from the risk of health and life by picking up a prostitute, than the finest declamation on the sordidness of the appetite.

[Vol. IV, part 1, 146.]

(d)
A Collection of Genteel and Ingenious Conversation

This treatise appears to have been written with the same view, as *The tritical essay on the faculties of the mind*, but upon a more general plan: the ridicule, which is there confined to literary composition, is here extended to conversation, but its object is the same in both; the repetition of quaint phrases picked up by rote either from the living or the dead, and applied upon every occasions to conceal ignorance or stupidity, or to prevent the labour of thoughts to produce native sentiment, and combine such words as will precisely express them.

[Vol. VI, part 1, 55.]

(e)
'A Sermon on the Trinity', Posthumous Prose

In defending the peculiar doctrines of christianity perhaps it is always best to insist upon the positive evidence, as the Dean has done in this sermon: for in every question he who undertakes to obviate objections must necessarily be foiled by him who puts them. By the human intellect little more than the surface of things can be known; and therefore speculative objections, which would puzzle an able philosopher, may be easily raised even against those truths which admit of practical demonstration. It was once objected to a philosopher, who was explaining the laws of motion, that there could be no such thing, for that a body must move either in the place in which it *is*, or in the place in which it is *not*, but both being impossible, there could be no motion: this objection the philosopher immediately removed by walking cross the room; and if none were to triumph in the strength of popular objections against christianity, but those who could otherwise shoew the falacy [sic] of this against motion, the number of *moral philosophers* among us would probably be very few.

[Vol. VI, part I, 172.]

30. W. H. Dilworth on Swift

1758

The Life of Dr. Jonathan Swift, Dean of St. Patrick's, Dublin, 1758.

W. H. Dilworth (*fl.* 1755–83) had a considerable output as a man of letters. He wrote lives of Pope and of Frederick III of Prussia and translated Pizzaro's *The Conquest of Peru* and Cortes's *History of the Conquest of Mexico.* He is represented here at some length because he is unusually conscientious, for his time, in dealing in chronological order with a large number of Swift's individual works, though he does borrow verbations from Orrery and Deane Swift.

The most remarkable productions of Swift's, which had been published in the reign of King William, are, *A Tale of a Tub; The Battle of the Books,* and, *The Discourse concerning the Mechanical Operation of the Spirit.* The first of those pieces, to wit, *A Tale of a Tub,* published in the year 1697, had been originally written by Dr. Swift, when a very young man, in the university of Dublin.

Wessendra Warren, Esquire, a gentleman of fortune in the neighbourhood of Belfast in the North of Ireland, and who was a person of undoubted veracity, often declared, that he had seen *A Tale of a Tub* in the hand-writing of Dr. Swift, when he was but nineteen years old; which, no doubt, received many alterations, amendments and improvements, before it appeared to the world in print.

Besides the abovementioned pieces of Dr. Swift, it is reported, that in the early part of his life he wrote several poems in the irregular kind of metre, miscalled by our moderns Pindaric odes; by which he acquired no reputation. . . .

However, while the Earl of Berkeley was in Ireland, Swift's true poetical vein (Pindaric flights being out of his way) began to discover itself in some occasional pieces which he writ in those times, particularly, *The Ballad on the game of traffick,* the ballad to the old tune of, *The cut-purse;* and,

The humble petition of Mrs. Frances Harris,
Who must starve and die a maid if it miscarries.

The petition of Mrs. Frances Harris, although it may be ranked in that class of poetry which is called low humour, abounds with entertaining raillery, and strong characterizing strokes, which is the distinguishing criterion of a truly original genius from mere imitators, the servile herd of the pen.

[25-9.]

[*A Discourse of the Contests and Dissensions between the Nobles and Commons in Athens and Rome*] consists of matter borrowed from the Greek and Latin history, applied (in favour of the cause which Swift intended to serve) with infinite judgment and sagacity to the contests and dissensions between the nobles and commons of England in those times. It is not to be considered as a defence, but rather as an apology for his supposed friends, and therein he has acted according to the best of his judgment, from the then appearance of things.

If we consider Swift's prose-works, we shall find a certain masterly conciseness of style, that has scarcely been equalled by any other writer. Politics were his favourite topic, as they gave him an opportunity of gratifying his ambition, and thirst of power. Yet even in this road he seldom continued long in one particular path.

He has written miscellaneously, and has chosen rather to appear a wandering comet than a fixed star. For had he applied the superior faculties of his mind to any one great and useful work, he must in consequence have made a more shining figure, and thrown out light sufficient to illumine an whole system of politics.

We shall now proceed to accompany Dr. Swift from the death of King William, or rather from the beginning of this century, to his final retirement from the state-affairs of England, to his deanery-house in Dublin.

Subsequent to the discourse concerning Athens and Rome, there appeared in the year 1703, a paper called, *Meditations upon a broomstick*, written in derision of the style and manner of Mr. Robert Boyle. Tho' we laugh at the humour, we cannot help censuring Swift for having so far indulged his satyrical vein, as to chuse unprovoked so good and excellent a man for the butt of his mirth, tending somewhat to buffoonery. That illustrious personage is revered by all scientific academies for his services rendered in physical enquiries. It was too much Swift's inclination to ridicule those sciences for which he found himself disqualified.

The Tritical Essay upon the Faculties of the Mind was written about the same time with the former; viz. in the year 1703, a piece wherein the spirit of ridicule is very highly displayed; and must force a smile from the most learned gravity. . . .

The genius of Dr. Swift broke forth in the year 1708, with such an astonishing burst of humour, politics, religion, patriotism, wit and poetry, that if the public had been totally unacquainted with all his former reputation, the productions of that one year would have been highly sufficient to have established his fame beyond the reach of envy's sacrilegious hands.

Swift commences the year 1708 with a series of papers relating to Partrige the *Almanack-maker*; wherein those who have a taste for mirth, raillery, and genuine humour, will find abundance of entertainment.

They are designed as a ridicule upon all that absurd tribe, who set up for astrologers, and, without the least ray of true learning, are mighty pretenders to science. The *Elegy on Partrige* can never be sufficiently relished by those who are unacquainted with these whimsical facts.

However, it is a point worth observing, that upon every occasion Dr. Swift is at the Fanaticks, and that so incessantly, that he would not allow a poor cobler, star-monger and quack, to go out of the world, *until upon his death-bed he had declared himself a Non-conformist, and had a fanatical preacher to be his spiritual guide.*

Moreover, it should not be forgotten, that the inquisition in Portugal was pleased, in their great wisdom, to burn the prediction of Isaac Bickerstaff, Esq; and to condemn the author and readers, as Dr. Swift was informed by Sir Paul Methuen, then embassador at the Portugueze court.

It is proper to observe here, that in one of the pamphlets published in the said year, to wit, *A letter from a member of the house of commons in Ireland, to a member of the house of commons in England, concerning the sacramental test*, Dr. Swift appears to have been the patron of Ireland, and to have therein asserted, tho' in a cursory way, the liberties of his country, upon the same noble and generous principles, so directly opposite to slavery and arbitrary power, which he pursued in a more abundant course of reasoning in the year 1724, the flagrant iniquity of the times requiring it.

We think it methodical for the present to wave entering into any particular remarks on the abovementioned letter, as far as it relates to the sacramental test, until we arrive at that period of his life, when he attacks the whole body of Fanatics, and all their inglorious partisans, in the year of our Lord 1733.

That piece, entitled, *The sentiments of a church of England-man, with respect to a religion and government*, was also written in the year 1708, and is adapted to that particular period. Its principal drift seems to tend to unite the parties, by checking that rage and violence which subsisted in those times between Whig and Tory. And perhaps, by recommending in the place of that abominable rancour and malice, which had broken all the laws of charity and hospitality among human-kind, those candid and salutary principles, with respect to religion and government, which, if, rightly comprehended, and vigorously pursued, might certainly preserve the whole constitution, both in church and state.

This tract is well worthy of attention, and serves to confirm an observation which will perpetually occur, that Swift excels in whatever manner or style he assumes. When he is in earnest, his strength of reason carries conviction with it. When he inclines to joke, all competitors, to raise a laugh, are far distanced by him.

The Argument against Abolishing Christianity, which is another production of the same year, is carried on with the highest wit and humour. It is one of the most delicate, and refined pieces of irony that has been wrote in any language, or on any subject.

Grave divines threaten their readers with future punishments; but Swift artfully exhibits a picture of present shame. He judged rightly in imagining, that a small treatise, written with a spirit of mirth and freedom, must be more efficacious than long sermons, or laborious lessons of morality. He endeavours to laugh us into religion, well knowing that we have been often laughed out of it.

The papers of the said year, that immediately follow, are entirely humorous, and relate to Patrige, the almanack-maker. And although they are not only temporary, but also local, yet, by an art peculiar to Swift, they are rendered of every place and time, so as to be read with universal pleasure.

There were likewise, besides, the *Elegy on Patrige*, three other copies of verses written in the same year. Two of them are pieces of wit and raillery against Sir John Vanbrugh.

The third is the tale of *Baucis and Philemon*; wherein there is not only abundance of wit and pleasantry, but some peculiar happy strokes; which, although but very rarely to be found in the works of the finest authors, are the distinguishing marks of an improved and consummate genius. . . .

He wrote, in the same year [1709], *A project for the advancement of religion, and the reformation of manners*; wherein he rebukes all ranks of men for their depravities and corruptions, their profaneness, their blasphemy, and their irreligion. A striking paragraph in this spirited performance gave the first hint to certain bishops, particularly to that most excellent prelate Doctor Atterbury, in the earl of Oxford's ministry, to procure a fund for building fifty new churches in London. . . .

He commenced the champion of Lord Oxford, and his party, so early as the month of November 1710, under the title of *The Whiggish Examiner*: besides which, he wrote several other papers in defence of the queen, constitution, and the ministry.

He wrote particularly, *Some advice to the members of the October club*; *The conduct of the allies*; *Remarks on the barrier treaty*; *The publick spirit of the Whigs*. In the last appears the consummate knowledge the doctor had of the several interests and designs of all the powers in Europe.

We have thought proper, for the use and benefit of those who are not acquainted with the course of the doctor's politics, during the latter part of the queen's reign, to mention the several tracts in that order, according to which they ought to be ranged in the publication of his works; whereby the reader may have a progressive view of this extraordinary genius.

The pieces subsequent to the before-mentioned are; *The preface to the bishop of* S A R U M'*s introduction*; *Some free thoughts upon the present state of affairs*. These pieces are not to be considered in the light of occasional pamphlets, or despicable essays, thrust upon the public by hackney scribblers, in the defence of corruption, and to serve the iniquitous designs of a party.

They are rather to be considered, and read over and over, as lectures of true, unprejudiced, constitutional politics, calculated to expose the enemies of the public, and to maintain, at the same time, the honour of the crown, and the sacred liberties of the people of England.

The several poems of Dr. Swift, relative to those times, and which, in truth, greatly illustrate his political tracts, ought to be read in the following order: *The virtues of* Sid Hamet, *the magician's rod*; *The table of Midas*; *Atlas, or the minister of state*; *Horace's ep.* vii. *book* i. *imitated, and addressed to the earl of Oxford*; *Horace's sat.* vi. *book* i, *part of it imitated*; *The Author on himself*; *The faggot*; *To the earl of Oxford, late lord treasurer, sent to him when he was in the Tower before his trial.*

What mighty reward, what recompence, or what dignities, have been conferred upon this heroic champion of a ministry, this indefatigable defender of the English Constitution, for all his labours? Not a thousandth part of what he deserved from the state, to whom he had done uncommon service, and which they were very sensible of.

The very ministry, whose battles he had fought with so much vigour and success, never once exerted their interest to get him any sort of promotion, either in church or state, in England.

What can such ingratitude be attributed to? Perhaps they dreaded those great abilities which had been their chief support; and therefore were not desirous that he should be raised to an English bishopric; which would have entitled him to a seat in the house of lords, where, very probably, his talents might have broke out on them, in a blaze of politics, that would have rendered him as much the idol of the public, as the wonder of all his cotemporaries.

They therefore, in their great wisdom, (as it were) banished him into Ireland, by giving him the deanery of St. Patrick's, Dublin; which, as he himself expresseth it, was the only small favour he had ever received at their hands, in return for the many eminent services he had done them; and which, when reminded thereof by any sanguine friend of his, they could not deny.

In the beginning of the year 1712, Dr. Swift wrote *A letter to the earl of Oxford, for correcting, improving, and ascertaining the English tongue.* It is a very useful performance. A work of this kind, carried into execution, is much wanted.

In this masterly epistle the doctor complains to his lordship, as *first minister*, in the name of all the learned and polite persons of the nation, that our language is extremely imperfect; that its daily improvements are, by no means, equal to its daily corruptions; that the pretenders to polish and refine it, have chiefly multiplied abuses and absurdities; and that, in many instances, it offends against every part of grammar.

He proves, with irresistible force of reason, that our language ought to be refined to a certain standard, and then fixed for ever. He judiciously remarks the several inconveniences which arise perpetually from our shameful, and unpardonable inattention to such matters.

He doth not however prescribe any methods for ascertaining the language; but throws out some general observations, leaving the rest to the inspection of that society which he hoped would have been speedily instituted by the lord treasurer.

But this noble and truly patriot scheme fell to the ground, partly by the dissensions among the great men at court; and chiefly by the lamented death of that glorious princess Queen Anne: in whose auspicious reign the glory of British arts and arms was at the summit, and is much feared will not be equalled, or even imitated by succeeding ages; so rapidly degenerate we seem to be.

We are now, courteous reader, to behold no more Dr. Swift of any importance in England: his hopes there are crushed for ever. His ministerial friends are degraded, banished, or imprisoned.

Indecent rage, sanguinary zeal, and ill-tempered loyalty, revelled at large throughout the three kingdoms, especially in Ireland: where duels were fought almost every week; and where party contagion was so universal, that the ladies there were as violent as the gentlemen. Even children at school, instead of fighting for apples, quarrelled for kings.

As Dr. Swift was known to have been attached to the queen's last ministry, and to have written against the Whigs, on his retreat to Ireland, he met with frequent indignities from the puritanic protestant part of the populace, and all whiggish parsons of higher rank.

Such a treatment soured his temper, confined his acquaintance, and added a bitterness to his style. From the year seventeen hundred and fourteen, till he appeared in the year twenty, his spirit of politics, and of patriotism, was kept almost closely confined within his own bosom.

His attendance upon the public service of the church was regular, and uninterrupted. Regularity, indeed, was peculiar to him in all his actions, even in the greatest trifles. His hours of walking, and reading, never varied. His motions were guided by his watch, which was so constantly held in his hand, or placed before him upon his table, that he seldom deviated many minutes in the daily revolution of his employments and exercises.

His works, from the year 1714 to 1720, are few in number, and of little importance. Poems to his beloved Stella, and nugatory pieces to Dr. Sheridan, fill up a great part of that period.

At last, in the year 1720, (notwithstanding the many gross affronts he had received) he resolved, as far as lay in his power, to correct the errors and the blunders of his deluded countrymen; and with that view he wrote short and lively proposals, *For the universal use of Irish manufacture in cloaths, and furniture of houses,* &c. *utterly rejecting and renouncing everything wearable that comes from England.*

On account of the said proposals, a prosecution was set on foot against Waters, the printer of them, and carried on with so much violence, that the then chief justice, Whitshed, a virulent Whig, thought proper, in a manner the most extraordinary, to keep the jury eleven hours, and send them back nine times out of courts, until he had wearied them into a special verdict.

Swift, fired with a zeal for *liberty* and *public interest*, was resolved to avenge his printer's prosecution on the petty tyrant who had been the promoter of it. Two or three lashes from his satyric genius, proved sufficient to make the chief justice thoroughly odious and contemptible in the eyes of the public for that time; more of him hereafter.

This national pamphlet turned the tide of popular favours entirely to him. The prejudiced rabble, that, not long since, used to throw dirt at him as he walked in the streets, now, wherever he went, bowed to him as to their guardian angel. His sayings of wit and humour were echoed from mouth to mouth by the people, now become idolatrous of him. In short, nothing was spoke of in Dublin but, *The dean*, by excellence, distinguished above all others.

Some little pieces of poetry, to the same purpose, were no less acceptable and engaging. The inviolable attachment which *the dean* bore to the true interest of Ireland, was no longer doubted. He was as much reverenced by the people, for his patriotism, as admired for his wit.

Joy preceded, and respect followed, wherever he passed. His popularity was become of such general influence, that most disputes about property, among his neighbours, were submitted to his arbitration; from which to appeal, would have been looked on as a kind of impiety. In fine, he was the darling oracle of the people.

Being alarmed, in the year 1724, with fresh matter of indignation, to resume his pen, he oposed, overturned, and totally defeated the scheme of an infamous projector; encouraged and supported in his villainy by those who were understood to be the chief directors in all public affairs, and which had derived its source from the then national calamity.

There having been a scarcity of copper coin in Ireland, to so great a degree that, for some time past, the chief manufacturers throughout the kingdom, had been obliged to pay in pieces of tin, or in other tokens of suppositious value. Such a method proved very disadvantageous to the lower parts of traffic, and was, in general, an impediment to the commerce of the kingdom.

To remedy this evil, the late King William (of therefore deservedly glorious, and immortal memory to Ireland) had granted a patent, for the term of fourteen years, to one William Wood, to coin half-pence and farthings, in England, to the value of a certain sum, for the use of

Ireland. These half-pence and farthings were to be received by those only who should chuse so to do, but to be forced upon none.

They were about eleven parts in twelve under the real value. But, supposing they had been made ever so good, no man living was obliged, or by virtue of the prerogative of the crown, could be compelled to receive them in any payment whatsoever; nothing being, in truth, the current coin of England or Ireland, besides gold and silver, of the right sterling, and standard.

The baser metals are only, by custom, accepted for the conveniency of change; which every man that pleases may refuse whenever he shall think proper.

This patent of Wood's appearing to be of such dangerous consequence to the public, and of such exorbitant advantage to the patentee, Dr. Swift, now known in Dublin by the unequivocal title of, *The Dean*, in order to expose the fraud to the competency of all understandings, wrote, and caused to be published, a short treatise, with this remarkable and humourous title:

A letter to the shopkeepers, tradesmen, farmers, and common people of Ireland, concerning the brass halfpence, coined by one William Wood, *Hardware-man, with a Design to have them pass in this Kingdom. By* M. B. Drapier.

In this letter, the judicious cannot but observe, that he hath adapted his style, his phrases, his humour, and his address, in a very surprizing manner, to the taste and apprehension of the populace. Nor indeed is the title page wholly void of that captivating rhetoric, which is admired by the common people; for it concludes like that of *The whole duty of man, very proper to be kept in every family*.

This first letter was succeeded by several others to the same purpose, but without confining his style and phrases to the taste of the multitude; and although through the whole of them he talks of liberty in a strain highly becoming a warm and zealous defender of the rights of his country, which he maintains with great force of law, reason, justice, and eloquence, he never once deviates, in the whole series of his arguments, from the distinguishing characteristics of a most loyal subject; whatever might have been insinuated to the contrary by some degenerate wretches, and sycophants to the pandars of power.

At the sound of the Drapier's patriot trumpet, the spirit of the Irish nation was rouzed. Most persons of every rank, party, and denomination, were convinced, that the admission of Wood's copper coin must prove the ruin of the kingdom.

The Whig, the Tory, the Papist, the Fanatic, all listed themselves volunteers under the Drapier's banner, and appeared all equally zealous to serve in the common cause. Much heat of blood, and many fiery speeches against the then administration, were the consequence of this union of parties; nor would the flames of commotion have been allayed, notwithstanding the many severe threats from the courts of law, and several government-proclamations, had not Wood withdrawn his patent; the timely cessation of which, perhaps, prevented the general insurrection of a most loyal people, when not too far provoked.

Such had been the iniquity of the prostitute delegates of power in those days, that a reward of three hundred pounds was offered for the author of the *Fourth Letter*; and chiefly, because he had maintained therein the liberty of his country, and declared, in very spirited terms, worthy of a brave and resolute mind, that he would continue firm and faithful to his sovereign lord the king, whatever turn, in the vicissitudes of this world, his majesty's affairs might possibly take in other parts of his dominions.

As the author of that *Fourth Letter* could not be discovered, Harding the Printer was indicted in the usual forms, and brought to the King's Bench to be tried before the abovementioned Chief Justice Whitshed. But the noble spirited jury, friends to their country and the public welfare, would not find the bill.

[32–56.]

At the close of the Drapier's letters, which are all very serious and political, is a piece of humour and ridicule, which occasioned a great deal of mirth and laughter in those times. The title of this whimsical tract is, *A full and true account of the solemn procession to the gallows, at the execution of* William Wood, *Esquire, and Hardware-man.* . . .

As the Drapier's letters, written in the year 1724, &c. are founded on the secure basis of the laws of our country, and supported throughout the whole with the warmest zeal for liberty, they will, nay must, for ever command the veneration of those, who are not unworthy to enjoy the blessings of our constitution.

The next piece of the Dean's is, *A short view of the state of* Ireland, written in the year 1727. In this pamphlet the author enumerates fourteen causes of any country's flourishing and growing rich; and then examines what effects arise from these causes in the kingdom of Ireland. It must be owned, that since the writing of this pamphlet, several alterations for the better have taken place in Ireland, through the universal encouragement given to industry, the præmiums of the Dublin society, &c. . . .

Subsequent to the former is a piece entitled, *An answer to a paper, called a memorial of the poor inhabitants, tradesmen, and labourers of the kingdom of Ireland*; written in the year 1728, which, as far as it relates to agriculture and grazing, displays the great evils relative to these two heads, under which the kingdom of Ireland still groans.

The pamphlet which comes next in order of succession, is written with Swift's usual peculiarity of humour, and is entitled *A modest proposal for preventing the children of poor people in* Ireland, *from being a burden to their parents and country; and for making them beneficial to the public*; written in the year 1729.

The extraordinary proposal is to fatten beggars children, and sell them for food to rich landlords, and persons of quality. This tragicomic treatise, equally the product of the author's despair and benevolence, seemeth to have been written in the bitterness of Swift's soul, and principally addressed to the consideration of those merciless tyrants, who starve, and oppress their fellow-creatures, even to the shame and destruction of their country.

Though this serio-comic proposal of fattening the children of beggars, cottagers, and farmers, as they do lambs and pigs for the markets, and selling their carcasses to the wealthy, may at first sight alarm all humane readers, yet it will on reflection appear to be the most effectual method of touching hard hearted landlords, the bane of Ireland, upon whom all mild arguments had failed, by recommending to them, as their properest food, and to which they were duly entitled, the childrens flesh, whose parents they had already devoured. . . .

Having heretofore observed, that Swift did not appear as a political writer from the year 1714 to the year 1720, the curious reader may desire us to inform him how he employed his leisure hours all that time, it being impossible for so great and active a genius to lie all that time fallow; little or nothing of his appearing in that space, but a few poetical pieces on domestic occurrences, to Dr. Sheridan and Stella, and to be looked on as sportive or complimentary trifles.

He employed all his leisure time of these five or six years in writing *The travels of* Lemuel Gulliver *into several remote nations of the world.* The work is divided into four parts, and is to be looked on in no other light, than as a direct, plain, and bitter satire against the innumerable follies and corruptions in law, politics, learning, morals, and religion.

In these travels the author has exerted a force of ridicule and satire, pointed so directly against the depravities of human kind, and supported with such abundance of pleasantry and wit, as, indeed, more than persuadeth us to believe that his intention was either to laugh vice and immorality (if possible) quite out of the world; or, at least, to avenge the cause of virtue, on all the abettors and patrons of iniquitous measures.

Let us proceed, by taking a joint view of the two first parts. In one, the inhabitants of Lilliput are represented, as if reflected from a convex mirror, by which every object is reduced to a despicable minuteness. In the other the inhabitants of Brobdingnag, by a contrary mirror, are enlarged to a shocking deformity.

In Lilliput we behold a set of puny insects, or animalcules in human shape, ridiculously engaged in affairs of importance. In Brobdingnag the monsters of enormous size are employ'd in trifles. There is observed throughout, by the ingenious author, a great exactness in the just proportion and appearances of the several objects thus lessened and magnified.

Lemuel's voyage to Lilliput, as well as that to Brobdingnag (the machinery, and some particular sallies of nature, wit, and humour, only excepted) are entirely political.

The author's meaning throughout, the whole, especially where he glances at the history of his own times, the wars of Europe, and the factions of Whig and Tory, is to be found so very near the surface, that it would almost be an affront to the common reason of those, who are at all versed in the affairs of the world, to offer at any farther explication.

The third part, that is, *Gulliver's voyage to Laputa*, is designed to turn into ridicule the absurd and vain pretensions, of projectors, chemists, and mathematicians, with all the rest of the idly speculative tribes, who waste their precious time in visionary studies, by no means calculated to improve the faculties of the mind, or to enlarge the number of ideas.

The mathematicians (particularly those entirely devoted to their circles, telescopes, &c.) are a race of mortals, so very abstracted from all the necessary affairs of life, that scarce one in a score of them can converse rationally. A certain degree of mathematical knowledge is of great use in several arts and sciences.

The account GULLIVER gives of his entertainment at Glubdubdrib, or the island of sorcerers, abounds with a noble extravagance of wit, and is most humourously entertaining.

The idly celebrated son of Philip of Macedon, called Alexander the great, at the head of his army, just after the battle of ARBELLA, assured

GULLIVER, upon his honour, that he was not poisoned, but died of a fever, by excessive drinking.

And afterwards, the boast of Carthage, and the terror of Rome, HANNIBAL, declared also to him, upon his honour, that when passing the Alps, he had not a drop of vinegar with him in his camp.

Lemuel Gulliver, in the eighth chapter of the voyage to Laputa, becomes curious to know the situation of poets and philosophers, who have as eagerly contended for fame as the abovementioned heroes. He desires that Homer and Aristotle may make their appearance at the head of their commentators.

HOMER, as Gulliver informs us, 'was the taller and comlier person of the two, walked very erect, for one of his age; and his eyes were the most quick and piercing he had ever beheld.' It is certain that Homer has rather gained than lost vigour by his years.

Two thousand six hundred years have not unbraced the nerves of his reputation, or given one wrinkle to the brow of his fame. All that our author means here by making Gulliver give Homer the most quick and piercing eyes he had ever beheld, is to insinuate that the great, father of *epic*, and therein of all other poetry, had the most quick and piercing genius of all the human race.

The description of Aristotle is very fine; for, in a few words, it represents the true nature of his works; 'He stooped much, and made use of a staff, His visage was meagre, his hair lank and thin, and his voice hollow.'

By not having the immortal spirit of HOMER, he was unable to keep his body erect: and the staff which weakly supported him, like his commentators, made that defect more conspicuous. He wanted not some useful qualifications; but their real ornaments, like his hair, were thin and ungraceful. His style was harsh, and, like his voice, had neither force nor harmony.

Aristotle was, without doubt, a man of great genius and penetration; but he has done infinite more prejudice than service to real literature. He studied words more than facts, and delivered his philosophy perplexed with such intricate, logical terms, as have laid a foundation for the endless scholastic disputations, which have corrupted and retarded the progress of learning.

He waged war with all his predecessors. He never quotes an author, except with a view to refute his opinion. Like the great Turk, he did not think his literary throne could stand in safety till after having first destroy'd his brethren.

The famous *Stagyrite* was as ambitious in science as his pupil Alexander was in arms. He aimed to be a despotic original, and not only the prince, but the tyrant of philosophy.

The description of the *Struld-brugs,* in the tenth chapter, is an instructive piece of morality; for, if considered in a serious light, as it ought to be, it tends to reconcile us to our final dissolution.

Death, when set in contrast with the immortality of the *Struldbrugs,* is no longer the king of terrors: he loses his sting. He appears to be a friend. We chearfully obey his summons, because it brings certain relief to the greatest miseries. Swift, in this description shines in a particular manner.

Alas! he felt, perhaps, in himself the effects of approaching age, and tacitly dreaded that period of life, in which, (by the weakness enfeebled flesh is heir to) he might become a representative of those miserable immortals. His apprehensions have been unfortunately fulfilled.

He lived to be the most melancholy sight that was ever beheld; yet, even in that condition, he continued to instruct, by appearing a striking instance of the frailty of our nature, and sufficient to mortify that vanity which is but too apt to dilate our bosoms upon any trivial advantage. . . .

The fourth and last part of Lemuel Gulliver's imaginary travels, is a voyage to the *Houynhnyhms.* Our general answer to all those whose mistaken delicacy, or rather affected squeamishness, may be offended thereat, is; that if the brutality and filthiness of the *Yahoes* be painted by the powerful genius of Dean Swift, in colours the most shocking and detestable, as these certainly are, and, in fact, they ought to have been; the picture is the more striking, as well as the more terrible: and upon that very account the more likely to enforce the obligation of religion and virtue upon the human mind.

Having thus far considered *The dean* as a politico-philosophical writer, let us now, *en passant*, say something of his poetical merit, which was really considerable.

His descriptions, wherein there constantly appear the distinguishing marks of his own peculiar talents, are extremely just and lively. Many of his groups are not to be excelled by any painter's imagination. His rhimes and his numbers are chaste and delicate.

In places when, rather by accident than choice, he rises from the earth, and soars into the regions of poetry, he is equal to the finest masters among the Greeks and Romans. His ideas are lofty, and his versification musically sonorous.

And yet, after all, he is not to be considered in the light of a professed poet. The multitude of his various writings, in various subjects, both in verse and prose, being an evident demonstration, that he was superior to any particular course of learning. He was born to be the encourager of virtue, and the terror of the wicked.

He never sat musing in his elbow chair in quest of new subjects, for the exercise of his genius, and the advancement of his fame; but writ occasionally, to please and reform the world, as either politics or humour gave the spur to his faculties.

There are but few of his poems that seem to have been the labour of more than one day; how greatly soever they might have been corrected and polished afterwards, to his own liking, before he transcribed them.

[62–76.]

If it cannot be denied on one hand, that there runs an unabating vein of satire throughout all the writings of Dean Swift, it must be owned on the other, as he himself declares, no age could have more deserved it than that in which he was destined to live.

He is, therefore, justly entitled to all the praise we can bestow upon him, for having exerted his abilities (which were uncommonly great) in the defence of honour, virtue, and his country.

An article worthy of special observation is, that in his general satire, wherein, perhaps, thousands were equally meant, he hath never once, through malice, inserted the name of any one person. The vice, nevertheless, he exposed to contempt, and ridicule.

But, in his particular satire, when egregious monsters, traitors to the commonwealth, and slaves to party, are the objects of his resentment, he cuts without mercy; in order that those, who trespass in defiance of laws, might live in fear of him.

If our readers expect that, in this work, we should enter into a minute detail of Swift's poetry, in order to point out his most striking beauties; our humble answer is, That, as for the dull or ignorant, such a disquisition would be quite fruitless: so all persons of taste and learning are enabled to judge for themselves, as well as to admire the real beauties of an author, and accompany his flights into the most distant regions of poetry, without guide or monitor.

From these considerations we shall be very sparing in references and quotations of that sort. It is proper, however, to observe, that, in general, Swift's poetical writings, which, in their present situation, are only a beautiful heap of confusion, rather distracting the eye, and flashing upon the imagination, than conducting our fancies into poetical scenes, and commanding our approbation, while they improve our faculties, might easily be reduced to a number of classes under proper heads; and those which are too miscellaneous for any particular scenes, might follow the rest to posterity, in a course by themselves. . . .

One of the most distinguishing characters of Dr. Swift was, a bright and clear genius; so extremely piercing, that every, the most striking, circumstance, arising from any subject whatever, quickly occurred to his happy imagination; and those he frequently so accumulated one upon another, that, perhaps, beyond all other poets, of all ages and countries, he deserves in this particular to be the most universally admired.

And this choice of circumstances (if any stress can be laid on the opinion of Longinus, that great director of our taste and judgment) renders a composition truly noble and sublime. For his masterly sentiments thereon, we refer our readers to his tenth section.

The most remarkable pieces of this sort are *The furniture of a woman's mind*; BETTY, *the Grizette*; *The journal of a modern lady*; *His poem on reading Dr. Young's satires*; *Mordanto*; *The description of a city shower*; *The description of Quilca*; *The description of the morning*; and *The place of the damned*.

His great powers of the mind gave him also that *desperate hand*, as Pope terms it, in taking off all sorts of characters. We shall omit, for the present, those of a political nature, and mention but *The progress of poetry*; the second part of *Traulus*; *The progress of love*; *The character of Corinna*; and, *The beautiful young nymph just going to bed*.

By the last of these poems it appears, that his imagination could even dream in the character of an old battered strumpet. From the same inexhaustible fund he acquired the historic arts, both of designing and colouring, either in groups or in single portraits.

For instance: how exact, how lively and spirited, is that group of figures in *The journal of a modern lady*! how admirable also in point of single-portrait, if we consider the design, the attitude, the drapery, or the colouring, is that excellent representation of Cassinus in *The tragical elegy*!

Throughout all Dean Swift's poetical productions, although many of them be dedicated immediately to the fair sex, there cannot be found, to the best of our recollection, one single distich addressed in the character of a lover to any person. If he wrote any poems of that sort in his younger days, they must have been destroyed; for, after the strictest research we have been able to make, we could never come to the knowledge of any.

Those verses upon women, which are deemed the most satirical, were written principally with a view to correct their foibles, to improve their taste, and to make them as agreeable companions at three score, as at the age of five and twenty.

By all that ever we could hear, the most exceptionable of his poems in that way, have produced some very extra-ordinary effects in the public world; which was, in truth, the ultimate design of his writing *The lady's dressing-room*, and other pieces, which are acknowledged to be somewhat liable to censure on account of their indelicacy.

It is impossible to remark on the poetical works of Dean Swift, without being somewhat particular on the piece entitled, *Cadenus and Vanessa*; for that poem is built on the finest model, supported with infinite humour, wit and gaiety, embellished with ideas the most lovely and delicate, beautifully adorned with variety of the most attractive images, and conducted, throughout the whole, with such perfect regularity, that, beyond all other pieces, whether of Dean Swift, or of any other poet that has writ in the English language, it appears the best calculated to abide the severest examination of the critics.

[80–6.]

That pamphlet, [*The publick Spirit of the Whigs*] which caused all this mighty bustle, was written in the year 1712, by the consent, nay, approbation and encouragement of the then ministry. In the style and conduct, this piece is one of the boldest, as well as one of the most masterly ever Swift wrote; and of whom it is peculiarly to be remarked, that on whatever topic he employed his pen, the subject which he treats is so excellently managed, as to seem to have been the whole study and application of his life: so that it may (without partiality) be asserted of him, that he is the greatest master through a greater variety of materials, than perhaps have ever been discussed by any other writer.

As for the amusing trifles, the *Minutissimae* of Swift's writings, which we incline to think, he would not have suffered to be published, fond as he appeared to be of seeing his reveries in print, if he had been in the full vigour of his understanding; or had duly considered, that such trifles, which are weak as feathers in supporting a reputation, are as heavy as lead in sinking it.

His epistolary correspondence was mostly with the greatest geniusses of England; to wit, Mr. Pope, whom he had a particular friendship for,

Lord Bolinbroke, &c. Swift has been often heard to say, 'When I sit down to write a letter, I never lean upon my elbow, till I have finished it.'

By this expression he meant, that he never studied for particular phrases, or polished paragraphs. His letters therefore are the true representatives of his mind. They are written in the warmth of his affections; and when they are considered in the light of kindness and sincerity, they illustrate his character to a very high degree.

Throughout his various correspondence, courteous reader, you will discover very strong marks of an anxious benevolent friend, and the misanthropic tincture of his mind gradually vanish in the good natured man.

On reading his letters to Mr. Gay, you will be of our sentiment; and on reading those to Dr. Sheridan, in the eighth volume, you will be farther confirmed in that opinion. We may therefore compound to lose satire and raillery, when we gain humanity and tenderness in their stead.

Yet even in some of Swift's highest scenes of benevolence, his expressions are delivered in such a manner, as to seem rather the effects of haughtiness than of good nature: but he is never to be looked upon as a traveller in the common road.

He must be viewed by a *camera obscura*, that turns all objects the contrary way. When he appears most angry, he is most pleased; when most humble, he is most assuming. Such was the man, and in such variegated colours must he be painted.

[96–9.]

As Dean Swift's works are now published, the tract, which immediately follows the will, is, *The directions to servants*. It is imperfect and unfinished. The editor tells us, that a preface and a dedication were to have been added to it. According to the best informations we have been able to get, this pamphlet was not published till after the dean's death. But it is said that the manuscript was handed about, and applauded in his life-time.

To say the most that can be offered in its favour, the tract is written in so facetious a kind of low humour, that it must please many readers: nor is it without some degree of merit, by pointing out with an amazing exactness (and what in a less trivial case must have been called judgment) the faults, tricks, blunders, lies, and various knaveries of domestic servants.

How much time must have been employed in putting together such a work! What an intenseness of thought must have been bestowed upon the lowest, and most slavish scenes of life? It is one of those subjects, that the utmost strain of wit can scarce sustain from sinking.

A man of Swift's exalted genius ought constantly to have soared into higher regions. He ought to have looked upon persons of inferior abilities as children, whom nature had appointed him to instruct, encourage, and improve.

Superior talents seem to have been intended by Providence as public benefits; and the person, who possesses such blessings, is certainly answerable to heaven for those endowments, which he enjoys above the rest of mankind.

[106–7.]

There are also published, in the same volume with the above tracts [minor Irish tracts], three sermons of the *dean*; and curious for such reasons as would make other works despicable. They were writ in a careless, hurried manner; and were the offspring of necessity, not of choice: so that the original force of his genius is to be seen more in those compositions, that were the legitimate sons of duty, than in other pieces, that were the natural sons of love.

They were held in such low esteem, in his own thoughts, that, some years before he died, he gave away the whole collection to Dr. Sheridan, with the utmost indifference: 'Here', says he, 'are a bundle of my old sermons; you may have them if you please. They may be of use to you; they have never been of any to me.'

The parcel given to Dr. Sheridan is said to have consisted of five and thirty sermons, of which the three above hinted at are the only published. The first is upon *Mutual subjection*, and that duty which is owing from one man to another. A clearer style, or a discourse more properly adapted to a public audience, can scarce be framed. Every paragraph is simple, nervous, and intelligible.

The next sermon, or rather moral essay, is upon the *Testimony of conscience*; in which the author inserts some very striking observations upon such false notions of honour as are too prevalent in the world. The third discourse, upon the *Trinity*, is indeed a sermon, and one of the best in its kind.

Let us now say somewhat of other productions of Swift, hitherto omitted by us; for it is almost impossible to be scrupulously methodical in giving an account of his writings, which are on such a variety of subjects, written at such different periods of time, and so confusedly huddled together in all the editions we have as yet had of them.

The *Battle of the books* took its rise from the controversy between Sir William Temple and Mr. Wotton: a controversy which made much noise, and employed many pens, towards the latter end of the last century.

This humorous treatise, is drawn up in an heroi-comic style; in which Swift, with great wit and spirit, gives the victory to the former. This is not an original invention of Swift's, but borrowed from a French work, called, *The way between the ancients and the moderns,* in an heroi-comic style, and divided into nine books.

The two chief heroes among Swift's modern generals, are Wotton and Bentley. Their figures are display'd in the most disadvantageous attitudes. The former is described, 'Full of spleen, dulness, and ill manners'. The latter; 'Tall, without shape or comliness; large, without strength or proportion.'

The *Battle of the books* is maintained by the antients with great superiority of strength, though not of numbers; and ends with the demolition of Bentley and his friend Wotton, by the lance of the late earl of Orrery, father of the present earl, of the same title, and also earl of Cork.

'*The fragment; or, A discourse concerning the mechanical operation of the Spirit.*' is a satire against enthusiasm, and those affected inspirations, which constantly begin in folly, and very often end in vice. In this treatise the author has revelled in too licentious a vein of sarcasm.

Many of his ideas are nauseous, some are indecent, and others have an irreligious tendency. In all those tracts, where Swift's splenetic disposition runs down, nay, degrades humanity, he tries to make us uneasy with ourselves, and unhappy in our present sphere of existence; there we think him undefensible; and that censure is justly pointed at such works. . . .

There are two letters of admonition in the dean's works; but we cannot ascertain the time when wrote. The one is 'To a young gentleman lately entered into holy orders;' the other, 'To a young lady on her marriage.' The former ought to be read by all the young clergymen in the three kingdoms; and the latter by all the new-married women.

Here again blazes forth, in a conspicuous manner, the peculiar happiness of Swift's singular knack of writing. These letters, though addressed only to a young clergyman, and a newly-married lady, are adapted to every age and understanding.

They contain observations that delight and improve every mind, and they will be read with pleasure, as well as advantage, by the oldest and most exemplary divines, and by the most distinguished and most accomplished ladies. . . .

Polite conversation is a ridiculous exposition of the quaint and absurd phrases that were in his time practised by the unfurnished heads of both sexes, miscalled *high life*, or people of fashion; though, by their phraseology, which is here exhibited, it appears that none could be lower in understanding.

We shall not take upon us to defend *The lady's dressing-room*, which hath been universally condemned as deficient in point of delicacy, even to the highest degree. However, the best apology that can be made for it, is to suppose that the author exhibited his *Celia* in the most hideous colours he could find, lest she might be mistaken for a goddess, when she was only a mortal.

It must, however, on the whole, be acknowledged, that whatever might have been Swift's views, designs, or motives in order to deter from impudicity, that his want of delicacy and decorum in this and many other pieces; such as,

> Corinna *high in Drury-lane*,
> *For whom no shepherd sighs in vain*, &c.

Must not hope to find even the shadow of an excuse. It would be the blindest partiality not to own that he too frequently forgot that politeness and tenderness of manners which are undoubtedly due to human kind.

[110–17.]

31. Edward Young on *Gulliver's Travels*

1759

Conjectures on Original Composition in a Letter to the Author of Sir Charles Grandison, 2nd ed., 1759.

Edward Young (1683–1765) is famous for *The Complaint, or Night-thoughts* as well as for the *Conjectures on Original Composition*, which went through two editions in 1759. Young knew Swift and was himself a verse satirist of some accomplishment, but he was of the more sentimental school of the eighteenth century, and to him *Gulliver's Travels* was not the comic satire which it seems to have been to Swift's friends, but a peevish 'blasphemy' against human nature.

Of Genius there are two species, an Earlier, and a Later; or call them *Infantine*, and *Adult*. An Adult Genius comes out of Nature's hand, as *Pallas* out of *Jove's* head, at full growth, and mature: *Shakespeare's* Genius was of this kind: On the contrary, *Swift* stumbled at the threshold, and set out for Distinction on feeble knees: His was an Infantine Genius; a Genius, which, like other Infants, must be nursed, and educated, or it will come to nought: Learning is its Nurse, and Tutor; but this Nurse may overlay with an indigested Load, which smothers common sense; and this Tutor may mislead, with pedantic Prejudice, which vitiates the best understanding. As too great admirers of the Fathers of the Church have sometimes set up their Authority against the true sense of Scripture; so too great admirers of the Classical Fathers have sometimes set up their Authority, or Example, against Reason.

[31–2.]

But as nothing is more easy than to write originally wrong; Originals are not here recommended, but under the strong guard of my first rule —*Know thyself*. *Lucian*, who was an Original, neglected not this rule, if we may judge by his reply to one who took some freedom with him.

He was, at first, an apprentice to a statuary; and when he was reflected on as such, by being called *Prometheus*, he replied, 'I am indeed the inventor of new work, the model of which I owe to none; and, if I do not execute it well, I deserve to be torn by twelve vultures, instead of one'.

If so, O *Gulliver*! dost thou not shudder at thy brother *Lucian's* vultures hovering o'er thee? Shudder on! they cannot shock thee more, than decency has been shock'd by thee. How have thy *Houyhnhnms* thrown thy judgment from its feat; and laid thy imagination in the mire? In what ordure hast thou dipt thy pencil? What a monster hast thou made of the

> *Human face divine?*
> > > Milton.

This writer has so satirised human nature, as to give a demonstration in himself, that it deserves to be satirised. But, say his wholesale admirers, Few could *so* have written; true, and Fewer *would*. If it required great abilities to commit the fault, greater still would have saved him from it. But whence arise such warm advocates for such a performance? From hence, *viz.* before a character is established, merit makes fame; afterwards fame makes merit. *Swift* is not commended for this piece, but this piece for *Swift*. He has given us some beauties which deserve all our praise; and our comfort is, that his faults will not become common; for none can be guilty of them, but who have wit as well as reputation to spare. His wit had been less wild, if his temper had not jostled his judgment. If his favourite *Houyhnhnms* could write, and *Swift* had been one of them, every horse with him would have been an ass, and he would have written a panegyrick on mankind, saddling with much reproach the present heroes of his pen: On the contrary, being born amongst men, and, of consequence, piqued by many, and peevish at more, he has blasphemed a nature little lower than that of angels, and assumed by far higher than they: But surely the contempt of the world is not a greater virtue, than the contempt of mankind is a vice. Therefore I wonder that, though forborn by others, the laughter-loving *Swift* was not reproved by the venerable Dean, who could sometimes be very grave.

For I remember, as I and others were taking with him an evening's walk, about a mile out of *Dublin*, he stopt short; we passed on; but, perceiving that he did not follow us, I went back; and found him fixed as a statue, and earnestly gazing upward at a noble elm, which in its uppermost branches was much withered, and decayed. Pointing at it, he said, 'I shall be like that tree, I shall die at top.' As in this he seemed to prophesy like the Sybils; if, like one of them, he had burnt part of his works, especially *this* blasted branch of a noble Genius, like her too, he might have risen in his demand for the rest.

[61–5.]

32. George Lord Lyttelton on Swift

1760

Dialogues of the Dead. The Works of George Lord Lyttelton (3 vols.), 3rd ed., 1776, Vol. II.
(a) Dialogue IV, 'Mr. Addison—Dr. Swift', 120–4.
(b) Dialogue XXIII, 'Rabelais—Lucian', 288–9.

Lyttelton (1709–73) is perhaps best known today for his verse epistle to Pope, which is prefixed to several editions of Pope's works. Though he was popular at Court, Lyttelton's notorious absent-mindedness and slowness in debate inhibited his political career. In literary circles Lyttelton was either greatly admired or greatly disliked. Fielding, Lyttelton's old schoolmate, dedicated Tom Jones to him, but Smollett burlesqued Lyttelton and made unkind allusions to him in his novels. Dialogues of the Dead was first published anonymously in 1760, and appeared in second and third editions in the same year; it includes some genuine critical judgements, in spite of its generally frivolous tone.

(a)

MERCURY.—Dr. Swift, I rejoice to see you.—How does my old lad! how does honest Lemuel Gulliver? have you been in Lilliput lately, or in the *flying island*, or with your good nurse, Glumdalclitch? Pray when did you *eat a crust with lord* Peter? is Jack as mad still as ever? I hear that, since you published the history of his cafe, the poor fellow, by more gentle usage, is almost got well. If he had but more food, he would be as much in his senses as *brother* Martin himself. But Martin, they tell me, has lately spawned a strange brood of Methodists, Moravians, Hutchinsonians, who are madder than ever Jack was in his worst days. It is a great pity you are not alive again, to make a new edition of your *Tale of the Tub* for the use of these fellows.—Mr. Addison, I beg your pardon. I should have spoken to you sooner; but I was so struck with the sight of my old friend the doctor, that I forgot for a time the respects due to you.

SWIFT. Addison, I think our dispute is decided, before the judge has heard the cause.

ADDISON. I own it is, in your favour;—but—

MERCURY—Dont be discouraged, friend Addison. Apollo perhaps would have given a different judgement. I am a wit, and a rogue, and a foe to all dignity. Swift and I naturally like one another. He worships me more than Jupiter, and I honour him more than Homer. But yet, I assure you, I have a great value for you.—Sir Roger de Coverley, Will Honeycomb, Will Wimble, the country gentleman in the Freeholder, and twenty more characters, drawn with the finest strokes of unaffected wit and humour in your admirable writings, have obtained for you a high place in the class of my *authors*, though not quite so high a one as that of the dean of St. Patrick's. Perhaps you might have got before him, if the decency of your nature and the cautiousness of your judgement would have given you leave. But, allowing that, in the force and spirit of his wit he has really the advantage, how much does he yield to you in all the elegant graces; in the fine touches of delicate sentiment; in developing the secret springs of the soul; in shewing the mildlights and shades of a character; in distinctly marking each line, and every soft gradation of tints, which would escape the common eye! Who ever painted like you the beautiful parts of human nature, and brought them out from under the shade even of the greatest simplicity, or the most ridiculous weaknesses; so that we are forced to admire, and feel that we *venerate*, even while we are *laughing!* Swift was able to do nothing that approaches to this.—He could draw an ill face, or caricature a good one, with a masterly hand: but there was all his power; and, if I be to speak as a *god*, a worthless power it is. Yours is divine. It tends to exalt human nature.

SWIFT. Pray, good Mercury, (if I may have liberty to say a word for myself) do you think that my talent was not highly beneficial to *correct* human nature? is whipping of no use, to mend naughty boys?

MERCURY—Men are generally not so patient of whipping as boys; and *a rough satirist* is seldom known to mend them. Satire, like antimony, if it be used as a medicine, must be rendered less corrosive. Yours is often rank poison. But I will allow that you have done some good in your way, though not half so much as Addison did in his.

ADDISON. Mercury, I am satisfied. It matters little what rank you assign me as a wit, if you give me the precedence as a friend and benefactor to mankind.

MERCURY—I pass sentence on the *writers*, not the *men*. And my decree is this. When any hero is brought hither, who wants to be humbled, let the task of lowering his arrogance be assigned to Swift. The same good office may be done to a philosopher vain of his wisdom and virtue, or to a bigot puffed up with spiritual pride. The doctor's discipline will soon convince the first, that, with all his boasted morality, he is but a *Yahoo*; and the latter, that to be *holy*, he must necessarily be *humble*. I would also have him apply his *anticosmetick wash* to the painted face of female vanity; and his rod, which draws blood at every stroke, to the hard back of insolent folly or petulant wit. But Addison should be employed to comfort those, whose delicate minds are dejected with too painful a sense of some infirmities in their nature. To them he should hold his fair and charitable mirrour; which would bring to their sight their hidden excellences, and put them in a temper fit for Elysium.— Adieu: continue to esteem and love each other as you did in the other world, though you were of opposite parties, and (what is still more wonderful) *rival wits*. This alone is sufficient to entitle you both to Elysium.

(b)

RABELAIS. . . . I don't despair of being proved, to the entire satisfaction of some future age, to have been, without exception, the profoundest *divine* and *metaphysician* that ever yet held a pen.

LUCIAN. I shall rejoice to see you advanced to that honour. But in the mean time I may take the liberty to consider you as one of our class. There you sit very high.

RABELAIS. I am afraid there is another, and a modern author too, whom you would bid to sit above me, and but just below yourself: I mean Dr. Swift.

LUCIAN. It was not necessary for him to throw so much nonsense into his history of Lemuel Gulliver, as you did into that of your two illustrious heroes: and his style is far more correct than yours. His wit never descended (as yours frequently did) into the lowest of taverns, nor ever wore the meanest garb of the vulgar.

RABELAIS. If the garb, which it wore, was not as *mean*, I am certain it was sometimes as *dirty* as mine.

LUCIAN. It was not always nicely clean. Yet, in comparison with you, he was decent and elegant. But whether there were not in your compositions more *fire*, and a more *comic spirit*, I will not determine.

RABELAIS. If you will not determine it, e'en let it remain a matter in dispute, as I have left the great question. *Whether Panurge should marry or not?* I would as soon undertake to measure the difference between the height and bulk of the giant Garagantua and his Brobdi-guanian majesty, as the difference of merit between my writings and Swift's. If any man take a fancy to like my book, let him freely enjoy the entertainment it gives him, and drink to my memory in a bumper. If another like Gulliver, let him toast Dr. Swift. Were I upon earth, I would pledge him in a bumper, *supposing the wine to be good.* If a third like neither of us, let him silently pass the bottle, and be quiet.

33. A French reissue of *Gulliver's Travels*

1762

L'Année Littéraire, iv (1762), pp. 259–63.

This late review of *Gulliver's Travels* appeared on the occasion of a reissue of Desfontaines's translation. Only extracts are given here, since, though the review is a long one, much of it is devoted to description or to quotation, either from the *Travels* or from Desfontaines's Preface. Doubtless the softening which the fourth voyage received at Desfontaines's hands made it easier for Frenchmen to see its philosophical content.

It is above all in the voyage to the country of the Houyhnhnms (horses) that Swift's philosophy bursts upon us, and here above all he is the equitable and enlightened judge of human nature. Moreover this voyage is the most curious and interesting; it is here that the subject of the pictures is no less than all tastes and all Nations. What the author makes Gulliver say is of a novel and interesting morality. . . .

I do not tire of repeating it, Sir; all which pertains to the voyage to Houyhnhnmland is of the greatest beauty; in it reason and imagination are reunited to please and instruct at the same time. It is not necessary, however, to conceal the faults of *Gulliver*; there is an unbearable monotony in the means that the author employs to set his philosopher hero travelling; he always returns to England and sets out again by sea to seek new regions. Another bad fault is the obscurity of many of the allegories, which have need of a Key. But in spite of all these observations, *Gulliver's Travels* must be put alongside the best books of censure and morality. A proof of their merit is that M. de Voltaire, who possesses the art of imitation in the happiest degree, has in many of his prose pieces made use of the substance and often the form of this production of the celebrated *Swift*.

34. Oliver Goldsmith on Swift

1764

An History of England, in a Series of Letters, 1787, ii, 153–4.

Goldsmith (1730–74) first published his *History of England* in 1764. His comments on the writers of the eighteenth century are necessarily brief, serving only as indications of the learning of the period.

Steele was Addison's friend and admirer: his comedies are perfectly polite, chaste, and genteel; nor were his other works contemptible: he wrote on several subjects, and yet it is amazing, in the multiplicity of his pursuits, how he found leisure for the discussion of any; ever persecuted by creditors, whom his profuseness drew upon him, or pursuing impracticable schemes, suggested by illgrounded ambition. Dean Swift was the professed antagonist of both Addison and him. He perceived that there was a spirit of romance mixed with all the works of the poets who preceded him; or, in other words, that they had drawn nature on the most pleasing side. There still therefore was a place left for him, who, careless of censure, should describe it just as it was, with all its deformities; he therefore owes much of his fame, not so much to the greatness of his genius, as to the boldness of it. He was dry, sarcastic, and severe; and suited his style exactly to the turn of his thought, being concise and nervous.

35. Ralph Griffiths on Swift's 'Cause'

1765

Monthly Review, xxxiii (1765), 149.

Ralph Griffiths (1720–1803) was for many years editor and pub-
lisher of the *Monthly Review* as well as a frequent contributor of
articles. These remarks on Swift are taken from a lengthy review of
Volume VIII of Swift's *Works*, the second of the eight 'posthumous' volumes edited by Deane Swift between 1763 and 1779
as a supplement to Hawkesworth's 1755 edition of Swift's
works. The volume consists chiefly of Irish tracts.

The patriot Dean here [in *A Letter to the Archbishop of Dublin, concerning
the Weavers*] takes a melancholy view of the then state of Ireland, and
with a spirited and manly commiseration, expatiates on the ruin of her
trade, the vast yearly remission of the rents into England, for the support of absentees, the destructive importation of foreign luxury and
vanity, the oppression of landlords, and the discouragement of agriculture. All these evils he considers as past the possibility of a cure; except
that of unnecessary importations of foreign silks, laces, teas, china-ware,
and other articles of luxury: and in order to endorce the remedy of this
grievance, he labours with becoming zeal, to recommend the wear of
Irish manufactures, both for men and women, and the use of the innocent and wholesome produce of their own soil.—Apologizing for the
acrimony with which he usually treats these subjects, (though he is
sometimes droll and ludicrous upon them too) he observes, that it is
hard for a man of common spirit to turn his thoughts to such speculations, without discovering a resentment which people are too delicate
to bear.—There were, indeed, people who could ill brook the rough
and manly freedoms which our excellent Author was apt to take, on
these occasions, because, more than their delicacy, their interests were
likely to be affected by his just remonstrances and keen invectives: and,
accordingly, in return, they gave him sufficient trouble, as far as lay in

their power, by setting on foot prosecutions against his printers, and offering rewards for discovery of the Author, in order to punish him as a Libeller.—But, as his cause was good, his resolution steady, his perseverance unshaken, he finally triumphed over all his opponents; who deservedly sunk into the infamy they so justly merited: while the patriot Dean became the idol and the glory of that kingdom, for the welfare of which he so worthily exerted those talents with which the Almighty had most bounteously endowed him. In truth, the Dean was, in this part of his character, whatever may be thought of him as a divine, or even as a wit, A TRULY GREAT AND GOOD MAN.

36. Horace Walpole and his circle on Swift

1771, 1780

Horace Walpole's Correspondence, the Yale edn., ed. W. S. Lewis, 1937.
(*a*) To Lady Ossory, 14 December 1771, 32 (1965), 71–3.
(*b*) From Mme du Deffand, 15 July 1780, 7 (1939), 237.

The personal and literary differences of Swift and Walpole (1717–97) did not prevent *Gulliver's Travels* from appealing to Walpole's imagination. Throughout his voluminous correspondence, Walpole refers to himself as a 'Strulbrug' [*sic*] and sometimes characterizes others in Gulliverian terms. He wrote this sequel to *Gulliver's Travels* for Lady Ossory, formerly Duchess of Grafton, who at the time was in seclusion in the country, following her scandalous divorce and remarriage. Mme du Deffand, who finds *Gulliver's Travels* so boring, had retired in 1754 to the Convent of St. Joseph, whence she corresponded with such important figures as D'Alembert, Montesquieu, and Voltaire.

(*a*)
The Sequel to 'Gulliver's Travels'

The two nations of the giants and the fairies had long been mortal enemies, and most cruel wars had happened between them. At last in the year 2000096 Oberon the 413th had an only daughter who was called Illipip, which signified the corking-pin, from her prodigious stature, she being full eighteen inches high, which the fairies said was an inch taller than Eve the first fairy. Gob, the Emperor of the giants, had an only son, who was as great a miracle for his diminutiveness, for at fifteen he was but seven and thirty feet high, and though he was fed with the milk of sixteen elephants every day, and took three hogsheads of jelly of lions between every meal, he was the most puny child that ever was seen, and nobody expected that he would ever be reared to man's estate. However as it was indispensably necessary to marry him, that the imperial family might not be extinct, and as an opportunity offered of terminating the long wars between the two nations by an union of the hostile houses, ambassadors were sent to demand the Princess of the Fairies, for the Prince of the Giants, who I forgot to say was called the Delicate Mountain. The Queen of the Fairies, who was a woman of violent passions, was extremely offended at the proposal, and vowed that so hopeful a girl as Corking-Pin should not be thrown away upon a dwarf—however as Oberon was a very sage monarch and loved his people, he overruled his wife's impetuosity and granted his daughter. Still the Queen had been so indiscreet as to drop hints of her dissatisfaction before the Princess, and Corking-Pin set out with a sovereign contempt for her husband, whom she said she supposed she should be forced to keep in her tooth-pick case for fear of losing him. This witticism was so applauded by all the Court of Fairy that it reached the ears of Emperor Gob and had like to have broken off the match.

On the frontiers of the two kingdoms the Princess was met by the Emperor's carriages. A litter of crimson velvet, embroidered with seed pearls as big as ostriches' eggs, and a little larger than a cathedral was destined for the Princess, and was drawn by twelve dromedaries. At the first stage she found the bridegroom, who for fear of catching cold, had come in a close sedan, which was but six and forty feet high. He had six under-waistcoats of bear-skin, and a white handkerchief about his neck twenty yards long. He had the misfortune of having weak eyes, and when the Princess descended from her litter to meet him he could not distinguish her. She was wonderfully shocked at his not saluting her, but when his governor whispered to him which was she, he spit upon his finger, and stretched out his hand to bring her nearer to his eye, but unluckily fixed upon the great Mistress of the Queen's Household and lifted her up in the air in a very unseemly attitude, to the great diversions of the young fairy lords. The lady squalled dreadfully, thinking the Prince was going to devour her. As misfortune would have it, notwithstanding all the Empress's precautions, the Prince had taken cold, and happening at that very instance to sneeze, he blew the old lady ten leagues off, into a mill-pond, where it was forty to one but she had been drowned. The whole cavalcade of the fairies was put into great disorder likewise by this untoward accident, and the cabinet councillors deliberated whether they should not carry back the Princess immediately to her father—but Corking-Pin it seems had not found the Prince quite so disagreeable as she had expected, and declaring that she would not submit to the disgrace of returning without a husband. Nay, she said, that to prevent any more mistakes, she would have the marriage solemnized that night. The nuptial ceremony was accordingly performed by the Archbishop of Saint Promontory, but the governor declaring that he had the Empress's express injunctions not to let them live together for two years in consideration of the Prince's youth and tender constitution, the Princess was in such a rage, that she swore and stamped like a madwoman, and spit in the Archbishop's face. Nothing could equal the confusion occasioned by this outrage. By the laws of Giantland it was death to spit in a priest's face. The Princess was immediately made close prisoner, and couriers were dispatched to the two courts to inform them of what had happened. By good fortune the chief of the law, who did not love the Archbishop, recollected an old law which said that no woman could be put to death for any crime committed on her wedding day. This discovery split the whole nation of giants into two parties, and occasioned a civil war which lasted till the whole nation of giants was exterminated; and as the fairies from a factious spirit took part with the one side or other, they were all trampled to death, and not a giant or fairy remained to carry on either race.

(b)

I cannot amuse myself with reading history, whose accounts of sieges and battles I find extremely boring; but what I hate most at present is moral books, especially when allegories are used to make them pleasing. I have just tried to read *Gulliver*, which I have already read, and which the translator, the Abbé Desfontaines, had dedicated to me. I do not think there is anything more disagreeable. The conversation with the horses is the most forced, the most frigid, the most tedious thing that one can imagine.

37. Lord Monboddo on *Gulliver's Travels*

1776

Of the Origin and Progress of Language, iii (2nd edn.), 1786, 195–6.

James Burnett, Lord Monboddo (1714–99), seriously pursued literary and philosophical studies during a distinguished career as both lawyer and judge in his native Scotland. He became known in English literary circles on visits to London. *Of the Origin and Progress of Language* appeared serially in six volumes from 1773 to 1792. Volume III, from which this extract is taken, first appeared in 1776.

The author, in English, that has excelled the most in this style [the simple style] is Dr. Swift, in his *Gulliver's Travels*; of which the narrative is wonderfully plain and simple, minute likewise, and circumstantial, so much, as to be disgusting to a reader without taste or judgment, and the character of an English sailor is finely kept up in it. In short, it has every virtue belonging to this style; and I will venture to say, that those monstrous lies so narrated, have more the air of probability than many a true story unskilfully told. And, accordingly, I have been informed, that they imposed upon many when they were first published. The voyage to Lilliput, in my judgment, is the finest of them all, especially in what relates to the politics of that kingdom, and the state of parties there. The debate in the King's council, concerning Gulliver, is a master-piece; and the original papers it contains, of which he says he was so lucky as to get copies, give it an air of probability that is really wonderful. When we add to all this; the hidden satire which it contains, and the grave ridicule that runs through the whole of it, the most exquisite of all ridicule, I think I do not go too far when I pronounce it the most perfect work of the kind, ancient or modern, that is to be found. For, as to Lucian's true history, which is the only antient work of the kind that has come down to us, it has nothing to recommend it, except the imitation of the grave style of the ancient historians, such as Herodotus; but it wants the satire and exquisite ridicule that is to be found in the Dean's work. . . .

[195–6.]

I would therefore advise our compilers of history, if they will not study the models of the historic style which the antients have left us, at least to imitate the simplicity of Dean Swift's style in his *Gulliver's Travels*, and to endeavour to give as much the appearance of credibility to what truth they relate as he has given to his monstrous fictions; not that I would be understood to recommend the style of these travels as a pattern for history, for which it never was intended, being indeed an excellent imitation of the narrative of a sailor, but wanting that gravity, dignity and ornament which the historical style requires.

[367–8.]

38. James Beattie on *Gulliver's Travels,*
A Tale of a Tub, and *The Day of Judgment*

1776, 1783

(*a*) 'Essays on Poetry and Music as they Affect the Mind',
    Essays . . . , 1776, 378–9, 387.
(*b*) 'On Fable and Romance', *Dissertations Moral and Critical,*
    1783, 514–18.

Beattie (1735–1803) was Professor of Moral Philosophy at Mari-
schal College, Aberdeen, and author of *The Minstrel.* He tells us
that the *Essays on Poetry and Music* were read to a private literary
society in the 1760s, and that the *Dissertations* were adapted from
a course of Prelections, delivered some time earlier to his students.

(*a*)

The Lilliputians of Swift may pass for probable beings; not so much
because we know that a belief in pygmies was once current in the
world, (for the true ancient pygmy was at least thrice as tall as those
whom Gulliver visited), but because we find, that every circumstance
relating to them accords with itself, and with their supposed character.
It is not the size of the people only that is diminutive; their country,
seas, ships, and towns, are all in exact proportion; their theological and
political principles, their passions, manners, customs, and all the parts
of their conduct, betray a levity and littleness perfectly suitable: and so
simple is the whole narration, and apparently so artless and sincere,
that I should not much wonder, if it had imposed (as I have been told
it has) upon some persons of no contemptible understanding. The same
degree of credit may perhaps for the same reasons be due to his giants.
But when he grounds his narrative upon a contradiction to nature;
when he presents us with rational brutes, and irrational men; when he
tells us of horses building houses for habitation, milking cows for food,
riding in carriages, and holding conversations on the laws and politics
of Europe; not all his genius (and he there exerts it to the utmost) is

able to reconcile us to so monstrous a fiction: we may smile at some of his absurd exaggerations; we may be pleased with the energy of style, and accuracy of description, in particular places; and a malevolent heart may triumph in the satire: but we can never relish it as a fable, because it is at once unnatural and self-contradictory. Swift's judgement seems to have forsaken him on this occasion:[1] he wallows in nastiness and brutality; and the general run of his satire is downright defamation.

[378-9.]

In Swift we see a turn of mind very different from that of the amiable Thomson, little relish for the sublime and beautiful, and a perpetual succession of violent emotions. All his pictures of life seem to show, that deformity and meanness were the favourite objects of his attention, and that his soul was a constant prey to indignation, disgust, and other gloomy passions arising from such a view of things. And it is the tendency of almost all his writings (though it was not always the author's design) to communicate the same passions to his reader; insomuch, that, notwithstanding his erudition, and knowledge of the world, his abilities as a popular orator and man of business, the energy of his style, the elegance of some of his verses, and his extraordinary talents in wit and humour, there is no reason to doubt, whether by studying his works any person was ever much improved in piety or benevolence.

[387.]

---

[1] There are improprieties in this narrative, which one would think a very slight attention to nature might have prevented; and which, without heightening the satire, serve only to aggravate the absurdity of the fable. *Houyhnhnms* are horses in perfection, with the addition of reason and virtue. Whatever, therefore, takes away from their perfection as horses, without adding to their rational and moral accomplishments, must be repugnant to the author's design, and ought not to have found a place in his narration. Yet he makes his beloved quadrupeds *dwell in houses* of their own building, and use *warm food* and the *milk of cows* as a delicacy: though these luxuries, supposed attainable by a nation of horses, could contribute no more to their perfection than brandy and imprisonment would to that of a man. Again, did Swift believe that religious ideas are natural to a reasonable being, and necessary to the happiness of a moral one? I hope he did. Yet has he represented his *Houyhnhnms* as patterns of moral virtue, as the greatest masters of reason, and withal as completely happy, without any religious ideas, or any views beyond the present life. In a word, he would make stupidity consistent with mental excellence, and unnatural appetites with animal perfection. These, however, are small matters, compared with the other absurdities of this abominable tale. But when a Christian Divine can set himself deliberately to trample upon that nature, which he knows to have been made but a little lower than the angels, and to have been assumed by One far more exalted than they; we need not be surprised if the same perverse habits of thinking which harden his heart, should also debase his judgement. [Beattie's note.]

(*b*)

Guilliver's Travels are a sort of allegory; but rather Satirical and Political, than Moral. The work is in every body's hands; and has been criticised by many eminent writers. As far as the satire is levelled at human pride and folly; at the abuses of human learning; at the absurdity of speculative projectors; at those criminal or blundering expedients in policy, which we are apt to overlook, or even to applaud, because custom has made them familiar; so far the author deserves our warmest approbation, and his satire will be allowed to be perfectly just, as well as exquisitely severe. His fable is well conducted, and, for the most part consistent with itself, and connected with probable circumstances. He personates a sea-faring man; and with wonderful propriety supports the plainness and simplicity of the character. And this gives to the whole narrative an air of truth; which forms an entertaining contraste, when we compare it with the wildness of the fiction. The style too deserves particular notice. It is not free from inaccuracy: but, as a model of easy and graceful simplicity, it has not been exceeded by any thing in our language; and well deserves to be studied by every person, who wishes to write pure English.—These, I think, are the chief merits of this celebrated work; which has been more read, than any other publication of the present century. Gulliver has something in him to hit every taste. The statesman, the philosopher, and the critick, will admire his keenness of satire, energy of description, and vivacity of language: the vulgar, and even children, who cannot enter into these refinements, will find their account in the story, and be highly amused with it.

But I must not be understood to praise the whole indiscriminately. The last of the four voyages, though the author has exerted himself in it to the utmost, is an absurd, and an abominable fiction. It is absurd: because, in presenting us with rational beasts, and irrational men, it proceeds upon a direct contradiction to the most obvious laws of Nature, without deriving any support from either the dreams of the credulous, or the prejudices of the ignorant. And it is abominable: because it abounds in filthy and indecent images; because the general tenor of the satire is exaggerated into absolute falsehood; and because there must be something of an irreligious tendency in a work, which, like this, ascribes the perfection of reason, and of happiness, to a race of beings, who are said to be destitute of every religious idea.—But, what is yet worse, if any thing can be worse, this tale represents human nature itself as the object of contempt and abhorrence. Let the ridicule of wit be pointed at the follies, and let the scourge of satire be brandished at the crimes of mankind: all this is both pardonable, and praiseworthy; because it may be done with a good intention, and produce good effects. But when a writer endeavours to make us dislike and despise, every one his neighbour, and be dissatisfied with that Providence, who has made us what we are, and whose dispensations toward the human race are so peculiarly, and so divinely beneficent; such a writer, in so doing, provides himself the enemy, not of man only, but of goodness itself; and his work can never be allowed to be innocent, till impiety, malevolence, and misery, cease to be evils.

A Tale of a Tub, at least the narrative part of it, is another Allegorical fable, by the same masterly hand; and, like the former, supplies no little matter, both of admiration, and of blame. As a piece of humorous writing, it is unequalled. It was the author's first performance, and, is in the opinion of many, his best. The style may be less correct, than that of some of his latter works; but in no other part of his writings has he displayed so rich a fund of wit, humour, and ironical satire, as in *A Tale of a Tub.* The subject is Religion: but the allegory, under which he typifies the Reformation, is too mean for an argument of so great dignity; and tends to produce, in the mind of the reader, some very disagreeable associations, of the most solemn truths with ludicrous ideas. Professed wits may say what they please; and the fashion, as well as the laugh, may be for a time on their side: but it is a dangerous thing, and the sign of an intemperate mind, to acquire a habit of making every thing matter of merriment and sarcasm. We dare not take such liberty with our neighbour, as to represent whatever he does or says in a ridiculous light; and yet some men (I wish I could not say, clergymen) think themselves privileged to take liberties of this sort with the most awful, and most benign dispensations of Providence. That this author has repeatedly done so, in the work before us, and elsewhere, is too plain to require proof.[1] The compliments he pays the Church of England I

[1] I know not whether this author is not the only human being, who ever presumed to speak in ludicrous terms of the Last Judgment. His profane verses on that tremendous subject were not published, so far as I know, till after his death: for Chesterfield's Letter to Voltaire, in which they are inserted, and spoken of with approbation (which is no more than one would expect from such a critick), and said to be copied from the original in Swift's hand-writing, is dated in the year one thousand and seven hundred and fifty-two. But this is no excuse for the Author. We may guess at what was in his mind, when he wrote them; and at what remained in his mind, while he could have destroyed them, and would not. Nor is it any excuse to say, that he makes Jupiter the agent: a Christian, granting the utmost possible favour to Poetick licence, cannot conceive a heathen idol to do that, of which the only information we have is from the word of God, and in regard to which we certainly know, that it will be done by the Deity himself. That humourous and instructive allegory of Addison, (*Spectator,* 558, 559) in which Jupiter is supposed to put it

allow to be very well founded, as well as part of the satire, which he levels at the Church of Rome; though I wish he had expressed both the one and the other with a little more decency of language. But, as to his abuse of the Presbyterians, whom he represents as more absurd and frantick, than perhaps any rational beings ever were since the world began, every person of sense and candour, whether Presbyterian or not, will acknowledge it, if he know any thing of their history, to be founded in gross misrepresentation. There are other faults in this work, besides those already specified; many vile images, and obscene allusions; such as no well-bred man could read, or endure to hear read, in polite company.

---

in every person's power to choose his own condition, is not only conformable to antient philosophy, but is actually founded on a passage of Horace.

I mean not to insinuate that Swift was favourable to infidelity. There is good reason to believe he was not; and that, though too many of his levities are inexcusable, he could occasionally be both serious and pious. In fact, an infidel clergyman would be such a compound of execrable impiety and contemptible meanness, that I am unwilling to suppose there can be such a monster. The profaneness of this author I impute to his passion for ridicule, and rage of witticism; which, when they settle into a habit, and venture on liberties with what is sacred, never fail to pervert the mind, and harden the heart. [Beattie's note.]

39. A French comment on *A Modest Proposal*

1777

Journal Anglais, iii, No. 17 (1 June 1777), 4.

Critical comments on this minor work by Swift are rare in eighteenth-century journals. Many critics confine themselves to *Gulliver's Travels* or *A Tale of a Tub*, but the anonymous contributor to the *Journal Anglais* gives both a full translation of the *Modest Proposal* and a brief comment on its purpose.

Having become Dean of the Cathedral in Dublin, constrained by his position to witness the ills of his country, but forced by his character not to endure them patiently, Swift consecrated his pen and his talents to the service of his fellow citizens. Joining wit to profound political knowledge and bitter irony to compelling reason, he made himself the scourge of the ministry and the idol of the people. The piece which we present to our readers was written to ridicule those schemes for reform with which the public was inundated at that time, and which often insulted the misery to which they affected a desire to bring consolation. It will be noticed that Swift has imitated the common expressions and the insinuating tone of the authors of these projects.

40. Dr. Johnson on Swift

1779, 1785, 1791

(a) Samuel Johnson, *The Lives of the Poets* (2 vols.), (1779–81) Everyman Edition, 1925.

(b) James Boswell, *Journal of a Tour to the Hebrides with Dr. Samuel Johnson, LL.D.*, 1785, ed. R. W. Chapman, 1934, 187.

(c) James Boswell, *The Life of Samuel Johnson, LL.D.* (2 vols.), 1791.

Samuel Johnson (1709–84) gives his opinion of Swift's writings both formally, in *The Lives of the Poets*, and informally in conversations with his biographer, James Boswell (1740–95). Boswell does not give his own opinion of Swift, but he does remark, accurately, on Johnson's 'unaccountable prejudice' against him, a prejudice which Boswell apparently tried to oppose.

(a)

Swift began early to think, or to hope, that he was a poet, and wrote Pindaric Odes to Temple, to the King, and to the Athenian Society, a knot of obscure men, who published a periodical pamphlet of answers to questions sent, or supposed to be sent, by letters. I have been told that Dryden, having perused these verses, said, 'Cousin Swift, you will never be a poet'; and that this denunciation was the motive of Swift's perpetual malevolence to Dryden. . . .

Swift was not one of those minds which amaze the world with early pregnancy: his first work, except his few poetical Essays, was the *Dissensions in Athens and Rome*, published (1701) in his thirty-fourth year. After its appearance, paying a visit to some bishop, he heard mention made of the new pamphlet that Burnet had written, replete with political knowledge. When he seemed to doubt Burnet's right to the work, he was told by the Bishop that he was 'a young man'; and, still persisting to doubt, that he was 'a very positive young man'.

Three years afterwards (1704) was published *A Tale of a Tub*: of this book charity may be persuaded to think that it might be written by a man of a peculiar character, without ill intention; but it is certainly of dangerous example. That Swift was its author, though it be universally believed, was never owned by himself, nor very well proved by any evidence; but no other claimant can be produced, and he did not deny it when Archbishop Sharp and the Duchess of Somerset, by showing it to the Queen, debarred him from a bishopric.

When this wild work first raised the attention of the public, Sacheverell, meeting Smalridge, tried to flatter him, seeming to think him the author; but Smalridge answered with indignation, 'Not all that you and I have in the world, nor all that ever we shall have, should hire me to write *A Tale of a Tub.*'

The digressions relating to Wotton and Bentley must be confessed to discover want of knowledge, or want of integrity; he did not understand the two controversies, or he willingly misrepresented them. But wit can stand its ground against truth only a little while. The honours due to learning have been justly distributed by the decision of posterity.

The Battle of the Books is so like the *Combat des Livres*, which the same question concerning the ancients and moderns had produced in France, that the improbability of such a coincidence of thoughts without communication is not, in my opinion, balanced by the anonymous protestation prefixed, in which all knowledge of the French book is peremptorily disowned.

For some time after Swift was probably employed in solitary study, gaining the qualifications requisite for future eminence. How often he visited England, and with what diligence he attended his parishes, I know not. It was not till about four years afterwards that he became a professed author; and then one year (1708) produced *The Sentiments of a Church of England Man*, the ridicule of astrology, under the name of 'Bickerstaff', the *Argument against Abolishing Christianity*, and the defence of the *Sacramental Test*.

The Sentiments of a Church of England Man is written with great coolness, moderation, ease, and perspicuity. The *Argument against Abolishing Christianity* is a very happy and judicious irony. . . .

In the year following [1709] he wrote a *Project for the Advancement of Religion*, addressed to Lady Berkeley, by whose kindness it is not unlikely that he was advanced to his benefices. To this project, which is formed with great purity of intention, and displayed with sprightliness and elegance, it can only be objected, that like many projects, it is, if not generally impracticable, yet evidently hopeless, as it supposes more zeal, concord, and perseverance than a view of mankind gives reason for expecting.

He wrote likewise this year [1709] a *Vindication of Bickerstaff*, and an explanation of an *Ancient Prophecy*, part written after the facts, and the rest never completed, but well planned to excite amazement. . . .

[II, 248-51.]

This important year [1727] sent likewise into the world *Gulliver's Travels*, a production so new and strange, that it filled the reader with a mingled emotion of merriment and amazement. It was received with such avidity, that the price of the first edition was raised before the second could be made; it was read by the high and the low, the learned and illiterate. Criticism was for a while lost in wonder; no rules of judgment were applied to a book written in open defiance of truth and regularity. But when distinctions came to be made, the part which gave the least pleasure was that which describes the Flying Island, and that which gave most disgust must be the history of the Houyhnhnms.

[II, 261.]

When Swift is considered as an author, it is just to estimate his powers by their effects. In the reign of Queen Anne he turned the stream of popularity against the Whigs, and must be confessed to have dictated for a time the political opinions of the English nation. In the succeeding reign he delivered Ireland from plunder and oppression; and showed that wit, confederated with truth, had such force as authority was unable to resist. He said truly of himself, that Ireland 'was his debtor'. It was from the time when he first began to patronise the Irish that they may date their riches and prosperity. He taught them first to know their own interest, their weight, and their strength, and gave them spirit to assert that equality with their fellow-subjects to which they have ever since been making vigorous advances, and to claim those rights which they have at last established. Nor can they be charged with ingratitude to their benefactor; for they reverenced him as a guardian and obeyed him as a dictator.

In his works he has given very different specimens both of sentiments and expression. His *Tale of a Tub* has little resemblance to his other pieces. It exhibits a vehemence and rapidity of mind, a copiousness of images, and vivacity of diction, such as he afterwards never possessed or never exerted. It is of a mode so distinct and peculiar, that it must be considered by itself; what is true of that, is not true of anything else which he has written.

In his other works is found an equable tenor of easy language, which rather trickles than flows. His delight was in simplicity. That he has in works no metaphor, as has been said, is not true; but his few metaphors seem to be received rather by necessity than choice. He studied purity; and though perhaps all his strictures are not exact, yet it is not often that solecisms can be found; and whoever depends on his authority may generally conclude himself safe. His sentences are never too much dilated or contracted; and it will not be easy to find any embarrassment in the complication of his clauses, any inconsequence in his connections, or abruptness in his transitions.

His style was well suited to his thoughts, which are never subtilised by nice disquisitions, decorated by sparkling conceits, elevated by ambitious sentences, or variegated by far-sought learning. He pays no court to the passions; he excites neither surprise nor admiration; he always understands himself, and his readers always understand him: the peruser of Swift wants little previous knowledge; it will be sufficient that he is acquainted with common words and common things; he is neither required to mount elevations nor to explore profundities; his passage is always on a level, along solid ground, without asperities, without obstruction.

This easy and safe conveyance of meaning it was Swift's desire to attain, and for having attained he deserves praise, though perhaps not the highest praise. For purposes merely didactic, when something is to be told that was not known before, it is the best mode; but against that inattention by which known truths are suffered to lie neglected, it makes no provision; it instructs, but does not persuade.

[II, 266–8.]

In the poetical works of Dr. Swift there is not much upon which the critic can exercise his powers. They are often humorous, almost always light, and have the qualities which recommend such compositions, easiness, and gaiety. They are, for the most part, what their author intended. The diction is correct, the numbers are smooth, and the rhymes exact. There seldom occurs a hard-laboured expression, or a redundant epithet; all his verses exemplify his own definition of a good style— they consist of 'proper words in proper places'.

To divide this collection into classes, and show how some pieces are gross, and some are trifling, would be to tell the reader what he knows already, and to find faults of which the author could not be ignorant, who certainly wrote not often to his judgment, but his humour.

It was said, in a Preface to one of the Irish editions, that Swift had never been known to take a single thought from any writer, ancient or modern. This is not literally true; but perhaps no writer can easily be found that has borrowed so little, or that in all his excellences and all his defects has so well maintained his claim to be considered as original.

[II, 273-4.]

(b)

He [Johnson] seemed to me to have an unaccountable prejudice against Swift; for I once took the liberty to ask him, if Swift had personally offended him, and he told me, he had not. He said to-day, 'Swift is clear, but he is shallow. In coarse humour, he is inferior to Arbuthnot; in delicate humour, he is inferior to Addison: So he is inferior to his contemporaries; without putting him against the whole world. I doubt if *A Tale of a Tub* was his: it has so much more thinking, more knowledge, more power, more colour, than any of the works which are indisputably his. If it was his, I shall only say, he was *impar sibi*.'

(c)

On Thursday, July 28, we again supped in private at the Turk's Head coffee-house. JOHNSON. 'Swift has a higher reputation than he deserves. His excellence is strong sense; for his humour, though very well, is not remarkably good. I doubt whether *A Tale of a Tub* be his; for he never owned it, and it is much above his usual manner.'

[I, 275.]

Swift having been mentioned, Johnson, as usual, treated him with little respect as an authour. Some of us endeavoured to support the Dean of St. Patrick's, by various arguments. One in particular praised his 'Conduct of the Allies.' JOHNSON. 'Sir, his "Conduct of the Allies" is a performance of very little ability.' 'Surely, Sir,' (said Dr. Douglas,) 'you must allow it has strong facts.' JOHNSON. 'Why yes, Sir; but what is that to the merit of the composition? In the Sessions-paper of the Old Bailey there are strong facts. Housebreaking is a strong fact; robbery is a strong fact; and murder is a *mighty* strong fact: but is great praise due to the historian of those strong facts? No, Sir. Swift has told what he had to tell distinctly enough, but that is all. He had to count ten, and he has counted it right.'—

[I, 306-7.]

Johnson was in high spirits this evening at the club, and talked with great animation and success. He attacked Swift, as he used to do upon all occasions. '*A Tale of a Tub* is so much superiour to his other writings, that one can hardly believe he was the authour of it. There is in it such a vigour of mind, such a swarm of thoughts, so much of nature, and art, and life.' I wondered to hear him say of *Gulliver's Travels*, 'When once you have thought of big men and little men, it is very easy to do all the rest.' I endeavoured to make a stand for Swift, and tried to rouse those who were much more able to defend him; but in vain. Johnson at last of his own accord allowed very great merit to the inventory of articles found in the pockets of the Man Mountain, particularly the description of his watch, which it was conjectured was his GOD, as he consulted it upon all occasions. He observed, that 'Swift put his name to but two things (after he had a name to put), "The Plan for the Improvement of the English Language," and the last "Drapier's Letter".'

[I, 462.]

41. Samuel Badcock on Swift's 'true wit'

1779

Review of John Nichols, ed., *A Supplement to Dr. Swift's Works*
. . . , ii, 1799, *Monthly Review* (1st series), lxi (November 1779),
356–65.

Badcock (1747–88) was a prolific reviewer for many of the major
perodicals of his day, including the *Gentleman's Magazine* and the
London Review as well as the *Monthly Review*. This extract is from
the beginning of the review, which is chiefly concerned with
summarizing the subject-matter of the volume. Here, however,
Badcock takes a more general overview of Swift and expresses
an unusually high opinion of Swift's creative imagination.

It is the province of true wit to cultivate the barren and beautify the
deformed. Nor doth it stop here. Its plastic hand forms worlds of its
own, and moulds them into whatever shape it pleaseth. It commands
the deep abyss of vacuity itself;—calls up new and unknown creations,
and (as the first Lord of this ideal empire beautifully expresses it) 'gives
to airy *nothings* a local habitation and a name.' Few writers have better
illustrated this remark than Swift. He was a man of native genius. His
fancy was inexhaustible. His conceptions were lively and comprehensive: and he had the peculiar felicity of conveying them in language
equally free, and perspicuous. His penetration was as quick as intuition:
and he was indeed the critic of nature. The high rank he holds in the
republic of letters was owing, not to the indulgence of the times in
which he wrote, but entirely to his own incontestable merit. Nothing
could suppress his genius. Nothing could hinder the world's seeing it.
The opposition of an unrelenting party in church and state, and the
personal enmity that was borne him by several of high rank and great
influence, could not eclipse the lustre of his name, nor sink in the smallest
degree, that authority in literature which he claimed, and the world
granted, as his right. By such opposers, a genius of less force would

have been totally crushed. But from him they were shaken, 'like dew-drops from a lion's mane'.

As his genius was of the first class, so were some of his virtues. He hath been accused of avarice, but with the same truth as he hath been been accused of infidelity. In *detached* views, no man was more liable to be mistaken. Even his genius and good sense might be questioned, if we were only to read some passages of his writings. To judge fairly, and pronounce justly of him, as a man, and as an author, we should examine the uniform tenor of his disposition and conduct, and the general nature and design of his productions. In the latter, he will appear great—and in the former, good—notwithstanding the puns and puerilities of the one, and the absurdities and inconsistencies of the other.

42. James Harris on *Gulliver's Travels*

1781

Philological Inquiries, in Three Parts, Part III (1781), 537.

Harris (1709–80) was a nephew of the third Earl of Shaftesbury. An M.P. and magistrate, he encouraged the arts in his home district of Salisbury and took special interest in the annual music festival there. Publication of his *Philological Inquiries* began in 1780 and continued into the next year. In view of Harris's comments on *Gulliver's Travels*, it is not hard to see why Dr. Johnson labelled him 'a prig and a bad prig'. The comments are contained in a note on the text, which at this point is concerned with the evils of misanthropy and the superiority of good humour.

MISANTHROPY is so dangerous a thing, and goes so far in sapping the very foundations of MORALITY and RELIGION, that I esteem the last part of *Swift's Gulliver* (that I mean relative to his *Hoyhnms* [sic] and *Yahoos*) to be a worse Book to peruse, than those which we forbid, as the most flagitious and obscene.

One absurdity in this Author (a wretched Philosopher, tho' a great Wit) is well worth remarking—in order to render the *Nature of* MAN *odious*, and *the Nature of* BEASTS *amiable*, he is compelled to give HUMAN *Characters* to his BEASTS, and BEASTLY *Characters* to his MEN—so that we are to *admire* THE BEASTS, *not for being Beasts*, but *amiable* MEN; and *to detest* THE MEN, *not for being* MEN, *but detetestable* BEASTS.

Whoever has been reading this *unnatural* Filth, let him turn for a moment to a *Spectator* of ADDISON, and observe the PHILANTHROPY of that *Classical Writer*; I may add the *superior* Purity of his *Diction* and his *Wit*.

43. Joseph Warton on Swift's descriptions

1782

An Essay on the Genius and Writings of Pope (2 vols.) 5th ed., 1806, ii, 49–50.

Joseph Warton (1722–1800) was the elder brother of Thomas Warton, Professor of Poetry at Oxford and subsequently Poet Laureate. Joseph was in Holy Orders and was for some years Headmaster of Winchester. He was a literary critic, best known for the essay on Pope from which this extract is taken, in which he distinguishes between a man of wit, like Pope, and a true poet. The two volumes of the Essay were published separately, first appearing in 1756 and 1782.

The Description of the Life of a Country Parson is a lively imitation of Swift, and is full of humour. The point of the likeness consists in describing the objects as they really exist in life, like Hogarth's paintings, without heightening or enlarging them, and without adding any imaginary circumstances. In this way of writing Swift excelled; witness his description of a morning in the city, of a city shower, of a house of Baucis and Philemon, and the verses on his own death. These are of the same species with the piece before us. In this also consists the chief beauty of Gay's Trivia, a subject Swift desired him to write upon, and for which he furnished him with many hints.

44. Swift's characteristics as a writer

1782

Gentleman's Magazine, iii (October 1782), 470.

The anonymous contributor to the *Gentleman's Magazine*, who claims to have known Swift, deals chiefly with biographical material, but he includes a general comment on his character as a writer.

His knowledge of men was general; it was not, however, deep, nor perfect. He was by no means a master of first causes, of original principles of action, but rather observed the result, and reported with an appearance of consummate judgment. His poetry, in the main, with all its beauties, is prostituted to the most trifling subject; his politics were *factious* in the extreme. . . . His writings to his friends have an incomparable beauty of style; but all his epistles to people in a higher sphere were unnatural, and laboured. From the whole survey of the man, I am inclined to think, that, like Rembrandt's figures he would have been lost in the shadows of his character, if the strength of the lights had not relieved him.

45. Hugh Blair on Swift's style

1783

Lectures on Rhetoric and Belles Lettres (2 vols.), 1783.
(*a*) Extract from Lecture XVII.
(*b*) Lecture XXIV (entire).
(*c*) Extract from Lecture XXXIV.

Hugh Blair (1718–1800) held the Chair of Rhetoric and Belles-lettres at Edinburgh. He resigned in 1783 and published the lectures in the same year. His interest in rhetoric makes him concentrate on stylistic matters, and he makes use of Swift's works to illustrate his points. Lecture XXIV, 'Critical Examination of the Style in a Passage of Dean Swift's Writings', deals with Swift's *Proposal for Correcting . . . the English Tongue* in a remarkably detailed fashion.

(*a*)

The difference between a dry and plain writer, is, that the former is incapable of ornament, and seems not to know what it is; the latter seeks not after it. He gives us his meaning, in good language, distinct and pure; any further ornament he gives himself no trouble about; either, because he thinks it unnecessary to his subject; or, because his genius does not lead him to delight in it; or, because it leads him to despise it.

THIS last was the case with Dean Swift, who may be placed at the head of those that have employed the Plain Style. Few writers have discovered more capacity. He treats every subject which he handles, whether serious or ludicrous, in a masterly manner. He knew, almost, beyond any man, the Purity, the Extent, the Precision of the English Language; and, therefore, to such as wish to attain a pure and correct Style, he is one of the most useful models. But we must not look for much ornament and grace in his Language. His haughty and morose genius, made him despise any embellishment of this kind as beneath his dignity. He delivers his sentiments in a plain, downright, positive manner, like the one who is sure he is in the right; and is very in-different whether you be pleased or not. His sentences are commonly negligently arranged; distinctly enough as to the sense; but, without any regard to smoothness of sound; often without much regard to compactness, or elegance. If a metaphor, or any other figure, chanced to render his satire more poignant, he would, perhaps, vouchsafe to adopt it, when it came in his way; but if it tended only to embelish and illustrate, he would rather throw it aside. Hence, in his serious pieces, his style often borders upon the dry and unpleasing; in his humourous ones, the plainness of his manner gives his wit a singular edge, and sets it off to the highest advantage. There is no froth, nor affectation in it; it flows without any studied preparation; and while he hardly appears to smile himself, he makes his reader laugh heartily. To a writer of such a genius as Dean Swift, the Plain Style was most admirably fitted. Among our philosophical writers, Mr. Locke comes under this class; perspicuous and pure, but almost without any ornament whatever. In works which admit, or require, ever so much ornament, there are parts where the plain manner ought to predominate. But we must remember, that when this is the character which a writer affects throughout his whole composition, great weight of matter, and great force of senti-ment, are required, in order to keep up the reader's attention, and prevent him from tiring of the author.

[I, 380–2.]

(b)

MY design, in the four preceeding Lectures, was not merely to appre-tiate the merit of Mr. Addison's Style, by pointing out the faults and the beauties that are mingled in the writings of that great Author. They were not composed with any view to gain the reputation of a Critic; but intended for the assistance of such as are desirous of studying the most proper and elegant construction of Sentences in the English Language. To such, it is hoped, they may be of advantage; as the proper application of rules respecting Style, will always be best learned by means of the illustration which examples afford. I conceived that examples, taken from the writings of an Author so justly esteemed, would, on that account, not only be more attended to, but would also produce this good effect, of familiarising those who study composition with the Style of a writer, from whom they may, upon the whole, derive great benefit. With the same view, I shall, in this Lecture, give one critical exercise more of the same kind, upon the Style of an Author of a different character, Dean Swift; repeating the intimation I gave formerly, that such as stand in need of no assistance of this kind, and who, therefore, will naturally consider such minute discussions concerning the propriety of words, and structure of Sentences, as beneath their attention, had best pass over what will seem to them a tedious part of the work.

I FORMERLY gave the general character of Dean Swift's Style. He is esteemed one of our most correct writers. His Style is of the plain and simple kind; free of all affectation, and all superfluity; perspicuous, manly, and pure. These are its advantages. But we are not to look for much ornament and grace in it. On the contrary, Dean Swift seems to have slighted and despised the ornaments of Language, rather than to have studied them. His arrangement is often loose and negligent. In elegant, musical, and figurative Language he is much inferior to Mr. Addison. His manner of writing carries in it the character of one who rests altogether upon his sense, and aims at no more than giving his meaning in a clear and concise manner.

THAT part of his writings, which I shall now examine, is the beginning of his treatise, entitled *A Proposal for Correcting, Improving, and Ascertaining the English Tongue*, in a Letter addressed to the Earl of Oxford, then Lord High Treasurer. I was led, by the nature of the subject, to choose this treatise: but, in justice to the Dean, I must observe, that, after having examined it, I do not esteem it one of his most correct productions; but am apt to think it has been more hastily composed than some other of them. It bears the title and form of a Letter; but it is, however, in truth, a Treatise designed for the Public: and, therefore, in examining it, we cannot proceed upon the indulgence due to an epistolary correspondence. When a man addresses himself to a Friend only, it is sufficient if he makes himself fully understood by him; but when an Author writes for the Public, whether he assume the form of an Epistle or not, we are always entitled to expect, that he shall express himself with accuracy and care. Our Author begins thus:

What I had the honour of mentioning to your Lordship, sometime ago, in conversation, was not a new thought, just then started by accident or occasion, but the result of long reflection; and I have been confirmed in my sentiments by the opinion of some very judicious persons with whom I consulted.

THE disposition of circumstances in a Sentence, such as serve to limit or to qualify some assertion, or to denote time and place, I formerly showed to be a matter of nicety; and I observed, that it ought to be always held a rule, not to crowd such circumstances together, but rather to intermix them with more capital words, in such different parts of the Sentence, as can admit them naturally. Here are two circumstances of this kind placed together, which had better have been separated, *Some time ago, in conversation*—better thus—*What I had the honour, sometime ago, of mentioning to your Lordship in conversation*—*was not a new thought*, proceeds our Author, *started by accident or occasion:* the different meaning of these two words may not, at first, occur. They have, however, a distinct meaning, and are properly used: for it is one very laudable property of our Author's Style, that it is seldom incumbered with superfluous, synonymous words. *Started by accident*, is, fortuitously, or at random; started *by occasion*, is, by some incident, which at that time gave birth to it. His meaning is, that it was not a new thought which either casually sprung up in his mind, or was suggested to him, for the first time, by the train of the discourse: but, as he adds, *was the result of long reflection*.—He proceeds:

> *They all agreed, that nothing would be of greater use towards the improvement of knowledge and politeness, than some effectual method, for correcting, enlarging, and ascertaining our Language; and they think it a work very possible to be compassed under the protection of a prince, the countenance and encouragement of a ministry, and the care of proper persons chosen for such an undertaking.*

THIS is an excellent Sentence; clear, and elegant. The words are all simple, well chosen, and expressive; and arranged in the most proper order. It is a harmonious period too, which is a beauty not frequent in our Author. The last part of it consists of three members, which gradually rise and swell above one another, without any affected or unsuitable pomp;—*under the protection of a prince, the countenance and encouragement of a ministry, and the care of proper persons chosen for such an undertaking*. We may remark, in the beginning of the Sentence, the proper use of the preposition *towards*—*greater use towards the improvement of knowledge and politeness*—importing the pointing or tendency of any thing to a certain end; which could not have been so well expressed by the preposition *for* commonly employed in place of *towards*, by Authors who are less attentive, than Dean Swift was, to the force of words.

ONE fault might, perhaps, be found, both with this and the former Sentence, considered as introductory ones. We expect, that an introduction is to unfold, clearly and directly, the subject that is to be treated of. In the first Sentence, our Author had told us, of a thought he mentioned to his Lordship, in conversation, which had been the result of long reflection, and concerning which he had consulted judicious persons. But what that thought was, we are never told directly. We gather it indeed from the second sentence, wherein he informs us, in what these judicious persons agreed; namely, that some method for improving the language was both useful and practicable. But this indirect method of opening the subject, would have been very faulty in a regular treatise; though the ease of the epistolary form, which our Author here assumes in addressing his patron, may excuse it in the present case.

I was glad to find your Lordship's answer in so different a style from what hath commonly been made use of, on the like occasions, for some years past: 'That all such thoughts must be deferred to a time of peace'; a topic which some have carried so far, that they would not have us, by any means, think of preserving our civil and religious constitution, because we are engaged in a war abroad.

THIS Sentence also is clear and elegant; only there is one inaccuracy, when he speaks of his Lordship's *answer* being in so different a style from what had formerly been used. His *answer* to what? or to whom? For from any thing going before, it does not appear that any application or address had been made to his Lordship by those persons, whose opinion was mentioned in the preceding Sentence; and to whom the answer, here spoken of, naturally refers. There is little indistinctness, as I before observed, in our Author's manner of introducing his subject here.— We may observe too, that the phrase—*glad to find your answer in so different a style*—though abundantly suited to the language of conversation, or of a familiar letter, yet, in regular composition, requires an additional word—*glad to find your answer run in so different a style.*

It will be among the distinguishing marks of your ministry, my Lord, that you have a genius above all such regards, and that no reasonable proposal, for the honour, the advantage, or ornament of your country, however foreign to your immediate office, was ever neglected by you.

THE phrase—*a genius above all such regards,* both seems somewhat harsh, and does not clearly express what the Author means, namely, the *confined views* of those who neglected every thing that belonged to the arts of peace in the time of war.—Bating this expression, there is nothing that can be subject to the least reprehension in this Sentence, nor in all that follows, to the end of the paragraph.

I confess, the merit of this candor and condescension is very much lessened, because your Lordship hardly leaves us room to offer our good wishes; removing all our difficulties, and supplying our wants, faster than the most visionary projector can adjust his schemes. And therefore, my Lord, the design of this paper is not so much to offer you ways and means, as to complain of a grievance, the redressing of which is to be your own work, as much as that of paying the nation's debts, or opening a trade into the South Sea; and, though not of such immediate benefit as either of these, or any other of your glorious actions, yet, perhaps, in future ages not less to your honour.

THE compliments which the Dean here pays to his patron, are very high and strained; and show, that, with all his surliness, he was as capable, on some occasions, of making his court to a great man by flattery, as other writers. However, with respect to the Style, which is the sole object of our present consideration, every thing here, as far as appears to me, is faultless. In these Sentences, and, indeed, throughout this paragraph, in general, which we have now ended, our Author's Style appears to great advantage. We see that ease and simplicity, that correctness and distinctness, which particularly characterise it. It is very remarkable, how few Latinised words Dean Swift employs. No writer, in our Language, is so purely English as he is, or borrows so little assistance from words of foreign derivation. From none can we take a better model of the choice and proper significancy of words. It is remarkable, in the Sentences we have now before us, how plain all the expressions are, and yet, at the same time, how significant; and, in the midst of that high strain of compliment into which he rises, how little there is of pomp, or glare of expression. How very few writers can preserve this manly temperance of Style; or would think a compliment of this nature supported with sufficient dignity, unless they had embellished it with some of those high-sounding words, whose chief effect is no other than to give their Language a stiff and forced appearance?

My Lord, I do here, in the name of all the learned and polite persons of the nation, complain to your Lordship, as First Minister, that our Language is extremely imperfect; that its daily improvements are by no means in proportion to its daily corruptions; that the pretenders to polish and refine it, have chiefly multiplied abuses and absurdities; and that, in many influences, it offends against every part of grammar.

THE turn of this Sentence is extremely elegant. He had spoken before of a grievance for which he had sought redress, and he carries on the allusion, by entering, here, directly on his subject, in the Style of a public representation presented to the Minister of State. One imperfection, however, there is in this Sentence, which, luckily for our purpose, serves to illustrate a rule before given, concerning the position of adverbs, so as to avoid ambiguity. It is in the middle of the Sentence;—*that the*

pretenders to polish and refine it, have chiefly multiplied abuses and absurdities.
—Now, concerning the import of this adverb, *chiefly*, I ask, whether
it signifies that these pretenders to polish the Language, have been the
chief persons who have multiplied its abuses, in distinction *from others*;
or, that the *chief thing* which these pretenders have done, is to multiply
the abuses of our Language, in opposition to their *doing any thing to
refine it?* These two meanings are really different; and yet, by the
position which the word *chiefly* has in the Sentence, we are left at a loss
in which to understand it. The construction would lead us rather to the
latter sense; that the chief thing which these pretenders have done, is to
multiply the abuses of our Language. But it is more than probable, that
the former sense was what the Dean intended, as it carries more of his
usual satirical edge; 'that the pretended refiners of our Language were,
in fact, its chief corruptors;' on which supposition, his words ought to
have run thus: *that the pretenders to polish and refine it, have been the chief
persons to multiply its abuses and absurdities*; which would have rendered
the sense perfectly clear.

PERHAPS, too, there might be ground for observing farther upon
this Sentence, that as Language is the object with which it sets out; *that
our Language is extremely imperfect*; and then follows an enumeration
concerning Language, in three particulars, it had been better if Language had been kept the ruling word, or the nominative to every verb,
without changing the scene; by making *pretenders* the ruling word, as
is done in the second member of the enumeration, and then, in the
third, returning again to the former word, Language—*That the pretenders to polish*—and that, *in many instances, it offends*—I am persuaded,
that the structure of the Sentence would have been more neat and happy,
and its unity more complete, if the members of it had been arranged
thus: 'That our Language is extremely imperfect; that its daily improvements are by no means in proportion to its daily corruptions; that, in
many instances, it offends against every part of grammar; and that the
pretenders to polish and refine it, have been the chief persons to multiply
its abuses and absurdities.'—This degree of attention seemed proper to
be bestowed on such a Sentence as this, in order to show how it might
have been conducted after the most perfect manner. Our Author, after
having said, *Lest your Lordship should think my censure too severe, I shall
take leave to be more particular*; proceeds in the following paragraph:

*I believe your Lordship will agree with me, in the reason why our Language is less
refined than those of Italy, Spain, or France.*

I AM sorry to say, that now we shall have less to commend in our Author. For the whole of this paragraph, on which we are entering, is, in truth, perplexed and inaccurate. Even, in this short Sentence, we may discern an inaccuracy—*why our Language is less refined than those of Italy, Spain, and France*; putting the pronoun *those* in the plural, when the antecedent substantive to which it refers is in the singular, *our Language.* Instances of this kind may sometimes be found in English authors; but they sound harsh to the ear, and are certainly contrary to the purity of grammar. By a very little attention, this inaccuracy could have been remedied; and the Sentence have been made to run much better in this way; 'why our Language is less refined than the Italian, Spanish, or French.'

It is plain, that the Latin tongue, in its purity, was never in this island; towards the conquest of which, few or no attempts were made till the time of Claudius; neither was that Language ever so vulgar in Britain, as it is known to have been in Gaul and Spain.

To say, that *the Latin Tongue, in its purity, was never in this island*, is very careless Style; it ought to have been, *was never spoken in this island*. In the progress of the Sentence, he means to give a reason why the Latin was never spoken in its purity amongst us, because our island was not conquered by the Romans till after the purity of their Tongue began to decline. But this reason ought to have been brought out more clearly. This might easily have been done, and the relation of the several parts of the Sentence to each other much better pointed out by means of a small variation; thus: 'It is plain, that the Latin Tongue, in its purity, was never spoken in this island, as few or no attempts towards the conquest of it were made till the time of Claudius.' He adds, *Neither was that Language ever so vulgar in Britain.*—*Vulgar* was one of the worst words he could have chosen for expressing what he means here; namely, that the Latin Tongue was at no time so *general*, or so much in *common use*, in Britain, as it is known to have been in Gaul and Spain.— *Vulgar*, when applied to Language, commonly signifies impure, or debased Language, such as is spoken by the low people, which is quite opposite to the Author's sense here; for, in place of meaning to say, that the Latin spoken in Britain was not so debased, as what was spoken in Gaul and Spain; he means just the contrary, and had been telling us, that we never were acquainted with the Latin at all, till its purity began to be corrupted.

Further, we find that the Roman legions here were at length all recalled to help their country against the Goths, and other barbarous invaders.

THE chief scope of this Sentence is, to give a reason why the Latin Tongue did not strike any deep root in this island, on account of the short continuance of the Romans in it. He goes on:

Meantime the Britons, left to shift for themselves, and daily harassed by cruel inroads from the Picts, were forced to call in the Saxons for their defence; who, consequently, reduced the greatest part of the island to their own power, drove the Britons into the most remote and mountainous parts, and the rest of the country, in customs, religion, and language, became wholly Saxon.

THIS is a very exceptional sentence. First, the phrase *left to shift for themselves*, is rather a low phrase, and too much in the familiar Style to be proper in a grave treatise. Next, as the Sentence advances—*forced to call in the Saxons for their defence, who, consequently, reduced the greatest part of the island to their own power.*—What is the meaning of *consequently* here? if it means 'afterwards,' or 'in the progress of time,' this, certainly, is not a sense in which *consequently* is often taken; and therefore the expression is chargeable with obscurity. The adverb, *consequently*, in its most common acceptation, denotes one thing following from another, as an effect from a cause. If he uses it in this sense, and means that the Britons being subdued by the Saxons, was a necessary consequence of their having called in these Saxons to their assistance, this consequence is drawn too abruptly, and needed more explanation. For though it has often happened, that nations have been subdued by their own auxiliaries, yet this is not a consequence of such a nature that it can be assumed, as seems here to be done, for a first and self-evident principle.—But further, what shall we say to this phrase, *reduced the greatest part of the island to their own power?* we say *reduce to rule, reduce to practice*—we can say, that *one nation reduces another to subjection*—But when *dominion* or *power* is used, we always, as far as I know, say, *reduce under their power. Reduce to their power,* is so harsh and uncommon an expression, that, though Dean Swift's authority in language be very great, yet, in the use of this phrase, I am of opinion, that it would be not safe to follow his example.

BESIDES these particular inaccuracies, this Sentence is chargeable with want of unity in the composition of the whole. The persons and the scene are too often changed upon us—First, the Britons are mentioned, who are harassed by inroads from the Picts; next, the Saxons appear, who subdue the greatest part of the island, and drive the Britons into the mountains; and, lastly, the rest of the country is introduced, and a description given of the change made upon it. All this forms a groupe of various objects, presented in such quick succession, that the mind finds it difficult to comprehend them under one view. Accordingly, it is quoted in the *Elements of Criticism*, as an instance of a sentence rendered faulty by the breach of unity.

> *This I take to be the reason why there are more Latin words remaining in the British than the old Saxon; which, excepting some few variations in the orthography, is the same in most original words with our present English, as well as with the German and other northern dialects.*

THIS Sentence is faulty, somewhat in the same manner with the last. it is loose in the connection of its parts; and, besides this, it is also too loosely connected with the preceding sentence. What he had there said, concerning the Saxons expelling the Britons, and changing the customs, the religion, and the language of the country, is a clear and good reason for our present language being Saxon rather than British. This is the inference which we would naturally expect him to draw from the premises just before laid down. But when he tells us, that *this is the reason why there are more Latin words remaining in the British tongue than in the old Saxon*, we are presently at a stand. No reason for this inference appears. If it can be gathered at all from the foregoing deduction, it is gathered only imperfectly. For, as he had told us, that the Britons had *some* connection with the Romans, he should have also told us, in order to make out his inference, that the Saxons never had *any*. The truth is, the whole of this paragraph concerning the influence of the Latin tongue upon ours, is careless, perplexed, and obscure. His argument required to have been more fully unfolded, in order to make it be distinctly apprehended, and to give it its due force. In the next paragraph, he proceeds to discourse concerning the influence of the French tongue upon our language. The Style becomes more clear, though not remarkable for great beauty or elegance:

> *Edward the Confessor having lived long in France, appears to be the first who introduced any mixture of the French tongue with the Saxon; the court affecting what the Prince was fond of, and others taking it up for a fashion, as it is now with us. William the Conqueror proceeded much further, bringing over with him vast numbers of that nation, scattering them in every monastery, giving them great quantities of land, directing all pleadings to be in that language, and endeavouring to make it universal in the kingdom.*

ON these two Sentences, I have nothing of moment to observe. The sense is brought out clearly, and in simple, unaffected language.

This, at least, is the opinion generally received; but your Lordship hath fully convinced me, that the French tongue made yet a greater progress here under Harry the Second, who had large territories on that continent both from his father and his wife; made frequent journeys and expeditions thither; and was always attended with a number of his countrymen, retainers at court.

IN the beginning of this Sentence, our Author states an opposition between an opinion generally received, and that of his Lordship; and, in compliment to his patron, he tells us, that his Lordship had convinced him of somewhat that differed from the general opinion. Thus one must naturally understand his words: *This, at least, is the opinion generally received; but your Lordship hath fully convinced me*—Now here there must be an inaccuracy of expression. For, on examining what went before, there appears no sort of opposition betwixt the generally received opinion, and that of the Author's patron. The general opinion was, that William the Conqueror had proceeded much farther than Edward the Confessor, in propagating the French language, and had endeavoured to make it universal. Lord Oxford's opinion was, that the French tongue had gone on to make a yet greater progress under Harry the Second, than it had done under his predecessor William: which two opinions are as entirely consistent with one another, as any can be; and therefore the opposition here affected to be stated between them, by the adversative particle *but*, was improper and groundless.

For some centuries after, there was a constant intercourse between France and England by the dominions we possessed there, and the conquests we made; so that our language, between two and three hundred years ago, seems to have had a greater mixture with France than at present; many words having afterwards been rejected, and some since the days of Spenser; although we have still retained not a few, which have been long antiquated in France.

THIS is a Sentence too long and intricate, and liable to the same objection that was made to a former one, of the want of unity. It consists of four members, each divided from the subsequent by a semicolon. In going along, we naturally expect the Sentence is to end at the second of these, or, at farthest, at the third; when, to our surprise, a new member pops out upon us, and fatigues our attention in joining all the parts together. Such a structure of a Sentence is always the mark of careless writing. In the first member of the Sentence, *a constant intercourse between France and England, by the dominions we possessed there, and the conquests we made*, the construction is not sufficiently filled up. In place of *intercourse by the dominions we possessed*, it should have been—*by* *reason of the dominions we possessed—or—occasioned by the dominions we possessed—*and in place of—*the dominions we possessed there, and the conquests we made,* the regular Style is—*the dominions which we possessed there, and the conquests which we made.* The relative pronoun *which,* is indeed in phrases of this kind sometimes omitted: But, when it is omitted, the Style becomes elliptic; and though in conversation, or in the very light and easy kinds of writing, such elliptic Style may not be improper, yet in grave and regular writing, it is better to fill up the construction, and insert the relative pronoun.—After having said—*I could produce several instances of both kinds, if it were of any use or entertainment*—our Author begins the next paragraph thus:

> *To examine into the several circumstances by which the language of a country may be altered, would force me to enter into a wide field.*

THERE is nothing remarkable in this Sentence, unless that here occurs the first instance of a metaphor since the beginning of this treatise; *entering into a wide field,* being put for beginning an extensive subject. Few writers deal less in figurative language than Swift. I before observed, that he appears to despise ornaments of this kind; and though this renders his Style somewhat dry on serious subjects, yet his plainness and simplicity, I must not forbear to remind my readers, is far preferable to an ostentatious and affected parade of ornament.

> *I shall only observe, that the Latin, the French, and the English, seem to have undergone the same fortune. The first from the days of Romulus, to those of Julius Cæsar, suffered perpetual changes; and by what we meet in those Authors who occasionally speak on that subject, as well as from certain fragments of old laws, it is manifest that the Latin, three hundred years before Tully, was as unintelligible in his time, as the French and English of the same period are now; and these two have changed as much since William the Conqueror (which is but little less than 700 years), as the Latin appears to have done in the like term.*

THE Dean plainly appears to be writing negligently here. This Sentence is one of that involved and intricate kind, of which some instances have occurred before; but none worse than this. It requires a very distinct head to comprehend the whole meaning of the period at first reading. In one part of it we find extreme carelessness of expression. He says, *it is manifest that the Latin, 300 years before Tully, was as unintelligible in his time, as the English and French of the same period are now.* By the English and French *of the same period,* must naturally be understood, *the English and French that were spoken three hundred years before Tully.* This is the only grammatical meaning his words will bear; and yet assuredly what he means, and what it would have been easy for him to have expressed with more precision, is, *the English and French that were spoken 300 years ago:* or at a period equally distant from our age, as the old Latin, which he had mentioned, was from the age of Tully. But when an author writes hastily, and does not review with proper care what he has written, many such inaccuracies will be apt to creep into his Style.

Whether our Language or the French will decline as fast as the Roman did, is a question that would perhaps admit more debate than it is worth. There were many reasons for the corruptions of the last; as the change of their government to a tyranny, which ruined the study of eloquence, there being no further use or encouragement for popular orators; their giving not only the freedom of the city, but capacity for employments, to several towns in Gaul, Spain, and Germany, and other distant parts, as far Asia, which brought a great number of foreign pretenders to Rome; the slavish disposition of the Senate and people, by which the wit and eloquence of the age were wholly turned into panegyric, the most barren of all subjects; the great corruption of manners, and introduction of foreign luxury, with foreign terms to express it, with several others that might be assigned; not to mention the invasion from the Goths and Vandals, which are too obvious to insist on.

In the enumeration here made of the causes contributing towards the corruption of the Roman Language, there are many inaccuracies— *The change of their government to a tyranny*—of whose government? He had indeed been speaking of the Roman language, and therefore we guess at his meaning; but the Style is ungrammatical; for he had not mentioned the Romans themselves; and therefore, when he says *their government*, there is no antecedent in the Sentence to which the pronoun, *their*, can refer with any propriety—*Giving the capacity for employments to several towns in Gaul*, is a questionable expression. For though towns are sometimes put for the people who inhabit them, yet to give a town *the capacity for employments*, sounds harsh and uncouth.—*The wit and eloquence of the age wholly turned into panegyric*, is a phrase which does not well express the meaning. Neither wit nor eloquence can be turned into panegyric; but they may be turned *towards panegyric*, or, *employed in panegyric*, which was the sense the Author had in view.

The conclusion of the enumeration is visibly incorrect—*The great corruption of manners, and introduction of foreign luxury, with foreign terms to express it, with several others that might be assigned*—He means, *with several other reasons*. The word *reasons*, had indeed been mentioned before; but as it stands at the distance of thirteen lines backward, the repetition of it here became indispensable, in order to avoid ambiguity.

Not to mention, he adds, *the invasions from the Goths and Vandals, which are too obvious to insist on.* One would imagine him to mean, that the invasions from the Goths and Vandals, are *historical facts* too well known and obvious to be insisted on. But he means quite a different thing, though he has not taken the proper method of expressing it, through his haste, probably, to finish the paragraph; namely, that these invasions from the Goths and Vandals *were causes of the corruption of the Roman Language too obvious to be insisted on.*

I SHALL not pursue this criticism any further. I have been obliged to point out many inaccuracies in the passage which we have considered. But, in order that my observations may not be constructed as meant to depreciate the Style or the Writings of Dean Swift below their just value, there are two remarks, which I judge it necessary to make before concluding this Lecture. One is, That it were unfair to estimate an Author's Style on the whole, by some passage in his writings, which chances to be composed in a careless manner. This is the case with respect to this treatise, which has much the appearance of a hasty production; though, as I before observed, it was by no means on that account that I pitched upon it for the subject of this exercise. But after having examined it, I am sensible that, in many other of his writings, the Dean is more accurate.

MY other observation, which applies equally to Dean Swift and Mr. Addison, is, that there may be writers much freer of such inaccuracies, as I have had occasion to point out in these two, whose Style, however, upon the whole, may not have half their merit. Refinement in Language has, of late years, begun to be much attended to. In several modern productions of very small value, I should find it difficult to point out many errors in Language. The words might, probably, be all proper words, correctly and clearly arranged; and the turn of the sentence sonorous and musical; whilst yet the Style, upon the whole, might deserve no praise. The fault often lies in what may be called the general cast, or complexion of the Style; which a person of a good taste discerns to be vicious; to be feeble, for instance, and diffuse; flimsy or affected; petulant or ostentatious; though the faults cannot be so easily pointed out and particularised, as when they lie in some erroneous, or negligent construction of a sentence. Whereas, such writers as Addison and Swift, carry always those general characters of good Style, which, in the midst of their occasional negligences, every person of good taste must discern and approve. We see their faults overbalanced by higher beauties. We see a writer of sense and reflection expressing his sentiments without affectation, attentive to thoughts as well as to words; and, in the main current of his Language, elegant and beautiful; and, therefore, the only proper use to be made of the blemishes which occur in the writings of such authors, is to point out to those who apply themselves to the study of composition, some of the rules which they ought to observe for avoiding such errors; and to render them sensible of the necessity of strict attention to Language and to Style. Let them imitate the ease and simplicity of those great authors; let them study to be always natural, and, as far as they can, always correct in their expressions; let them endeavour to be, at some times, lively and striking; but carefully avoid being at any time ostentatious and affected.

[I, 475-96.]

(c)

SOME Authors there are, whose manner of writing approaches nearer to the Style of Speaking than others; and who, therefore, can be imitated with more safety. In this class, among the English authors, are Dean Swift, and Lord Bolingbroke. The Dean, throughout all his writings, in the midst of much correctness, maintains the easy natural manner of an unaffected Speaker; and this is one of his chief excellencies.

[II, 238.]

46. Thomas Sheridan on Swift

1784

The Life of the Reverend Jonathan Swift. The Works of the Rev. Jonathan Swift, D.D. Dean of St. Patrick's, Dublin (19 vols.), 1801, i.

Sheridan (1719–88) was the third son of Swift's friend and the father of Richard Brinsley Sheridan, the dramatist. Known to his contemporaries primarily as an actor, Sheridan wrote a dissertation on grammar (1762) and *A Plan of Education for the Young Nobility and Gentry* (1769). His *Life of Swift* comprises Vol. I of his 1784 edition of Swift's works, which was larger and more complete than Hawkesworth's 1755 edition and which was subsequently reissued in several revised and enlarged versions. It is intended as yet another attempt to rectify the inaccuracies of Lord Orrery. Isaac Hawkins Browne (1705–60), whose opinion Sheridan cites on the 'oratory' of the *Drapier's Letters*, was the author of a long didactic poem on the immortality of the soul, but he owed his popularity to an ode, 'A Pipe of Tobacco', which he composed as an imitation of Pope, Swift, and Thomson.

[*A Tale of a Tub*] was first published in the following year 1704; and though without a name, yet the curiosity excited by the appearance of such a wonderful piece of original composition, could not fail of finding out the author, especially as not only the bookseller knew him, but as the manuscript had at different times been shown to several of sir William Temple's relations, and most intimate friends. When it is considered that Swift had kept this piece by him eight years, after it had been, by his own confession, completely finished, before he gave it to the world; we must stand astonished at such a piece of self-denial, as this must seem, in a young man, ambitious of distinction, and eager after fame; and wonder what could be his motive for not publishing it sooner. But the truth is, Swift set but little value on his talents as a writer, either at that time, or during the whole course of his life, farther than as they might contribute to advance some nobler ends, which he had always in view. Unsolicitous therefore about fame merely literary, or the reputation of an author, he could with the most perfect *sang froid* lock up this admirable piece in his desk, and wait, with the most philosophick patience, for a favourable season to produce it, when it might answer some more important purpose. After the time he had given the last finishing to it, the violence of parties ran so high for some years, and their disputes were carried on with such animosity, that he did not think the publick in a temper fit to receive the work, so as to produce the effects which he proposed from it. But as the rage of party began to cool at that time, and the opposition from the tories grew daily more feeble, as the power of the whigs increased; and as a firm establishment of the whig interest seemed to threaten, upon their principles, an entire disregard to, and neglect of all religion; Swift thought this a proper juncture to revive the topick of religion, and to show the excellency of the Established Church, over its two rivals, in a new way, adapted to common capacities, with regard to the understanding; and calculated to make way to the heart, through the pleasure which it afforded to the fancy. And without some artifice of that sort, it would have been impossible to have gained any attention at all to the topick of religion. People were quite wearied out with the continual repetition of the same dull arguments; or sore, on account of the ill temper with which the disputes were carried on, and the ill blood which they occasioned. The bulk of mankind were therefore in a fit disposition to fall in with the principle of moderation held out by the whigs; but as it was easy to see from some of their political measures, that moderation was not the point at which they intended to stop; but that an indifference with regard to any form of religion was likely to ensue, in consequence of some of their tenets; Swift thought it high time that the attention of the people toward the security of the established church should be roused, that they might be guarded against the undermining artifices of its enemies, secretly carried on under covert of her pretended friends; who in their hearts were little solicitous about her interests, being wholly absorbed in worldly pursuits. And surely nothing could be contrived better to answer this end, than to make religion once more a general topick of conversation; but of such conversation as no longer excited the disagreeable and malevolent passions, but gave rise to cheerfulness and mirth. Stripped of the frightful mask with which her face had been covered by bigotry and enthusiasm, and adorned with all the graces of the comick muse, she became a welcome guest in all companies. The beauty of the church of England, by a plain and well conducted allegory, adapted to all capacities, was shown, in the most obvious light, by the characters of simplicity and moderation, which are the true marks of christianity, in opposition to the pageantry, superstition, and tyranny of the church of Rome, on the one hand; and the spleen, hypocrisy, and enthusiasm of Calvinism, on the other. This had been often done before in a serious way, but it was the new manner of treating the subject that produced the great effect. While the English divines had for more than a century been engaged in a constant state of warfare with their antagonists, and attacked them with serious reasoning, and vehemence of argumentation, their antagonists were always considered as powerful and formidable; and though often foiled, were never looked upon as subdued. While these different religions were rendered odious or terrible to the imaginations of people, the very feelings of that hatred and fear, were accompanied with the ideas of danger and power in the objects which excited them, and of course gave them a consequence. But the instant they were rendered ridiculous, they became contemptible, and their whole power vanished; nor was there ever a stronger instance of the truth of Horace's rule,

Ridiculum acri
Fortius & melius magnas plerumque secat res;[1]

than in the effects produced by *A Tale of a Tub*, with regard to the weakening of the powers of popery and fanaticism in this country. Effects not merely temporary, but which, with their cause, are likely to last, as long as the English language shall be read.

After the publication of this work, Swift wrote nothing of consequence for three or four years; during which time his acquaintance was much sought after by all persons of taste and genius. There was, particularly, a very close connexion formed between Mr. Addison and him, which ended in a sincere and lasting friendship, at least on Swift's part. Addison's companionable qualities were known but to a few, as an invincible bashfulness kept him for the most part silent in mixed companies; but Swift used to say of him, that his conversation in a *tête-à-tête*, was the most agreeable he had ever known in any one; and that in the many hours which he passed with him in that way, neither of them ever wished for the coming in of a third person.

In the beginning of the year 1708, Swift started forth from his state of inactivity, and published several pieces upon religious and political

---

[1] 'Jesting oft cuts hard knots more forcefully and effectively than gravity', Horace, *Satires*, I, x, 14–15, Loeb Classical Library, trans. H. Rushton Fairclough, 1926, 116–17.

subjects, as also in the humourous way. That which regarded religion chiefly, was, *An Argument against abolishing Christianity*; in which he pursues the same humourous method, which was so successfully followed in *A Tale of a Tub*. Perhaps there never was a richer vein of irony than runs through that whole piece; nor could any thing be better calculated to second the general impression made by *A Tale of a Tub*. It is certain, that Swift thought the state of the church in great danger, notwithstanding any vote of parliament to the contrary; and this chiefly from a sort of lethargick disorder, which had in general seized those who ought to have been its watchful guardians. To rouse them from this state, he found tickling to be more effectual than lashing; and that the best way to keep them wakeful, was to make them laugh.

[45–50.]

Early in the following year, Swift published that admirable piece, called, *A Project for the Advancement of Religion*. In which, after enumerating all the corruptions and depravities of the age, he shows that the chief source of them was the neglect, or contempt of religion, which so generally prevailed. Though at first view this pamphlet seemed to have no other drift, but to lay down a very rational scheme for a general reformation of manners, yet upon a closer examination it will appear to have been a very strong, though covert attack, upon the power of the whigs. It could not have escaped a man of Swift's penetration, that the queen had been a long time wavering in her sentiments, and that she was then meditating that change in the ministry, which some time afterward took place. To confirm her in this intention, and to hasten the execution of it, appears, from the whole tenour of the pamphlet, to have been the main object he had in view, in publishing it at that time. For though it seems designed for the use of the world in general, and is particularly addressed to the countess of Berkeley, yet that it was chiefly calculated for the queen's perusal, appears from this; that the whole execution of his project depended upon the impression which it might make upon her mind; and the only means of reformation proposed, were such as were altogether in her own power. . . .

Nothing could have been better contrived to work upon the queen's disposition, than the whole of this tract. In which the author first shows all the corruptions and wickedness of the times, arose from irreligion: he shows that it is in her majesty's power alone, without other aid, to restore religion to its true lustre and force, and to make it have a general influence on the manners and conduct of her people: and then he urges the strongest motives, of honour, of interest, and of duty, to induce her to enter upon the immediate exercise of that power. And to render what he offered upon that head more forcible, it was apparently written by some disinterested hand, from no other principle but a due regard to religion and morality. For the author artfully suppressed all mention of party: and yet, upon a closer examination, it would appear, that nothing could be more directly, though covertly, aimed at the destruction of the power of the whigs. For, the first step proposed to render the design effectual, was, that the queen should employ none in her ministry, or in any offices about her person, but such as had the cause of religion at heart: now this was in effect to say, that she must begin with turning out the whigs, or low church party, who in general professed either an indifference to, or contempt of religion; and choose her officers from among the tories, or high church party, with whom the support of the interests of religion was the first and most generally avowed principle. . . .

Having expatiated on this topick [the Queen's ability to make religion fashionable, if she would do so], and shown how easily such a design might be carried into execution, if the queen would only form such a determination, he proceeds to enforce his arguments by conscientious motives; which were likely to have the strongest effects upon one of such a truly religious turn as the queen was.

[55-9.]

Whoever examines the *Drapier's Letters* with attention will find, that the great talents of Swift never appeared in a more conspicuous light than on this occasion. He saw that a plan was formed by the British minister to bring his country into the utmost distress. Notwithstanding the apparent opposition given to it by the Irish parliament and privy council, he knew too well the servile disposition of all men in office at that time, and their abject dependance on the minister, to suppose they would continue firm in their opposition, at the certain loss of their places, if he was determined to carry the point. He saw therefore no possible means of preventing the evil, but raising such a spirit in the whole body of the people, as would make them resolve on no account whatsoever to receive this coin. His writings in the character of a drapier were in such plain language, as rendered them perfectly intelligible to the meanest capacities. His arguments were so naturally deduced, and in such an easy series, from simple and evident principles, as carried the fullest conviction to every mind. But as it was necessary

to his purpose to rouse the feelings, as well as convince the understandings of mankind; without ever appearing to apply at all to the passions,
he raises them to the highest pitch, by seemingly casual strokes here and
there interspersed. So that the whole, on a transient view, appeared
what it professed to be, the work of an honest shopkeeper, of plain
common sense, who started out of his sphere to commence writer,
upon a view of the imminent danger with which his country was
threatened; and who could not, now and then, in the course of his
argument, suppress the honest indignation which rose in his breast, at
the unparalleled insolence of power, in treating a great and loyal kingdom with such indignity as would have been thought intolerable, even
by the inhabitants of the Isle of Man. Yet plain and simple as these
writings seem to be at first view, and such as every common reader
would imagine he could produce himself, upon a closer inspection they
would be found to be works of the most consummate skill and art; and
whoever should attempt to perform the like, would be obliged to say
with Horace:

> *Sudet multum, frustraque laboret*
> *Quivis speret idem.*[1]

I remember to have heard the late Hawkins Browne say, that the
Drapier's Letters were the most perfect pieces of oratory ever composed
since the days of Demosthenes. And indeed, upon a comparison, there
will appear a great similitude between the two writers. They both made
use, of the plainest words, and such as were in most general use
which they adorned only by a proper and beautiful arrangement
of them. They both made choice of the most obvious topicks, which,
by the force of genius they placed in a new light. They were equally
skilful in the arrangement and closeness of their arguments; equally
happy in the choice and brevity of their allusions: each so entirely master of his art, as entirely to conceal the appearance of art, so that they
seized on the passions by surprise. Nor were the effects produced by the
orations of Demosthenes on the Athenians, though set off with all the
advantage of a most powerful elocution, greater than what followed
from the silent pen of Swift. For in a nation made up of the most dis-
cordant materials, who never before agreed in any one point, he produced such a unanimity, that English and Irish, protestant, presbyterian,

---

[1] '. . . anybody [who] may hope for the same success, may sweat much and yet toil
in vain when attempting the same', Horace, *Ars Poetica*, 241–2, Loeb Classical Library,
470–1.

and papist, spoke the same language, and had but one voice. There is one advantage indeed which Swift had over Demosthenes, in that admirable vein of wit and humour, peculiar to himself, at which the other often made unsuccessful attempts; and of which, though sparingly, we find some shining instances scattered through those letters. One of which is so excellent, that I am tempted to present the passage to the reader. Where, speaking in the assumed character of the drapier, he says,

I am very sensible that such a work as I have undertaken, might have worthily employed a much better pen: but when a house is attempted to be robbed, it often happens that the weakest in the family, runs first to stop the door. All my assistance, were some informations from an eminent person; whereof I am afraid I have spoiled a few, by endeavouring to make them of a piece with my own productions; and the rest I was not able to manage. I was in the case of David, who could not move in the armour of Saul, and therefore I rather chose to attack this uncircumcised Philistine (Wood I mean) with a sling and a stone. And I may say for Wood's honour, as well as my own, that he resembles Goliah in many circumstances, very applicable to the present purpose: for, *Goliah had a helmet of brass upon his head, and he was armed with a coat of mail, and the weight of the coat was five thousand shekels of brass, and he had greaves of brass upon his legs, and a target of brass between his shoulders.*—In short he was, like Mr. Wood, all over *brass, and he defied the armies of the living God.*— Goliah's conditions of combat, were likewise the same with those of Wood: if he prevail against us, *then shall we be his servants.* But if it happens that I prevail over him, I renounce the other part of the condition; he shall never be a servant of mine; for I do not think him fit to be trusted in any honest man's shop. [*Drapier's Letters*, ed. Herbert Davis (1941), 48.]

Nothing showed the generalship of Swift in a higher point of view, during this contest, than his choice of ground both for attack and defence. He well knew of what importance it was to steer clear of party; and that if he had attacked the British minister as the real author, promoter, and abettor of this project, he would immediately have been stigmatized with the name of jacobite, and his writings of course disregarded. He therefore treated the matter all along as if there were no parties concerned but William Wood hardwareman, on the one side; and the whole kingdom of Ireland on the other. Or, as he himself expresses it, it was *bellum atque virum*, a kingdom on one side, and William Wood on the other. Nay he went farther, and finding that Wood in his several publications had often made use of Mr. Walpole's name, he takes upon him the defence of the latter in several passages of his fourth letter, which he concludes thus:

But I will now demonstrate, beyond all contradiction, that Mr. Walpole is against this project of Mr. Wood, and is an entire friend to Ireland, only by this one invincible argument; that he has the universal opinion of being a wise man, an able minister, and in all his proceedings pursuing the *true interest* of the king his master: and that as his integrity is above all *corruption*, so is his *fortune* above all *temptation*. [*Drapier's Letters*, ed. Herbert Davis (1941), 68.]

By the use of this irony, a double edged weapon, which he knew how to manage with peculiar dexterity, his argument cut both ways. To the bulk of readers it might pass for a real acquittal of Mr. Walpole of the charge brought against him, which would answer one end; and to those of more discernment, it obliquely pointed out the true object of their resentment; but this so guardedly, that it was impossible to make any serious charge against the author of his having such a design.

In the course of these writings, Swift took an opportunity of laying open his political principles, declaring the most zealous attachment to the protestant succession in the house of Hanover, and utter abhorrence of the pretender: by which means he removed the chief prejudice conceived against him, on account of the ill-founded charge of his being a jacobite, and opened the way for that tide of popular favour which afterwards flowed in upon him from all sides.

[230-4.]

The last charge, as before mentioned against Swift, and which has gained most general credit, is that of perfect misanthropy; and this is chiefly founded upon his supposed satire on human nature, in the picture he has drawn of the yahoos. This opinion has been so universally adopted by almost all who have read *Gulliver's Travels*, that to controvert it would be supposed to act in opposition to the common sense and reason of mankind. And yet I will undertake to overthrow it, by appealing to that very reason and common sense, upon which they suppose it to be founded. I shall only beg of my reader that he would lay aside for a while any prepossession he may have entertained of that kind, and candidly examine what I shall advance in support of the opposite side of the question; and if he finds the arguments there laid down unanswerable, that he will not obstinately persist in errour, by whatever numbers it may be supported, but ingenuously yield to conviction. The position I mean to prove is, that the whole apologue of the Houyhnhnms and Yahoos, far from being intended as a debasement of human nature, if rightly understood, is evidently designed to show in what the

233

true dignity and perfection of man's nature consists, and to point out the way by which it may be attained.

In order to this, let us first see with what design the fourth book of the *Travels* was written. In the first three books he has given various views of the different vices, follies, and absurdities of mankind, not without some mixture of good qualities, of virtue and wisdom, though in a small proportion to the others, as they are to be found in life. In his last book, he meant to exhibit two new portraits; one, of pure unmixed vice; the other, of perfect unadulterated virtue. In order that the native deformity of the one, might excite in us a deeper abhorrence of evil; and the resplendent charms of the other, allure us to what is good. To represent these to us in sensible forms, he clothes the one with the body of a man; the other with that of a horse. Between these two he divides the qualities of the human mind, taking away the rational soul from the Yahoo, and transferring it to the Houyhnhnm. To the Yahoo he leaves all the passions and evil propensities of man's nature, to be exerted without any check or control, as in the case of all other animals. The rational soul in the Houyhnhnm, acts unerringly as by instinct; it intuitively perceives what is right, and necessarily acts up to the dictates of reason. The Yahoo, as here described, is a creature of fancy, the product of the author's brain, which never had any thing similar to it upon earth. It has no resemblance to man, but in the make of its body, and the vicious propensities of its nature. It differs from him wholly in all the characteristical marks which distinguish man from the rest of the animal world. It has not a ray of reason, it has no speech, and it goes, like other quadrupeds, upon all four. Now, as reason, speech, and walking upright on two legs, are the universal properties of the human race, even in the most savage nations, which peculiarly mark their superiority over brutes, how, in the name of Heaven, has it come to pass, that by almost all who have read *Gulliver*, the Yahoos have been considered as beings of the human species, and the odious picture drawn of them, as intended to vilify and debase our nature? But it is evident from the whole account given of this creature of his fancy, that the author intended it should be considered as a mere beast, of a new species; for he has not only deprived it of all the characteristical distinctions of man before recited, but has superadded some material differences even in his bodily organs and powers, sufficient to distinguish it from the human race. He says,—
'They climbed high trees as nimbly as a squirrel, for they had strong extended claws before and behind, terminating in sharp points, and hooked.' Now it is well known, that the human nails, when suffered

to grow to any considerable length, never assume that shape, and unless pared, disable the hands from discharging their office. He says in another place,—'They are prodigiously nimble from their infancy.' This is directly opposite to the nature of the children of men, who are the most helpless in infancy, and the slowest in arriving at any degree of strength or agility, of all living creatures. Indeed it was necessary to the author's end, that of showing the vicious qualities of man's nature in their pure unmixed state, that the creature in whom they were placed should be a mere brute, governed as all others are by an irresistible instinct, without any control from a superiour faculty; and accordingly he seems to have thrown in these additional circumstances to distinguish it from any thing human. At the same time it was also necessary to give this creature the human form, in order to bring the lesson home to man, by having the vicious part of his nature reflected back to him from one in his own shape; for in the form of any other creature, he would not think himself at all concerned in it. Yet it is on account of its bodily form only, represented as it is in so hideous a light, that the pride of man was alarmed, and made him blind to the author's design, so as to charge him with an intention of degrading and vilifying the whole of human nature below that of brutes. I have already shown that the whole of human nature has no concern in what is related of this creature, as he is entirely deprived of all the characteristick properties of man which distinguish him from, and elevate him above all other animals. I have also shown, that even his body, however resembling in outward form, is not the body of a man, but of a beast. In the first place it is prone, like all other beasts, which never was the case in any human creature.

Os homini sublime dedit, cœlumque tueri Jussit.[1]

In the next, he has long hooked claws, which enable him to climb the the highest trees with the nimbleness of a squirrel, and to dig holes in the earth for his habitation. Their faces too, as in some other tribes of animals, were all alike, being thus described: 'The face of this animal indeed was flat and broad, the nose depressed, the lips large, and the mouth wide.' When we consider too, that these features were never enlivened by the rational soul, nor the countenance lighted up by the benevolent sensations in man, which constitute the chief beauty of the human face, but on the contrary were continually distorted by a variety

---

[1] 'He gave to man an upturned face and bade him [stand erect and] turn his eyes to heaven', Ovid, *Metamorphoses*, I, 85–6, Loeb Classical Library, trans. Frank Justus Miller, 1916, I, 8–9.

of malevolent passions, we must conclude with Gulliver, that such a man beast must be the most odious animal that ever crawled upon the face of the earth; and that his description of it, disgusting as it is, is not in the least exaggerated. At first sight they had so little resemblance to any thing human, that Gulliver mistook them for some new species of cattle belonging to the inhabitants. After having given a description of them as they appeared to him when he first saw a number of them near him, where he lay concealed behind a thicket, in order to mark their form more distinctly, he says,

So that thinking I had seen enough, full of contempt and aversion, I got up and pursued the beaten road, hoping it might direct me to the cabin of some Indian, I had not got far, when I met one of these creatures, full in my way, and coming up directly to me. The ugly monster, when he saw me, distorted several ways every feature of his visage, and started as at an object he had never seen before; then approaching nearer, *lifted up his fore paw*, whether out of curiosity or mischief, I could not tell: but I drew my hanger, and gave him a good blow with the flat side of it, for I durst not strike with the edge, fearing the inhabitants might be provoked against me, if they should come to know that I had killed or maimed any of *their cattle*. [*Gulliver's Travels*, ed. Herbert Davis (1941), Part IV, I, 224.]

And it was not till afterward, when he had an opportunity of examining one of them more closely in his kennel, that he perceived its resemblance to the human figure. But it may be asked, to what end has such an odious animal been produced to view? The answer is obvious: The design of the author, in the whole of this apologue, is, to place before the eyes of man a picture of the two different parts of his frame, detached from each other, in order that he may the better estimate the true value of each, and see the necessity there is that the one should have an absolute command over the other. In your merely animal capacity, says he to man, without reason to guide you, and actuated only by a blind instinct, I will show you that you would be degraded below the beasts of the field. That very form, that very body, you are now so proud of, as giving you such a superiority over all other animals, I will show you owe all their beauty, and all their greatest powers, to their being actuated by a rational soul. Let that be withdrawn, let the body be inhabited by the mind of a brute, let it be prone as theirs are, and suffered like theirs to take its natural course, without any assistance from art, you would in that case be the most deformed, as to your external appearance, the most detestable of all creatures. And with regard to your internal frame, filled with all the evil dispositions, and malignant passions of mankind, you would be the most miserable of beings, living in a continued state of internal vexation, and of hatred and warfare with each other.

On the other hand, I will show another picture of an animal endowed with a rational soul, and acting uniformly up to the dictates of right reason. Here you may see collected all the virtues, all the great qualities, which dignify man's nature, and constitute the happiness of his life. What is the natural inference to be drawn from these two different representations? Is it not evidently a lesson to mankind, warning them not to suffer the animal part to be predominant in them, lest they resemble the vile Yahoo, and fall into vice and misery; but to emulate the noble and generous Houyhnhnm, by cultivating the rational faculty to the utmost; which will lead them to a life of virtue and happiness.

It is not very extraordinary that mankind in general should so readily acknowledge their resemblance to the Yahoo, whose similitude to man consists only in the make of its body, and the evil dispositions of its mind; and that they should see no resemblance to themselves, in a creature possessed of their chief characteristical marks, reason and speech, and endowed with every virtue, with every noble quality, which constitute the dignity of man's nature, which distinguish and elevate the human above the brute species? Shall they arraign the author of writing a malignant satire against human nature, when reduced to its most abject brutal state, and wholly under the dominion of the passions; and shall they give him no credit for the exalted view in which he has placed the nobler part of our nature, when wholly under the direction of right reason? Or are mankind so stupid, as in an avowed fable, to stop at the outside, the vehicle, without diving into the concealed moral, which is the object of all fable? Do they really take the Yahoo for a man, because it has the form of a man; and the Houyhnhnm for a horse, because it has the form of a horse? But we need not wonder that the bulk of mankind should fall into this errour, when we find men pretending to the utmost depths of wisdom, avowing themselves of the same mind. The learned Mr. Harris, in his *Philological Inquiries*, has the following passage:

Misanthropy is so dangerous a thing, and goes so far in sapping the very foundations of morality and religion, that I esteem the last part of Swift's *Gulliver* (that, I mean, relative to his Houyhnhnms and Yahoos) to be a worse book to peruse, than those which we are forbid, as the most flagitious and obscene. One absurdity in this author (a wretched philosopher, though a great wit) is well worth remarking—in order to render the nature of man odious, and the nature of beasts amiable, he is compelled to give human characters to his beasts, and beastly characters to his men: so that we are to admire the beasts, not for being beasts, but amiable men; and to detest the men, not for being men, but detestable beasts. ['James Harris on *Gulliver's Travels*', No. 42, p. 208, above.]

I believe so strange an interpretation of an author's meaning, never fell from the pen of any commentator. He first assumes that the end proposed by Swift in this fable, is, to render the nature of man odious, and the nature of beasts amiable. This surely was a most unaccountable design in any human creature; and before it can be admitted, it ought to be first proved that Swift was of a beastly disposition, which engaged him on the side of his fellow brutes. And if this were his object, no mortal ever used more unlikely means to attain it, and no one ever more completely failed of his end. By representing a beast in a human form, without any one characteristical mark of man, he could hardly expect to render human nature itself odious: and by exhibiting so strange a phenomenon as the soul of man actuating a quadruped, and regulating his conduct by the rules of right reason, he could as little hope to render the nature of irrational beasts more amiable. And accordingly I believe no mortal ever had a worse opinion of human nature, from his description of the Yahoos; nor a better of the brute creation, from that of the Houyhnhnms. And all the ill effect produced by this fable, has been turned on the author himself, by raising the general indignation of mankind against him, from a mistaken view of his intention: so that the writer of the above remarks, need not have prohibited the reading of that part of *Gulliver* with such solemnity, as it never did, nor never can make one proselyte to misanthropy, whereof he seems so apprehensive; but on the contrary may be productive of great good, from the moral so evidently to be deduced from it, as has already been made appear.

In one paragraph of the above quoted passage, the author, wrapped up in the pride of philosophy, seems to look down upon Swift with sovereign contempt; where he says,—'One absurdity in this author (a *wretched philosopher*, though a great wit) is well worth remarking,' &c. But it has been already shown, that the absurdity belongs to the commentator, not to the author; and it will be difficult to persuade the world, that Swift is not one of the greatest adepts in the first philosophy, the science of mankind; of which he has given such ample proofs throughout his works, and more particularly in this very book, so superciliously decried by this *soi disant* philosopher; and which will be of more real benefit to mankind, than the labours of a thousand such writers as the author of *Philological Inquiries*, employed about splendid trifles, and useless metaphysicks.

Another writer of no small eminence has attacked Swift with great virulence on the same account. In a pamphlet of Dr. Young's, entitled *Conjectures on Original Composition*, there is the following passage:

If so, O Gulliver! dost thou not shudder at thy brother Lucian's vultures hovering o'er thee? Shudder on! they cannot shock thee more, than decency has been shocked by thee. How have thy Houyhnhnms thrown thy judgment from its seat, and laid thy imagination in the mire? In what ordure hast thou dipped thy pencil? What a monster hast thou made of the

Human face divine?

MILTON

This writer has so satirized human nature, as to give a demonstration in himself, that it deserves to be satirized. ['Edward Young on *Gulliver's Travels*', No. 31, p. 178, above.]

In answer to which I shall address him in his own way—O doctor Young, how has thy prejudice thrown thy judgment from its seat, and let thy imagination hurry thee beyond all bounds of common sense! In what black composition of spleen and envy hast thou dipped thy pen! What a monstrous character hast thou given of

One of the noblest men
That ever lived in the tide of times.
SHAKSPEARE.

Thou hast so satirized this great man, as to show that thou thyself deservest the utmost severity of satire. After such a string of poetical epiphonemas, what is the charge which he brings against Swift? It is all contained in these words—'What a monster hast thou made, of the human face divine!' Now as Dr. Young himself, and all the world must have allowed, that the human face can have no claim to the epithet of divine, unless when animated by the divine particle within us, how can he be said to make a monstrous representation of the human face divine, who first supposes the divine part to be withdrawn, which entitles it to that appellation, and substitutes in its place the mind of a brute? Must not the human countenance in this case lose all that beauty and expression, which it derives from the soul's looking out at the eyes, and animating every feature? On the contrary, what more deformed or shocking object can be exhibited to view, than the human face distorted by all the vile and malevolent passions belonging to man's nature? Let any one reflect what sensations he has had on the sight of an idiot, an outrageous madman, or one possessed by ungovernable fury, extreme hatred, or implacable revenge, and he must allow that the picture Swift gives of the Yahoo face, always expressive of some one or other of similar passions, however hideous it may be, is yet a just likeness.

What then is the meaning of the general clamour raised against Swift, unless it be thought criminal in him to suppose it possible, even in a fable, that the human frame, upon which we value ourselves so highly, might be the receptacle of a brutal soul? I should not wonder if such men should arraign the Almighty also, for having really effected this in the case of Nebuchadnezzar; or exhibiting another instance of it to our view, without a miracle, in that of Peter the wild man, caught in the woods of Germany; in whom was to be found a perfect image of that man beast which Swift supposes in his Yahoo. Nor should I be surprised if they who value themselves chiefly on their outward form, should mutter complaints against their Creator, for giving certain animals so near a resemblance to them, as is to be found in some species of baboons, but more particularly in the mantiger; who not only is formed exactly like man in his bodily organs, but, like him too, often walks erect upon two legs, with a staff in his hand, sits down upon chairs, and has the same deportment in many other points.

But while they so squeamishly take offence at this nonentity, this chimera of the brain, does it never occur to them that there really exist thousands and ten thousands of their own species, in different parts of this peopled earth, infinitely more detestable than the Yahoos. In whatever odious light their form has been portrayed, can it excite higher disgust than that of the Hottentot, decorated with guts, which are used for food when in a state of putrefaction; and who loads his head with a mixture of stinking grease and soot, to make a secure lodgement for swarms of the most filthy vermin? or than those savages, who lash, mangle, and deform, with a variety of horrid figures, the *human face divine*, in order to strike a greater terrour into their enemies? Are there any actions attributed to the miserable Yahoo so diabolical as are constantly practised in some of these savage nations, by exposing their children, murdering their parents in their old age, and roasting and eating their captives taken in war, with many other abominations? In all which instances we see, that human reason, in its state of depravity, is productive of infinitely worse consequences, than can proceed from a total deprivation of it. This lesson Gulliver has taken care to inculcate, where his master Houyhnhnm, after having received an account from him of the manners and customs of the Europeans, makes the following observation:

That although he hated the Yahoos of this country, yet he no more blamed them for their odious qualities, than he did a *gnnayh* (a bird of prey) for its cruelty, or a sharp stone for cutting his hoof. But when a creature, pretending to reason, could be capable of such enormities, he dreaded lest the corruption of that faculty, might be worse than brutality itself. [*Gulliver's Travels*, ed. Herbert Davis (1941), Part IV, V, 248.]

It may be said that the instances of depravity above quoted, are only to be found among savages, whose minds, unenlightened by knowledge, are governed wholly by their brutal appetites and passions; and that a true picture of human nature is only to be taken from the more civilized states. Let us see, therefore, whether in our own dear country, while we boast so much of the extraordinary lights drawn from philosophy, and the divine illumination of the Gospel, we do not abound in crimes more numerous, and more fatal to society, even than those of savages. Of these Swift has given us a long muster-roll, where he describes the happy life he led among the Houyhnhnms, free from the odious scenes of vice in his own country, in the following passage:

I enjoyed perfect health of body, and tranquillity of mind; I did not feel the treachery or inconstancy of a friend, nor the injuries of a secret or open enemy. I had no occasion of bribing, flattering, or pimping, to procure the favour of any great man, or his minion. I wanted no fence against fraud or oppression; here was neither physician to destroy my body, nor lawyer to ruin my fortune; no informer to watch my words and actions, or forge accusations against me for hire: here were no gibers, censurers, backbiters, pickpockets, highwaymen, housebreakers, attornies, bawds, buffoons, gamesters, politicians, wits, spleneticks, tedious talkers, controvertists, ravishers, murderers, robbers, virtuosoes: no leaders or followers of party and faction; no encouragers to vice by seducement or example; no dungeons, axes, gibbets, whippingposts, or pillories; no cheating shopkeepers or mechannicks; no pride, vanity, or affectation; no fobs, bullies, drunkards, strolling whores, or poxes; no ranting, lewd, expensive wives; no stupid proud pedants; no importunate, overbearing, quarrelsome, noisy, roaring, empty, conceited, swearing companions; no scoundrels raised from the dust upon the merit of their vices, or nobility thrown into it on account of their virtues; no lords, fidlers, judges, or dancingmasters. [*Gulliver's Travels*, ed. Herbert Davis (1941), Part IV, X, 276.]

In another place, after having brought the whole state of affairs in England before the judgment seat of the king of Brobdingnag, he thus relates the sentiments of that wise and virtuous monarch on the occasion:

He was perfectly astonished with the historical account I gave him of our affairs during the last century, protesting it was only a heap of conspiracies, rebellions, murders, massacres, revolutions, banishments, the very worst effects that avarice, faction, hypocrisy, perfidiousness, cruelty, rage, madness, hatred, envy, lust, malice, and ambition could produce. His majesty in another audience was at the pains to recapitulate the sum of all I had spoken; compared the questions with the answers I had given; then taking me into his hands, and stroking me gently, delivered himself in these words, which I shall never forget, nor the manner he spoke them in: 'My little friend *Grildrig*, by what I have gathered from your own relation, and the answers I have with much pains wringed and extorted from you, I cannot but conclude the bulk of your natives to be the most pernicious race of little odious vermin, that nature ever suffered to crawl on the surface of the earth.' [*Gulliver's Travels*, ed. Herbert Davis (1941), Part II, VI, 132.]

Is it not strange, that so bold a satire on human nature, in its actual state of existence, should excite no resentment in mankind, and that they should so readily take the alarm at an imaginary representation of it? But in the former case men are ready enough to see and allow all manner of vices and bad qualities of the mind in others, though they are so blinded by self-love as not to find the resemblance to themselves; but when their bodily form, common to all men, is vilified and debased, each individual brings the attack home to himself; his self-love takes fire at the view, and kindles his indignation against the author, as an enemy to the whole human species. That this opinion, however ill founded, became so general, is easily to be accounted for, as taking its rise from two of the most prevailing passions in human nature, pride and envy. The former called the universal passion by Dr. Young; and the latter partaking of its nature, as springing from the same root. Their pride instantly took fire upon seeing that part of their frame, whereof in general men are most vain, represented in so odious a light; and envy seized the occasion of making so heavy a charge as that of misanthropy, against a man of such uncommon talents. This broke forth chiefly among authors, jealous of that high degree of fame obtained by the superiority of his genius; and as he was unassailable on that side, they thought to bring him down more on a level with themselves, by attributing some of the finest exertions of that genius to a malevolent disposition: and as the prejudices of mankind were of their side, they cheaply purchased credit to themselves, from appearing champions for the dignity of human nature.

Yet there were not wanting others of clearer discernment, and a more liberal turn of mind, who saw this whole affair in its true light.

Among these the benevolent and judicious Dr. Hawksworth, steps
forth as an advocate for Swift, and decidedly gives judgment in his
faviour. In one of his notes on *Gulliver*, he says,

Whoever is disgusted with this picture of a *Yahoo*, would do well to reflect,
that it becomes his own in exact proportion as he deviates from virtue; for
virtue is the perfection of reason: the appetites of those abandoned to vice, are
not less brutal and sordid than those of a Yahoo, nor is their life a state of less
abject servility. ['John Hawkesworth on Swift', No. 29, p. 149, above.]

And in another of his comments upon a passage wherein Swift had
given a lively and true description of the horrours of war, stripped of all
the glare and false colouring thrown over it by vain glory and ambition,
he explains, justifies, and applauds the author's motive, for exhibiting
here, as well as in all other parts of this admirable work, such true
pictures of the vicious practices and habits of mankind, however
sanctified by custom, or embellished by fashion. His words are these,—

It would perhaps be impossible by the most laboured arguments, or forcible
eloquence, to show the absurd injustice and horrid cruelty of war, so effectually,
as by this simple exhibition of them in a new light: with war, including every
species of iniquity, and every art of destruction, we become familiar by degrees,
under specious terms; which are seldom examined, because they are learned at
an age in which the mind receives and retains whatever is imprest on it. Thus it
happens, that when one man murders another to gratify his lust, we shudder at
it; but when one man murders a million to gratify his vanity, we approve and
admire, we envy and applaud. If, when this and the preceding pages are read,
we discover with astonishment, that when the same events have occurred in
history, we felt no emotion, and acquiesced in wars which we could not but
know to have been commenced for such causes, and carried on by such means;
let not him be censured for too much debasing his species, who has contributed
to their felicity and preservation, by stripping off the veil of custom and prejudice, and holding up, in their native deformity, the vices by which they become wretched, and the arts by which they are destroyed. ['John Hawkesworth
on Swift', No. 29, p. 149, above.]

Such is the construction which will be put by all men of candour, taste,
and judgment, upon these, and all other passages in Swift of a similar
kind. But if there are still any who will persist in finding out their own
resemblance in the Yahoo, in the name of God, if the cap fits, let them
wear it, and rail on. I shall only take my leave of them with an old Latin
sentence, *Qui capit ille facit.*

[478-95.]

47. Incidental comments on *Gulliver's Travels*

1789

The Analytical Review, iv (May–August 1789), 77–8.

The unsigned notice from which this extract is taken is of *Mammuth; or, Human Nature displayed on a grand Scale . . .* by The Man in the Moon, the sentiments of which are compared favourably with those taken to be implied in the *Travels*.

THE author of this philosophic tour certainly took Swift for his model; but surveying human nature with a less prejudiced eye, the reader does not rise from the perusal of the remarks made by the Man in the Moon, with that painful sensation of disgust, and even distrust of Providence, which *Gulliver's Travels* never fail to excite in a mind possessed of any sensibility. That kind of fellow-feeling which attaches men to their species, Swift's caricature pictures, drawn indeed with a masterly hand by a misanthrope, whom disappointed ambition had stung to the quick, tends to tear up by the roots. We are led to detest, instead of compassionating, beings under the influence of vices obtruded on us in such glaring colours, and wonder, viewing mankind in this brutalized light, why they were created to contradict what appears in shining characters throughout the universe, that God is wise and good. It is not decent thus to expose wantonly the nakedness of our parent; nay, the disgust the representation inspires, silently destroys its force.

Though we agree that the real nature of all sentiments and passions is best understood when they are magnified to extravagance by the microscope of enthusiasm, yet, in magnifying them, a trite, but just remark, ought never to be lost sight of, that there is a uniform variety in the numerous modifications of human passions. In sketches of life, a degree of dignity, which distinguishes man, should not be blotted out; nor the prevailing interest undermined by a satirical tone, which makes the reader forget an acknowledged truth, that in the most vicious, vestiges may be faintly discerned of a majestic ruin, and in the most virtuous, frailties which loudly proclaim, that like passions unite the two extremities of the social chain, and circulate through the whole body.

48. George-Monck Berkeley on Swift

1789

Literary Relics: Containing Original Letters . . . To which is prefixed an Inquiry into the Life of Dean Swift, 1789, xxii–xxvi.

Berkeley (1763–93) was a grandson of Swift's friend, Bishop Berkeley, and so took an interest in Swift's life. He was a man of letters whose *Literary Relics*, including letters of his grandfather, of Swift, and of other famous people, are of some interest. In the *Inquiry*, Berkeley takes issue with hostile biographers of Swift, defending the 'Voyage to the Houyhnhnms' and *A Tale of a Tub*.

HAVING now concluded my remarks on the principal writers who have made any mention of Swift, I shall proceed to inquire with what degree of justice he has been charged with being a misanthrope.

THE authors of this charge have ever depended on the Yahoos for support: And where could those who wished to *throw dirt* have found more proper allies? for it seems to have been a favourite amusement among that celebrated nation. 'How,' exclaim the enemies of Swift, 'could a man that possessed one spark of benevolence paint human nature in such colours?' They then proceed to declaim for an hour on the *dignity of human nature;* a term which, though generally used, I could never comprehend: nor have I found, among those who were most frequent in the use of it, one person able to favour me with a satisfactory definition.

THE only meaning I can affix to the term is, that it alludes to a certain portion of dignity which is *innate* in us, and consequently *inseparable* from our *nature*. Now, if this definition be allowed to be just, it will be incumbent on the patrons of innate dignity to show in what it consists; and whether it be discernable in our state of infancy, which is more helpless than that of any other creature; or at a more advanced period of our lives, when we are slaves to our passions? or whether its splendor is more evident when our sun sets, enveloped in the cheerless clouds of dotage? Till this point be determined, I shall beg leave to remain an infidel with respect to the existence of this much injured DIGNITY.

THE writers on this subject seem to have involved themselves in an error by not distinguishing between the terms *natural* and *acquired*. That human nature is, by the practice of virtue, capable of acquiring great dignity, is what I most readily admit; but the dignity of an individual, thus acquired by himself, cannot be said to be the dignity of the species. No man who sees two mares at ASTLY's dancing a minuet will affirm that dancing is common to the whole species; or, because some men are born with a power of erecting their ears, that therefore it is a power common to the whole race. But admitting that this same DIGNITY existed any where but in the imaginations of those who declaim about it, the History of the Yahoos can by no means be considered as offering any insult to our nature. It only paints mankind in that state to which habits of vice must necessarily sink them. And it is surely not very reprehensible part of Swift's character, that, being by profession a teacher of morals, he should paint the deformity of vice in colours the most glaring, and in situations the most disgusting. It therefore remains with the public to determine, how far he is culpable who attempts to correct by satire those who are invulnerable to reproof, and deaf to persuasion; and how far a wish to make mankind better, and consequently happier, is a proof of misanthropy.

I SHALL not trespass on the reader's attention by recapitulating the many instances of benevolence and mercy that adorned the life of the illustrious Dean. They are *too* well known to need repetition, and are recorded where they will one day be amply rewarded. I shall therefore conclude this subject by observing, that of *his* benevolence no one can entertain a doubt, who sees him resigning the only preferment he possessed to relieve the wants of honest indigence; who sees him quitting the splendid mansions of the great, to visit the dreary residence of sequestered wo; exchanging the applause of peers and of princes for the inarticulate thanks of grateful poverty; whilst the smile which he frequently withheld from the great, beamed spontaneous on every child of sorrow.

I SHALL now proceed to the consideration of the second charge; namely, that of *Impiety*.

THE first and the most important argument on which the patrons of this charge rest their hopes of success, is the tendency said to be observable in *A Tale of a Tub*.

'OF this work,' says Johnson, 'charity may be persuaded to think, that it might be written by a man of a peculiar character without bad intention; but it is certainly of dangerous example.' I confess myself unable to discern the danger. *A Tale of a Tub* holds up to ridicule superstitious and fanatical absurdities, which having no weak side of common sense, defy argument, and are unassailable by learning: but the essentials of religion are never attacked; and that church, for which Johnson entertained the highest veneration, is every where treated with the respect which is due to the glory of the reformation. If, in the book, a flight of fancy now and then occurs which a serious mind would wish away, before Swift be convicted of impiety, the following circumstances ought to be impartially weighed.

IN the *first* place, *A Tale of a Tub* was the work of a very young man; and although the rule of Horace, *Nonum prematur in annum*, was observed, it still made its appearance at an early period of the author's life. To say that he whose youth is not totally exempt from levity will be disgraced by an old age of blasphemy, is perhaps not perfectly consistent with that first of human virtues, *charity*. But of that virtue the persecutors of Swift seem to have had little or no idea. *Secondly*, I maintain, that in the work before us there is not a single passage which implies a disbelief of revelation. At the same time I must confess, there are many passages that, with the assistance of *well-meaning* and *able commentators*, might be so construed as to prove, that the author was an admirer of the *Gentoo* tenets, and not wholly averse to the *God of Toibet*. For although my reading cannot as yet have been very extensive, I have read enough to know, that there is not the least necessity for *any sort of connection* between the *text* and the *commentary*.

49. Thomas Ogle on Swift and misanthropy

1790

Review of George-Monck Berkeley's *Literary Relics, The Monthly Review*, 2nd Series, iii (November 1790), 242.

Thomas Ogle, Surgeon Extraordinary to the Prince of Wales and a prolific reviewer for several of the periodicals of his day, comments here on Berkeley's defence of Swift's treatment of the Yahoos. Thus his remarks contain criticism of Swift as well as of Berkeley. Unlike many eighteenth-century critics, Ogle differentiates between Swift's writings and his moral character.

Swift has been charged with being a misanthrope; and as a proof of it, his character of the Yahoos has been quoted. In answer to this charge, we have a long discussion about the dignity of human nature; and we are told, that dignity is not inherent in mankind, because some men are dignified; any more than dancing is inherent in horses, because two mares at Astley's dance a minuet. What trifling is this! The simple question is, whether Man, such as he is, is superior, in the scale of existance [*sic*], to the other animals, by which he is surrounded. If he is, there is neither wisdom nor truth in representing him as their inferior;—and as for the argument, that Swift, 'being a teacher of morals, did right to paint the deformity of vice in colours the most glaring, and in situations the most disgusting;' it will appear futile, when we reflect that the morals of any individual are not likely to be amended by indiscriminate censure on the whole species. What inducement for an alteration in conduct, will the worthless man find, in seeing his virtuous neighbour held up to derision? Or what instruction will the honest well-meaning man derive from seeing himself degraded below the rank of a brute, and from being referred to brutes for a system of improved manners?—We mean not, however, to cast any severe censure on Swift for this part of his writings, which, in our opinion reflects neither honour nor reproach on his moral character.

The next charge which is combated, is that of impiety. We are acquainted with no part of Swift's writings which can justify such a charge; yet, if the stories related of him be true, there was in his actions, as well as in his writings, an occasional levity of manner, which might be censured, by some, as arising from an indifference about religion. Mr. Berkeley here curiously defends his conduct. Swift, he tells us, very early in life, conceived a violent disgust at that despicable vice, hypocrisy; and therefore carefully concealed his sense of religion, that he might not be thought an hypocrite! Is it not equal dissimulation, at least, if not hypocrisy, to be religious and seem impious?

50. Swift as satirist and poet

1790

(*a*) 'Some Outlines of the Character of Dr. Swift,' *European Magazine*, xviii (September 1790), 184–5.
(*b*) 'Character of Jonathan Swift, D.D., Dean of St. Patrick's, Dublin', *European Magazine*, xviii (November 1790), 329–32.

Of the two anonymous essays on Swift from which these extracts are taken, the first compares Swift to Dryden and other satirists; the second shows the bias of its time in taking as the criteria for imaginative writers the sublime and the pathetic, to neither of which Swift attains.

(*a*)

'*That great genius Doctor Swift*' is become almost appropriated to him, though by no eminent writers I confess; yet, I think, was never more improperly applied. I cannot find, in my own notion of the term, above two or three names with which it can agree; and when I have named Aristotle, Bacon, and Newton, I am nearly at the end of my catalogue. An all-comprehending mind, that sees every object on every side; sees the different relations (and, to an ordinary observer, contradictory) that it bears to other things we contemplate, seems to me alone worthy of the name. If Swift had this large comprehension and clear discernment, it is not to be collected from his writings: it is plain, whatever he had in contemplation, he remarked only on one side, and put together such ideas in his writings, as, standing in juxta-position, formed the burlesque or ridicule; in which talent, I believe, he may be allowed an original; for either we are ignorant of the circumstances and mode of the times in which Aristophanes, Plautus and Lucian wrote, or else he is, by a great interval, in that talent superior to them all. His satire is neither that of Horace, Persius, or Juvenal, though more like the last than any; his wit, otherwise called invention, is not the wit of Dryden, Addison, or Pope. Dryden is a better satirist than Swift, and much of what is

251

clever in Pope's Satires is manifestly derived from Dryden; though a late poetry balance-master places Pope above him as a poet. It is obvious to observe, that had Dryden studied the foibles of mankind as Swift did, he had been as great a master of ridicule, with ten times his versifying talent. Whether his prose be better than Dryden's I shall not say; more chaste, as critics term it, less adulterated with foreign words, and correct, it certainly is; but I have more pleasure in reading Dryden, where I rove thro' a wilderness of fruits and flowers, than in pacing through a garden laid out by line, and trimmed by art, as is Pope's artificial prose.

To consider Swift as a poet only, were doing him injustice; his whole talent that way consisted in finding out rhymes that surprise by their oddness, and was little more than an excellent crambo player, if we except the good sense he abounds with. How it comes that he is more admired as a poet (I am sure it is so in Ireland) than in any other part of his author-character, is not very difficult to account for. Nine in every ten readers think the jingling of words is the sublimest part of poetry, and I have many people now in my eye, who pass for clever scholars, that can read a canto of Hudibras (who, perhaps, is the most universal wit we know of) without conceiving any entertainment but from his rhymes.

To finish what I fear grows tedious to the reader, it must be owned Swift was a genius, though neither a great nor sublime one; and to characterise him in one word, he was, to use the expression of a late real wit, though no author, the first *left-handed* genius in the world. The metaphor is taken from fencing, where a left-handed adversary makes the wickedest pass, and the most difficult to be parried.

(b)

Full of the enthusiasm which this [reading the classics at Moor Park] inspired, and of attachment for his patron, who was involved in the controversy of Wotton and Bentley, he produced that beautiful satire, *The Battle of the Books*. It was at the same time that he entered upon his very celebrated and extraordinary work, *A Tale of a Tub*. None but a young man would probably have undertaken to concenter in one volume, a satire upon the various abuses in religion and in learning. He has performed, however, what he designed, we will venture to affirm, in a manner more complete than perhaps could have been done by any other writer in any age. The performance is enriched with an exuberance of wit and the happiest vein of irony. No publication can rise to the highest eminence without being the object of much censure. We

believe, however, that a judicious and impartial critic would find little
to object to the principal allegory upon the subject of christianity. In
the other parts of the work there is, what can little be pardoned by the
reader of elegance and taste, much obscurity; and what will less be
passed over by the friend of decency and morality, much obscenity.
Upon the whole, however, we believe that few minds at the age of
thirty years ever produced a more comprehensive and vigorous performance than *A Tale of a Tub*. . . .

About the year 1720 Dr. Swift formed the plan of his last, and, as it
has usually been considered, his best production. We need not say that
we mean the *Travels of Gulliver*. The work is founded in the utmost
wantonness of invention. It has a liveliness of description and a simplicity of narrative that render it equally interesting to persons of both
sexes, and of all ages. It instantly became the only subject of conversation; everybody wondered, everybody admired, and everybody sought
for meanings that were never intended. The performance, though
highly polished, is unequal. The 'Voyage to Laputa' is much inferior to
the other parts of the work: That to the Houyhnhnms seems to be the
favourite of the author, and has much merit in its composition. But the
lesson it is designed to inculcate is so hateful, as to render it a disgrace
to any book, and to any author. The 'Voyage to Brobdingnag' is by
far the most excellent. . . .

That he understood the genius of the English language better than
most of his contemporaries, we are firmly persuaded. His style is pure,
serious, and manly, beyond the example of any of his predecessors. But
something we have gained in purity and something in strength, since he
wrote. That we have been also gainers in elegance, in melody, in grace,
is to say little; for these were qualities after which Swift did not aspire.
His genius was rigid and severe. He rejected the flowers of rhetoric; he
disdained the flow of eloquence and the rounded period. Precision is his
chief aim, and perspicuity his principal praise.

But there is another character of which Swift was ambitious, to
which his claim is not so eminent. We mean that of originality. He had
more originality than Addison, and more than Pope. His style is highly
peculiar and characteristic, and this is the first proof of genius. But his
fancy was not rich and luxuriant; he does not lose himself in fields of his
own creation. The mind that is not turned either to the sublime or the
pathetic, cannot certainly rank in the first class of writers of imagination. The fictions of Lilliput and Brobdingnag will appear, to a vulgar
reader, as belonging to the highest species of invention. But in reality

they are of all fictions the most simple and obvious; and the genius of Swift is rather to be acknowledged in supporting, than in producing them.

The understanding of Swift was strong and manly. His penetration was great; his mode of reasoning clear, vigorous, attractive, and convincing. But these do not rank among the highest and most original powers of the mind. His chief praise is that of humour. His humour was perfectly his own, and was never excelled. Cervantes does not keep his countenance better; and the stores of allusion by which Butler was characterized, are not more inexhaustible. It has a march, plain, dry, and unambitious, that is absolutely irresistable. . . .

Something must be said of the poetry of Swift: and in his productions in verse there is nothing wire-drawn and insipid, jejune and bombast, like those poetical remains which have disgraced some of the most celebrated prose-writers in the world. The versification is easy, and the humour is natural. But in reality they are to be regarded in the very same light with his other compositions. They are nothing more than prose in rhyme. Imagination, metaphor, and sublimity constitute no part of their merit. Sir Isaac Newton was within a trifle as great a poet as Dr. Swift.

51. William Godwin on Swift's style

1797

Essay XII, 'Of English Style', Section 5, 'Age of Queen Anne',
The Enquirer . . . *a Series of Essays*, 1797, 443–6.

Though Godwin (1756–1836) is best known to students of literature for his eccentricity, his personal influence on the Romantic
poets, and his radical *Political Justice* (1793), his writings also include much historical, literary, and philosophical material.
Caleb Williams, his novel of social commentary, and his two-
volume *Life of Geoffrey Chaucer* were both well received. Robert
Lowth (1710–87), the 'great authority' Godwin cites here, was
Professor of Poetry at Oxford before becoming Bishop of
London, and was a respected critic of both Hebrew and English
letters.

We now come to Swift, respecting whom the great authority of Lowth
has pronounced that 'he is one of the most correct, and perhaps the best
of our prose writers.' No author was ever more applauded by his
contemporaries: no author ever produced a greater public effect, than
he is supposed to have done, by his *Conduct of the Allies*, and his *Drapier's
Letters*. For his solicitude about accuracy, he deserves to be considered
with respect. For the stern and inflexible integrity of his principles, and
the profound sagacity of his speculations, he will be honoured by a
distant posterity.

We will confine ourselves in our specimens, to his *A Tale of a Tub*
and *Gulliver's Travels*, the two best of his works; the former written
with all the rich exuberance of youthful imagination; the latter in his
last stage of intellectual cultivation, and, as Milton expresses it, 'the
most consummatt act of his fidelity and ripeness.'

A Tale of a Tub is a work of perhaps greater felicity of wit, and more
ludicrous combinations of ideas, than any other book in the world. It is
however, written in so strange a style of 'banter' to make use of one of

the author's words, or rather in so low and anomalous a slang, which perhaps Swift considered as the necessary concomitant of wit; that it is by no means proper to be cited as an example of just composition. The reader however may not be aware of this; and, to remove the scruples with which he may possibly be impressed, I will adduce a few instances. . . .

Gulliver's Travels is a book in which the author seems to have called up all his vigilance and skill in the article of style: and, as the plan of his fiction led to that simplicity in which he delighted, no book can be taken as a fairer specimen of the degree of cultivation at which the English language had at that time arrived. Swift was perhaps the man of the most powerful mind of the time in which he lived.

52. John Nichols on Swift

1801, 1828

(a) *The Works of the Reverend Jonathan Swift* (19 vols.), 1801.
  1. Note on *Gulliver's Travels*, Book III, viii, 397.
  2. Introduction to Swift's Sermons, ix, 99.
(b) *Illustrations of the Literary History of the Eighteenth Century* (8 vols.), 1828, 396–7.

After editing several supplementary volumes to Sheridan's 1784 edition of Swift's works, John Nichols (1745–1826) published his own edition in 1801. Like the earlier editions by Hawkesworth and Sheridan, it included notes by many critics, along with a biography of Swift. Nichols's attitude toward his own editorship is revealed in his comments in *Illustrations of the Literary History of the Eighteenth Century* on Sir Walter Scott's edition. *Illustrations . . .* is a sequel to Nichols's nine-volume *Literary Anecdotes of the Eighteenth Century* (1812–15); each work is a compendium of information on the printing and publishing world of the day and contains many incidental critical comments.

(a)

Dr. *Swift* seems to have borrowed several hints, in his Voyage to *Laputa* from a novel written by the learned Dr. *Francis Godwin*, Bishop of *Landaff*, called *Man in the Moon, or a Discourse of a Voyage Thither*, by *Domingo Gonsales*, 1638, 8vo. This philosophic romance, which has been several times printed, shows that Bishop *Godwin* had a creative genius. His *Nuncius Inanimatus*, which contains instructions to convey secret intelligence, is very scarce. He died in April 1633.

Though the Dean's first and most laudable ambition was to excel as a preacher, he frequently declared that he had not talents for it; and therefore would not publish any sermons, though often pressed by his friends to do it. He was, however, well attended by a crowded audience every fifth Sunday at his cathedral, when the preaching came to his turn, which was well known in Dublin; and his 'sermons', lord Orrery observes,

are certainly curious, for such reasons as would make other works despicable. They were written in a careless hurrying manner, the offspring of necessity, not of choice; so that we see the original force of his genius more in these compositions, that were the legitimate sons of duty, than in other pieces, that were the natural sons of love. They were held in such low esteem in his own thoughts, that, some years before he died, he gave away the whole collection to Dr. Sheridan, with the utmost indifference. 'Here,' says he, 'are a bundle of my old sermons; you may have them if you please: they may be of use to you; they have never been of any to me.' The parcel given to Dr. Sheridan consisted of about five-and-thirty sermons.

Twelve of these, having come to light at different periods of time, are here collected; and a perusal of any one of them must excite a wish for those which we have not been so happy as to recover.

(b)

Thus matters rested till 1801, when, at the request of the London Booksellers, many of whom had given large sums for the purchase of shares in the Dean's Works, I undertook to incorporate the various scattered articles which I had collected, and to make a complete arrangement of the whole Work, which was accordingly completed in Nineteen 8vo volumes; re-printed in Twenty-four small volumes in 1804; and again in Nineteen octavo volumes in 1808; . . .

Here ends my own Literary History as Editor of the Works of the far-famed Dean of St. Patrick's; for, about that period, the great Magician of the North, [not then *Unknown*,] having made a solid breakfast on John Dryden, conceived the idea of a pleasant dinner and supper on Jonathan Swift; which, from the entertainment I had prepared, he found a task of no great difficulty. Laying his potent wand on my humble labours, he very soon, by a neat shuffling of the cards, and by abridging my tedious annotations, (turning lead to gold)[1] he presented to the Booksellers of Edinburgh an Edition somewhat similar to mine, and consisting of the same number of volumes; condescending, however, to honour me with this brief compliment:

The valuable and laborious Edition of Mr. *Nicol* [the misnomer is of no consequence] was the first which presented to the publick any thing resembling a

---

[1] The pecuniary remuneration to Sir Walter Scott was precisely *thirty* times as much as I had received, or expected, for my Three Editions.

complete collection of Swift's Works; and unquestionably those who peruse it, must admire the labour and accuracy of the Editor.

It would be unjust to the talents of Sir Walter Scott, were I not to add that he has, by condensing the various Memoirs of the Dean which had been given by preceding Writers, exerted his usual ability in an elegant Life of Swift; and that he was fortunate enough to obtain some useful contributions from Theophilus Swift, Esq., of Dublin, son of Deane Swift, the near kinsman and biographer of the celebrated Dean of St. Patrick's . . .

53. Alexander Chalmers on Swift's style and character

1803

The British Essayists: with Prefaces Historical and Biographical (38 vols.), 1803, i, 53–59 *passim*.

Chalmers (1759–1834), a prolific editor and biographer, introduced many eighteenth-century works to nineteenth-century readers, often in co-operation with the printer John Nichols. In addition to the collection of periodical literature which appeared in *The British Essayists*, Chalmers prepared editions of the works of numerous authors, including Fielding, Gibbon, and Dr. Johnson, and a comprehensive enlargement of *The General Biographical Dictionary* (1812–17).

Among the occasional contributors to *The Tatler*, Swift has been often mentioned. It is not improbable that he frequently gave hints, but there is not much that can be assigned to his pen. He wrote, in No. 9, the 'Description of the Morning;' in No. 32, the history of Madonella; in No. 35, from internal evidence, the family of Ix; in No. 59, the letter signed Obadiah Greenhat: in No. 63, Madonella's Platonic College: in No. 66, the first article, on pulpit oratory: in No. 67, the proposal for a Chamber of Fame: in No. 68, a continuation of the same: in No. 70, a letter on oratory signed Jonathan Rosehat: in No. 71, a letter on the irregular conduct of a clergyman: No. 230, entire; in No. 238, the poetical description of a shower; and No. 258, a short letter on the words 'Great Britain.' These are all the communications that can with any confidence be ascribed to Swift, a writer who, with a rich fund of humour, an easy and flowing style, perhaps more correct than that of any of his contemporaries, with habits of observation, and a keen discernment of folly and weakness, was nevertheless ill qualified for this species of composition. His wit was so licentious, that no subject, however sacred, and no character however amiable, were safe; his invective has more of malignity than virtuous indignation: his characters are drawn in hideous distortion; and perhaps no man ever attempted to ridicule vice or folly with less of the salutary and gentle spirit of correction. . . .

Mr. Sheridan's defence of the Fourth part of *Gulliver's Travels*, is ingenious; but when he censures the opposition to this work as prejudice, he forgets that is not the prejudice of the vulgar, but the opinion of every writer of piety or taste who has considered the subject. With respect to his attack on Dr. Johnson, except where he has corrected some mistakes in point of fact, it may safely be left unanswered. In this he was too obviously imitating one of the *virtues* of his idol. He was taking that vengeance for which he had long prepared his mind. As a critic, Mr. Sheridan has not always been successful. Swift's style was, beyond all precedent, pure and precise, yet void of ornament or grace, and partook in some instances of the pride and dogmatism of its author: nor does his Biographer seem to be aware, that his most incorrect composition is his *Proposal for correcting the English tongue*.

Those who wish to appreciate Swift's character with justice, must derive their information from his voluminous writings, which undoubtedly place him among the most illustrious ornaments of literature, as an author of incomparable ability, of multiform talent, and inexhaustible fancy.

54. *Swiftiana*
1804

Charles Henry Wilson, *Swiftiana* (2 vols.), 1804 i, lxxxv–lxxxvi.

This book is a collection of anecdotes (often spurious) about Swift, witty passages from his works, and critical comments, made by Charles Henry Wilson (1756–1808). Wilson also edited collections of songs and selections from the writings of Edmund Burke and Tom Brown. *Swiftiana* was followed by a similar work. *Brookiana: Anecdotes of Henry Brooke* (2 vols.), 1804.

Swift was well acquainted with human nature in high and low scenes; but his knowledge more resembled that of Homer, Shakespeare, Addison, and Fielding, than that of Aristotle, of Locke, of Hucheson, or of Reed. He used to declare that he never could understand logic, physics, metaphysics, natural philosophy, mathematics, or any thing of that sort. His style is characterized by a masterly conciseness. He was the first writer who attempted to express his meaning without subsidiary words and corroborative phrases. He nearly laid aside the use of synonyms, in which even Addison had in small degree indulged, and without being solicitous for the structure or harmony of his periods, devoted all his attention to illustrate the force of individual words. Scarcely one metaphor is to be found in his works. His images are surprizingly unexpected, and exhibited in their genuine native form. Politics were his favourite topic; and in party writing he was far superior to any man of his time, not excepting Addison.—Of his poetry, a flowing ease is its leading feature; he had not taste for heroics, and hated an Alexandrine. His poems were written either to please or to vex particular persons; and he is in general severely useful rather than politely engaging. Swift has been called the Rabelais of England. He was less learned than Rabelais, but his wit is more pointed, and in general more delicate. He is the Rabelais of high life, for *cum magnis Vixisse* was not more applicable to Horace than to Swift. He used to say, 'When I sit down to write a letter, I never lean upon my elbow until I have finished it.' His letters, therefore, must be taken as affording a true representation of his mind. They greatly illustrate his character, and shew the misanthrope often lost in the good-natured man; but as it has been justly observed, he must never be looked upon as a traveller in the common road. When he appears most angry, he is most pleased, and when he is most assuming, he is most humble.

55. John Aikin on Swift's poetry

1804, 1820

(*a*) *Letters to a Young Lady on a Course of English Poetry*, 1804, 62–76.

(*b*) *Select Works of the British Poets*, 1820, 390.

John Aikin (1747–1822), a physician, is the author of numerous essays on English poetry. Like many of his contemporaries, he felt that the chief end of criticism of eighteenth-century works was to make them palatable to the delicate tastes of nineteenth-century readers. As an editor Aikin finds the selection of Swift's poems 'perplexing', and as a critic he warns the reader to leave much of Swift's poetry 'unvisited'. However, once he has made a careful selection of poems to discuss 'safely', Aikin's comments are specific and rather detailed.

(*a*)

Dean SWIFT is in our language the master in *familiar poetry*. Without the perusal of his works no adequate conception can be formed of wit and humour moving under the shackles of measure and rhyme with as much ease as if totally unfettered; and even borrowing grace and vigour from the constraint. In your progress hitherto, although it has been through some of our most eminent poets, you cannot but have observed, that the necessity of finding a termination to a line of the same sound with that of the preceding, has frequently occasioned the employment of an improper word, such as without this necessity would never have suggested itself in that connexion. Indeed, it is not uncommon in ordinary versifiers to find a whole line thrown in for no other purpose than to introduce a rhyming word. How far rhyme is a requisite decoration of English verse, you will judge from your own perceptions, after perusing the best specimens of blank verse. It is manifest, however, that when employed, its value must be in proportion to its exactness, and to its coincidence with the sense. In these respects, Swift is without exception the most perfect rhymer in the language; and you will admire how the very word which by its meaning seems most fit for the occasion, slides in without effort as the echo in sound to the terminating word of the preceding line. Even double and triple rhymes are ready at his call, and, though suggesting the most heterogeneous ideas, are happily coupled by some of those whimsical combinations in which comic wit consists.

The diction of Swift is the most complete example of colloquial ease that verse affords. In aiming at this manner, other writers are apt to run into quaintness and oddity; but in Swift not a word or phrase occurs which does not belong to the natural style of free conversation. It is true, this freedom is often indecorous, and would at the present day be scarcely hazarded by any one who kept good company, still less by a clergyman. Yet he has known how to make distinctions; and while many of his satirical and humorous pieces are grossly tainted with in-delicacies, some of his best and longest compositions are void of any thing that can justly offend. It is evident, indeed, that Swift, though destitute of genius for the sublimer parts of poetry, was sufficiently capable of elegance, had he not preferred indulging his vein for sarcastic wit. No one could compliment more delicately when he chose it, as no one was a better judge of proprieties of behaviour, and the graces of the female character.

From the preceding representation, you will conclude that I cannot set you to read Swift's works straight forwards. In fact, your way through them must be picked very nicely, and a large portion of them must be left unvisited. It should be observed, however, to do him justice, that their impurities are not of the moral kind, but are chiefly such as it is the scavenger's office to remove.

The first of his poems which I shall point out to your notice is the longest and one of the most serious of his compositions. Its title, 'Cadenus and Vanessa,' denotes his own concern in the subject; for *Cadenus* is Decanus (the Dean) transposed; and *Vanessa* is the poetical name of miss Vanhomrigh, a young lady whose unfortunate love for him met with a cold return. This piece, under an ingenious mythological fiction, contains a fine compliment to the lady, and much severe satire on the greater part of her sex, as well as on the foppish part of ours. You must, indeed, in reading Swift, arm yourself with patience to endure the most contemptuous treatment of your sex; for which, if really justified by the low state of mental cultivation among the females of that period, you may console yourself by the advantageous comparison afforded by that of the present age. The poem does not finish the real story; for it says,

> what success Vanessa met
> Is to the world a secret yet.

The melancholy truth was, that after uniting himself secretly with another woman, he continued to visit Vanessa, and she retained her hopes of softening his obduracy, till a final explanation broke her heart. This poem was in her possession, and by her direction was published after her death.

The 'Poems to Stella' will naturally follow. This was the lady to whom the former was sacrificed; but she seems to have had little enjoyment in the preference. His pride, or his singularity, made him refuse his consent to the publication of their marriage, and they continued to live apart as mere friends. Yet he appears to have sincerely loved her, probably beyond any other human being; and almost the only sentiments of tenderness in his writings are to be found in the poems addressed to her. This affection, however, does not in general characterize them, and the writer's disposition to raillery breaks out in the midst of his most complimentary strains. A Frenchman would be shocked at his frequent allusions to her advancing years. His exposure of her defects, too, may seem much too free for a lover, or even a husband; and it is easy to conceive that Stella's temper was fully tried in the connection. Yet a woman might be proud of the serious approbation of such a man, which he expresses in language evidently coming from the heart. They are, indeed,

> Without one word of Cupid's darts,
> Of killing eyes and bleeding hearts;

but they contain topics of praise which far outlive the short season of youth and beauty. How much superior to frivolous gallantry is the applause testified in lines like these!

> Say, Stella, feel you no content
> Reflecting on a life well spent?
> Your skilful hand employ'd to save
> Despairing wretches from the grave,
> And then supporting with your store
> Those whom you dragg'd from death before?
> Your generous boldness to defend
> An innocent and absent friend;
> That courage which can make you just

> To merit humbled in the dust;
> The detestation you express
> For vice in all its glittering dress;
> That patience under tort'ring pain
> Where stubborn stoics would complain?
> ['Stella's Birthday, 13 March,
> 1726,' Swift's *Poems*, ed. Harold
> Williams (1937), II, 764–5.]

In the lines 'To Stella visiting him in sickness,' there is a picture of *honour*, as influencing the female mind, which is morally sublime, and deserves attentive study:

> Ten thousand oaths upon record
> Are not so sacred as her word;
> The world shall in its atoms end
> Ere Stella can deceive a friend; &c.
> [*Poems*, ed. Harold
> Williams (1937), II, 724.]

There is something truly touching in the description of Stella's ministring in the sick chamber, where

> with a soft and silent tread
> Unheard she moves about the bed.

In all these pieces there is an originality which proves how much the author's genius was removed from any thing trite and vulgar: indeed, his life, character and writings were all singularly his own, and distinguished from those of other men.

May I now, without offence, direct you by way of contrast to the 'Journal of a Modern Lady?' It is, indeed, an outrageous satire on your sex, but one perfectly harmless with respect to yourself or any whom you love. I point it out as an admirable example of the author's familiar and colloquial manner. It also exhibits a specimen of his powers in that branch of poetical invention which is regarded as one of the higher efforts of the art. A more animated group of *personifications* is not easily to be met with than the following lines exhibit:

> When, frighted at the clamorous crew,
> Away the God of Silence flew,
> And fair Discretion left the place,
> And Modesty, with blushing face.
> Now enters overweening Pride,

267

And Scandal ever gaping wide,
Hypocrisy with frown severe,
Scurrility with gibing air,
Rude Laughter, seeming like to burst,
And Malice, always judging worst,
And Vanity with pocket-glass,
And Impudence with front of brass,
And study'd Affectation came,
Each limb and feature out of frame,
While Ignorance, with brain of lead,
Flew hov'ring o'er each female head.

[*Poems*, ed. Harold
Williams (1937), II, 448.]

The poems of Swift are printed in a different order in different editions;
I shall therefore attend to no particular order in mentioning them to
you. As I have commended the last for the easy familiarity of its style,
I shall next refer to one which perhaps stands the first in this respect;
and in which, not only the language of the speakers, but their turn of
thinking, is imitated with wonderful exactness. This is, 'The Grand
Question debated, whether Hamilton's Bawn should be turned into a
Barrack or a Malt-house.' The measure is that which is classically called
anapaestic, chiefly consisting of feet or portions composed of two short
and one long syllable. Next to that of eight syllables, it is the most used
for light and humorous topics; and no kind of English verse runs so
glibly, or gives so much the air of conversation. The satire of the piece
is chiefly directed against the gentlemen of the army, for whom Swift,
probably through party prepossessions, seems always to have entertained both aversions and contempt. It is, however, irresistibly pleasant.

Another conversation piece which rivals the last in ease, though not
in humour, is 'Mrs. Harris's Petition.' The singularity of it is the long
loose measure in which it is written, and which indeed is scarcely to be
called verse, though divided into lines terminated with rhyme. Swift
was fond of oddities of all kinds, some of which sink into mere puerilities. The number of these, raked together by injudicious editors, would
have injured his reputation, had it not been solidly founded upon pieces
of real excellence.

The story of 'Baucis and Philemon', imitated from Ovid, is one of
the happiest examples of that kind of humour which consists in mod-
ernising an antient subject in the way of parody. It will be worth your
while first to read a translation of the original tale, which you will find

in Dryden's *Fables*. The dexterity with which Swift has altered it to his purpose, cannot fail to strike you upon the comparison. The particulars of the transformation are fancied with all the circumstantial propriety for which this author is famous, and are described with great pleasantry. The *personifying* of Philemon gives occasion to some sarcastic strokes against his own profession, in which he frequently indulged, though he could not readily bear them from others.

His imitations from Horace, those, especially, which begin 'Harley the nation's great support,' and 'I've often wish'd that I had clear,' are equally excellent. They do not, like the former, borrow a subject from antiquity, but follow allusively the train of thought and incident presented by the original. You must, I fear, be content to lose the pleasure derived from this allusive resemblance; but you cannot fail of being entertained by the ease and humour with which he tells his story. In these qualities he is certainly unrivalled; and the pieces in question would afford an useful study to one who should investigate the means by which this air of facility is obtained. The colloquial touches in the following lines are admirable in this view:

> 'Tis (let me see) three years and more,
> (October next it will be four.)—

> My lord—the honour you design'd—
> Extremely proud—but I had din'd.—

Though many more entertaining *pickings* may be made from this author, and even some pieces of considerable length might be safely recommended to your perusal, (as, for example, the 'Rhapsody on Poetry,' and the 'Beast's Confession'), yet I shall bring my remarks to a conclusion, with the 'Verses on his own Death,' a piece written in the maturity of his powers, and upon which he evidently bestowed peculiar attention. Its foundation is a maxim too well suited to Swift's misanthropical disposition; and he must be allowed to have illustrated it with much knowledge of mankind, as well as with a large portion of his characteristic humour. Yet it may be alleged, that his temper was too little calculated to inspire a tender affection in his friends, to render the manner in which his death would be received, an example for all similar cases. Still it is, perhaps, generally true, that in the calamities of others,

> Indifference clad in wisdom's guise
> All fortitude of mind supplies;

and that the ordinary language of lamentation at the decease of one not intimately connected with us, and whose life was not greatly important to our happiness, is little more than, as he has represented it, the customary cant of feeling. We must likewise assent to the remark on the force that selfishness gives to sympathy, which he has so finely expressed in the following lines:

> Yet should some neighbour feel a pain
> Just in the parts where I complain,
> How many a message he would send?
> What hearty prayers that I should mend?
> Inquire what regimen I kept,
> What gave me ease, and how I slept?
> And more lament when I was dead
> Than all the snivellers round my bed.
> [*Poems*, ed. Harold
> Williams (1937), II, 557.]

The lamentations of his female friends over their cards will amuse you, as one of his happiest conversation-pieces. The greater part of the poem is devoted to the justification of his character and conduct; and, unless you have acquainted yourself with his life, will not greatly interest you. Indeed, I recollect reading it with greater pleasure in the earlier editions, when there was less detail of this kind.

So much may suffice for an author who, upon the whole, is regarded rather as a man of wit than as a poet. Though inimitable in one style of writing, his excellence is limited to that style. His works are extremely amusing, but the pleasure we taken in them is abated by a vein of malignity which is too apparent even when he is most sportive.

(b)

Of the poems of Swift, some of the most striking were composed in mature life, after his attainment of his deanery of St. Patrick; and it will be admitted that no one ever gave a more perfect example of the easy familiarity attainable in the English language. His readiness in rhyme is truly astonishing; the most uncommon associations of sounds coming to him as it were spontaneously, in words seemingly the best adapted to the occasion. That he was capable of high polish and elegance, some of his works sufficiently prove; but the humorous and sarcastic was his habitual taste which he frequently indulged beyond the bounds of decorum; a circumstance which renders the task of selection from his works somewhat perplexing. In wit, both in verse and prose, he stands foremost in grave irony, maintained with the most plausible air of serious simplicity, and supported by great minuteness of detail. His *Gulliver's Travels* are a remarkable exemplification of his powers in this kind, which have rendered the work wonderfully amusing, even to childish readers, whilst the keen satire with which it abounds may gratify the most splenetic misanthropist. In general, however, his style in prose, though held up as a model of clearness, purity, and simplicity, has only the merit of expressing the author's meaning with perfect precision.

56. Richard Payne Knight on the plausibility of *Gulliver's Travels*

1805

An Analytical Inquiry into the Principles of Taste, 2nd ed., 1805, 285.

Knight (1750–1824) was a connoisseur of gems, coins, and sculpture as well as a writer on aesthetics and antiquities. He gathered extensive materials on these subjects on his European travels. Though generally respected as an authority on ancient art and mythology, Knight was not appreciated as an English poet. His didactic poems, *The Landscape* (1794) and *The Progress of Civil Society* (1796), plunged him into disputes with Walpole and others. The *Analytical Inquiry*, published twice in 1805, had appeared in four editions by 1808.

We have a work, in our own language, in which the most extravagant and improbable fictions are rendered, by the same means [probability of detail], sufficiently plausible to interest, in a high degree, those readers, who do not perceive the moral or meaning of the stories. I mean the *Travels of Gulliver*; with which, I have known ignorant and very young persons, who read them without even suspecting the satire, more really entertained and delighted, than any learned or scientific readers, who perceived the intent from the beginning, have ever been.

57. Nathan Drake on Swift

1805

Essays, Biographical, Critical, and Historical, Illustrative of the Tatler, Spectator, and Guardian (3 vols.), 1805, iii, 133–82 *passim*.

Nathan Drake (1766–1836), like John Aikin, was a physician as well as a literary critic, and the two doctors share an extremely moralistic attitude toward Swift. The series of essays quoted here was followed in 1809 by two volumes of *Essays Illustrative of the Rambler, Adventurer, Idler, etc.,* and in 1810 by *The Gleaner, a Series of Periodical Essays, Selected* . . . in four volumes. These works present eighteenth-century periodical literature to an audience which Drake seems to feel is much more refined and discriminating than that of Swift's day. Drake's disdain for the 'coarse' works of Swift is also seen in his review of a 1795 edition of Catullus's works: 'Voluptuous ideas in a young poet when clothed in fascinating language will, as in Catullus, receive pardon, but to conception at which even Swift would have sickened, what mercy can be conceded!' (*Literary Hours: or Sketches Critical, Narrative, and Poetical*, 3rd ed., 1804, ii, 108).

On the living of Laracor, Swift usually resided when in Ireland, and here he at length embraced the resolution of publishing his *Tale of a Tub*. This celebrated work he had commenced so early as at the age of nineteen, and during his residence at Dublin college; he completed it whilst with Sir William Temple, and kept it by him nearly eight years in its finished state; a piece of forbearance very unusual with a young author.

This keen but humorous satire appeared anonymously in 1704, and speedily excited very considerable attention, some applauding, and some vehemently reprobating its tendency and design. The invective, however, which has been so lavishly poured upon this production, seems to have been greatly misplaced; and what is somewhat extraordinary, considering the purport of the work, the members of the

273

church of England were its severest adversaries, and carried their resentment to such a pitch, that, some years subsequent to its publication, our author was precluded the honours of a bishopric through the representations of Archbishop Sharpe to the Queen, on the supposed hostility of this fiction to the church. The idea could only have arisen from the occasional, and certainly, in some instances, indecent levity of the author; for the incidents of the tale form an allegory, which places in a very conspicuous light the beauty and simplicity of the established worship of this kingdom, when compared with the gorgeous superstitions of popery on the one hand, and the stern fanaticism of presbyterianism on the other.

There was a peculiarity in the character of Swift, which, both in his writings and conduct, frequently laid him open, in the eyes of common observers, to the charge of levity or even impiety; he had such a rooted abhorrence of hypocrisy, that, rather than be liable, in the smallest degree, to its imputation, he would conceal his religious feelings and habits with the most scrupulous care; and a friend has been known to have resided under his roof for six months, before he discovered that the Dean regularly read prayers to his servants morning and evening. . . .

The literary merit of *A Tale of a Tub* is great, and, in this respect, exceeding every thing which he afterwards produced. The style has more nerve, more imagery, and spirit, than any other portion of his works: the wit and humour are perfectly original, and supported throughout with undiminished vigour; but, it must be confessed, occasionally coarse and licentious; and the digressions exhibit erudition of no common kind, though not always applied in illustration of that side of the question on which justice and impartiality have since arranged themselves. . . .

Four years elapsed ere Swift again ventured before the bar of the public; and of the pieces which he then published, and which belong to our present department (the literary class), may be mentioned his ridicule of Partridge the almanack-maker, published under the signature of Isaac Bickerstaff, Esq. an effusion of pleasantry that obtained so much popularity as to induce Steele (as we have already related in his life) to adopt that name for the leading character of his *Tatler*. . . .

In the year 1712 our author published, in a letter to the Earl of Oxford, a *Proposal for Correcting, Improving, and Ascertaining the English Tongue*. The mode by which he meant to effect his purpose was, through the institution of an academy; in the formation of which he had proceeded so far as to have named twenty persons of both parties for its members. The ministers were, however, too much involved in political warfare to have leisure for any consideration of this kind; they praised the design, but did nothing more, and of course the project was dropped. Swift does not appear, indeed, to have been well qualified for the task that he proposed to undertake; he had little or no acquaintance with the languages on which the superstructure of the English tongue is chiefly founded; and it is singularly unfortunate, that the very pamphlet in which his scheme is proposed, is, in point of grammar and style, the most defective and erroneous of any production in his voluminous works.

As we are in this place considering the *principal literary* compositions of Swift, we must pass over a series of fourteen years before we reach his *second* capital work, his *Gulliver's Travels*; a book, which, in style, matter, and manner, bears little resemblance to *A Tale of a Tub*, but which acquired a popularity even still more extended than that humorous satire. It was also, like every other effusion of the Dean, save the letter to Lord Oxford, published anonymously, and occasioned therefore on its appearance (November 1726) a variety of conjecture as to the author of such an original and eccentric volume. Even his most intimate friends were unacquainted with its origin; and though they might suspect him as the founder of the feast, were cautious about absolutely declaring themselves. Thus Gay, in a letter to Swift, dated November 17, 1726, speaks with hesitation, though it is apparent, from the tenor of his epistle, that he had nearly arranged his creed upon the subject. . . .

This singular work displays a most fertile imagination, a deep insight into the follies, vices, and infirmities of mankind, and a fund of acute observation on ethics, politics, and literature. Its principal aim appears to have been to mortify the pride of human nature, whether arising from personal or mental accomplishments: the satire, however, has been carried too far, and degenerates into a libel on the species. The fourth part, especially, notwithstanding all that has been said in its defence by Sheridan and Berkeley, apparently exhibits such a malignant wish to degrade and brutalize the human race, that with every reader of feeling and benevolence it can occasion nothing but a mingled sensation of abhorrence and disgust. Let us hope, though the tendency be such as we have described, that it was not in the contemplation of Swift; but that he was betrayed into this degrading and exaggerated picture, by that habitual and gloomy discontent which long preyed upon his spirits, which at length terminated in insanity, and which for ever veiled from his eyes the fairest portion of humanity.

As it is not within the scope of our design to notice every separate publication of the Dean, we shall close our observations on his mere literary labours, by a brief discussion of his merits as a poet and epistolary writer.

The poetry of Swift occupies nearly two octavo volumes of the last edition of his works, and is entirely confined to those species which may be termed the *humorous* and *familiar*. In these, however, he had attained a degree of perfection, of which English rhyme, before the appearance of his productions, had not been thought susceptible. The language is, in general, that of conversation; and so complete a master is he of similar terminations, that scarcely a single word appears to have been introduced for the sake of consentaneous sound, but strikes the reader as the very one which he should have chosen in plain prose as best adapted to express his meaning. The pleasure and surprise are likewise greatly enhanced, when it is found that no writer has equalled our bard in the accuracy and correspondency of his rhymes.

With these technical beauties he has, in his best pieces, combined the most poignant wit and humour, and a rich display of character; and these, so far from suffering from the necessary restrictions of metre and rhyme, are, in fact, rendered more graceful and impressive by their adoption.

The same blemish, however, which has injured many of his prose compositions, is still more apparent in his poetry, much of which abounds in the grossest indelicacies, and in the most disgusting physical impurities. There are, notwithstanding, several poems, and of some length, which are not only free from any thing which ought to revolt a correct taste, but exhibit much elegance, urbanity, and well-turned compliment. Of this kind are the productions addressed to *Stella,* or descriptive of his passion for *Vanessa;* his *Baucis and Philemon,* and his imitations of Horace, written in 1713 and 1714.

A very great majority of the poetry of Swift is written in lines of eight syllables, a measure in which he moves with peculiar spirit and facility. He possesses also equal excellence in what may be termed the anapaestic metre, which he has employed with uncommon success in the delineation of broad humour.

The letters of Swift have been usually admired for their colloquial and unaffected ease; and they certainly do possess, when compared with those of his correspondents, a larger portion of the lighter graces which should characterize epistolary compositions. Yet are they deficient in many very impressive qualities; they are querulous and splenetic; and want both the tenderness and dignity which distinguish many of the letters of Pope, Arbuthnot, and Gay, as well as the eloquence and energy which pervade the correspondence of Bolingbroke.

Swift for several years acted an important part upon the great national theatre, and his political life was a scene of much activity and address. It may be said to have commenced in the year 1710, at which period the Primate of Ireland commissioned him to solicit the Queen for a remission of the first Fruits and Twentieth Parts to the Irish Clergy. He had, previous to this, however, attained some reputation as a writer upon political and ecclesiastical affairs; so early as 1701 he had published a pamphlet entitled *Dissensions in Athens and Rome*, which attracted the notice of several public characters; and in 1708 he produced *The Sentiments of a Church-of-England-Man with respect to Religion and Government*; the *Argument against abolishing Christianity*; and *A Letter concerning the Sacramental Test*. All these tracts have the merit of much sound reasoning, argument, and perspicuity, and were followed during the subsequent year by a *Project for the Advancement of Religion*, addressed to Lady Berkeley. His delegation relative to the First-Fruits was, however, the foundation of his political eminence; for Mr. Harley, to whom he applied on this account, very speedily discovered his genius and talents, and very shortly afterwards admitted him to the most unbounded confidence and familiarity.

In consequence of this connection with the Tory ministers of Queen Anne, Swift, who had hitherto been esteemed a Whig, now eagerly embraced the measures of government; and, on the 2d of November, 1710, wrote and published the thirteenth number of the *Examiner*, a paper of great warmth and virulence, in defence of Tory principles, and which he continued without interruption until June 7, 1711.

From this period to the death of Queen Anne in 1714, our author continued the confidential friend of St. John and Harley; planned and directed many of the most efficient measures of the state, and became one of a select ministerial association which met weekly under the appelation of Brothers. His pen was of course strenuously employed in the support of his party, and sometimes with a success which exceeded even the most sanguine expectations of government. Thus, in 1712, when it was the aim of administration to reconcile the nation to a peace, he published the *Conduct of the Allies*; a pamphlet which so completely answered the purpose for which it was written, that it produced an entire revolution in the opinions of the people; and Marlborough, who had hitherto been the favourite, and almost idol of the kingdom, was now generally believed, in consequence of Swift's representation, to have protracted the war merely with a view to his own interest. Such was the eagerness to peruse this celebrated treatise, that it passed through seven editions in the course of a few days, and eleven thousand copies were sold in less than a month.

The demand upon the abilities of our author increased with the danger which threatened the ministers; they were assailed on all sides by a formidable body of Whigs; and the single arm of Swift was employed to disperse a host. He continued to defend the cause with unabated vigour, and published in its support *Reflections on the Barrier Treaty; Remarks on the Bishop of Sarum's Introduction to his third Volume of the History of the Reformation;* and, in the commencement of 1714, *The Public Spirit of the Whigs,* in answer to Sir Richard Steele's *Crisis.* These tracts display a fund of humour, ridicule, and wit; but the last so offended the Scotch nation, that, through the solicitations of its Lords, a proclamation was issued, offering a reward of three hundred pounds for the discovery of the author. Swift, however, remained concealed; and the Scotch, a short time subsequent to this transaction, were happy to secure him in their interest. . . .

His pen during this seclusion was not altogether idle; he drew up *Memoirs relating to that Change which happened in the Queen's Ministry in the Year 1710,* written in October, 1714; and *An Inquiry into the Behaviour of the Queen's last Ministry, with relation to their Quarrels among themselves, and the Design charged upon them of altering the Succession to the Crown.* It is probable also, that during this period he revised, corrected, and enlarged, his *History of the Four last Years of Queen Anne,* a work which had been destined for publication in 1713, but which political circumstances at that time, and, in the subsequent year, the decease of the Queen, arrested in its way to the press; obstacles which occasioned its consignment to the desk for nearly half a century. Much information, and much developement of mystery, were expected from its appearance; but when printed in 1758 it is said to have greatly disappointed the public expectations.

It was in the year 1720 that the Dean resumed his consequence with the public, by issuing a pamphlet, entitled *A Proposal for the Universal Use of Irish Manufactures;* in which he points out, in a most clear and convincing manner, the wealth and prosperity which would accrue to the Irish from wearing their own manufactures, and rejecting those of England. This attempt, as might have been foreseen, brought upon the author the vengeance of the English traders; the printer was prosecuted, and imprisoned; but the result of this ill-judged resentment was a tide of popularity in favour of Swift; and, after the Chief Justice had in vain endeavoured to procure a verdict of guilty, permission was at length obtained from England to grant a *noli prosequi*.

Four years after this event the Dean became almost an object of idolatry to the Irish by rescuing them from the artifice and rapacity of one William Wood, who had by sinister means procured a patent for coining halfpence for the use of Ireland to the enormous amount of one hundred and eighty thousand pounds. In an address to both houses of parliament, drawn up by our author, he states the petitioners as alledging the fraudulent obtaining and executing of Wood's patent; the baseness of his metal; and the prodigious sum to be coined, which might be encreased by stealth, from foreign importation, and his own counterfeits, as well as those at home; whereby, say they, we must infallibly lose all our little gold and silver, and all our poor remainder of a very limited and discouraged trade.

To enforce these representations, Swift commenced the publication of a series of letters, under the feigned name of *M. B. Drapier,* and placed the ruinous consequences which must necessarily attend the enforcement of the patent in so striking a light, that the nation, through all its ranks, became alarmed and clamorous against the measure. So universally indeed were these letters read and admired, that, it is said, there was scarcely an individual in the kingdom, independent of the creatures of government, but what had formed from their perusal a fixed resolution never to receive one piece of Wood's coin in payment. The consequence was, that, though the printer was imprisoned, and a bill of indictment ordered to be prepared against him, no Grand Jury could be prevailed upon to find it; nor could the proclamation of a reward of three hundred pounds for the discovery of the author, avail in the least toward his detection. The triumph of Swift was complete; government became apprehensive of the consequences of pressing a project so deservedly detested; the patent was annulled, and the halfpence withdrawn.

The style of these celebrated letters is a proof of the most consummate art and judgment; they were meant to appear as the production of an honest shopkeeper of plain good sense, and, of course, it was requisite that the language should correspond with the character; it is, accordingly, perfectly plain and simple; and to every individual, however moderate his capacity, in the highest degree perspicuous and intelligible. The arguments likewise, and their arrangement, were as clear and evident as the diction in which they were clothed; and, considering the persons to whom these epistles were addressed, and the purport they were written to answer, the opinion of Hawkins Browne will not probably be deemed hyperbolical, when he asserted, that 'the *Drapier's Letters* were the most perfect pieces of oratory ever composed since the days of Demosthenes.' As a specimen of their style and humour, and of the happy facility with which our author supported the character that he had assumed, the following passage may be adduced:

'I am very sensible', says the Drapier, 'that such a work as I have undertaken, might have worthily employed a much better pen: but when a house is attempted to be robbed, it often happens that the weakest in the family runs first to stop the door. All the assistance I had were some informations from an eminent person whereof I am afraid I have spoiled a few, by endeavouring to make them of a piece with my own productions; and the rest I was not able to manage. I was in the case of David, who could not move in the armour of Saul, and therefore I rather chose to attack this uncircumcised Philistine (Wood, I mean) with a sling and a stone. And I may say for Wood's honour, as well as my own, that he resembles Goliah in many circumstances very applicable to the present purpose: *for Goliah had a helmet of* BRASS *upon his head, and he was armed with a coat of mail, and the weight of the coat was five thousand shekels of* BRASS; *and he had greaves of* BRASS *upon his legs, and a target of* BRASS *between his shoulders.* In short he was, like Mr. Wood, all over BRASS, *and he defied the armies of the living God.*—Goliah's conditions of combat were likewise the same with these of Wood: if he prevail against us, *then shall we be his servants.* But if it happens that I prevail over him, I renounce the other part of the condition; he shall never be a servant of mine; for I do not think him fit to be trusted in any honest man's shop.' [*Drapier's Letters*, ed. Herbert Davis (1941), 48.]

Of the character of Swift, the representations have been various and opposed; at one time his portrait has been tinted with the colours of friendship, at another with those of aversion. He was, without doubt, a man of commanding and powerful intellect; almost unparalleled in wit and humour; intimately acquainted with the human heart, and a keen observer of the manners, the vices, and follies of his species. He was from principle charitable; free from hypocrisy; and a strenuous defender of the rights of an oppressed people.

These great and estimable qualities were sullied and debased by pride, dogmatism, and misanthropy; by a temper harsh, gloomy, and discontented. Such is the malignancy of a disposition prone to vilify and degrade human nature, that no abilities, however pre-eminent, can atone for such a tendency. The soul of Swift seems to have delighted in the accumulation of objects of meanness, deformity, and filth; in the display of man as the seat of brutal passions, and malignant propensities.

58. John Dunlop on the background of
Gulliver's Travels

1814

The History of Fiction (3 vols.), 1814, iii, 349–50.

The comprehensive *History of Fiction*, by John Dunlop (d. 1842), was an influential work throughout the nineteenth century, appearing in four English editions as well as a German translation. It is cited by Sir Walter Scott in his edition of Swift's *Works*, and it is a valuable source of early nineteenth-century attitudes toward world literature 'from the earliest Greek romances to the novels of the present age'. A lawyer and sheriff during much of his life, Dunlop is also known for his history of Latin literature and his English translations of Latin poetry. In this extract Dunlop discusses the possible influence of Cyrano de Bergerac on Swift.

Such is the abstract of the *Histoire Comique des estats et Empire de la Lune*, a work which, like all those of which the satire is in any degree temporary, has lost a good deal of its first relish. It is, however, still worthy of perusal, especially by those who are acquainted with the philosophical history of the period in which it was composed. And the interest which it excites, must, to an English reader, be increased by its having served in many respects as a prototype to the most popular work of a writer so celebrated as Swift. Nor has it only directed the plan of the Dean of St. Patrick's; since even in the summary of the Lunar Voyage that has been presented, many points of resemblance will at once be discerned to the journey to Brobdingnag. Gulliver is beset, on his first landing on that strange country, by a number of the inhabitants, who are of similar dimensions with the people of the moon, and who are astonished at his diminutive stature—he is exhibited as a sight at one of the principal towns—he amuses the spectators with various mountebank tricks—and acquires an imperfect knowledge of the language—

afterwards he is carried to court, where he is introduced to the queen's favourite dwarf, and where great disputes arise concerning the species to which he belongs, among the chief scholars, whose speculations are ridiculed in a manner extremely similar to the reasonings of the lunar sages. The general turn of wit and humour is besides the same, and seems to be of a description almost peculiar to these two writers. The Frenchman, indeed, wanted the advantages of learning and education possessed by his successor, and hence his imagination was, perhaps, less guarded and correct; in many respects, however, it is more agreeably extravagant, and his aerial excursion is free from what is universally known to be the chief objections to the satire contained in the four voyages of Gulliver.

As Cyrano's *Journey to the Moon* is the origin of Swift's Brobdingnag, so the *Histoire des Estats du Soleil* seems to have suggested the plan of the voyage to Laputa. This second expedition of Cyrano is much inferior in merit to his former one, but, like the third excursion of Gulliver, is in a great measure intended to expose the vain pursuits of schemers and projectors in learning and science.

59. Sir Walter Scott on Swift

1814

The Works of Jonathan Swift, D.D., Dean of St. Patrick's Dublin
(12 vols.), 2nd ed., 1824.

Sir Walter Scott (1771–1832) edited an annotated edition of
Swift's works in 1814. It was reissued, with minor changes, in
1824. Scott is one of the more just and perceptive early critics of
Swift, and his comments, rather detailed for his time, are still of
interest. These extracts are from Scott's Life of Swift, which comprises the first volume of the edition, and from his introductory
remarks to the Journal to Stella (Vol. III), Swift's Sermons (Vol.
VII), and Gulliver's Travels (Vol. XI).

This celebrated production [A Tale of a Tub] is founded upon a simple
and obvious allegory, conducted with all the humour of Rabelais, and
without his extravagance.[1] The main purpose is to trace the gradual
corruptions of the church of Rome, and to exalt the English reformed
church at the expence both of the Roman catholic and presbyterian
establishments. It was written with a view to the interests of the high
church party, and it succeeded in rendering them the most important
services; for what is so important to a party in Britain, whether in

[1] Among the Dean's books, sold by auction 1745, was an edition of Rabelais' works,
with remarks and annotations in his own hand. This, could it be recovered, would be a
work of no little interest, considering that the germ, both of the Tale and of Gulliver's
Travels, may be traced in the works of the French Lucian. Swift was not, indeed, under the
necessity of disguising his allegory with the buffoonery and mysticism affected by Rabelais; but the sudden and wide digressive excursions, the strain of extraordinary reading and
uncouth learning which is assumed, together with the general style of the whole fable, are
indisputably derived from the humorous philosopher of Chinon. . . .
  While on this subject, the Editor cannot suppress his opinion, that Swift's commentators have, in some instances, overstrained his allegory, and attempted to extort deep and
recondite allusions, from passages where the meaning lay near the surface. Thus, the wars
between the Eolists and the monster Moulinavent, appear to mean nothing more than that
the fanatics, described under the former denomination, spent their time in combating
imaginary spiritual obstacles to their salvation, as the distempered imagination of Don
Quixote converted windmills into giants. [Scott's note.]

church or state, as to gain the laughers to their side. But the raillery was considered, not unreasonably, as too light for a subject of such grave importance; and it cannot be denied, that the luxuriance of Swift's wit has, in some parts of the *Tale*, carried him much beyond the bounds of propriety. Many of the graver clergy, even among the Tories, and particularly Dr. Sharpe, the archbishop of York, were highly scandalized at the freedom of the satire; nor is there any doubt that the offence thus occasioned, proved the real bar to Swift's attaining the highest dignities in the church. King and Wotton, in their answers to the *Tale*, insisted largely upon the inconsistence between the bold and even profane turn of the satire, and the clerical character of the reputed author. For similar reasons, *A Tale of a Tub* was hailed by the infidel philosophers on the Continent, as a work well calculated to advance the cause of scepticism, and, as such, was recommended by Voltaire to his proselytes, because the ludicrous combinations which are formed in the mind by the perusal, tend to lower the respect due to revelation. Swift's attachment to the real interests of religion are so well known, that he would doubtless rather have burned his manuscript, than incurred the slightest risk of injuring them. But the indirect consequences of ridicule, when applied to subjects of sacred importance, are more extensive, and more prejudicial than can be calculated by the author, who, with his eye fixed on the main purpose of his satire, is apt to overlook its more remote effects.

A Tale of a Tub had for some years attracted the notice of the public, when Dr. Thomas Swift, already mentioned as Swift's relation and fellow-student at Trinity College, set up pretensions to a share in that humorous composition. These he promulgated, in what he was pleased to entitle, *A Complete Key to A Tale of a Tub*, printed in 1710, containing a flimsy explanation of the prominent points of the allegory, and averring the authors to be 'Thomas Swift, grandson to Sir William Davenant, and Jonathan Swift, cousin-german to Thomas Swift, both retainers to Sir William Temple.' *Our* Swift, it may be easily imagined was not greatly pleased by an arrangement, in which his cousin is distinguished as a wit, and an author by descent, and he himself only introduced as his relative; and still less could he endure his arrogating the principal share of the composition, and the corresponding insinuation, that the work had suffered by his cousin Jonathan's inability to support the original plan. The real author, who, at the time the *Key* appeared, was busied in revising a new edition of the book, wrote a letter to his bookseller, Benjamin Tooke, sufficiently expressive of his feelings. 'I have just now your last, with the *Complete Key*. I believe it so perfect a Grub Street piece, it will be forgotten in a week. But it is strange that there can be no satisfaction against a bookseller for publishing names in so bold a manner, I wish some lawyer could advise you how I might have satisfaction; for at this rate there is no book, however vile, which may not be fastened on me. I cannot but think that little parson-cousin of mine is at the bottom of this; for, having lent him a copy of some part of, &c. and, he showing it, after I was gone for Ireland, and the thing abroad, he affected to talk suspiciously, as if he had some share in it.'

[I, 82–8.]

The first three letters of M.B., Drapier in Dublin, dwell . . . upon arguments against Wood's halfpence, derived from their alleged inferiority in weight and value, and the indifferent or suspicious character of the projector himself. These arguments, also, had the advantage of being directly applicable to the grosser apprehensions of the 'tradesmen, shopkeepers, farmers, and country people,' to whom they are professedly addressed. Such persons, though incapable of understanding, or being moved by the discussion of a theoretical national right, could well comprehend, that the pouring into Ireland a quantity of copper coinage, alleged to be so base in denomination, that twelve pence were not intrinsically worth more than a penny, must necessarily drain the country of gold and silver, and occasion great individual loss, as well as national distress. The bitter and satirical passages against Wood himself were also well adapted to the taste of the vulgar, whose callous palate is peculiarly excited by the pungency of personal satire. Whether Swift himself believed the exaggerated reports which his tracts circulated concerning the baseness of the coin, and the villainy of the projector, we have no means of discovering. Once satisfied of the general justice of his cause, he may have deemed himself at liberty to plead it by such arguments as were most likely to afford it support, without rigid examination of their individual validity, or, (which is more likely,) like most warm disputants, he may himself have received, with eager faith, averments so necessary to the success of his plan. But it is certain, that, in these first three letters, the king, the minister, the mistress, and the British privy council, are not mentioned, or treated with studied respect; while the whole guilt and evil of the scheme are imputed to the knavery of William Wood, who, from an obscure ironmonger, had become an avaricious and unprincipled projector, ready and eager to ruin the whole kingdom of Ireland, in order to secure an exorbitant profit to himself.

The ferment produced by a statement so open to the comprehension, and so irritating to the feelings of the nation at large, became unspeakably formidable. Both the Irish houses of Parliament joined in addressing the Crown against Wood's scheme. Parties of all denominations, whether religious or political, for once united in expressing their abhorrence of the detested halfpence. The tradesmen to whom the coin was consigned refused to receive them, and endeavoured, by public advertisement, to remove the scandal of being concerned in the accursed traffic. Even Wood's near relatives were compelled to avert public indignation by disavowing all concern for his contract. Associations were formed for refusing their currency; and these extended from the wealthy corporation of Dublin down to the hawkers and errand-boys, who announced to their employers, that they would not receive nor offer in change Wood's drossy halfpence, since they could 'neither get news, ale, tobacco, nor brandy for such cursed stuff.' The matter being thus adopted by the mob, they proceeded, according to their usual custom, made riotous processions, and burned the unfortunate projector in effigy. In short, such was the state of the public mind, that it was unsafe for any one to be supposed favourable to Wood's project.

Swift, finding the people in a disposition so favourable for the maintaining their rights, did not suffer their zeal to cool for lack of fuel. Not satisfied with writing, he preached against Wood's halfpence. One of his sermons is preserved, and bears the title 'On doing good.' It verifies his own account, that he preached not sermons, but political pamphlets. At his instigation, also, the the grand jury, and principal inhabitants of the liberty of St Patrick's joined in an association for refusing this odious coin. Besides the celebrated Drapier's letters, he supplied the hawkers with a variety of ballads and prose satires, seasoned with all the bitterness and pungency of his wit, directing the popular indignation against the contractor, without sparing some very intelligible inuendos against his patrons and abbettors in England. By such means the timid were encouraged, the doubtful confirmed, the audacious inflamed, and the attention of the public so rivetted to the discussion, that it was no longer shocked at the discussion of the more delicate questions which it involved; and the viceroy and his advisers complained that any proposition, however libellous and treasonable, was now published without hesitation, and perused without horror, providing that Wood and his halfpence could be introduced into the tract. The Duke of Grafton (then lord-lieutenant,) found himself unable to stem the popular torrent; and it became evident, that the scheme, if enforced, would occasion a civil war. . . .

It was now obvious, from the temper of Ireland, that the true point of difference between the countries might safely be brought before the public. In the Drapier's fourth letter, accordingly, Swift boldly treats of the royal prerogative, of the almost exclusive employment of natives of England in places of trust and emolument in Ireland; of the dependency of that kingdom upon England, and the power assumed, contrary to truth, reason, and justice, of binding her by the laws of a Parliament in which she had no representation. It is boldly affirmed, (though in terms the most guarded,) that the revolutions of England no farther affected Ireland, than as they were consonant to freedom and liberty; and that, should an insurrection fix a new prince on the throne of the sister kingdom, the Irish might still lawfully resist his possessing himself of theirs. The threats of the English ministers to enforce the currency of Wood's halfpence by violent measures, are next alluded to; and the Drapier concludes this part of his reasoning in the following very marked passage:

The remedy is wholly in your own hands, and, therefore, I have digressed a little, in order to refresh and continue that spirit so seasonably raised among you, and to let you see, that, by the laws of GOD, of NATURE, of NATIONS, and of your COUNTRY, you ARE, and OUGHT to be as FREE a people as your brethren in England.

This tract pressed at once upon the real merits of the question at issue, and the alarm was instantly taken by the English government. . . .

When the bill against the printer of *The Drapier's Letters* was about to be presented to the grand jury, Swift addressed to that body a paper, entitled *Seasonable Advice*, exhorting them to remember the story of the league made by the wolves with the sheep, on condition of their parting with their shepherds and mastiffs, after which they ravaged the flock at pleasure. A few spirited verses addressed to the citizens at large, and enforcing similar topics, are subscribed by the Drapier's initials, and are doubtless Swift's own composition. . . .

Three other Drapier's letters were published by Swift, not only in order to follow up his victory, but for explaining more decidedly the cause in which it had been won. The fifth letter is addressed to Lord Molesworth, and has for its principal object a justification of the former letters, and a charge of oppression and illegality, founded upon the proceedings against the author and printer. The sixth letter is addressed to Lord Chancellor Middleton, who strenuously opposed Wood's project, and resigned his office in consequence of the displeasure of the court being expressed on account of such resistance. It is written in the Dean's person, who pleads the cause of the Drapier, and, from several passages, does not appear anxious to conceal this identity. This also relates chiefly to the conduct of Whitshed, and the merits of the prosecution against Harding. The seventh letter, though last published, appears to have been composed shortly after the fourth. It enters widely into the national complaints of Ireland, and illustrates what has been already mentioned, that the project of Wood was only chosen as an ostensible and favourable point on which to make a stand against principles of aggression which involved many questions of much more vital importance. This letter was not published until the Drapier's papers were collected into a volume. Meantime Carteret yielded to the storm,—Wood's patent was surrendered,—and the patentee indemnified by a grant of £3000, yearly for twelve years. Thus victoriously terminated the first grand struggle for the independence of Ireland.

[I, 286–301.]

We have endeavoured elsewhere to make some remarks on those celebrated *Travels*. Perhaps no work ever exhibited such general attractions to all classes. It offered personal and political satire to the readers in high life, low and coarse incident to the vulgar, marvels to the romantic, wit to the young and lively, lessons of morality and policy to the grave, and maxims of deep and bitter misanthropy to neglected age, and disappointed ambition. The plan of the satire varies in the different parts. The voyage to Liliput refers chiefly to the court and politics of England, and Sir Robert Walpole is plainly intimated under the character of the Premier Flimnap, which he afterwards probably remembered to the prejudice of the Dean's view of leaving Ireland. The factions of High-Heels and Low-Heels express the factions of Tories and Whigs, the Small-Endians and Big-Endians the religious divisions of Papist and Protestant; and when the Heir-Apparent was described as wearing one heel high and one low, the Prince of Wales, who at that time divided his favour between the two leading political parties of England, laughed very heartily at the comparison. Blefescu is France, and the ingratitude of the Liliputian court, which forces Gulliver to take shelter there rather than have his eyes put out, is an indirect reproach upon that of England, and a vindication of the flight of Ormond and Bolingbroke to Paris. Many other allusions may be traced by those well acquainted with the secret history of the reign of George I. The scandal which Gulliver gave to the Empress, by his mode of extinguishing the flames in the royal palace, seems to intimate the author's own disgrace with Queen Anne, founded upon the indecorum of *A Tale of a Tub*, which was remembered against him as a crime, while the service which it had rendered the cause of the high church was forgotten. It must also be remarked, that the original institutions of the empire of Liliput are highly commended, as also their system of public education, while it is intimated, that all the corruptions of the court had been introduced during the three last reigns. This was Swift's opinion concerning the English Constitution.

In the 'Voyage to Brobdingnag' the satire is of a more general character; nor is it easy to trace any particular reference to the political events or statesmen of the period. It merely exhibits human actions and sentiments as they might appear in the apprehension of beings of immense strength, and, at the same time, of a cold, reflecting, and philosophical character. The monarch of these sons of Anak is designed to embody Swift's ideas of a patriot king, indifferent to what was curious, and cold to what was beautiful, feeling only interest in that which was connected with general utility and the public weal. To such a prince, the intrigues, scandals, and stratagems, of an European court, are represented as equally odious in their origin, and contemptible in their progress. A very happy effect was also produced by turning the telescope, and painting Gulliver, who had formerly been a giant among the Liliputians, as a pigmy amidst this tremendous race. The same ideas are often to be traced, but, as they are reversed in the part which is performed by the narrator, they are rather illustrated than repeated. Some passages of the court of Brobdingnag were supposed to be intended as an affront upon the maids of honour, for whom, Delany informs us, that Swift had very little respect.

The 'Voyage to Laputa' was disliked by Arbuthnot, who was a man of science, and probably considered it as a ridicule upon the Royal Society; nor can it be denied that there are some allusions to the most respectable philosophers of the period. An occasional shaft is even said to have been levelled at Sir Isaac Newton. The ardent patriot had not forgot the philosopher's opinion in favour of Wood's halfpence. Under the parable of the tailor, who computed Gulliver's altitude by a quadrant, and took his measure by a mathematical diagram, yet brought him his clothes very ill made and out of shape, by the mistake of a figure in the calculation, Swift is supposed to have alluded to an error of Sir Isaac's printer, who, by carelessly adding a cypher to the astronomer's computation of the distance between the sun and the earth, had increased it to an incalculable amount. Newton published, in the *Amsterdam Gazette*, a correction of this typographical error, but the circumstance did not escape the malicious acumen of the Dean of St Patrick's. It was also believed by the Dean's friends, that the office of flapper was suggested by the habitual absence of mind of the great philosopher. The Dean told Mr D. Swift that Sir Isaac was the worst companion in the world, and that, if you asked him a question, 'he would revolve it in a circle in his brain, round, and round, and round, (here Swift described a circle on his own forehead,) before he could produce an answer.'

But, although Swift may have treated with irreverence the first philosopher of the age, and although it must be owned that he evinces, in many parts of his writings, an undue disrespect for mathematics, yet the satire in *Gulliver* is rather aimed against the abuse of philosophical science than at its reality. The projectors in the academy of Laputa are described as pretenders, who had acquired a very slight tincture of real mathematical knowledge, and eked out their plans of mechanical improvement by dint of whim and fancy. The age in which Swift lived had exhibited numerous instances of persons of this description, by whom many of the numerous *bubbles*, as they were emphatically termed, had been set on foot, to the impoverishment of credulous individuals, and the general detriment of the community. In ridiculing this class of projectors, whose character was divided between self-confidence in their own chimæras, and a wish to impose upon others, Swift, who peculiarly hated them, has borrowed several illustrations, and perhaps the general idea, from Rabelais, Book v, cap. xxiii, where Pantagruel inspects the occupations of the courtiers of Quinte-Essence, Queen of Entelechie.

The professors of speculative learning are represented as engaged in prosecution of what was then termed Natural and Mathematical Magic, studies not grounded upon sound principles, or traced out and ascertained by experiment, but hovering between science and mysticism. Such are the renowned pursuits of alchemy—the composition of brazen images that could speak; or wooden birds that could fly; of powders of sympathy, and salves, which were applied, not to the wound, but to the weapon by which it was inflicted; of vials of essence, which could manure acres of land, and all similar marvels, of which imposters propagated the virtue, and which dupes believed to their cost. The machine of the worthy professor of Lagado, for improving speculative knowledge, and composing books on all subjects, without the least assistance from genius or knowledge, seems to be designed in ridicule of the art invented by Raimond Lully, and advanced by his sage commentators; the mechanical process, namely, by which, according to Cornelius Agrippa, (himself no mean follower of Lully) 'everye man might plentifullye dispute of what matter he wolde, and with a certain artificial and huge heap of nownes and verbes invente and dispute with ostentation, full of trifling deceites upon both sides.'[1] A reader might supposed himself transported to the grand academy of Lagado when they read of this 'Brief and great art of invention and demonstration,' which consisted in adjusting the subject to be treated of, according to a machine composed of divers circles, fixed and moveable. The principle circle was fixed, and inscribed with the substances of all things that may be treated of, arranged under general heads, as GOD, ANGEL, EARTH, HEAVEN, MAN, ANIMAL, &c. Another circle was placed within it, which is moveable, bearing inscribed thereon what logicians call the accidents, as QUANTITY, QUALITY, RELATION, &c. Other circles again contained the predicates absolute and relative, &c. and the forms of the questions; and by turning the circles, so as to bring the various attributes to bear upon the question proposed, there was effected a species of mechanical logic, which it cannot be doubted was in Swift's mind when he described the celebrated machine for making books. Various refinements upon this mechanical mode of composition and ratiocination were contrived for the purpose of improving this Art of arts, as it was termed. Kircher, the teacher of an hundred arts, modernized and refitted the machine of Lully. Knittel, the Jesuit, composed, on the same system, his Royal Road to all sciences and arts; Brunus invented the art of logic on the same mechanical plan; and Kuhlman makes our very hair bristel, by announcing such a machine as should contain, not only an art of knowledge, comprehending a general system of all sciences, but the various arts of acquiring languages, of commentary, of criticism, of history, sacred and profane, of biography of every kind, not to mention a library of libraries, comprehending the essence of all the books that ever were written. When it was gravely announced by a learned author, in tolerable latinity, that all this knowledge was to be acquired by the art

[1] Cornelius Agrippa of the *Vanity of Sciences*, Englished by Ja. San. Gent., Lond. 1575. [Scott's note.]

of a mechanical instrument, much resembling a child's whirligig, it was time for the satirist to assume the pen. It was not real science, therefore, which Swift attacked, but those chimerical and spurious studies with which the name has been sometimes disgraced. In the department of the political projectors we have some glances of his Tory feelings; and when we read the melancholy account of the Struldbrugs, we are affectingly reminded of the author's contempt of life, and the miserable state in which his own was at length prolonged.

The voyage to the land of the Houynhms is what an editor of Swift must ever consider with pain. The source of such a diatribe against human nature could only be, that fierce indignation which he has described in his epitaph as so long gnawing his heart. Dwelling in a land where he considered the human race as divided between petty tyrants and oppressed slaves, and being himself a worshipper of that freedom and independence which he beheld daily trampled upon, the unrestrained violence of his feelings drove him to loath the very species by whom such iniquity was done and suffered. To this must be added, his personal health, broken and worn down by the recurring attacks of a frightful disorder; his social comfort destroyed by the death of one beloved object, and the daily decay and peril of another; his life decayed into autumn, and its remainder, after so many flattering and ambitious prospects, condemned to a country which he disliked, and banished from that in which he had formed his hopes, and left his affections:—when all these considerations are combined, they form some excuse for that general misanthrophy which never prevented a single deed of individual benevolence. Such apologies are personal to the author, but there are also excuses for the work itself. The picture of the Yahoos, utterly odious and hateful as it is, presents to the reader a moral use. It was never designed as a representation of mankind in the state to which religion, and even the lights of nature, encourage men to aspire, but of that to which our species is degraded by the wilful subservience of mental qualities to animal instincts, of man, such as he may be found in the degraded ranks of every society, when brutalized by ignorance and gross vice. In this view, the more coarse and disgusting the picture, the more impressive is the moral to be derived from it, since, in proportion as an individual indulges in sensuality, cruelty, or avarice, he approaches in resemblance to the detested Yahoo. It cannot, however, be denied, that even a moral purpose will not justify the nakedness with which Swift has sketched this horrible outline of mankind degraded to a bestial state; since a moralist ought to hold with the Romans, that crimes of atrocity should be exposed when punished, but those of flagitious impurity concealed. In point of probability, too, for there are degrees of probability proper even to the wildest fiction, the fourth part of *Gulliver* is inferior to the three others. Giants and pigmies the reader can conceive; for, not to mention their being the ordinary machinery of romance, we are accustomed to see, in the inferior orders of creation, a disproportion of size between those of the same generic description, which may parallel (among some reptile tribes at least) even the fiction of *Gulliver*. But the mind rejects, as utterly impossible, the supposition of a nation of horses placed in houses which they could not build, fed with corn which they could neither sow, reap, nor save, possessing cows which they could not milk, depositing that milk in vessels which they could not make, and, in short, performing an hundred purposes of rational and social life, for which their external structure altogether unfits them.

But under every objection, whether founded in reason or prejudice, the *Travels of Gulliver* were received with the most universal interest, merited indeed by their novelty, as well as their internal merit. Lucian, Rabelais, More, Bergerac, Alletz, and many other authors, had indeed composed works, in which may be traced such general resemblance as arises from the imaginary voyage of a supposed traveller to ideal realms. But every Utopia which had hitherto been devised, was upon a plan either extravagant from its puerile fictions, or dull from the speculative legislation of which the story was made the vehicle. It was reserved for Swift to enliven the morality of his work with humour; to relieve its absurdity with satire; and to give the most improbable events an appearance of reality, derived from the character and stile of the narrator. Even Robinson Crusoe (though detailing events so much more probable,) hardly excels Gulliver in gravity and verisimilitude of narrative. The character of the imaginary traveller is exactly that of Dampier, or any other sturdy nautical wanderer of the period, endowed with courage and common sense, who sailed through distant seas, without losing a single English prejudice which he had brought from Portsmouth or Plymouth, and on his return gave a grave and simple narrative of what he had seen or heard in foreign countries. The character is perhaps strictly English, and can be hardly relished by a foreigner. The reflections and observations of Gulliver are never more refined or deeper than might be expected from a plain master of a merchant-man, or surgeon in the Old Jewry; and there was such a reality given to his whole person, that one seaman is said to have sworn he knew Captain Gulliver very well, but he lived at Wapping, not at Rotherhithe. It is the contrast between the natural ease and simplicity of such a stile, and the marvels which the volume contains, that forms one great charm of this memorable satire on the imperfections, follies, and vices of mankind. The exact calculations preserved in the first and second part, have also the effect of qualifying the extravagance of the fable. It is said that in natural objects, where proportion is exactly preserved, the marvellous, whether the object be gigantic or diminutive, is lessened in the eyes of the spectator, and it is certain, in general, that proportion forms an essential attribute of truth, and consequently of verisimilitude, or that which renders a narration probable. If the reader is disposed to grant the traveller his postulates as to the existence of the strange people whom he visits, it would be difficult to detect any inconsistence in his narrative. On the contrary, it would seem that he and they conduct themselves towards each other, precisely as must necessarily have happened in the respective circumstances which the author has supposed. In this point of view, perhaps the highest praise that could have been bestowed on *Gulliver's Travels* was the censure of a learned Irish prelate, who said the book contained *some* things which he could not prevail upon himself to believe. It is a remarkable point of the author's art, that, in Liliput and Brobdignag, Gulliver seems gradually, from the influence of the images by which he was surrounded, to lose his own ideas of comparative size, and to adopt those of the pigmies and giants by whom he was surrounded. And, without further prolonging these reflections, I would only request the reader to notice the infinite art with which human actions are divided between these two opposite races of ideal beings, so as to enhance the keenness of the satire. In Liliput political intrigue and *tracasserie*, the chief employment of the highest ranks in Europe, are ridiculed by being transferred to a court of creatures about six inches high. But in Brobdignag, female levities, and the lighter follies of a court, are rendered monstrous and disgusting, by being attributed to a race of such tremendous stature. By these, and a thousand masterly touches of which we feel the effect, though we cannot trace the cause without a long analysis, the genius of Swift converted the sketch of an extravagant fairy tale into a narrative, unequalled for the skill with which it is sustained, and the genuine spirit of satire of which it is made the vehicle.

The renown of Gulliver's travels soon extended into other kingdoms. Voltaire, who was at this time in England, spread their fame among his correspondents in France, and recommended a translation. The Abbé

Desfontaines undertook the task, but with so many doubts, apprehensions, and apologies, as make his Introduction a curious picture of the mind and opinions of a French man of letters. He admits, that he was conscious of offending against rules; and, while he modestly craves some mercy for the prodigious fictions which he had undertaken to clothe in the French language, he confesses, that there were passages at which his pen escaped his hand, from actual horror and astonishment at the daring violations of all critical decorum: then he becomes alarmed, lest some of Swift's political satire might be applied to the Court of Versailles, and protests, with much circumlocution, that it only concerns the *Toriz and Wigts*, as he is pleased to term them, of the factious kingdom of Britain. Lastly, he assures his readers, that not only has he changed many of the incidents, to accommodate them to the French taste, but moreover, they will not be annoyed, in his translation, with the nautical details, and minute particulars, so offensive in the original. Notwithstanding all this affectation of superior taste and refinement, the French translation is very tolerable.

[I, 326–42.]

The occasional poems which the Dean published about this time, were numerous and of various kinds. Some were satirical, and such were almost universally given to the public anonymously by means of the hawkers. Under this description fall the various political poems already mentioned; and such as we have still to allude to, the attacks upon Lord Allen and Tighe, published in *The Intelligencer*, or in single sheets or broadsides, as they are generally termed, which were consigned to the hawkers. These may be classed with his political satires in prose, since the Dean seldom was offended to the extent of making a public assault upon his adversary, without attacking him at once with both weapons of prose and verse.

There was another class of fugitive pieces in which the Dean neglected both the decency due to his station as a clergyman and a gentleman, and his credit as a man of literature. These were poems of a coarse and indelicate character, where his imagination dwelt upon filthy and disgusting subjects, and his ready talents were employed to embody its impurities in humorous and familiar verse. The best apology for this unfortunate perversion of taste, indulgence of caprice, and abuse of talent, is the habits of the times and the situation of the author. In the former respect, we should do great injustice to the present day, by comparing our manners with those of the reign of George I. The writings even of the most esteemed poets of that period, contain passages which, in modern times, would be accounted to deserve the pillory. Nor was the tone of conversation more pure than that of composition; for the taint of Charles II's reign continued to infect society until the present reign, when, if not more moral, we have become at least more decent than our fathers: and although Swift's offences of this description certainly far exceeded those of contemporary authors, the peculiarities of his habits and state of mind are also to be received in extenuation of his grossness. This unfortunate propensity seems nearly allied to the misanthropy which was a precursor of his mental derangement; and notwithstanding the talent employed upon those coarse subjects, 'The Ladies' Dressing-Room,' 'Cassinus and Peter,' 'Cloe,' and other poems of that class, are to be ranked with the description of the Yahoos, as the marks of an incipient disorder of the mind, which induced the author to dwell upon degrading and disgusting subjects, from which all men, in possession of healthful taste and sound faculties, turn with abhorrence. If it be true, as alleged by Delany, that this propensity only distinguished the latter years of Swift's life, it may be more readily accounted for from this cause, than by supposing that Swift acquired from Pope a habit of thinking and writing, in which he far exceeded Pope himself. It may be lastly remembered, that neither in this or other cases, (unless when he had some particular point in view,) did the Dean write with a view to publication. He produced and read his poems to the little circle of friends, where he presided as absolute dictator, where all applauded the manner, and none, it may be presumed, ventured to criticize the subject. Copies were requested and frequently granted. If refused, the auditors contrived to write down from memory an imperfect version. These, in the usual course of things, were again copied repeatedly, until at length they fell into the hands of some hackney author or bookseller, who, for profit, or to affront the author, or with both views, gave them to the public. It would seem that, even to Pope himself, Swift refused an explicit acknowledgement of his having written them.

[I, 384–7.]

As an AUTHOR, there are three peculiarities remarkable in the character of Swift. The first of these has been rarely conceded to an author, at least by his contemporaries. It is the distinguished attribute of ORIGINALITY, and it cannot be refused to Swift by the most severe critic. Even Johnson has allowed that perhaps no author can be found who has borrowed so little, or has so well maintained his claim to be considered as original. There was indeed nothing written before his time which could serve for his model, and the few hints which he has adopted from other authors bear no more resemblance to his compositions than the green flax to the cable which is formed from it.

The second peculiarity, which has indeed been already noticed, is his total indifference to literary fame. Swift executed his various and numerous works as a carpenter forms wedges, mallets, or other implements of his art, not with the purpose of distinguishing himself by the workmanship bestowed on the tools themselves, but solely in order to render them fit for accomplishing a certain purpose, beyond which they were of no value in his eyes. He is often anxious about the success of his argument, and angrily jealous of those who debate the principles and the purpose for which he assumes the pen, but he evinces, on all occasions, an unaffected indifference for the fate of his writings, providing the end of their publication was answered. The careless mode in which Swift suffered his works to get to the public, his refusing them the credit of his name, and his renouncing all connection with the profits of literature, indicate his disdain of the character of a professional author.

The third distinguishing mark of Swift's literary character is, that, with the exception of history, (for his fugitive attempts in Pindaric and Latin verse are too unimportant to be noticed,) he has never attempted any stile of composition in which he has not obtained a distinguished pitch of excellence. We may often think the immediate mode of exercising his talents trifling, and sometimes coarse and offensive; but his Anglo-latin verses, his riddles, his indelicate descriptions, and his violent political satires, are in their various departments as excellent as the subjects admitted, and only leave us room occasionally to regret that so much talent was not uniformly employed upon nobler topics.

As a poet Swift's post is pre-eminent in the sort of poetry which he cultivated. He never attempted any species of composition, in which either the sublime or the pathetic were required of him. But in every department of poetry where wit is necessary, he displayed, as the subject chanced to require, either the blasting lightning of satire, or the lambent and meteor-like coruscations of frolicsome humour. His powers of versification are admirably adapted to his favourite subjects. Rhyme, which is a hand-cuff to an inferior poet, he who is master of his art wears as a bracelet. Swift was of the latter description; his lines fall as easily into the best grammatical arrangement, and the most simple and forcible expression, as if he had been writing in prose. The numbers and the coincidence of rhymes, always correct and natural, though often unexpected, distinguish the current of his poetical composition, which exhibits, otherwise, no mark of the difficulty with which these graces are attained. In respect of matter, Swift seldom elevates his tone above a satirical diatribe, a moral lesson, or a poem on manners; but the former are unrivalled in severity, and the latter in ease. Sometimes, however, the intensity of his satire gives to his poetry a character of emphatic violence, which borders upon grandeur. This is peculiarly distinguishable in the Rhapsody on Poetry. Yet this grandeur is founded, not on sublimity either of conception or expression, but upon the energy of both; and indicates rather ardour of temper, than power of imagination. *Facit indignatio versus*. The elevation of tone arises from the strong mood of passion rather than from poetical fancy. When Dryden told Swift he would never be a poet, he only had reference to the Pindaric odes, where power of imagination was necessary for success. In the walk of satire and familiar poetry, wit, and knowledge of mankind, joined to facility of expression, are the principal requisites for excellence, and in these Swift shines unrivalled. 'Cadenus and Vanessa' may be considered as Swift's *chef-d'œuvre* in that class of poems which is not professedly satirical. It is a poem on manners; and, like one of Marmontelle's *Contes Moraux*, traces the progress and involutions of a passion, existing between two persons in modern society, contrasted strongly in age, manners, and situation. Yet even here the satirical vein of Swift has predominated. We look in vain for depth of feeling or tenderness of sentiment; although, had such existed in the poet's mind, the circumstances must have called it forth. The mythological fable, which conveys the compliments paid to Vanessa, is as cold as that addressed to Ardelia or to Miss Floyd. It is, in short, a kind of poetry which neither affects sublimity nor pathos, but in which the graceful facility of the poet unites with the acute observation of the observer of human nature, to commemorate the singular contest between Cadenus and Vanessa, as an extraordinary chapter in the history of the mind.

The Dean's promptitude in composition was equal to his smoothness and felicity of expression. At Mr Gore's, in the county of Cavan, he heard the lively air called the Feast of O'Rourke, and, obtaining a literal translation of the original Irish song from the author, Mr Macgowran, executed with surprising rapidity the spirited translation which is found in his works.

Of the general stile of Swift's poems, Dr Johnson has said, in language not to be amended—

They are often humorous, almost always light, and have the qualities which recommend such compositions, easiness and gaiety. They are, for the most part, what their author intended. The diction is correct, the numbers are smooth, and the rhymes exact. There seldom occurs a hard-laboured expression, or a redundant epithet; all his verses exemplify his own definition of a good stile—they consist of 'proper words in proper places'.

As an historian Swift is entitled to little notice. . . . But although his political treatises raised his fame when published, and are still read as excellent models of that species of composition, it is to his *Tale of a Tub*, to *The Battle of the Books*, to his moral romance of *Gulliver*, and to his smaller, but not less exquisite satires upon men and manners, that Swift owes the extent and permanency of his popularity as an English classic of the first rank. In reference to these works, Cardinal Polignac, to whom Swift was well known, used the remarkable expression, *Qu'il avoit l'esprit createur*. He possessed, indeed, in the highest perfection, the wonderful power of so embodying and imaging forth 'the shadowy tribes of mind,' that the fiction of the imagination is received by the reader as if it were truth. Undoubtedly the same keen and powerful intellect, which could sound all the depths and shallows of active life, had stored his mind with facts drawn from his own acute observation, and thus supplied with materials the creative talent which he possessed; for although the knowledge of the human mind may be, in a certain extent, intuitive, and subsist without extended acquaintance with the living world, yet that acquaintance with manners, equally remarkable in Swift's productions, could only be acquired from intimate familiarity with the actual business of the world.

In fiction he possessed, in the most extensive degree, the art of veri-similitude;—the power, as we observed in the case of *Gulliver's Travels*, of adopting and sustaining a fictitious character, under every peculiarity of place and circumstance. A considerable part of this secret rests upon minuteness of narrative. Small and detached facts form the foreground of a narrative when told by an eye-witness. They are the subjects which immediately press upon his attention, and have, with respect to him as an individual, an importance, which they are far from bearing to the general scene in which he is engaged; just as a musket-shot, passing near the head of a soldier, makes a deeper impression on his mind, than all the heavy ordnance which has been discharged throughout the engage-ment. But to a distant spectator all these minute incidents are lost and blended in the general current of events; and it requires the discrimina-tion of Swift, or of De Foe, to select, in a fictitious narrative, such an enumeration of minute incidents as might strike the beholder of a real fact, especially such a one as has not been taught, by an enlarged mind and education, to generalize his observations. I am anticipated in a sort of parallel which I intended to have made between the romances of *Gulliver* and *Robinson Crusoe* by the ingenious author of the *History of Fiction*, whose words I adopt with pleasure, as expressing an opinion which I have been long induced to hold. After illustrating his proposition, by showing how Crusoe verifies his narrative of a storm, through means of a detail of particular incidents, he proceeds:

Those minute references immediately lead us to give credit to the whole narrative, since we think they would hardly have been mentioned unless they had been true. The same circumstantial detail of facts is remarkable in *Gulliver's Travels*, and we are led on by them to a partial belief in the most improbable narrations.[1]

The genius of De Foe has never been questioned, but his sphere of information was narrow; and hence his capacity of fictitious invention was limited to one or two characters. A plain sailor, as Robinson Crusoe, —a blunt soldier, as his supposed 'Cavalier'—a sharper in low life, like some of his other fictitious personages, were the only disguises which the extent of his information permitted him to assume. In this respect he is limited, like the sorcerer in the Indian tale, whose powers of transformation were confined to assuming the likeness of two or three animals only. But Swift seems, like the Persian dervish, to have possessed the faculty of transfusing his own soul into the body of any one whom he selected,—of seeing with his eyes, employing every organ of his sense, and even becoming master of the powers of his judgment. Lemuel Gulliver the traveller, Isaac Bickerstaff the astrologer, the Frenchman who writes the new *Journey to Paris*, Mrs Harris, Mary the cook-maid, the projector who proposes a plan for relieving the poor by eating their children, and the vehement Whig politician who remonstrates against the enormities of the Dublin signs, are all persons as distinct from each other as they are in appearance from the Dean of St Patrick's. Each maintains his own character, moves in his own sphere, and is stuck with those circumstances which his situation in life, or habits of thinking, have rendered most interesting to him as an individual.

The proposition I have ventured to lay down, respecting the art of giving verisimilitude to a fictitious narrative, has a corollary resting on

1 Dunlop's *History of Fiction*, Vol. III, p. 400. [Scott's note.]

the same principles. As minute particulars, pressing close upon the observation of the narrator, occupy a disproportionate share of his narrative and of his observation, so circumstances more important in themselves, in many cases, attract his notice only partially, and are therefore but imperfectly detailed. In other words, there is a distance as well as a foreground in narrative, as in natural perspective, and the scale of objects necessarily decreases as they are withdrawn from the vicinity of him who reports them. In this particular, the art of Swift is equally manifest. The information which Gulliver acquires from hearsay, is communicated in a more vague and general manner than that reported in his own knowledge. He does not, like other voyagers into Utopian realms, bring us back a minute account of their laws and government, but merely such general information upon these topics, as a well-informed and curious stranger may be reasonably supposed to acquire, during some months residence in a foreign country. In short, the narrator is the centre and main-spring of the story, which neither exhibits a degree of extended information, such as circumstances could not permit him to acquire, nor omits those minute incidents, which the same circumstances rendered of importance to him, because immediately affecting his own person.

Swift has the more easily attained this perfection of fictitious narrative, because, in all his works of whatever description, he has maintained the most undeviating attention to the point at issue. What Mr Cambridge has justly observed of *The Battle of the Books* is equally true as a general characteristic of Swift's writings; whoever examines them will find, that, through the whole piece, no one episode or allusion is introduced for its own sake, but every part appears not only consistent with, but written for the express purpose of strengthening and supporting the whole.

[I, 481–92.]

The Journal to Stella, from 2d September 1710 to 6th June 1713, forms a natural introduction to the political pieces by which Swift supported the last ministry of Queen Anne. But it may also be thought a fit preface to his works in general, as affording the closest insight into his temper, principles, and habits, during the busiest and happiest period of his life. It contains, indeed, documents for his private history, of a nature equally curious and authentic. The letters of literary men are usually written under some feeling, that they may one day become public; at least they are calculated so as to bear relation to the habits and feelings of their correspondents; and thus far the writer is necessarily under a degree of restraint. In a private diary, on the other hand, the journalist pays some attention to the arranging and methodizing his thoughts; for, supposing that it is intended for the writer's sole use, there are few who care to review even their own sentiments in absolute dishabille: But *The Journal to Stella* is as unconstrained as conversation the most intimate and familiar, nearly as much so, indeed, as thought itself. To account for this, we must recollect, that Swift had united the destiny of Mrs Johnson so closely to his own, that his hopes, fears, wishes, and expectations, were sure to be identified with those of his correspondent. The strange and peculiar relation in which they had now for some years stood to each other, had produced between them all the confidence and mutual interest of marriage, while their affection was unchilled by familiarity, or by possession. Swift, therefore, wrote to Stella, alike without coldness or suspicion, with all the intimacy of a husband, but with all the feelings of a lover. Nothing was too precious to be withheld from her; and, at the same time, nothing so trifling in which she was not to find interest, if it related to him. Hence that curious and diverting mixture of the meanest and most common domestic details with state secrets, court intrigues, and the fate of ministries; where the history of the Duke of Marlborough's disgrace is hardly detailed with more minute accuracy than the progress and cure of the doctor's broken shin. This miscellaneous mode of writing is a warrant to the reader, that he has the real sentiments of the author. He who bends his mind to a single subject, will gradually, and even unconsciously, become guarded in his mode of treating it, and, consequently, will rather plead a cause than deliver an opinion. But, while throwing into his *Journal* the ideas as they rose in his mind, grand or minute, important or trifling, Swift insures us, that he had not even that very harmless motive for a certain disguise of sentiment, which arises from the wish of doing all things in order. His ideas, upon subjects of importance, break from him at intervals; and, as he was under no necessity to preserve an appearance of uniformity, the attentive reader may perceive when he judges coolly; when he is swayed by passion, or prejudice; when he alters or revokes an opinion; and when, without doing so, his opinions are inconsistent with each other. In short, it is a picture of the man, the author, and the politician.

[II, 3–4.]

IT has been usually reported that Swift, though originally studious of his character as a preacher, was never satisfied with his own Sermons.

He preached, however, regularly as his turn of duty recurred, and always to a crowded congregation. Some years before his death, he gave thirty-five Sermons to Dr Sheridan, saying, slightly, 'There are a bundle of my old Sermons. You may have them if you please; they may be of use to you, they never were of any to me.' There are several reasons, which, without disparagement to the real value of these discourses, may have induced the author to think of them with indifference. They contain obvious marks of haste and carelessness; were the objects, says Lord Orrery, of necessity, not of choice; and it is not usual for writers to rate compositions highly on which they have bestowed neither time nor labour. But they are, besides, as Sermons, inferior to many written by Swift's contemporaries, and he was too much accustomed to pre-eminence to view with complacency compositions, which tended to place him in a secondary and subordinate situation. They are deficient also in those qualities of oratory which must ever be most valued by the preacher, since, through them, he is to produce his effect upon the congregation at the moment when he himself is addressing them. The Sermons of Swift have none of that thunder which appals, or that resistless and winning softness which melts, the hearts of an audience. He can never have enjoyed the triumph of uniting hundreds in one ardent sentiment of love, of terror, or of devotion. His reasoning, however powerful, and indeed unanswerable, convinces the understanding, but is never addressed to the heart; and, indeed, from his instructions to a young clergyman, he seems hardly to have considered pathos as a legitimate ingredient in an English sermon. Occasionally, too, Swift's misanthropic habits break out even from the pulpit; nor is he altogether able to suppress his disdain of those fellow mortals, on whose behalf was accomplished the great work of redemption. With such unamiable feelings towards his hearers, the preacher might indeed command their respect, but could never excite their sympathy. It may be feared that his Sermons were less popular from another cause, imputable more to the congregation than to the pastor. Swift spared not the vices of rich or poor; and, disdaining to amuse the imaginations of his audience with discussion of dark points of divinity, or warm them by a flow of sentimental devotion, he rushes at once to the point of moral depravity, and upbraids them with their favourite and predominant vices in a tone of stern reproof, bordering upon reproach. In short, he tears the bandages from their wounds, like the hasty surgeon of a crowded hospital, and applies the incision knife and caustic with salutary, but rough and untamed severity. But, alas! the mind must be already victorious over the worst of its evil propensities, that can profit by this harsh medicine. There is a principle of opposition in our nature, which mans itself with obstinacy even against avowed truth, when it approaches our feelings in a harsh and insulting manner. And Swift was probably sensible, that his discourses, owing to these various causes, did not produce the powerful effects most grateful to the feelings of the preacher, because they reflect back to him those of the audience.

But although the Sermons of Swift are deficient in eloquence, and were lightly esteemed by their author, they must not be undervalued by the modern reader. They exhibit, in an eminent degree, that powerful grasp of intellect which distinguished the author above all his contemporaries. In no religious discourses can be found more sound good sense, more happy and forcible views of the immediate subject. The reasoning is not only irresistible, but managed in a mode so simple and clear, that its force is obvious to the most ordinary capacity. Upon all subjects of morality, the preacher maintains the character of a rigid and inflexible monitor; neither admitting apology for that which is wrong, nor softening the difficulty of adhering to that which is right; a stern stoicism of doctrine, that may fail in finding many converts, but leads to excellence in the few manly minds who dare to embrace it.

In treating the doctrinal points of belief, (as in his Sermon upon the Trinity,) Swift systematically refuses to quit the high and pre-eminent ground which the defender of Christianity is entitled to occupy, or to submit to the test of human reason, mysteries which are placed, by their very nature, far beyond our finite capacities. Swift considered, that, in religion, as in profane science, there must be certain ultimate laws which are to be received as fundamental truths, although we are incapable of defining or analysing their nature; and he censures those divines, who, in presumptuous confidence of their own logical powers, enter into controversy upon such mysteries of faith, without considering that they give thereby the most undue advantage to the infidel. Our author wisely and consistently declared reason an incompetent judge of doctrines, of which God had declared the fact, concealing from man the manner. He contended, that he who, upon the whole, receives the Christian religion as of divine inspiration, must be contented to depend upon God's truth, and his holy word, and receive with humble faith the mysteries which are too high for comprehension. Above all, Swift points out, with his usual forcible precision, the mischievous tendency of those investigations which, while they assail one fundamental doctrine of the Christian religion, shake and endanger the whole fabric, destroy the settled faith of thousands, pervert and mislead the genius of the learned and acute, destroy and confound the religious principles of the simple and ignorant.

It cannot be denied, that Swift's political propensities break forth more keenly in many of these discourses, than, perhaps, suited the sacred place where they were originally delivered. The Sermons on the Martyrdom of Charles, on the Condition of Ireland, and on Doing Good, approach too nearly to the character of political essays. In those on Brotherly Love, on False Witness, and some others, traces of the same party violence are to be found. The Dean's peculiar strain of humour sometimes, too, displays itself without rigid attention to decorum, of which the singular Sermon on Sleeping in Church is a curious instance.

[VII, 403–5.]

[Gulliver's Travels]

THIS celebrated Satirical Romance has extended the name and the reputation of its author to nations who might never have heard of the favourite of Lord Oxford, the champion of the Church of England, or even the protector of the liberties of Ireland. The first sketch of the work occurs in the proposed *Travels of Martinus Scriblerus*,[1] devised in that

---

[1] Pope has not forgotten to intimate this in the concluding chapter of the *Memoirs of Scriblerus*. 'It was in the year 1699 that Martin set out on his travels. Thou wilt certainly be very curious to know what they were. It is not yet time to inform thee. But what hints I am at liberty to give, I will.

'Thou shalt know then, that, in his first voyage, he was carried by a prosperous storm to a discovery of the remains of the ancient Pygmæan empire.

'That, in his second, he was happily shipwrecked on the land of the Giants, now the most humane people in the world.

'That, in his third voyage, he discovered a whole kingdom of philosophers, who govern by the mathematics; with whose admirable schemes and projects he returned to benefit his own dear country; but had the misfortune to find them rejected by the envious ministers of Queen Anne, and himself sent treacherously away.

'And hence it is, that, in his fourth voyage, he discovers a vein of melancholy proceeding almost to a disgust of the species; but, above all, a mortal detestation to the whole flagitious race of ministers, and a final resolution not to give in any memorial to the Secretary of State, in order to subject the lands he discovered to the Crown of Great Britain.

'Now, if, by these hints, the reader can help himself to a farther discovery of the nature and contents of these Travels, he is welcome to as much light as they afford him: I am obliged, by all the ties of honour not to speak more openly.

'But if any man shall see such very extraordinary voyages, into such very extraordinary nations, which manifest the most distinguishing marks of a philosopher, a politician, and a legislator, and can imagine them to belong to a surgeon of a ship, or a captain of a merchantman, let him remain in his ignorance.

agreeable society where the rest of the miscellanies were planned. Had the work been executed under the same auspices, it would probably have been occupied by that personal satire upon obscure and unworthy contemporaries to which Pope was but too much addicted. But when the Dean mused in solitude over the execution of his plan, it assumed at once a more grand and a darker complexion. The spirit of indignant hatred and contempt with which he regarded the mass of humanity; his quick and powerful perception of their failings, errors, and crimes; his zeal for liberty and freedom of thought, tended at once to generalize, while it embittered, his satire, and to change traits of personal severity for that deep shade of censure which *Gulliver's Travels* throw upon mankind universally. This tone of mind gained upon the author, as we shall have occasion to remark when we examine the voyages separately.

The general idea of the work is unquestionably borrowed from the *True History* of Lucian, a fictitious journey through imaginary countries, prefaced by an introduction, in an exquisite vein of irony, upon the art of writing history. The allusions which this work probably contained to the histories of the time are lost to us; but there is a pleasing luxuriance of imagination which runs through the whole, and renders it still agreeable to the modern reader, notwithstanding the extravagance of some parts of the fiction, and the flatness of others. From the *True History* of Lucian, Cyrano Bergerac took his idea of *A Journey to the Moon*, and Rabelais derived his yet more famous *Voyage of Pantagruel*. Swift has consulted both, as well as their common original, but is more particularly indebted to the work of Rabelais, which satirizes severely the various orders of the law and clergy of his period. In a tract, republished in the *Harleian Miscellany*, said to have been written by Dr Francis Goodwin, Bishop of Llandaff, who died in 1633, called *The Man in the Moon, or the Discourse of a Voyage thither by Domingo Gonsalez*, we have men of enormous stature and of prodigious longevity; a flying chariot also, and some other slight points of resemblance to the *Travels of Gulliver*. But none of those works either approach in excellence, or anticipate in originality, the romance of Swift. They are, in comparison, eccentric, wild, and childish fables, neither conveying a useful moral nor an amusing satire. The passages of satirical allusion are few, and thrown

---

'And, whoever he be, he shall farther observe, in every page of such a book, that cordial love of mankind, that inviolable regard to truth, that passion for his dear country, and that particular attachment to the excellent Princess Queen Anne:—Surely that man deserves to be pitied, if, by all those visible signs and characters, he cannot distinguish and acknowledge the Great Scriblerus'.—(POPE's Works, edit. 1806, 8vo, vol. VI. p.171-173.) [Scott's note.]

at random, among a scattered mass of incoherent fiction. But no word drops from Gulliver's pen in vain. Where his work ceases for a moment to satirize the vices of mankind in general, it becomes a stricture upon the parties, politics, and court of Britain; where it abandons that subject of censure, it presents a lively picture of the vices and follies of the fashionable world, or of the vain pursuits of philosophy, while the parts of the narrative which refer to the traveller's own adventures form a humorous and striking parody of the manner of old voyagers; their dry and minute style, and the unimportant personal incidents with which their journals are encumbered. These are inserted with an address, which, abstracted from the marvellous part of the narrative, would almost induce us to believe we are perusing a real story. This art of introducing trifling and minute anecdotes, upon which nothing depends, or is made to turn, was perhaps imitated by Swift from the romances of De Foe, who carried the air of authenticity to the highest pitch of perfection in his *Robinson Crusoe*, and *Memoirs of a Cavalier*. It is, indeed, a marked difference between real and fictitious narrative, that the latter includes only such incidents as the author conceives will interest the reader, whereas the former is uniformly invested with many petty particulars, which can only be interesting to the narrator himself. Another distinction is, that, in the course of a real story, circumstances occur which lead neither to consequences nor to explanations; whereas the novelist is, generally speaking, cautious to introduce no incident or character which has not some effect in forwarding his plot. For example, Crusoe tells us, in the beginning of his history, that he had a second brother, an adventurer like himself, of whom his family could never learn the fate. Scarcely a man but De Foe himself would have concluded the adventures of Crusoe without again introducing this brother. But he was well aware that the course of human life is as irregular and capricious as the process of natural vegetation; and that a trim parterre does not more accurately point out the operation of art, than a story in which all the incidents are combined with, and depend upon each other with epic regularity, leads us to infer its being the offspring of invention. In these particulars, Gulliver was probably somewhat indebted to Robinson Crusoe. In the pretended Journey to Paris, however, Swift had already given an example of his capacity of identifying himself, in feelings, sentiments, and powers of comprehension and observation, with the fictitious character he then thought fit to assume. The style and character of Gulliver are founded upon those of the hardy and intrepid Dampier; a navigator who, although trained among the buccaneers, and following, upon many occasions, their lawless profession, displayed the patience, persevering fortitude, and zeal for adding to our knowledge of the globe which we inhabit, that form the first and most valuable points in the character of a nautical discoverer. We have, accordingly, a very accurate notion of Gulliver's character, who carries, through all the wonderful scenes he visits, the courage of a seaman, the curiosity of a traveller, and the prejudices of a thorough-bred Englishman.

The subject of the satire itself varies in the different voyages into which the work is subdivided.

The 'Voyage to Lilliput' is founded upon the well-known fiction of the pigmies. Herodotus, Aristotle, Pliny, Solinus, and other ancient authors, had averred the existence of this diminutive race of beings: Paulus Jovius, Pagafeta, and some of the earlier modern travellers, had confirmed the fable: Even Scripture had been appealed to for its truth, by those commentators who translate the word *Gammadim* (Ezekiel xxvii. 11,) by the term Pigmies. One hint seems to be taken from a passage in Philostratus, an author whom Swift must have perused with care, as he has made a brief character of the work upon the copy which he used, and marked on the margin such passages as he chiefly approved of. From a quotation taken from that author in Tyson's dissertation on the Pigmies, I have very little doubt that the Dean was indebted to Philostratus for the idea of the first scene between Gulliver and the Lilliputians:

The Pigmies, to revenge the death of Antæus, having found Hercules napping in Libya, mustered up all their forces against him. One phalanx (he tells us) assaulted his left hand; but against his right hand, that being the stronger, two phalanxes were appointed. The archers and slingers besieged his feet, admiring the hugeness of his thighs: But against his head, as the arsenal, they raised batteries, the king himself taking his post there. They set fire to his hair, put reaping-hooks in his eyes; and that he might not breathe, clapped doors to his mouth and nostrils; but all the execution that they could do was only to awake him, which when done, deriding their folly, he gathered them all up into his lion's skin, and carried them (Philostratus thinks) to Euristhenes.

In every point of view, therefore, the traditional belief was sufficiently established to render it an agreeable vehicle of fiction. The great scope and tendency of the satire is here levelled against the court and ministry of George I. In some points the parallel is very closely drawn, as where the parties in the church and state are described, and the mode in which offices and marks of distinction are conferred in the

Lilliputian court. The tone of the satire is there strictly personal; and the character of the Lord-treasurer Flimnap will be generally found to correspond with that which Swift wished to present of Sir Robert Walpole. Nothing could have been more happily imagined to ridicule the pursuits, passions, and intrigues of a court, than supposing them transferred to creatures only six inches high; and the extreme importance with which Gulliver continues to treat these subjects, even when agitated by beings 'less than smallest dwarfs;' his veneration for the person of the Emperor; his sense of the high favours and rank conferred upon him; his disputing precedence with Flimnap, in virtue of his title of Nardac, though giving way to him as an officer of state; above all, the inimitable gravity with which he vindicates the honour of a great lady from a supposed intrigue with him, throw an air of absurdity upon such discussions, well calculated to ridicule the interest which they are usually found capable of exciting. The secession of Gulliver to Blefuscu under the terrors of a prosecution for high treason, seems intended to reprobate the proceedings against Bolingbroke and Atterbury, who, in similar circumstances, were, as Swift's partiality led him to believe, unjustly compelled to take refuge in France.

In the Second Voyage, the author turns the opposite end of the telescope; and, as he had held up to the derision of ordinary beings the intrigues, cabals, wars, and councils of a Lilliputian court and ministry, he now shews us in what manner a people of immense stature, and gifted with a soundness and coolness of judgment in some degree corresponding, might be likely to regard the principles and politics of Europe. Swift's King of Brobdingnag is a patriot monarch, governing his people on the principles of reason and philanthropy; separated, by his situation, and his subjects' immense superiority in physical force, from either the necessity or the temptation of war and conquest; a stoic in appetite and in ambition; holding everything of little importance, except what directly tended to the real benefit of his subjects. This vision, as vain and improbable as the size of the personage so gifted, is maintained with singular art through the whole section. The monarch's coldness and indifference, while he considered the traveller as a mere play-thing, or subject of idle curiosity, joined to his earnest and anxious colloquies with Gulliver, so soon as he discovered him to be a rational and thinking being, convey some traits of William III. If there be any resemblance in the portrait, it must have escaped the pen of Swift unconsciously; for though his youth was taught to admire that monarch, it is well known William's panegyric was the last the Dean would have drawn, in the latter stage of his life. The portrait of the queen, who is represented as amiable and inquisitive, the protectress of the pigmy stranger, is unquestionably designed as a compliment to Queen Caroline, whom Swift was then desirous to gratify. The voyage to Brobdingnag differs from that to Lilliput in this material particular, that it contains few personal or temporary allusions. There are no circumstances mentioned which have not been, more or less, common attributes of the British court for two centuries, either in reality or according to popular report, or, indeed, which may not be considered as applicable to courts in general. All the usual topics of censure are run over with unqualified severity; and the unrelenting conclusion is summed up by the King of Brobdingnag, in the celebrated declaration, that the bulk of Gulliver's countrymen are the 'most pernicious race of little odious vermin, that Nature ever suffered to crawl upon the surface of the earth.'

The vehicle of the allegory, both in the First and Second Voyage, is less shocking to the understanding than might at first have been conceived. Our infancy has been accustomed to tales of giants and pigmies; and a thousand entertaining instances of the author's genius, in combining and arguing upon the very impossibilities of his tale, give it, at every turn, a new and additional interest. In fact, the work rests upon an axiom, in itself certain, that there is no such thing in nature as an absolute standard of size, and that all our ideas upon the subject are relative, and founded upon comparison. On this ground, the author successfully labours to exhibit all the whimsical consequences which might attend a contrast so violent as is offered to the usual standard of proportion in the inhabitants of Lilliput and Brobdingnag. The great accuracy with which proportions are preserved, has often been noticed as one of these interesting particulars. Another consists in the curious mode in which the traveller's mind seems to conform to the dimensions around him, and think of what is great or small, not according to the English standard, but that of Lilliput or Brobdingnag. Thus Gulliver talks with solemnity of the stately trees in his Majesty's park at Lilliput, the tops of some of which he could hardly reach with his clenched fist; and celebrates, with becoming admiration, the prodigious leap of one of the imperial huntsmen over his foot, shoe and all. In like manner, he undervalues the tower of the great temple in the capital of Brobdingnag, which, though three thousand feet in height, is, he thinks, hardly equal in proportion to Salisbury steeple. And he notices the lock of his box as remarkably small and neatly executed, because he had seen one rather larger on a gentleman's gate in England. It is by this imperceptible mode of assimilating our ideas of proportion to those of his dwarfs and giants, that Swift renders lively and consistent a fable, which, in other hands, would only have seemed monstrous and childish. The sort of re-action, too, which is produced upon the traveller's mind when restored to persons of his own size, (particularly after his return from the land of giants,) greatly reconciles us to a deception maintained with such accuracy and truth of description. It may be said of most similar fictions, that every incident is a new demand upon the patience and credulity of the reader, and a fresh shock to probability. But if, on the contrary, Gulliver's first postulates can be granted; if, that is, we are contented to suppose the existence of such nations as those to which he travels, every other step of the story is so consistent with their probable conduct to him, and to each other; his hopes, fears, and wishes, are pointed out with such striking accuracy; the impressions which he makes on the natives, and which he receives from them, are so distinct and lively, that we give way to the force of the author's genius, and are willing to allow him credit for an ideal world, in which the improbability of the original conception is palliated by the exquisitely artificial combination of the detail.

The 'Voyage to Laputa', as it was the part in which the world took the least pleasure, is that in which the author most required assistance. It is intended to ridicule the pursuits of philosophy, as the two first voyages were levelled against the government of Great Britain, both in its general administration, and as conducted under the auspices of Sir Robert Walpole. The Abbé des Fontaines, therefore, was grievously deceived when he supposed the mathematical court of Laputa was intended to designate that of Great Britain, 'because,' as he expresses himself, 'it resembles no other court whatever.' The satire was not, on this occasion, levelled against statesmen, but against philosophers. But Swift's learning as a student of Belles Lettres, and even his extensive knowledge of mankind, and of the human heart, were insufficient to guide him in a task which required depth of science, and where, above all, the assistance of Arbuthnot was indispensable to success. His ridicule of mathematical science, and his supposing that the knowledge of the theory of geometrical demonstrations either leads to, or is consistent with, the misapplication of them in mechanical arts, only shews his want of acquaintance with the very principles on which these arts depend. The satire, also, on experimental philosophy, shews ignorance as well as injustice. If it was a noble and patriotic object of the King of Brobdingnag to make two spikes of corn, or blades of grass, grow where the ground bore but one before, that object can only be attained by an appeal to first principles, and to those philosophers whose useful and indefatigable research deduces from them practical inferences, for the guidance of the mere farmer. Pope, as a student of polite learning, and Swift as a man of the world, accustomed to live with statesmen, and to witness the transactions of public business, looked down with the contempt of ignorance upon the pursuits of speculative philosophy. The gross blunders made by the former respecting the nature and purpose of mathematical research, is kept in countenance by Swift's account of the mathematicians of Laputa. It must be owned, however, that if the author's contempt for speculative science hurried him too far, he has fallen with just severity upon a class of men whom the circumstances of England at the time furnished ample food for satirizing—those quack pretenders, namely, whose projects were, for a time, so greedily received and fostered by all ranks. The plans of these projectors, or undertakers, as they were called, were usually founded upon some smattering of science, or some supposed discovery, which they had neither information nor honesty sufficient to verify by experience, before they set afloat their bubble. The extensive ruin in which the South-Sea scheme involved the nation must have made a strong impression on the mind of Swift, as honest as he was ardent; nor was it extraordinary that he should have extended his undeserved dislike to schemes founded on a less questionable basis, and conducted with greater probity. It may be also remarked, that some of the wildest hallucinations of the college of Lagado were revived in the middle of the last century by Maupertuis, who thereby subjected himself to the lash of Voltaire's satire. The censure, therefore, upon philosophical research, although it cannot hurt that which is conducted upon the principle of experiment, is richly merited by the wild hypothesis of the projector or sophist.

The Voyage to the Land of Houyhnhnms, is, beyond contest, the basest and most unworthy part of the work. It holds mankind forth in a light too degrading for contemplation, and which, if admitted, would justify or palliate the worst vices, by exhibiting them as natural attributes, and rendering reformation from a state of such base depravity a task too desperate to be attempted. As no good could possibly be attained by the exhibition of so loathsome a picture of humanity, as it may even tend to great evil, by removing every motive for philanthropy, the publication has been justly considered as a stain upon the character of the ingenious author. Allowance, however, is to be made for the soured and disgusted state of Swift's mind, which doubtless was even then influenced by the first impressions of that incipient mental disease which, in his case, was marked by universal misanthropy, as in many others by particular and individual antipathy. Even when he was plunged into total idiocy, Swift's temper continued irritable in the highest degree, however ineffectual his indignation; but while he retained mind to conceive, and ability to express, the fervour of his angry passions, their explosion was as powerful as violent. We are, accordingly, frequently compelled to admire the force of his talents, even while thus unworthily employed, in exposing the worst parts of our nature with the art of an anatomist dissecting a mangled and half-putrid carcase. As the previous departments of the satire were levelled against the court of George I., against statesmen, and against philosophers, the wider sweep of this last division comprehends human nature in every stage and variety, and, with an industry as malicious as the author's knowledge of life is extensive, holds it up to execration in all.

It is some consolation to remark, that the fiction on which this libel on human nature rests, is, in every respect, gross and improbable, and, far from being entitled to the praise due to the management of the first two parts, is inferior in plan even to the third. The voyage to Laputa, if we except the flying island, which has often been regarded as an unnecessary violation of the laws of nature, the picture of the Strulbrugs, and the powers of the governor of Balnibarbi, (from both of which an excellent moral is extracted,) falls within the rank of such ideal communities as the republic of Plato, and the Utopia of Sir Thomas More. But the state of the Houyhnhnms is not only morally but physically impossible, and, as Dr Beattie has remarked, self-contradictory also, since these animals are represented with attributes inconsistent with their natural structure. We may grant to the framer of an apologue that beasts may be endured with reason, but we can hardly conceive a horse riding in a carriage, and much less milking cows, building houses, and performing other functions of the same kind, to which its limbs are not adapted. This circumstance is sufficient of itself to refute the reflections thrown upon the conformation of the human body, since the meanest and most simple of the works which our configuration enables us to execute, cannot, without the grossest violation of probability, be imputed to almost any species of the inferior creation.

Severe, unjust, and degrading as this satire is, it was hailed with malignant triumph by those, whose disappointed hopes and expectations had thrown them into the same state of gloomy misanthropy which it

argues in its author. Swift's old antagonist, Sarah, Duchess of Marlborough, who had so often smarted under the lash of his political
sarcasms, and had lived to brave the successors in a court where she
had domineered, forgot all her former resentment against the favourite
of Oxford and Bolingbroke, in order to make common cause with the
author of *Gulliver* against mankind. So true it is, that disappointed
ambition can do more than distress itself to spite us at the world.

[XI, 3–13.]

60. Francis Jeffrey on Swift

1816

The Edinburgh Review, xxvii (September 1816), 1–58 *passim.*

Francis Jeffrey (1773–1850) was a lawyer, but is now most famous as editor of the *Edinburgh Review*, which he helped to establish. His brilliant and vigorous reviews made him a literary power to be reckoned with. This extract is from Jeffrey's unsigned review of Sir Walter Scott's edition of *The Works of Jonathan Swift, D.D., Dean of St. Patrick's Dublin . . . ,* 1814. As Jeffrey almost confesses, his detestation of Swift's life makes him an undependable critic of the works.

Of these ingenious writers [the Augustans] whose characteristic certainly was not vigour, any more than tenderness or fancy, SWIFT was indisputably the most vigorous—and perhaps the least tender or fanciful. The greater part of his works being occupied with politics and personalities that have long since lost all interest, can now attract but little attention, except as memorials of the manner in which politics and personalities were then conducted. In other parts, however, there is a vein of peculiar humour and strong satire, which will always be agreeable—and a sort of heartiness of abuse and contempt of mankind, which produces a greater sympathy and animation in the reader than the more elaborate sarcasms that have since come into fashion. Altogether his merits appear to be more *unique* and inimitable than those of any of his contemporaries—and as his works are connected in many parts with historical events which it must always be of importance to understand, we conceive that there are none, of which a new and careful edition is so likely to be acceptable to the public, or so worthy to engage the attention of a person qualified for the undertaking. . . .

. . . whether we look to the fortune, or the conduct of this extraordinary person, we really recollect no individual who was less entitled to be either discontented or misanthropical—to complain of men or of accidents. Born almost a beggar, and neither very industrious nor very engaging in his early habits, he attained, almost with his first efforts, the very height of distinction, and was rewarded by appointments, which placed him in a state of independence and respectability for life. He was honoured with the acquaintance of all that was distinguished for rank, literature, or reputation;—and, if not very generally beloved, was, what he probably valued far more, admired and feared by most of those with whom he was acquainted. When his party was overthrown, neither his person nor his fortune suffered;—but he was indulged, through the whole of his life, in a license of scurrility and abuse, which has never been permitted to any other writer,—and possessed the exclusive and devoted affection of the only two women to whom he wished to appear interesting. In this *history*, we confess, we see but little apology for discontent and lamentation;—and, in his *conduct*, there is assuredly still less for misanthropy. In public life, we do not know where we could have found any body half so profligate and unprincipled as himself, and the friends to whom he finally attached himself;—nor can we conceive that complaints of venality, and want of patriotism, could ever come with so ill a grace from any quarter as from him who had openly deserted and libelled his party, without the pretext of any other cause than the insufficiency of the rewards they bestowed upon him, —and joined himself with men who were treacherous, not only to their first professions, but to their country and to each other, to all of whom he adhered, after their mutual hatred and villanies were detected? In private life, again, with what face could he erect himself into a rigid censor of morals, or pretend to complain of men in general, as unworthy of his notice, after breaking the hearts of two, if not three, amiable women, whose affections he had engaged by the most constant assiduities,—after brutally libelling almost all his early friends and bene-factors, and exhibiting, in his daily life and conversation, a picture of domineering insolence and dogmatism, to which no parallel could be found, we believe, in the history of any other individual, and which rendered his society intolerable to all who were not subdued by their awe of him, or inured to it by long use? He had some right, perhaps, to look with disdain upon men of ordinary understandings; but for all that is the proper object of reproach, he should have looked only within: and whatever may be his merits as a writer, we do not hesitate to say, that he was despicable as a politician, and hateful as a man.

With these impressions of his personal character, perhaps it is not easy for us to judge quite fairly of his works. Yet we are far from being insensible to their great and very peculiar merits. Their chief peculiarity is, that they were almost all what may be called occasional productions —not written for fame or for posterity—from the fulness of the mind, or the desire of instructing mankind—but on the spur of the occasion— for promoting some temporary and immediate object, and producing a practical effect, in the attainment of which their whole importance centered. With the exception of *A Tale of a Tub, Gulliver,* the *Polite Conversation,* and about half a volume of poetry, this description will apply to almost all that is now before us;—and it is no small proof of the vigour and vivacity of his genius, that posterity should have been so anxious to preserve these careless and hasty productions, upon which their author appears to have set no other value than as means for the attainment of an end. The truth is, accordingly, that *they are* very extra- ordinary performances: And, considered with a view to the purposes for which they were intended, have probably never been equalled in any period of the world. They are written with great plainness, force and intrepidity—advance at once to the matter in dispute—give battle to the strength of the enemy, and never seek any kind of advantage from darkness or obscurity. Their distinguishing feature, however, is the force and the vehemence of the invective in which they abound;— the copiousness, the steadiness, the perseverance, and the dexterity with which abuse and ridicule are showered upon the adversary. This, we think, was, beyond all doubt, Swift's great talent, and the weapon by which he made himself formidable. He was, without exception, the greatest and most efficient *libeller* that ever exercised the trade; and possessed, in an eminent degree, all the qualifications which it requires: —a clear head—a cold heart—a vindictive temper—no admiration of noble qualities—no sympathy with suffering—not much conscience— not much consistency—a ready wit—a sarcastic humour—a thorough knowledge of the baser parts of human nature—and a complete familiarity with everything that is low, homely, and familiar in language. These were his gifts;—and he soon felt for what ends they were given. Almost all his works are libels; generally upon indi- viduals, sometimes upon sects and parties, sometimes upon human nature. Whatever be his end, however, personal abuse, direct— vehement, unsparing invective, is his means. It is his sword and his shield, his panoply and his chariot of war. In all his writings, accordingly, there is nothing to raise or exalt our notions of human nature,—but every thing to vilify and degrade. We may learn from them, perhaps, to dread the consequences of base actions, but never to love the feelings that lead to generous ones. There is no spirit, indeed, of love or of honour in any part of them; but an unvaried and harassing display of insolence and animosity in the writer, and villany and folly in those of whom he is writing. Though a great polemic, he makes no use of general principles, nor ever enlarges his views to a wide or comprehensive conclusion. Every thing is particular with him, and, for the most part, strictly personal. To make amends, however, we do think him quite without a competitor in personalities. With a quick and sagacious spirit, and a bold and popular manner, he joins an exact knowledge of all the strong and the weak parts of every cause he has to manage; and, without the least restraint from delicacy, either of taste or of feeling, he seems always to think the most effectual blows the most advisable, and no advantage unlawful that is likely to be successful for the moment. Disregarding all the laws of polished hostility, he uses, at one and the same moment, his sword and his poisoned dagger—his hands and his teeth, and his envenomed breath,—and does not even scruple, upon occasion, to imitate his own yahoos, by discharging on his unhappy victims a shower of filth, from which neither courage nor dexterity can afford any protection.—Against such an antagonist, it was, of course, at no time very easy to make head; and accordingly his invective seems, for the most part, to have been as much dreaded, and as tremendous as the personal ridicule of Voltaire. Both were inexhaustible, well directed, and unsparing; but even when Voltaire drew blood, he did not mangle the victim, and was only mischievous when Swift was brutal; any one who will compare the epigrams on M. Franc de Pompignan with those on Tighe or Bettesworth, will easily understand the distinction.

Of the few works which he wrote in the capacity of an author, and not of a party zealot or personal enemy, *A Tale of a Tub* was by far the earliest in point of time, and has, by many, been considered as the first in point of merit. We confess we are not of that opinion. It is by far too long and elaborate for a piece of pleasantry;—the humour sinks, in many places, into mere buffoonery and nonsense;—and there is a real and extreme tediousness arising from the too successful mimicry of tediousness and pedantry. All these defects are apparent enough even in the main story, in which the incidents are without the shadow of verisimilitude or interest, and by far too thinly scattered; but they become unsufferable in the interludes or digressions, the greater part of which are to us utterly illegible, and seem to consist almost entirely of cold and forced conceits, and exaggerated representations of long exploded whims and absurdities. The style of this work, which appears to us greatly inferior to the history of John Bull or even of

Martinus Scriblerus, is evidently more elaborate than that of Swift's other writings,—but has all its substantial characteristics. Its great merit seems to consist in the author's perfect familiarity with all sorts of common and idiomatical expressions, his unlimited command of established phrases, both solemn and familiar, and the unrivalled profusion and propriety with which he heaps them up and applies them to the exposition of the most fantastic conceptions. To deliver absurd notions or incredible tales in the most authentic, honest and direct terms, that have been used for the communication of truth and reason, and to luxuriate in all the variations of that grave, plain and perspicuous phraseology, which dull men use to express their homely opinions, seems to be the great art of this extraordinary humourist, and that which gives their character and their edge to his sly strokes of satire, his keen sarcasms and bitter personalities.

The voyages of Captain Lemuel Gulliver is indisputably his greatest work. The idea of making fictitious travels the vehicle of satire as well as of amusement, is at least as old as Lucian; but has never been carried into execution with such success, spirit, and originality, as in this celebrated performance. The brevity, the minuteness, the homeliness, the unbroken seriousness of the narrative, all give a character of truth and simplicity to the work which at once palliates the extravagance of the fiction, and enhances the effect of those weighty reflections and cutting severities in which it abounds. Yet though it is probable enough, that without those touches of satire and observation the work would have appeared childish and preposterous, we are persuaded that it pleases chiefly by the novelty and vivacity of the extraordinary pictures it presents, and the entertainment we receive from following the fortunes of the traveller in his several extraordinary adventures. The greater part of the wisdom and satire at least appears to us to be extremely vulgar and common-place; and we have no idea that they could possibly appear either impressive or entertaining, if presented without these accompaniments. A considerable part of the pleasure we derive from the voyages of Gulliver, in short, is of the same description with that which we receive from those of Sinbad the sailor, and is chiefly heightened, we believe, by the greater brevity and minuteness of the story, and the superior art that is employed to give it an appearance of truth and probability, in the very midst of its wonders. Among these arts, as Mr Scott has judiciously observed, one of the most important is the exact adaptation of the narrative to the condition of its supposed author. . . .

That the interest does not arise from the satire but from the plausible description of physical wonders, seems to be farther proved by the fact, that the parts which please the least are those in which there is most satire and least of those wonders. In the voyage to Laputa, after the first description of the flying island, the attention is almost exclusively directed to intellectual absurdities; and every one is aware of the dulness that is the result. Even as a satire, indeed, this part is extremely poor and defective; nor can any thing show more clearly the author's incapacity for large and comprehensive views than his signal failure in all those parts which invited him to such contemplations. In the multitude of his vulgar and farcical representations of particular errors in philosophy, he nowhere appears to have any sense of its true value or principles; but satisfies himself with collecting or imagining a number of fantastical quackeries, which tend to illustrate nothing but his contempt for human understanding. Even where his subject seems to invite him to something of a higher flight, he uniformly shrinks back from it, and takes shelter in commonplace derision. What, for instance, can be poorer than the use he makes of the evocation of the illustrious dead—in which Hannibal is brought in just to say, that he had not a drop of vinegar in his camp; and Aristotle, to ask two of his commentators, 'whether the rest of the tribe were as great dunces as themselves?' The voyage to the Houyhnhnms is commonly supposed to displease by its vile and degrading representations of human nature; but, if we do not strangely mistake our own feelings on the subject, the impression it produces is not so much that of disgust as of dulness. The picture is not only extravagant, but bald and tame in the highest degree; while the story is not enlivened by any of those numerous and uncommon incidents which are detailed in the two first parts, with such an inimitable air of probability as almost to persuade us of their reality. For the rest, we have observed already, that the scope of the whole work, and indeed of all his writings, is to degrade and vilify human nature; and though some of the images which occur in this part may be rather coarser than the others, we do not think the difference so considerable as to account for its admitted inferiority in the power of pleasing.

His only other considerable works in prose, are the *Polite Conversation*, which we think admirable in its sort, and excessively entertaining; and the *Directions to Servants*, which, though of a lower pitch, contains as much perhaps of his peculiar, vigorous and racy humour, as any one of his productions. The *Journal to Stella*, which was certainly never intended for publication, is not to be judged of as a literary work at all—

but to us it is the most interesting of all his productions—exhibiting not only a minute and masterly view of a very extraordinary political crisis, but a truer, and, upon the whole, a more favourable picture of his own mind, than can be gathered from all the rest of his writings—together with innumerable anecdotes characteristic not only of various eminent individuals, but of the private manners and public taste and morality of the times, more nakedly and surely authentic than any thing that can be derived from contemporary publications.

Of his Poetry, we do not think there is much to be said;—for we cannot persuade ourselves that Swift was in any respect a poet. It would be proof enough, we think, just to observe, that, though a popular and most miscellaneous writer, he does not mention the name of Shakespeare above two or three times in any part of his works, and has nowhere said a word in his praise. His partial editor admits that he has produced nothing which can be called either sublime or pathetic; and we are of the same opinion as to the beautiful. The merit of correct rhymes and easy diction, we shall not deny him; but the diction is almost invariably that of the most ordinary prose, and the matter of his pieces no otherwise poetical, than that the Muses and some other persons of the Heathen mythology are occasionally mentioned. He has written lampoons and epigrams, and satirical ballads and abusive songs in great abundance, and with infinite success. But these things are not poetry;—and are better in verse than in prose, for no other reason than that the sting is more easily remembered, and the ridicule occasionally enhanced, by the hint of a ludicrous parody, or the drollery of an extraordinary rhyme. His witty verses, where they are not made up of mere filth and venom, seem mostly framed on the model of Hudibras; and are chiefly remarkable, like those of his original, for the easy and apt application of homely and familiar phrases, to illustrate ingenious sophistry or unexpected allusions. One or two of his imitations of Horace, are executed with spirit and elegance, and are the best, we think, of his familiar pieces; unless we except the verses on his own death, in which, however, the great charm arises, as we have just stated, from the singular ease and exactness with which he has imitated the style of ordinary society, and the neatness with which he has brought together and reduced to metre such a number of natural, characteristic and common-place expressions. The Cadenus and Vanessa is, of itself, complete proof that he had in him none of the elements of poetry. It was written when his faculties were in their perfection, and his heart animated with all the tenderness of which it was ever capable—and yet it is as cold and as flat as the ice of Thulé. Though describing a real passion, and a real perplexity, there is not a spark of fire, nor a throb of emotion in it from one end to the other. All the return he makes to the warm-hearted creature who had put her destiny into his hands, consists in a frigid, mythological fiction, in which he sets forth, that Venus and the Graces lavished their gifts on her in her infancy, and moreover got Minerva, by a trick, to inspire her with wit and wisdom. The style is mere prose—or rather a string of familiar and vulgar phrases tacked together in rhyme, like the general tissue of his poetry. . . .

The Legion Club is a satire, or rather a tremendous invective on the Irish House of Commons, who had incurred the reverend author's displeasure for entertaining some propositions about alleviating the burden of the tythes in Ireland; and is chiefly remarkable, on the whole, as a proof of the extraordinary liberty of the press which was indulged to the disaffected in those days—no prosecution having been instituted, either by that Honourable House itself, or by any of the individual members, who are there attacked in a way in which no public men were ever attacked, before or since. It is also deserving of attention, as the most thoroughly animated, fierce and energetic, of all Swift's metrical compositions; and though the animation be altogether of a ferocious character, and seems occasionally to verge upon absolute insanity, there is still a force and a terror about it which redeems it from ridicule, and makes us shudder at the sort of demoniacal inspiration with which the malison is vented. The invective of Swift appears in this, and some other pieces, like the infernal fire of Milton's rebel angels, which

Scorched and blasted and o'erthrew—

and was launched even against the righteous with such impetuous fury,

That whom it hit none on their feet might stand,
Though standing else as rocks—but down they fell
By thousands, angel on archangel rolled.

It is scarcely necessary to remark, however, that there is never the least approach to dignity or nobleness in the style of these terrible invectives; and that they do not even pretend to the tone of a high-minded disdain or generous impatience of unworthiness. They are honest, coarse, and violent effusions of furious anger and rancorous hatred; and their effect depends upon the force, heartiness, and apparent sincerity with which those feelings are expressed. The author's object is simply to vilify his opponent,—by no means to do honour to him-self. If he can make his victim writhe, he cares not what may be thought of his tormentor;—or rather, he is contented, provided he can make *him* sufficiently disgusting, that a good share of the filth which he throws should stick to his own fingers; and that he should himself excite some of the loathing of which his enemy is the principal object....

We have not left ourselves room now to say much of Swift's style, or the general character of his literary genius:—But our opinion may be collected from the remarks we have made on particular passages, and from our introductory observations on the school or class of authors, with whom he must undoubtedly be rated. On the subjects to which he confines himself, he is unquestionably a strong, masculine, and perspicuous writer. He is never finical, fantastic, or absurd—takes advantage of no equivocations in argument—and puts on no tawdriness for ornament. Dealing always with particulars, he is safe from all great and systematic mistakes; and, in fact, reasons mostly in a series of small and minute propositions, in the handling of which, dexterity is more requisite than genius; and practical good sense, with an exact know-ledge of transactions, of far more importance than profound and high-reaching judgment. He did not write history or philosophy, but party pamphlets and journals;—not satire, but particular lampoons;—not pleasantries for all mankind, but jokes for a particular circle. Even in his pamphlets, the broader questions of party are always waved, to make way for discussions of personal or immediate interest. His object is not to show that the Tories have better principles of government than the Whigs,—but to prove Lord Oxford an angel, and Lord Somers a fiend,—to convict the Duke of Marlborough of avarice, or Sir Richard Steele of insolvency;—not to point out the wrongs of Ireland, in the depression of her Catholic population, her want of education, or the discouragement of her industry; but to raise an outcry against an amendment of the copper or the gold coin, or against a parliamentary proposition for remitting the tithe of *agistment*. For those ends, it cannot be denied, that he chose his means judiciously, and used them with incomparable skill and spirit: But to choose such ends, we humbly conceive, was not the part either of a high intellect or a high character; and his genius must share in the disparagement which ought perhaps to be confined to the impetuosity and vindictiveness of his temper.

Of his style, it has been usual to speak with great, and, we think, exaggerated praise. It is less mellow than Dryden's—less elegant than Pope's or Addison's—less free and noble than Lord Bolingbroke's—and utterly without the glow and loftiness which belonged to our earlier masters. It is radically a low and homely style—without grace, and without affectation; and chiefly remarkable for a great choice and profusion of *common* words and expressions. Other writers, who have used a plain and direct style, have been for the most part jejune and limited in their diction, and generally give us an impression of the poverty as well as the tameness of their language; but Swift, without ever trespassing into figured or poetical expressions, or ever employing a word that can be called fine, or pedantic, has a prodigious variety of good set phrases always at his command, and displays a sort of homely richness, like the plenty of an old English dinner, or the wardrobe of a wealthy burgess. This taste for the plain and substantial was fatal to his poetry, which subsists not on such elements; but was in the highest degree favourable to the effect of his humour, very much of which depends on the imposing gravity with which it is delivered, and on the various turns and heightenings it may receive from a rapidly shifting and always appropriate expression. Almost all his works, after *A Tale of a Tub*, seem to have been written very fast, and with very little minute care of the diction. For his own ease, therefore, it is probable they were all pitched on a low key, and set about on the ordinary tone of a familiar letter or conversation; as that from which there was little hazard of falling, even in moments of negligence, and from which any rise that could be effected must always be easy and conspicuous. A man fully possessed of his subject, indeed, and confident of his cause, may almost always write with vigour and effect, if he can get over the temptation of writing finely, and really confine himself to the strong and clear exposition of the matter he has to bring forward. Half of the affectation and offensive pretension we meet with in authors, arises from a want of matter,—and the other half, from a paltry ambition of being eloquent and ingenious out of place. Swift had complete confidence in himself; and had too much real business on his hands, to be at leisure to intrigue for the fame of a fine writer;—in consequence of which, his writings are more admired by the judicious than if he had bestowed all his attention on their style. He was so much a man of business indeed, and so much accustomed to consider his writings merely as means for the attainment of a practical end—whether that end was the strengthening of a party, or the wounding a foe—that he not only disdained the reputation of a composer of petty sentences, but seems to have been thoroughly indifferent to all sorts of literary fame. He enjoyed the notoriety and influence which he had procured by his writings; but it was the glory of having carried his point, and not of having written well, that he valued. As soon as his publications had served their turn, they seem to have been entirely forgotten by their author;—and, desirious as he was of being richer, he appears to have thought as little of making money as immortality by means of them. He mentions somewhere, that except 300*l.* which he got for *Gulliver*, he never made a farthing by any of his writings. Pope understood his trade better,— and not only made knowing bargains for his own works, but occasionally borrowed his friends' pieces, and pocketed the price of the whole. This was notoriously the case with three volumes of *Miscellanies*, of which the greater part were from the pen of Swift.

In humour and in irony, and in the talent of debasing and defiling what he hated, we join with all the world in thinking the Dean of St Patrick's without a rival. His humour, though sufficiently marked and peculiar, is not to be easily defined. The nearest description we can give of it, would make it consist in expressing sentiments the most absurd and ridiculous—the most shocking and atrocious—or sometimes the most energetic and original—in a sort of composed, calm, and unconscious way, as if they were plain, undeniable, commonplace truths, which no person could dispute, or expect to gain credit by announcing —and in maintaining them, always in the gravest and most familiar language, with a consistency which somewhat palliates their extravagance, and a kind of perverted ingenuity, which seems to give pledge for their sincerity. The secret, in short, seems to consist in employing the language of humble good sense, and simple undoubting conviction, to express, in their honest nakedness, sentiments which it is usually thought necessary to disguise under a thousand pretences—or truths which are usually introduced with a thousand apologies. The basis of the art is the personating a character of great simplicity and openness, for whom the common moral or artificial distinctions of society are supposed to have no existence; and making use of this character as an instrument to strip vice and folly of their disguises, and expose guilt in all its deformity, and truth in all its terrors. Independent of the moral or satire, of which they may thus be the vehicle, a great part of the entertainment to be derived from works of humour, arises from the contrast between the grave, unsuspecting indifference of the character personated, and the ordinary feelings of the world on the subjects which he discusses. This contrast it is easy to heighten, by all sorts of imputed absurdities: in which case, the humour degenerates into mere farce and buffoonery. Swift has yielded a little to this temptation in *A Tale of a Tub*; but scarcely at all in *Gulliver*, or any of his later writings in the same style. Of his talent for reviling, we have already said at least enough, in some of the preceding pages.

61. William Hazlitt on Swift

1818

Lectures on the English Poets, 1818, 217–24.

Hazlitt (1778–1830) comments perceptively on the method of *Gulliver's Travels* and differentiates between Swift, Rabelais, and Voltaire.

Swift's reputation as a poet has been in a manner obscured by the greater splendour, by the natural force and inventive genius of his prose writings; but if he had never written either *A Tale of a Tub* or *Gulliver's Travels*, his name merely as a poet would have come down to us, and have gone down to posterity with well-earned honours. His Imitations of Horace, and still more his Verses on his own Death, place him in the first rank of agreeable moralists in verse. There is not only a dry humour, an exquisite tone of irony, in these productions of his pen; but there is a touching, unpretending pathos, mixed up with the most whimsical and eccentric strokes of pleasantry and satire. His Description of the Morning in London, and of a City Shower, which were first published in *The Tatler*, are among the most delightful of the contents of that very delightful work. Swift shone as one of the most sensible of the poets; he is also distinguished as one of the most non-sensical of them. No man has written so many lack-a-daisical, slip-shod, tedious, trifling, foolish, fantastical verses as he, which are so little an imputation of the wisdom of the writer; and which, in fact, only shew his readiness to oblige others, and to forget himself. He has gone so far as to invent a new stanza of fourteen and sixteen syllable lines for Mary the cookmaid to vent her budget of nothings, and for Mrs. Harris to gossip with the deaf old housekeeper. Oh, when shall we have such another Rector of Laracor!—*A Tale of a Tub* is one of the most masterly compositions in the language, whether for thought, wit, or style. It is so capital and undeniable a proof of the author's talents, that Dr. Johnson, who did not like Swift, would not allow that he wrote it.

It is hard that the same performance should stand in the way of a man's promotion to a bishopric, as wanting gravity, and at the same time be denied to be his, as having too much wit. It is a pity the Doctor did not find out some graver author, for whom he felt a critical kindness, on whom to father this splendid but unacknowledged production. Dr. Johnson could not deny that *Gulliver's Travels* were his; he therefore disputed their merits, and said that after the first idea of them was conceived, thay were easy to execute; all the rest followed mechanically. I do not know how that may be; but the mechanism employed is something very different from any that the author of *Rasselas* was in the habit of bringing to bear on such occasions. There is nothing more futile, as well as invidious, than this mode of criticising a work of original genius. Its greatest merit is supposed to be in the invention; and you say, very wisely, that it is not *in the execution*. You might as well take away the merit in the invention of the telescope, by saying that, after its uses were explained and understood, any ordinary eyesight could look through it. Whether the excellence of *Gulliver's Travels* is in the conception or the execution, is of little consequence; the power is somewhere, and it is a power that has moved the world. The power is not that of big words and vaunting common places. Swift left these to those who wanted them; and has done what his acuteness and intensity of mind alone could enable any one to conceive or to perform. His object was to strip empty pride and grandeur of the imposing air which external circumstances throw around them; and for this purpose he has cheated the imagination of the illusions which the prejudices of sense and of the world put upon it, by reducing every thing to the abstract predicament of size. He enlarges or diminishes the scale, as he wishes to show the insignificance or the grossness of our overweening self-love. That he has done this with mathematical precision, with complete presence of mind and perfect keeping, in a manner that comes equally home to the understanding of the man and of the child, does not take away from the merit of the work or the genius of the author. He has taken a new view of human nature, such as a being of a higher sphere might take of it; he has torn the scales from off his moral vision; he has tried an experiment upon human life, and sifted its pretensions from the alloy of circumstances; he has measured it with a rule, has weighed it in a balance, and found it, for the most part, wanting and worthless—in substance and in show. Nothing solid, nothing valuable is left in his system but virtue and wisdom. What a libel is this upon mankind! What a convincing proof of misanthropy! What presumption and what *malice prepense*, to show men what they are, and to teach them what they ought to be! What a mortifying stroke aimed at national glory, is that unlucky incident of Gulliver's wading across the channel and carrying off the whole fleet of Blefuscu! After that, we have only to consider which of the contending parties was in the right. What a shock to personal vanity is given in the account of Gulliver's nurse Glumdalclitch! Still, notwithstanding the disparagement to her personal charms, her good-nature remains the same amiable quality as before. I cannot see the harm, the misanthropy, the immoral and degrading tendency of this. The moral lesson is as fine as the intellectual exhibition is amusing. It is an attempt to tear off the mask of imposture from the world; and nothing but imposture has a right to complain of it. It is, indeed, the way with our quacks in morality to preach up the dignity of human nature, to pamper pride and hypocrisy with the idle mockeries of the virtues they pretend to, and which they have not: but it was not Swift's way to cant morality, or any thing else; nor did his genius prompt him to write unmeaning panegyrics on mankind!

I do not, therefore, agree with the estimate of Swift's moral or intellectual character, given by an eminent critic, who does not seem to have forgotten the party politics of Swift. I do not carry my political resentments so far back: I can at this time of day forgive Swift for having been a Tory. I feel little disturbance (whatever I might think of them) at his political sentiments, which died with him, considering how much else he has left behind him of a more solid and imperishable nature! If he had, indeed, (like some others) merely left behind him the lasting infamy of a destroyer of his country, or the shining example of an apostate from liberty, I might have thought the case altered.

The determination with which Swift persisted in a preconcerted theory, savoured of the morbid affection of which he died. There is nothing more likely to drive a man mad than the being unable to get rid of the idea of the distinction between right and wrong, and an obstinate, constitutional preference of the true to the agreeable. Swift was not a Frenchman. In this respect he differed from Rabelais and Voltaire. They have been accounted the three greatest wits in modern times; but their wit was of a particular kind in each. They are little beholden to each other; there is some resemblance between Lord Peter in *A Tale of a Tub*, and Rabelais' Friar John; but in general they are all authors of a substantive character in themselves. Swift's wit (particularly in his chief prose works) was serious, saturnine, and practical; Rabelais' was fantastical and joyous; Voltaire's was light, sportive, and verbal. Swift's wit was the wit of sense; Rabelais', the wit of nonsense; Voltaire's, of indifference to both. The ludicrous in Swift, arises out of his keen sense of impropriety, his soreness and impatience of the least absurdity. He separates, with a severe and caustic air, truth from false-hood, folly from wisdom, 'shews vice her own image, scorn her own feature,' and it is the force, the precision, and the honest abruptness with which the separation is made that excites our surprise, our admira-tion, and laughter. He sets a mark of reprobation on that which offends good sense and good manners, which cannot be mistaken, and which holds it up to our ridicule and contempt ever after. His occasional disposition to trifling (already noticed) was a relaxation from the excessive earnestness of his mind. *Indignatio facit versus*. His better genius was his spleen. It was the biting acrimony of his temper that sharpened his other faculties. The truth of his perceptions produced the pointed coruscations of his wit; his playful irony was the result of inward bitterness of thought; his imagination was the product of the literal, dry, incorrigible tenaciousness of his understanding. He endeavoured to escape from the persecution of realities into the regions of fancy, and invented his Lilliputians and Brobdingnagians, Yahoos, and Houyn-nhyms, as a diversion to the more painful knowledge of the world around him: *they* only made him laugh, while men and women made him angry. His feverish impatience made him view the infirmities of that great baby the world, with the same scrutinizing glance and jealous irritability that a parent regards the failings of its offspring; but, as Rousseau has well observed, parents have not on this account been supposed to have more affection for other people's children than their own. In other respects, and except from the sparkling effervescence of his gall, Swift's brain was as 'dry as the remainder biscuit after a voyage.' He hated absurdity—Rabelais loved it, exaggerated it with supreme satisfaction, luxuriated in its endless varieties, rioted in nonsense, 'reigned there and revelled.' He dwelt on the absurd and ludicrous for the pleasure they gave him, not for the pain.

62. Coleridge on Swift

1818, 1825, 1830

(a) 'Lecture IX: On the Distinctions of the Witty, the Droll, the Odd, and the Humorous . . .', *The Literary Remains of Samuel Taylor Coleridge,* ed. Henry Nelson Coleridge (3 vols.), 1836, i, 140.

(b) 'Lecture XIV: On Style', op. cit., 239.

(c) 'Moral and Religious Aphorisms', *Aids to Reflection,* 1825, 76.

(d) 'June 15 1830: Rabelais—Swift . . .', *Specimens of the Table Talk of the Late Samuel Taylor Coleridge* (2 vols.), 1835, 177–9.

(e) Aitken, G. A., 'Coleridge on *Gulliver's Travels', The Athenaeum,* xi (15 August 1896), 224.

Samuel Taylor Coleridge (1772–1834) delivered a course of lectures on the English poets in 1818. These were transcribed imperfectly in note form and include brief observations on *Gulliver's Travels* and on the prose style of poets. The extract from 'Moral and Religious Aphorisms' is taken from a passage following Coleridge's fairly lengthy quotation from *A Tale of a Tub*; his use of the work as an example of 'profound sense and steady observation' provides a striking contrast to the attitudes of earlier critics, who were often preoccupied with that which 'pollutes the imagination'. The last entry was found by G. A. Aitken, written in Wordsworth's copy of *Gulliver's Travels,* and it was printed in a letter to *The Athenaeum* in 1896. It makes some very acute criticisms of Swift's handling of the Houyhnhnms, though Coleridge does not draw the conclusion (which some later critics have drawn) that the Houyhnhnm failure to understand the nature of man may be part of a deliberate effect.

(a)
SWIFT: *born in Dublin, 1667; died 1745*

In Swift's writings there is a false misanthropy grounded upon an exclusive contemplation of the vices and follies of mankind, and this

331

misanthropic tone is also disfigured or brutalized by his obtrusion of physical dirt and coarseness. I think *Gulliver's Travels* the great work of Swift. In the voyages to Lilliput and Brobdingnag he displays the little-ness and moral contemptibility of human nature; in that to the Houy-hnhnms he represents the disgusting spectacle of man with the under-standing only, without the reason or the moral feeling, and in his horse he gives the misanthropic ideal of man—that is, a being virtuous from rule and duty, but untouched by the principle of love.

(b)

It is, indeed, worthy of remark that all our great poets have been good prose writers, as Chaucer, Spenser, Milton; and this probably arose from their just sense of metre. For a true poet will never confound verse and prose; whereas it is almost characteristic of indifferent prose writers that they should be constantly slipping into scraps of metre. Swift's style is, in its line, perfect; the manner is a complete expression of the matter, the terms appropriate, and the artifice concealed. It is simplicity in the true sense of the word.

(c)

Were it my task to form the mind of a young man of talent, desirous to establish his opinions and belief on solid principles, and in the light of distinct understanding,—I would commence his theological studies, or, at least, that most important part of them respecting the aids which Religion promises in our attempts to realize the ideas of Morality, by bringing together all the passages scattered throughout the writings of Swift and Butler, that bear on Enthusiasm, Spiritual Operations, and pretences to the Gifts of the Spirit, with the whole train of New Lights, Raptures, Experiences, and the like. For all that the richest Wit, in intimate union with profound Sense and steady Observation, can supply on these topics, is to be found in the works of these satirists; though unhappily alloyed with much that can only tend to pollute the im-agination.

(d)

Rabelais is a most wonderful writer. . . . Some of the commentators talk about his book being all political; there are contemporary politics in it, of course, but the real scope is much higher and more philosophi-cal. It is in vain to look about for a hidden meaning in all that he has written; you will observe that, after any particularly deep thrust, as the Papimania, for example, Rabelais, as if to break the blow, and to appear

unconscious of what he has done, writes a chapter or two of pure buffoonery. He, every now and then, flashes you a glimpse of a real face
from his magic lantern, and then buries the whole scene in mist. The
morality of the work is of the most refined and exalted kind; as for the
manners, to be sure, I cannot say much.

Swift was *anima Rabelaisii habitans in sicco*—the soul of Rabelais
dwelling in a dry place.

Yet Swift was rare. Can anything beat his remark on King William's
motto—*Recepit, non rapuit*—'that the receiver was as bad as the thief?'

(e)

The great defect of the Houyhnhnms is not its misanthropy, and those
who apply this word to it must really believe that the essence of human
nature, that the *anthropus misoumenos*, consists in the shape of the body.
Now, to show the falsity of this was Swift's great object: he would
prove to our feelings and imaginations, and thereby teach *practically*,
that it is Reason and Conscience which give all the loveliness and
dignity not only to Man, but to the shape of Man; that deprived of
these, and yet retaining the Understanding, he would be as the most
loathsome and hateful of all animals; that his understanding would
manifest itself only as malignant cunning, his free will as obstinacy and
unteachableness. And how true a picture this is every madhouse may
convince any man; a brothel where highwaymen meet will convince
every philosopher. But the defect of the work is its inconsistency; the
Houyhnhnms are not rational creatures, *i.e.*, creatures of perfect reason;
they are not progressive; they have servants without any reason for
their natural inferiority or any explanation how the difference acted(?);
and, above all, they—*i.e.*, Swift himself—has a perpetual affectation of
being wiser than his Maker [see postscript], and of eradicating what
God gave to be subordinated and used; *ex. gr.*, the maternal and paternal
affection (οργή). There is likewise a true Yahooism in the constant
denial of the existence of Love, as not identical with Friendship, and yet
distinct always and very often divided from Lust. The best defence is
that it is a Satyr; still, it would have been, felt a thousand times more
deeply if Reason had been truly pourtrayed and a finer imagination
would have been evinced if the author had shown the effect of the
possession of Reason and the moral sense in the outward form and
gestures of the Horses. In short, critics in general complain of the
Yahoos; I complain of the Houyhnhnms.

As to the *wisdom* of adopting this mode of proving the great truths here exemplified, that is another question, which no feeling mind will find a difficulty in answering who has read and understood the Paradise scenes in *Paradise Lost*, and compared the moral effect on his heart and his virtuous aspirations of Milton's Adam with Swift's horses; but different men have different turns of genius; Swift's may be good, tho' very inferior to Milton's; they do not stand in each other's way.

S. T. C.

A case in point, and besides utterly inconsistent with the boasted Reason of the Houyhnhnms, may be seen, pp. 194, 195 [chap. IV], where the Horse discourses on the human frame with the grossest prejudices that could possibly be inspired by vanity and self-opinion. That Reason which commands man to admire the fitness of the horse and stag for superior speed, of the bird for flight, &c., &c.—must it not have necessitated the rational horse to have seen and acknowledged the admirable aptitude of the human hand, compared with his own fetlocks, of the human limbs for climbing, for the management of tools, &c.? In short, compare the *effect* of the Satire, when it is founded in truth and good sense (chap. V, for instance), with the wittiest of those passages which have their only support in spleen and want of reverence for the original frame of man, and the feelings of the Reader will be his faithful guide in the reperusal of the work, which I still think the highest effort of Swift's genius, unless we should except *A Tale of a Tub*. Then I would put Lilliput; next Brobdingnag; and Laputa I would expunge altogether. It is a wretched abortion, the product of spleen and ignorance and self-conceit.

63. William Monck Mason on
Gulliver's Travels and *A Modest Proposal*

1819

The History and Antiquities of the Collegiate and Cathedral Church of St. Patrick, near Dublin, from Its Foundation in 1190, to the Year 1819 . . . , 1819.

William Monck Mason (1775–1859) devoted most of his life to the study of the history and philology of Ireland, and he acquired a sizeable collection of original documents and works of art pertaining to his subject. He planned an exhaustive 'Topographical Account of Ireland, and a History of all the Establishments in that Kingdom, Ecclesiastical, Civil, and Monastic, drawn chiefly from sources of original record.' The book quoted here was to have been the first volume in this ambitious work. Another volume on Christ Church Cathedral, Dublin, was never completed, although special engravings were prepared for it. Much of Mason's commentary on Swift's works consists of quotations from Hawkesworth, Scott, and Hazlitt, but his own contributions are often noteworthy.

In the month of November following, *The Travels of Captain Lemuel Gulliver* were given to the world; the publication of this celebrated work was shadowed with that cloud of mystery, with which Swift delighted to envelope all his works of consequence, upon their first appearance. On this occasion, the effect upon the public was greatly heightened by this mode of publication, we may easier imagine than describe the sensations of surprise which this piece must have given rise to, displayed as it was before the world by an unknown hand. No work ever communicated such universal satisfaction, or received such general applause, for no other work was ever so perfectly addressed to all ages, and all ranks, of society. To frame a narrative capable of amusing the fastidious taste of the literary adept, and of gratifying, at the same time, the most vulgar or infantine capacity, was a task which no one but Swift could ever accomplish: but to amuse was not its sole object; to instruct the whole race of mankind, was the benevolent purpose of its philanthropic author.

In the voyage to Lilliput, religious and political divisions are humorously burlesqued; the importance often attached to these sources of civil discord is contrasted with the factions of High-heels and Low-heels, Big-endians and little-endians; the cause of humanity is served by this animated representation of the insignificance of those objects, for which the blood of thousands has been copiously shed. Besides reflections of a general nature, the voyage to Lilliput contains particular allusions to the court and politics of England. Sir Robert Walpole is plainly designated by the Premier, Flimnap; the Lilliputian treasurer's fall from the tight rope, which was broken by one of the king's cushions, seems to intimate the English minister's dismissal from office in 1717, when he was supposed to have been saved from utter disgrace, by the interest of the duchess of Kendal. By the ceremony of leaping over the coloured strings, the revival of the orders of the Garter, Bath, and Thistle is alluded to: the high-heels and low-heels express the political parties of tories and whigs, the small-endians and big-endians, the religious sects of papist and protestant. When the emperor's heels are described as lower than any of his court, the preference shewn by King George I to the whigs is glanced at; and where the heir apparent is said to wear one heel higher than the other, the conduct of the Prince of Wales is alluded to, who acted, at that time, in opposition to his father's ministers, and divided his favours between the discontented of these two political parties: the resemblance, Mrs. Howard informs Swift in one of her letters, was recognized by his royal highness, who laughed heartily at this passage, which represents him as halting between the two political creeds which divided the kingdom. Many other allusions might be traced, which have reference, chiefly, to the reign of George I, but, where he mentions the offence the empress took at his manner of extinguishing the flames in the royal palace, he appears, manifestly, to glance at the character of queen Anne, who paid greater regard to court ceremonial than was quite consistent with good sense; Mr. Walter Scott thinks that Swift meant to intimate thereby, his own disgrace with that queen, 'founded upon the indecorum of *A Tale of a Tub*, which was remembered against him as a crime, while the service, which it rendered the cause of the high church, was forgotten.' Swift's remarks on the institutions of the empire of Lilliput are not the least important part of this voyage, they serve as useful comments upon the legal policy of his own country; where he mentions, that the Lilliputians looked upon fraud as a greater crime than theft, and alludes to their policy in rewarding merit as well as punishing vice, he points out matters which are not, perhaps, undeserving of public attention.

In the voyage to Brobdingnag, Swift, as Mr. Scott remarks, 'turns the opposite end of the telescope, and, as he had held up to the derision of ordinary beings the intrigues, cabals, wars, and councils of a Lilliputian court and ministry, he now shews us in what manner a people of immense stature, and gifted with a soundness and coolness of judgment in some degree corresponding, might be likely to regard the principles and politics of Europe.' To exhibit a human creature, displaying the actions of mankind to the view of a cooly reflecting and philosophical monarch, 'a stoic in appetite and ambition'; to represent that faultless person pronouncing judgment upon those actions, and deciding on their importance or merit, by the criterion of the real benefit they might produce to mankind, was to effect a moral purpose, by means before unthought of; how truly prophetic was the following remark of lord Bolingbroke, expressed in his letter to Swift, of 1st January 1721–2. 'I long to see your *Travels*, for, I will undertake to find, in two pages of your *bagatelles*, more good sense, useful knowledge, and true religion, than you can show me in the works of nineteen in twenty of the profound divines and philosophers of the age.'—In this part the satire is of a more general nature, there are no particular references to political events, no circumstances mentioned which are not applicable, equally, to all courts. . . .

In the voyage to Laputa, the satire is aimed at the abuses of science, against those grave projectors, who, leaving behind them the landmarks of common sense, wander, without the guide of reason, into the immeasurably extended regions of speculative philosophy. Those qualities, by means of which Swift rose to pre-eminence, his profound skill in ethics, his extensive knowledge of the world and of the human heart, served him but to little purpose in a task, which required rather a deep insight into the science of physics: the satire, however, is not aimed, as has been unjustly insinuated, at true science, but at its abuses;

The projectors in the academy of Lagado are described as pretenders, who had acquired a very slight tincture of real mathematical knowledge, and eked out their plans of mechanical improvement by dint of whim and fancy. The age in which Swift lived had exhibited numerous instances of persons of this description, by whom many of the numerous *bubbles*, as they were emphatically termed, had been set on foot, to the impoverishment of credulous individuals, and the general detriment of the community.

The satire contained in the voyage to the Houyhnhnms is more intense than in any of the preceding. Swift, who had, in the former voyages, satirized the mental degradation of the human race, proceeds, in this, to vilify the debasement of the corporeal part of our nature. Although it was a necessary part of his scheme, and the intention was equally laudable, this portion is nevertheless executed with less ability. It exhibits mankind in a light too degraded for contemplation, the satire is too much exaggerated to be stiled a resemblance; 'That magnifying-glass', says Dr. Delany, 'which enlarges all the deformed features into monstrous dimensions, defeats its own purpose; for no man will ever know his own likeness in it; and consequently, though he be shocked, he will not be amended.'—If, however, the picture of the Yahoos be disgusting, it is what the author intended; but, in that of the Houyhnhnms, which he meant, doubtless, should be inviting, he has totally failed; the representation is cold and insipid, it wants both light and shade; there is a mediocrity of character, in his representation of those animals, which renders, them quite uninteresting; their virtues are all negative, they act inoffensively, but they have neither motive nor power to act otherwise; they are void of all those tender passions and affections, without which life becomes a burthen. It is true, some exalted virtues, and even some splendid accomplishments, are attributed by Swift to those animals; 'in poetry,' he tells us, 'they excel all animals,' he talks of their 'exalted notions of friendship and benevolence,' but he does not illustrate those matters, and indeed, to imagine how they could exercise them is beyond the power of comprehension.

The voyage to the Houyhnhnms is defective, likewise, in being quite destitute of verisimilitude, a charm which is the principal embellishment of his other works. 'The state of the Houyhnhnms,' says Mr. Scott, 'is not only morally but physically impossible;' the unsuitableness of their animal formation to the purposes of art and ingenuity are too manifest, too impossible even for fiction.

There are improprieties in the narrative [says Dr. Beattie], which, without heightening the satire, serve to aggravate the absurdity of the fable. Houyhnhnms are horses in perfection, with the addition of reason and virtue. Whatever, therefore, takes away from their perfection as horses, without adding to their rational and moral accomplishments, must be repugnant to the author's design, and ought not to have found a place in his narration; yet he makes his beloved quadrupeds dwell in houses of their own building, and use warm food and the milk of cows, as a delicacy; though these luxuries, supposed attainable by a nation of horses, could not attribute to their perfection.

This satire upon human corruptions, has been unjustly represented to be, a libel on human nature. 'The voyage to the land of Houyhnhnms,' says the last editor of Swift's *Works*, [Scott] 'holds mankind forth in a light too degrading for contemplation, and which, if admitted, would justify or palliate the worst vices, by exhibiting them as natural attributes:' how vices, by being represented in an odious light, should be, therefore, palliated or justified, this writer has not explained; Swift meant to produce, and has, I apprehend, succeeded in producing an effect precisely opposite.

[354–61.]

To represent, in strong colours, the actually degraded state of human nature, and yet, to shew the great value of charitable forbearance towards the faults of particular individuals, seems to be the moral which Swift had in view, and that which *The Travels of Captain Lemuel Gulliver* were intended chiefly to inculcate. The following passage of this letter to Pope, written 29th Sept. 1725, is remarkably illustrative of those principles.

I have ever hated all nations, professions, and communities; and all my love is toward individuals: for instance, I hate the tribe of lawyers, but I love counsellor such-a-one, and judge such-a-one: it is so with physicians. (I will not speak of my own trade), soldiers, English, Scotch, French, and the rest. But principally, I hate and detest that animal called man; although I heartily love John, Peter, Thomas, and so forth. This is the system upon which I have governed myself many years (but do not tell) and I shall go on till I have done with them. I have got materials toward a treatise, proving the falsity of that definition, *animal rationale*, and to show it should be only *rationis capax*. Upon this great foundation of misanthropy (though not in Timon's manner) the whole building of my travels is erected; and I never will have peace of mind till all honest men are of my opinion: by consequence you are to embrace it immediately, and procure that all who deserve my esteem may do so too. The matter is so clear that it will admit of no dispute; nay, I will hold a hundred pounds that you and I agree in the point.

[351, n.]

The Travels of Captain Lemuel Gulliver, by Swift, can only be compared to the *Life and Adventures of Robinson Crusoe*, by Defoe: between these two writers there are many points of resemblance; both are remarkable for the unaffected simplicity of their narratives, the variety of their incidents, but, most of all, for the air of truth with which they have enveloped the whole; a circumstance which was incomparably more difficult to Swift than to the other, because the matters whereof he treated were marvellous beyond credibility, whereas the events related by Defoe were mere ordinary occurrences. This appearance of truth is effected by the intermixture of minute circumstances, which state, particularly, dates, names of places, and persons, some of whom are referred to as actually living; the incidents too are described in so circumstantial a manner, and embellished with so many minute particulars, which we are apt to think would hardly be mentioned if they were not true, that we are induced to believe what we are perusing is a real story.

[355 n.]

The cold, phlegmatic style [in *A Modest Proposal*] of a political projector, who waves the consideration of all the finer feelings of humanity, or makes them subservient, as matters of slight moment, to the general advantages proposed in his plan of financial improvement, is admirably well satirized. . . . The cool, 'business-like' manner, in which the calculations are stated, is equally admirable. . . .

These calculations are every where interspersed with satirical allusions to the vices, follies, and prejudices which it was Swift's business, as well as his amusement, to expose. . . .

That unconsciousness of the barbarity of his own project, which he so well feigns, greatly encreases the effect, and produces a high degree of amusement, particularly when it is contrasted with the great compassion which he sometimes affects. . . .

He concludes this admirable specimen of comic humour with the following protestation of personal disinterestedness,—'I profess, in the sincerity of my heart, that I have not the least personal interest in endeavouring to promote this necessary work, having no other motive than the public good of my country.—I have no children by which I can propose to get a single penny; the youngest being nine years old and my wife past child-bearing.'

[375-6.]

It was, however, in the art of verisimilitude, the power of sustaining a fictitious character under every peculiarity of place and circumstance, that Swift excelled all writers, ancient or modern. This talent, exercised as it is by Swift, is directly opposite to that quality of the mind, denominated abstraction. The difference is particularly well illustrated in the admirable romance of *Gulliver*, and in this consists the difference between it and all other Utopean fables. The authors of these latter have given us abstract notions of laws and governments, information of a mere general nature, nothing individual, either in person, or circumstance, or event; Swift, however, goes beyond all others in this respect, he clothes the abstract idea of a peculiar description of people with all the circumstances and incidents of actual existance; thus is the deluded reader held by magic chains, the picture is so entirely filled with individual representation, that, for the time, he believes it true; nor is he awakened from the trance, by any distorsion in the proportions, which are all surprisingly well preserved throughout the whole narrative.

[434–5.]

Bibliography

This short select bibliography of works deals with Swift's critical reception.

BERWICK, DONALD M., *Reputation of Jonathan Swift, 1781–1882*. New York: Haskell House, 1941.

CLUBB, MERREL D., 'The Criticism of Gulliver's "Voyage to the Houyhnhnms", 1726–1914', pp. 203–32 in *Stanford Studies in Language and Literature*, ed. Hardin Craig. Stanford University Press, 1941.

GOULDING, SYBIL MAUD, *Swift en France: essai sur le fortune et l'influence de Swift en France* . . . Paris: E. Champion, 1924.

KLIGMAN, ELSIE, 'Contemporary Opinion of Swift', unpublished M.A. thesis, Columbia University, 1932.

PONS, EMILE, *Swift: les années de jeunesse et le 'Conte du tonneau'*. London: Oxford University Press, 1925.

VOIGT, MILTON, *Swift and the Twentieth Century*. Detroit: University of Michigan Press, 1964.

Index

Traulus (1730), 147, 172
*Tritical Essay upon the Faculties of
the Mind* (c. 1707), 119, 155, 159
Verses on the Death of Dr. Swift
(1731), 16–17, 136, 209, 269–70,
327
Swift, Theophilus, 259
Swift, Thomas, 35, 37, 50, 284

Taine, Hippolyte, 26
Tasso, Torquato, 80
Tatler, The, 47
Temple, Sir William, 37, 50, 58,
115, 130, 176, 226, 284
Thackeray, William, 3, 26
Thomson, James, 195, 226
Trelawny, Jonathan, Bp. of Exeter,
36
Tyler, Thomas, 16, 26–7

Van Effen, Juste, 5, 54
Preface to *Le Conte du Tonneau,*
54–8
Virgil, 81, 117, 130
Voigt, Milton
Swift in the Twentieth Century, 26,
28n
Voltaire, 5–6, 11–12, 73, 77, 78, 185
189, 191, 284, 294, 311, 318,

329–30
Correspondence, 73–4
Lettres . . . sur Rabelais et sur
d'autres auteurs, 75–6
Mélanges, 74–5
Siècle de Louis XIV, 75

Walpole, Horace
Correspondence, 189–91
Walpole, Sir Robert, 6, 11, 69–70,
93, 94, 232–3, 272, 288, 309,
311, 336
Warburton, William, 6, 10, 71, 149
A Critical and Philosophic
Enquiry . . ., 71–2
Warton, Joseph, 209
Essay on the Genius and Writings of
Pope, 209
Warton, Thomas, 209
Wilson, Charles Henry, 262
Swiftiana, 23, 262–3
Wotton, William, 4, 6, 37, 50, 51,
50, 115, 130, 176, 201, 252
A Defense . . . with Observations
on The Tale of a Tub, 37–46, 284

Young, Edward, 19, 20, 65, 178
Conjectures on Original Composition,
178–80, 239